Lies

Lies

The Science behind Deception

Rachelle M. Smith

BLOOMSBURY ACADEMIC
NEW YORK • LONDON • OXFORD • NEW DELHI • SYDNEY

BLOOMSBURY ACADEMIC
Bloomsbury Publishing Inc, 1359 Broadway, New York, NY 10018, USA
Bloomsbury Publishing Plc, 50 Bedford Square, London, WC1B 3DP, UK
Bloomsbury Publishing Ireland, 29 Earlsfort Terrace, Dublin 2, D02 AY28, Ireland

BLOOMSBURY, BLOOMSBURY ACADEMIC and the Diana logo
are trademarks of Bloomsbury Publishing Plc

First published in the United States of America by ABC-CLIO 2022
Paperback edition published by Bloomsbury Academic 2026

Cover design by Deanna Buley

Bloomsbury Publishing Inc does not have any control over, or responsibility for,
any third-party websites referred to or in this book. All internet addresses given
in this book were correct at the time of going to press. The author and publisher
regret any inconvenience caused if addresses have changed or sites have
ceased to exist, but can accept no responsibility for any such changes.

Library of Congress Cataloging-in-Publication Data
Names: Smith, Rachelle M., author.
Title: Lies : the science behind deception / Rachelle M. Smith.
Description: Santa Barbara, California : Greenwood, [2022] |
Includes bibliographical references and index.
Identifiers: LCCN 2021025288 (print) | LCCN 2021025289 (ebook) |
ISBN 9781440867590 (hardcover ; alk. paper) | ISBN 9781440867606 (ebook)
Subjects: LCSH: Deception. | Truthfulness and falsehood.
Classification: LCC BF637.D42 S655 2022 (print) | LCC BF637.D42 (ebook) | DDC 177/.3—dc23
LC record available at https://lccn.loc.gov/2021025288
LC ebook record available at https://lccn.loc.gov/2021025289

ISBN: HB: 978-1-4408-6759-0
PB: 979-8-2164-5214-0
ePDF: 978-1-4408-6760-6
eBook: 979-8-2161-1150-4

For product safety related questions contact productsafety@bloomsbury.com.

To find out more about our authors and books visit www.bloomsbury.com
and sign up for our newsletters.

Contents

List of Entries   vii

Preface   xi

Acknowledgments   xiii

Introduction   xv

Entries   1

Index   311

List of Entries

Academic Cheating

Advertising

Age Differences

Alternative Facts

Anderson, Anna

Antisocial Personality Disorder

Art of War, The

Astroturfing

Autism Spectrum Disorder

Bait and Switch

Bald-Faced Lies

Behavior Analysis Interview

Bending the Truth

Benefits of Lying

Betrayal

Black Lies

Blue Lies

Bluffs

Borderline Personality Disorder

Brokaw Hazard

Butler Lies

Camouflage

Careless Liars

Categories of Deception

Catfishing

Chadwick, Cassie

Charlatans

Clickbait

Coercion

Cognitive Changes while Lying

Cognitive Dissonance

Cognitive Distortion

Commission, Lies of

Competition

Compulsive Lying

Concealed Information Test

Conscience

Consequences of Lying

Conspiracy Theories

Control Questions Test

Corruption

Costs of Lying

Cultural Differences

Dark Triad

Dating

Deceiver Stereotype

Deception in Animals

Deception in Research

Defamation

Delusions

Dementia

Denial

DePaulo, Bella

Detecting Deception

Development of Deception

Diversionary Tactics

Doublespeak

Ekman, Paul

Emotional Effects

Equivocation

Erotomania

Espionage

Ethics

Evolution of Deception

Exaggeration

Eye Gaze

Fabrication

Facial Cues

Fact-Check

Fake News

False Confessions

False Memory

Fibs

Fifth Amendment

Fine Print

Fraud

Gaslighting

Half-Truths

Hoax

Hwang Woo-Suk

Hypocrisy

Impersonator

Infidelity

Instrumental Lies

Intelligence

Language

Lightfoot, Lucy

Linguistic Inquiry and Word Count
Analysis Program

Loch Ness Monster

Locus of Control

Lying

Lying at Work

Lying to Children

Lying to Parents

Machiavellianism

Malingering

Manipulation

Media

Memory

Mental Effort

Meyer, Pamela

Microexpressions

Milgram's Obedience Experiments

Mimicry

Minimization

Models of Lying

Motivational Impairment Effect

Motives for Lying

Munchausen Syndrome

Narcissism

Neuroscience

Noble Lies

Nonverbal Behavior

Omission, Lies of

Online Dating

Optimism Bias

Othello Error

Parkinson's Disease

Paternalistic Lies

Perjury

Personality

Phishing

Physiology

Piltdown Man

Placebo Effect

Plagiarism

Polite Lies

Politics

Polygraph Tests

Prevalence of Lying

Primates

Prisoner's Dilemma

Propaganda

Prosocial Lying

Puffery

Reaction Time

Reality Monitoring

Recursive Awareness

Red Herring

Reid Technique

Reverse Psychology

Romantic Relationships

Saarni, Carolyn

Saxe, Leonard

Scams

Self-Deception

Sex Differences in Lying Behavior

Sherlock Holmes Effect

Signaling Theory

Smoke and Mirrors

Social Intelligence

Social Media

Sockpuppets

Suspension of Disbelief

Tactical Deception

Theory of Mind

Transparent Lies and the Illusion of Transparency

Trolling

Truth-Default Theory

Tuskegee Syphilis Study

Vocal Changes when Lying

Vrij, Aldert

White Lies

Wizard's Project

Preface

Lies: The Science behind Deception provides a broad overview of 100 years' worth of research on the intricacies of deception. It is organized in an encyclopedic format and introduces over 160 topics associated with dishonesty and deception. Throughout the text, I examine why deception evolved, its costs and benefits in personal interactions, and how it is used in everyday life. I also present data outlining changes in deceptive abilities across the life span and the physical and mental health effects associated with lying behavior. To understand the breadth and depth of the field, over 30 types of lies, including prosocial, white, black, noble, and paternalistic, are described. Psychological disorders associated with increased lying behavior, such as antisocial personality disorder and borderline personality disorder; and disorders associated with decreased lying behavior, such as autism spectrum disorder and Parkinson's disease, are also highlighted. Personality traits that correlate with lying behavior, such as extroversion, neuroticism, and dark triad traits, are analyzed and interconnected. Because deception is of particular interest in criminal investigations, polygraph procedures such as the Behavior Analysis Interview, the Control Questions Test, the Concealed Information Test, and the Reid Technique are introduced and evaluated.

Political deception also features throughout the text with specific sections on topics such as alternative facts, blue lies, conspiracy theories, espionage, fake news, propaganda, and politics. I also introduce foundational researchers who have dedicated their lives to studying deception and examine classic psychological research studies that further our understanding of deceptive behavior. The impact of social media on the breadth and extent of deception is examined in sections such as online dating, clickbait, academic cheating, and advertising. Additionally, sidebars are included throughout the text, highlighting how research findings may be applied in the readers' own lives. Among a range of other topics, readers can learn about how to spot fake news, how to raise honest children, and how to be a better bluffer.

The primary audience for *Lies: The Science behind Deception* are those interested in why we lie, the physical and psychological effects of lying, and how lying is studied. Since the average adult lies on a daily basis, understanding the reasons, signals, and psychology of lying can help readers understand their own behavior as well as the behavior of social partners. The text covers how to be more savvy at detecting lies in personal relationships and identifying deception in propaganda, news reports, or advertising. I review the most common lies, the difference between low-stakes and high-stakes lies, and the typical physiological and neurological changes that accompany lying behavior. Readers are prompted to reevaluate their own behaviors as well as the behaviors of those around them. Throughout the text, I also introduce famous hoaxes and charlatans throughout history and explore why conspiracy theorists can be so resistant to altering their beliefs in light of empirical data.

Each entry within the text introduces and discusses a topic of interest and connects it with other topics via a *See Also* section, creating an integrated web of understanding deceit. A *Further Reading* section is also included in each entry, directing the reader to primary studies on each topic, for those who are interested in learning more. Sidebars are included throughout the text, allowing readers to see how the research may apply to their own lives. This organization allows for *Lies: The Science behind Deception* to be read in its entirety or used as a reference for topics of interest. The information provided in the text is designed to heighten the reader's awareness of how to more effectively identify and confront dishonesty and how to avoid being deceived.

My hope is that readers can benefit from understanding the verbal and nonverbal signals associated with lying as well as the impact that dishonesty has on intimacy, relationship satisfaction, and psychological health. Understanding and identifying self-deception can also help readers cultivate healthier interactions and stronger intimacy within relationships. Finally, awareness of concepts such as phishing, clickbait, false advertising, and fake news can help readers critically evaluate deceptive messages online, in the news, or from other media sources. Deception is a topic that is interesting and relevant to most individuals, and I hope readers find the information in this text to be engaging and applicable to their own lives.

Acknowledgments

This project has allowed me to delve more deeply into the research, applications, and outcomes of deception in everyday life, and it would not have been possible without a great deal of support. The extent of research needed to compile this collection was an enormous undertaking, and I appreciate the assistance extended by students, colleagues, friends, and family in finding articles, editing drafts, and listening to research findings. Thank you to all who were tremendously supportive in my research efforts. I would like to specifically thank Dr. Christine Selby for initially recommending me to ABC-CLIO and all of my colleagues at Husson University for understanding the importance of protecting time for scholarship. I would also like to thank Maxine Taylor of ABC-CLIO. Her responsiveness and support have been instrumental in keeping me motivated and confident along this journey. Finally, I want to thank Peg Killian who provided invaluable insights and edits throughout the text as well as devoted considerable time to creating the index for this book.

Introduction

The endeavors to deceive others and to detect deceptive attempts are universal and uniquely human abilities that pose complex challenges in everyday social life. The demands of typical social interactions call for honed abilities to inhibit information, modify expressive behavior, and occasionally provide misinformation. Such abilities are not only used during competition and conflict but are also regularly applied to enhance cooperative alliances, in negotiations, and to form and maintain relationships. Such abilities contribute to social intelligence and rely on complex cognitive skills including the ability to take multiple perspectives, understand competing goals, and control verbal and nonverbal presentations. Successful deceivers must recognize when deception is needed, construct believable lies, plan ahead, manipulate language, and control their emotional expressions and nonverbal behaviors. Effective deception relies on memory resources, executive functioning skills, advanced brain development, inhibitory control, and a mature theory of mind to understand and manipulate the perspective of the social partner.

Social interactions are rife with deception. The average adult tells one to two lies a day while more prolific liars lie almost constantly. Deception is used in personal relationships, business relationships, and even during interactions with strangers. Deception likely emerged as a by-product of human's social nature because it can convey a distinctive advantage to a savvy deceiver when interacting with both competitive and cooperative partners. The ability to control what information is shared with partners can allow one to control the outcome of an exchange, negotiation, or disagreement. This ability can shape interactions, strengthen relationships, and secure benefits for the deceiver. Though deception generally undermines true intimacy, when artfully applied, it can increase social status and regulate outcomes, conveying mutual benefits.

Though almost everyone lies, the ability to detect deception is a very difficult task for most people. The ability to recognize when someone else is lying can help an individual make better choices and prevent one from being manipulated by others. However, most adults have a truth bias and can only detect deception about 50 percent of the time or at about chance levels. Researchers argue that this inability to detect deception is likely connected to the fact that the vast majority of deceptive attempts are prosocial. Individuals lie to avoid hurting others, to prevent embarrassment, and to conform to social norms. Since the bulk of lies are designed to promote social interactions and to bolster self-esteem, it is not ultimately rewarding or beneficial to detect such lies. Accepting a compliment or believing an excuse is generally more advantageous than catching a liar, so most individuals do not put energy into honing their lie detection skills. Some lies, however, are for nefarious and selfish means, so the ability to detect such deception becomes necessary to maintain social order. Since humans are notoriously bad at detecting deception naturally, a field of research dedicated to learning how to detect deception more efficiently and successfully has emerged in psychology.

Research on deception has demonstrated that there are predictable changes in the ability to deceive and detect deception across the life span. Children under the age of eight tend to be relatively ineffective deceivers because they are not yet aware of the intricacies involved in shaping someone else's beliefs. Throughout later childhood and adolescence, individuals hone the skill of influencing the perceptions of others, and for most, use of deception peaks in early adolescence and then decreases with age. The ability to navigate and mediate social situations without lying takes skill and requires high confidence in one's own self-efficacy, so those with less experience and less confidence tend to resort to lying more readily. So, though the ability to lie effectively increases with age, reliance on lies to mediate interactions typically decreases with development in healthy adults.

The types of lies told also tend to change over the life span. Children tend to tell reactive lies to avoid punishment or to obtain a reward, while older teens and adults tell more prosocial lies to protect the feelings of others or to maintain relationships. Lies told for selfish reasons tend to be the least common type of lie told, but because they can have widespread negative and salient consequences, they may seem more prevalent. These lies tend to be used by individuals who have particular personality traits such as neuroticism, manipulativeness, and psychopathy. These traits are all associated with more frequent than average lying behavior and more high-stakes lying behavior across the life span. In some instances, these individuals may be categorized as prolific liars. Prolific liars are relatively rare, making up about 5 percent of the population, yet they tell almost half the lies told. Being able to identify and avoid such individuals may be the best means of dealing with such liars.

Though less common, selfish, high-stakes lies emerge in diverse realms of social experience such as warfare, commerce, and politics and can radically impact interactions at the individual, organizational, and international level. Thus, understanding the cues to deception and how to prevent falling victim to such deceptive attempts is a broad and applicable area of study. Furthermore, the pervasiveness of social media in current society requires an understanding of deception in the online world to negate the effects of sockpuppets, phishers, catfish, and trolls. Online deceptive schemes cost individuals and organizations billions of dollars each year and can shape perceptions and behavior at a global level. These wide-ranging consequences make the study of deception a necessity for industries and governments.

Research on deception demonstrates that lying behavior predictably correlates with heightened physiological and emotional arousal and increased experiences of stress and anxiety, particularly for high-stakes lies. These changes in heart rate, sweating, and breathing are some of the characteristics measured during a polygraph test. Various procedures have been developed to elicit physiological changes in order to detect lying during criminal investigations, with varying levels of effectiveness. These predictable changes in stress and emotionality also impact the physical and mental health of an individual. Individuals who lie frequently tend to have greater than average complaints of headaches, digestive problems, and high blood pressure. They also have lower than average ratings of relationship satisfaction and self-esteem and higher levels of anxiety, stress, and depression. These complaints significantly lessen when individuals consciously choose to discontinue lying behavior.

Deception is universal, and everyone has experience either lying or being the target of deceptive attempts. Though most adults are relatively poor lie detectors, deception detection is a skill that can be improved and honed through conscious effort and experience. Developing an awareness of common lies, environments that tend to elicit lying, empirically supported signals of lying, and signs that one is engaging in self-deception can facilitate development of lie detection skills. Additionally, such understanding can help one curb lying behavior, recoup health benefits of being more honest, and protect oneself from being deceived by others.

A

Academic Cheating

Academic cheating involves the use of dishonest actions to perform better on an exam or assignment. Successful cheaters receive the reward of a higher grade or better performance through dishonest means. A review of research completed by Dr. Angela Miller and colleagues revealed that the statistics on academic cheating in the United States are surprisingly high. Almost 100 percent of students admit to some type of cheating, including copying homework and getting help with papers. Over 60 percent of secondary school students admit to cheating on tests, and just under 60 percent admit to some form of plagiarism. The predominance of electronic devices may facilitate cheating in the digital age. Now students can purchase papers online, find answers to homework problems, or carry devices into the classroom that have digitized notes or preprogrammed answers.

Statistics show that cheating tends to increase with age. Only one-third of elementary-aged students endorse cheating behaviors, but 60 percent of middle school students, and upward of 75 percent of high school students admit to cheating. In college, rates of cheating reach 95 percent. The increase in cheating with age seems to be tied to the level of competitiveness within the classroom. As classes become more competitive and students become more grade-focused, cheating behaviors increase. The most common reasons given for cheating include fear of failure and lack of time to complete the work independently. Nontraditional college students are less likely to cheat than their traditional counterparts. These older students tend to be more focused on their education whereas traditional students are more focused on their grades.

Students with lower academic ability tend to engage in cheating behaviors more regularly. However, as pressure increases, even serious and capable students may resort to cheating, particularly in the subjects of the hard sciences, math, and technology. Level of self-efficacy, however, moderates this effect. Self-efficacy is how effectively individuals believe they can complete an assignment or exam. Individuals who are more confident have higher self-efficacy scores and are less likely to engage in cheating behaviors, even for difficult assignments. Those with lower senses of self-efficacy are less likely to study or attend class, and report less control over their performance. They are more likely to cheat and then use rationalization, neutralization, and deflection to make themselves feel better about cheating.

Dr. Miller demonstrated that the top students were the least likely to cheat. There were no A-level students in her study who endorsed engaging in cheating behaviors. However, 4 percent who earned Bs admitted to cheating, 23 percent who received Cs, 75 percent of those who earned Ds, and 67 percent of those who earned Fs cheated. In this group, lower scores on intelligence tests and lower scores on self-efficacy measures correlated with cheating behaviors. Interestingly, those individuals with more close friendships were also more likely to cheat. This may be due to simply having the opportunity.

Dr. Ann Bushway and Dr. William Nash from Texas A&M University noted that there are a few measures that can be used to decrease likelihood of cheating behaviors within a classroom. Asking for a commitment not to cheat or threatening punishment for cheaters was effective in lessening the incidence of cheating. Likelihood of detection and follow-through of consequences also decreased cheating behaviors. However, witnessing others cheat without detection or consequence increased the likelihood of cheating. Furthermore, students who cheated once were more likely to cheat again.

Online education may also lend itself to new methodologies of cheating. However, most research thus far does not show evidence that online classes invite more cheating. One reason for lack of cheating online may be the more consistent use of online resources to detect plagiarism. Furthermore, online students tend to be older than traditional college-aged populations, and older students are less likely to cheat or share work. Differences in cheating behavior seem to be more influenced by student demographics than course format. Online students also may have fewer personal connections in the class that give fewer opportunities to share work.

See also: Age Differences; Cognitive Dissonance; Ethics; Intelligence; Locus of Control; Minimization; Personality; Plagiarism.

Further Reading

Bushway, A., & Nash, W. R. (1977). School cheating behavior. *Review of Educational Research, 47*(4), 623–632.

Miller, A. D., Murdock, T. B., Anderman, E. M., & Poindexter, A. L. (2007). *Who are all these cheaters? Characteristics of academically dishonest students.* In E. M. Anderman & T. B. Murdock (Eds.), *Psychology of Academic Cheating* (pp. 9–32). Elsevier Academic Press.

Pilgrim, C., & Scanlon, C. (2018, July 27). *Don't assume online students are more likely to cheat. The evidence is murky.* Retrieved from https://phys.org/news/2018 -07-dont-assume-online-students-evidence.html

Advertising

The Federal Trade Commission (FTC), formed in 1914, sets specific standards and laws for advertising in the United States. Under their provision, advertisements must be evidence based and must not be deceptive or unfair. Despite their guidelines, however, almost 2.7 million consumers registered complaints with the FTC in 2017. These complaints included fraud, scams, and false advertising. Advertising can be deemed deceptive if it gives the consumer an impression of the advertised product that is untrue or misleading. The most common types of deception in advertising are ads that omit information, ads that use semantic confusion to mislead, ads that falsely imply positive characteristics about products, and ads that use the appearance of convincing sources.

In ads that omit information, consumers receive an unbalanced review of the product. Advertisers may neglect to mention side effects or report only the good qualities to encourage purchase. For example, advertisements for freecreditreport. com advertise that you can check your credit for free. However, the advertisements omit the fact that those who check their credit via the site are automatically signed up for additional services and charged $80 if they do not cancel within 30 days. This information is omitted in the advertisement, and unsuspecting consumers could easily be deceived.

Advertisements that engage in semantic confusion use words that have more than one meaning to suggest something that is untrue. Some advertisements use the word "fresh," implying that the ingredients are unprocessed, when in fact they are only claiming they taste fresh. Others use the word "lite," implying that the product has fewer calories, when in fact it is just lighter in color than comparison brands. The way advertisements are phrased can also have an effect on consumers. Lean Cuisine, for example, claims that their entrées have fewer than 300 calories, low fat, and less than 1 gram of sodium. Though they are not lying, consumers may be deceived by the phrasing, not recognizing that 1 gram of sodium is 1000 milligrams, which is almost a full daily recommended allowance in one serving. A pharmaceutical company was found guilty of such semantic confusion when they made claims that their black currant drink was made from natural black currants, which have more vitamin C than oranges. Though it is true that black currants do have more vitamin C than oranges, their drink did not contain enough black currants to make it have more vitamin C than orange juice, as was implied in the advertisements.

Advertisements also may use phrasing to imply that their product is better than it was in the past or in comparison to competitors. Mazola vegetable oil added a claim of "no cholesterol" to its product label, when in fact no vegetable oil contains cholesterol. Though the claim is not untrue, it leads to inferences about the product that are not true (that it is healthier than other oils). Advertisements for other foods may claim "contains fiber" or "lower fat" even if the fiber content is negligible and the "lower" fat is still extremely high. Furthermore, claims such as a product being low in fat may also lead consumers to believe it is also low in cholesterol or low in calories, when that may not be true. Advertisements may also use actors who appear happier, healthier, or more popular after using the product. This gives the consumer an impression that the product will convey these positive qualities without the advertiser telling an outright lie.

A final common source of deception in advertisements is using "experts" to endorse products. Frequently, experts are actually actors in lab coats or statistics have been manipulated to support the product. Four out of five dentists endorsing a product may omit to mention the other dentists who failed to support the product. Typically, advertisers will only use those endorsements that support their product.

Other research illustrates the impact of incomplete comparison claims. Advertisers commonly make claims that particular brands are the "best" or "premium quality," insinuating they are better than the other brands of similar products, though no other brand is named. Claims may be made that a product is better or faster, but the advertisement does not provide a comparison point (e.g., faster than what?). Being able to make inferences or draw implications is a large part of understanding text. Advertisers can exploit this ability and cause audiences to make inferences from their advertising to better sell their products. Though the advertisement may be semantically true, the implications that are drawn are misleading. Such semantic manipulation makes the FTC's job more difficult.

Advertisers have a reputation for skewing reality, and viewers are aware that advertisers may be spinning information to sell their products. Therefore, many consumers have a healthy skepticism when viewing commercials or print ads. Awareness of deceptive advertising makes consumers defensive and distrusting of advertising in general. Between 1997 and 2001, Ad Standards, a Canadian organization that offers services to administer the Canadian code of advertising standards, received twice as many complaints from people who realized they were deceived by advertisements that made incomplete or vague claims about their product. Such misleading advertisements make all advertising less effective and cause consumers to have a negative and defensive bias toward advertisements.

Recently, a new type of deception in advertising has emerged, known as embedded advertising. In television shows or Internet videos, companies pay to have their products integrated into the content. This may include a product being named, discussed, or used during an episode of a show, a movie, or video game. With new technologies that allow consumers to skip commercials, embedded advertising is escalating. This type of advertising can be considered deceptive because it may be undisclosed and less likely to activate the skepticism used when viewing traditional advertisements. This makes these advertisements more persuasive and the watcher more malleable. In response to this new mode of advertising, shows must now disclose when a sponsor has paid for a product to be in a show (e.g., "promotional consideration was provided by . . .").

Though the FTC has helped eliminate outright fraud in advertisements, monitoring and eliminating the other types of deception are more difficult. Use of humor, for example, allows advertisers to make outlandish, wildly untrue claims that everyone understands to be exaggerations. However, the implication is that the product has some of the quality that is being displayed, and thus the ads may be persuasive, making these ads influential for even suspicious viewers.

See also: Alternative Facts; Astroturfing; Bait and Switch; Clickbait; Competition; Consequences of Lying; Detecting Deception; Exaggeration; Fine Print; Fraud; Media; Omission, Lies of; Puffery; Scams.

Further Reading

Cain, R. M. (2011). Embedded advertising on television: Disclosure, deception, and free speech rights. *Journal of Public Policy and Marketing, 30*(2), 226–238.

Darke, P. R., & Ritchie, J. B. (2007). The defensive consumer: Advertising, deception, defensive processing, and distrust. *Journal of Marketing Research, 44*, 114–127.

DePaulo, P. J. (1988). Research on deception in marketing communications: Its relevance to the study of nonverbal behavior. *Journal of Nonverbal Behavior, 12*(4), 252–273.

Federal Trade Commission. (2018). *Advertising and marketing.* Retrieved from https://www.ftc.gov/tips-advice/business-center/advertising-and-marketing

Hastak, M., & Mazis, M. B. (2011). Deception by implication: A typology of truthful but misleading advertising and labeling claims. *Journal of Public Policy and Marketing, 30*(2), 157–167.

Johar, G. V. (1995). Consumer involvement and deception from implied advertising claims. *Journal of Marketing Research, 32*, 267–279.

Shabbir, H., & Thwaites, D. (2007). The use of humor to mask deceptive advertising: It's no laughing matter. *Journal of Advertising, 36*(2), 75–85.

Age Differences

The ability to deceive varies predictably over the life span. Due to the cognitive demands required to successfully deceive, brain development over childhood correlates with increases in deceptive ability. Similarly, cognitive declines across older adulthood correlate with a decline in deceptive ability. Deception draws on cognitive resources such as prefrontal cortex activity, executive control, working memory, mental flexibility, and inhibition. Age-related changes in these skills likely underlie age-related deceptive abilities.

To lie convincingly, one must inhibit true information and fabricate convincing false information. One must also align verbal and nonverbal behavior. These tasks require a mature theory of mind, which is an awareness of another's thoughts, feelings, and beliefs. This is an area where young children struggle, and thus, their lies are frequently less convincing than those told by older children or adults. For simple lies, such as saying "no" when asked a direct question, children can be quite convincing. However, their ability to successfully deceive breaks down if they have to concoct a longer response or if they are asked follow-up questions.

In childhood, deception is reinforced through immediate rewards and avoidance of punishment. Toddlers learn to divert blame through emotionally driven non-premeditated lies. By age four, children lie about behaviors to avoid punishment or earn rewards or because it is funny to trick a social partner. School-age kids are more likely to lie about homework, teachers, or friends. At this point, children are also likely to notice instances when their parents lie. By the preteen years, children feel more guilt about lying, but they also start to understand the importance of polite lies. Over adolescence, teens become more adept at lying and are more likely to lie to their parents or friends about behaviors or intentions. In adulthood, most adults lie less frequently than in childhood, but do so more effectively. In older adulthood, lying ability declines as a result of decreases in working memory and reaction time.

Dr. Evelyne Debey and colleagues surveyed over 1000 individuals from ages 6 to 77 for lying proficiency, reaction time, and frequency of lying. As expected, lying proficiency and speed increased over childhood, peaked in young adulthood, and decreased throughout adulthood. These findings correlate with age-related changes in inhibitory control and executive functioning. Younger children and older adults struggle to control and inhibit information and are more likely to leak information they are attempting to conceal. Lying frequency, similarly, increased throughout childhood, peaked during the adolescent years, and then decreased over adulthood.

The ability to detect lies also showed age-related changes over the life span. Children tend to be relatively oblivious to lies and score at or below chance levels when assessing whether another individual is lying. Furthermore, younger children have difficulty distinguishing lies from other types of statements such as mistakes, exaggerations, and jokes. It is not until late adolescence that individuals start scoring above chance on such skills. Adults were particularly effective at evaluating deceptive attempts when the lies were probed with follow-up questions. Dr. Debey demonstrated that all groups relied more on verbal statements rather than on the nonverbal cues that might prove more effective in detecting deception.

All groups were more effective at detecting when children were lying than when adults were lying, though most individuals demonstrate a truth bias for older adults and are less likely to rate an older adult as deceptive. Dr. Michelle Eskritt and Dr. Kang Lee from Mount St. Vincent University and the University of Toronto compared adults' and children's ability to detect lies. Adults and children were asked to say they liked examples of artwork provided in the study, whether they did or not, and their responses were videotaped. Some were simply asked whether or not they liked the artwork, and others were probed with follow-up questions, asking them to explain why they liked it. Then children and adults were asked to view the videos and rate each as truthful or not.

Adult participants were better at detecting lies than the younger or older groups. However, participants of all ages were better at detecting deception when assessing the youngest liars. Since all videotaped individuals said "yes" when asked if they liked the art, as directed, there must have been nonverbal leakage in the youngest groups. When judging the truthfulness of the older children or adults, participants' abilities to tell whether they were telling lies or telling the truth were only at chance levels.

Older adults were not able to detect lies as readily as younger adults. In addition to a decline in executive functioning abilities, there is also evidence to suggest that older adults spend less time looking at the eyes and the overall facial expression and spend more time looking at the mouth of the speaker. This is potentially due to decreases in hearing and increased reliance on looking at lips to understand words. Since older adults do not assess the nonverbal cues, they are less likely to detect lies.

See also: Detecting Deception; Development of Deception; Lying to Parents; Neuroscience; Nonverbal Behavior; Polite Lies; Reaction Time; Recursive Awareness; Theory of Mind; Truth-Default Theory.

Further Reading

Bussey, K. (1999). Children's categorization and evaluation of different types of lies and truths. *Child Development, 70*(6), 1338–1347.

Debey, E., De Schryver, M., Logan, G. D., Suchotzki, K., & Verschuere, B. (2015). From junior to senior Pinocchio: A cross-sectional lifespan investigation of deception. *Acta Psychologica, 160*, 58–68.

Eskritt, M., & Lee, K. (2017). The detection of prosocial lying by children. *Infant and Child Development, 26*, 1–17.

Ruffman, T., Murray, J., Halberstadt, J., & Vater, T. (2011). Age-related differences in deception. *Psychology and Aging, 27*(3), 543–549.

Sweeney, C. D., & Ceci, S. J. (2014). Deception detection, transmission, and modality in age and sex. *Frontiers in Psychology, 5,* 1–10.

Alternative Facts

Alternative facts are claims made through erroneous interpretations of data or through unscientific conclusions based on incomplete data. Though such claims may be easily discredited through empirical validation, simple exposure to such claims can have a long-term impact on the publics' perceptions of events or data. Furthermore, most individuals do not independently verify data or sources, and many erroneous claims are never contradicted. Due to the extent of alternative facts present in various media sources, practice and support for development of critical thinking and analytic skills are needed so that the general public has basic fact-checking abilities.

The term "alternative facts" was coined during an interview with U.S. Counselor to President Donald Trump, Kellyanne Conway, when she attempted to justify false statements made about the size of the president's inauguration in 2017. Retrospectively, she claimed she merely used the term to mean that there is more than one way to view an event and that the claims were made by drawing the best conclusions possible given the limited data. However, most criticized her and the president as attempting to misrepresent reality in order to convince the public of information that was obviously and demonstrably false.

Though the term "alternative facts" was popularized during the abovementioned political scandal, it can refer to any situation where information is presented as fact that is shown to be invalid. For example, erroneous claims that vaccines lead to autism have caused large groups of people to have an inaccurate understanding of the possible side effects of vaccines. This use of alternative facts has influenced public opinion and has been relatively resistant to correction by subsequent scientific research.

To examine the danger of exposure to alternative facts, Dr. Andrew Gordon and colleagues from the University of Bristol completed psychological research on examining the impact of alternative facts on people's beliefs. They demonstrated that presentation of misinformation, such as alternative facts or fake news, has long-term effects on judgments and reasoning. This effect is known as the continued influence effect of misinformation (CIEM). CIEM occurs when corrections to misinformation are not fully processed, and, therefore, the previous judgments are not corrected. Frequently alternative facts are attention-grabbing, satisfying, or emotionally provoking, making them more salient and resistant to change. Emotionally charged information is difficult to replace in memory stores, even if more accurate information is provided. The problem likely lies in the demand on memory stores to hold both correct and incorrect information in memory simultaneously and the difficulty of overcoming emotionally charged beliefs. To change such a belief, an individual would need to systematically process the new information rather than rely on the gut instinct. An example would be believing that someone is guilty of a crime and then struggling to overcome that belief in light of new information that supports the suspect's innocence.

Dr. Gordon found that the continued influence effect of misinformation (CIEM) was persistent even when participants were warned that they would be exposed to incorrect information and when the corrections to the misinformation were repeatedly emphasized. This is likely due to the cognitive effort needed to overwrite previously held beliefs. Disregarding new information is a more simplistic and less effortful process than replacing or integrating new information into cognitive or memory stores. Those who do acknowledge and attempt to process new information struggle. New information may not replace the old information, but may be held in memory concurrently, and thus, the individual would have competing information for the same topic. Likely, the more emotionally charged information would be called to mind more readily.

Additionally, previously held beliefs can strengthen the continued influence effect of misinformation (CIEM), particularly if the initial, incorrect information is in line with one's worldview. A desire to believe information that supports one's beliefs about the world can cause misinformation to be accepted more readily. Repetition of the misinformation can also radically increase its strength in long-term memory.

Alternative facts can gain traction through mechanisms that are becoming more and more common in society. Especially in the United States, there is growing diversity and variety in media sources of varying quality. There is also an increasing division in political ideology and an increase in the statistics used in reporting on topics, which puts increasing demands on readers' quantitative literacy. One way to combat this may be through increasing quantitative reasoning and critical thinking instruction in the U.S. education system.

See also: Blue Lies; Cognitive Distortion; Costs of Lying; Detecting Deception; Fake News; Gaslighting; Neuroscience; Politics; Propaganda; Reality Monitoring; Self-Deception; Social Media.

Further Reading

Blake, A. (2017, January 22). *Kellyanne Conway says Donald Trump's team has 'alternative facts.' Which pretty much says it all*. Retrieved from https://www.washington post.com/news/the-fix/wp/2017/01/22/kellyanne-conway-says-donald-trumps -team-has-alternate-facts-which-pretty-much-says-it-all/

Branson, M. (2019). Fighting alternative facts: Teaching quantitative reasoning with social issues. *Problems, Resources, and Issues in Mathematics Undergraduate Studies, 29*(3–4), 228–243.

Gordon, A., Quadflieg, S., Brooks, J. C. W., Ecker, U. K. H., & Lewandowsky, S. (2019). Keeping track of 'alternative facts': The neural correlates of processing misinformation corrections. *NeuroImage, 193*, 46–56.

Altruistic Lies (See Prosocial Lying)

Anastasia Romanov (See Anna Anderson)

Anderson, Anna

Anna Anderson is the most famous individual who claimed to be the Grand Duchess Anastasia (Nikolaevna) Romanov, the youngest daughter of Tsar Nicholas II of Russia. During the Russian Civil War, following the Bolshevik revolution in the early twentieth century, the Romanov family were taken captive and murdered. Rumors followed, however, that Anastasia may have escaped, and several women, including Anna Anderson, came forward over the next few years claiming to be the missing Grand Duchess. Anna claimed that she feigned death and was assisted by a guard who helped her escape. Anna continued to avow her identity as Anastasia until her death in 1984 despite not having enough evidence to satisfy the courts.

Anna Anderson's claim of being the missing Grand Duchess was initiated in 1920 during a mental hospital stay after an attempted suicide. Initially Anna refused to identify herself, and her photograph was circulated to no avail. Anna remained at the mental hospital for two years. During her stay, she revealed she was Anastasia, and living family members of the Grand Duchess were asked to come to identify her. However, many of the surviving family members did not know young Anastasia well enough to conclusively identify her after the intervening years. Given that the entire household was executed together, most remaining family members had not had enough contact with her during her life to conclusively confirm or deny her identity. Those who did claim to recognize her would not commit their support, likely for political or financial reasons. During the 1950s, Anastasia's good friend from childhood accepted Anna as the true Anastasia, though thirty years and hopeful thinking likely clouded her memory.

Concurrently with Anna's hospital stay, a woman called Franziska Schanskowska was reported missing from her boarding house. Franziska's family were told that she was likely murdered by serial killer Georg Karl Grossman, who ate or sold the meat of his victims. Once Anna began to claim to be the missing Grand Duchess, the surviving Romanovs hired a private detective to investigate. The private detective made the connection that Anna was most likely the missing Polish factory worker, Franziska. Franziska's family were asked to identify her in the late 1920s, almost 10 years after her disappearance, and though both her brother and sister claimed to recognize her, neither would sign a paper affirming her identity, likely to avoid the responsibility of her care.

In 1955, *Life* magazine published an article about Anna, highlighting her as the lost Grand Duchess. In the article, she was named Anastasia and sympathized with for missing out on the Tsar's fortune and for the powder burns and bayonet scars she received during the assassination attempt. In the interview, she reported that she was rescued by a soldier, whom she later married. After he was killed, she attempted suicide and grew so despondent that she was unable to assert her identity for the intervening two years.

When the Romanov grave was discovered in the late twentieth century, it added to the controversy because the remains of the son and one daughter were missing. Over the next 40 years, archeologists continued to search for a second grave, and in 2007, amateur archeologists discovered bone shards not far from the original grave. This led to the discovery of a second grave containing the missing daughter and Prince Alexei, Romanov's son. The bones belonged to a girl and boy about the age of the two missing children, and tests show that they died at the same time as the rest of their family. There is still controversy over whether the girl is Maria or Anastasia, but between the two graves, both girls are accounted for.

Though many people wanted to believe that Anna was the missing Grand Duchess, a DNA analysis after Anna Anderson's death provided conclusive proof that she was not genetically related to the Romanov line. In fact, in the 1990s, a DNA test concluded that Anna's remains were a 99.9% match with Franziska's great-nephew, supporting the idea that Anna was the missing factory worker, not the missing Grand Duchess. Thus, a century-long deception was exposed by both archeological and genetic evidence, and the biggest mystery that remains is whether or not Anna believed her own claims by the time of her death.

See also: Chadwick, Cassie; Charlatans; Fraud; Hoax; Impersonator; Motives for Lying; Scams; Self-Deception.

Further Reading

Coble, M. D., Loreille, O. M., Wadhams, M. J., Edson, S. M., Maynard, K., Meyer, C. E., Niederstatter, H., Berger, C., Berger, B., Falsetti, A. B., Gill, P., Parson, W., & Finelli, L. N. (2009). Mystery solved: The identification of the two missing Romanov children using DNA analysis. *PLoS One, 4*(3), e4838. https://doi.org/10.1371/journal.pone.0004838

Is this princess alive? (14 Feb 1955) *Life, 38*(7), 31–35.

Massie, R. K. (1996). *The Romanovs: The Final Chapter.* The Random House.

Rogaev, E. I., Grigorenko, A. P., Moliaka, Y. K., Faskhutdinova, G., Goltsov, A., Lahti, A., Hildebrandt, C., Kittler, E. L. W., & Morozova, I. (2009). Genomic identification in the historical case of the Nicholas II royal family. *Proceedings of the National Academy of Sciences, 106*(13), 5258–5263.

Antisocial Lies (See Black Lies; Instrumental Lies)

Antisocial Personality Disorder

Antisocial personality disorder, commonly called sociopathy, is a mental health disorder in which an individual has limited empathy for others and an abnormal sense of right and wrong. These individuals are much more likely than the average person to readily use deception to achieve goals or to manipulate others. Individuals with antisocial personality disorder tend to not feel a sense of guilt when lying, which makes their deceptive attempts very effective. Most tests to detect deception measure the changes in arousal that typically accompany lying behavior, so lack of such emotional arousal makes these liars more difficult to detect.

Some clues that may help one identify lies told by those with antisocial personality disorder are in the contradictions between their words and behaviors. Those with antisocial personality disorder frequently make big promises but then do not engage in behaviors that signal moving toward such goals. They talk in extremes and may swing from extreme cooperation and care to extreme anger and threats as they attempt to get what they want and manipulate others. They have a tendency to arouse the emotions of listeners, likely without even intending to do so. There is a contradiction between what they say and the emotions they provoke, and a savvy observer may be able to detect deception by paying attention to their own emotional response.

Individuals with antisocial personality disorder range in their behaviors and intelligence levels. High-functioning sociopathic liars tend to be quite intelligent, energetic, and charming, which aids their lying effectiveness. They are able to hide antisocial behaviors behind charm and deception. While functioning in regular society, they subtly manipulate people and situations to gain an advantage, without concern for the harm that such behavior may have on others. Rather than simply using threats, coercion, or intimidation to get what they want, they mask such behaviors to more effectively manipulate others. Alternatively, they can also act impulsively and frequently opt to violate social and legal boundaries for personal pleasure and without respect for personal property. They seem to enjoy the pain or hardship of others, show positive emotions in situations that would typically arouse sympathy, and react in atypical ways, such as smiling or nodding, when others are suffering.

Antisocial personality disorder is very difficult to treat, predominantly because most individuals who engage in such behaviors show little insight into their behavior patterns and little interest in the feelings of others, so they are not motivated to seek help. These individuals tend to fall into a pattern of manipulating others and are arrogant and aggressive. They do not show guilt, nor do they care about the consequences of their actions, even if they impact the safety or feelings of others. Since most do not acknowledge that they have a problem, the most effective way to deal with sociopathic liars is to minimize contact with them. Due to the constellation of traits, individuals with antisocial personality disorder are more likely to engage in criminal behavior, violate the rights of others, and engage in remorseless violence. Due to these tendencies, many end up in jail and may receive forced psychological treatment during incarceration. Such therapy can help those with the disorder become more aware of their patterns of behavior, but many use that insight to more effectively manipulate others. They tend to have poor-quality personal relationships characterized by a lack of true intimacy because they are not honest with themselves or others.

Individuals with antisocial personality disorder typically show symptoms prior to the age of 15. They may abuse animals and lack respect for property and for the law. Generally, the severity of symptoms decreases over time, but the damage to relationships tends to be long-lasting. Risk factors include family history of the disorder, childhood abuse or neglect, and instability during development. Around 3 percent of men and 1 percent of women meet the criteria for the disorder. In general, individuals with antisocial personality disorder tend to demonstrate frequent use of deception to exploit others and have little conscience for their behaviors.

See also: Coercion; Compulsive Lying; Dark Triad; Intelligence; Machiavellianism; Manipulation; Narcissism; Personality; Polygraph Tests; Scams; Tactical Deception.

Further Reading

Begun, J. H. (1976). The sociopathic or psychopathic personality. *International Journal of Social Psychiatry, 22*(1), 25–46.

Grohol, J. M. (2020). Differences between a psychopath vs. sociopath. *PsychCentral.* Retrieved from https://psychcentral.com/blog/differences-between-a-psychopath -vs-sociopath#1

Hughes, C. J., Tom, F. D., Hopwood, M.-C., Pratt, A., Hunter, M. D., & Spence, S. A. (2005). Recent developments in deception research. *Current Psychiatry Reviews, 1*(3), 273–379.

Werner, K. B., Few, L. R., & Bucholz, K. K. (2005). Behavioral genetics of antisocial personality disorder and psychopathy. *Psychiatric Annals, 45*(4), 195–199.

Arnold, Benedict (See Espionage)

Art of War, The

The Art of War is a military tactical strategy manual credited to Sun Tzu of China from the fifth century BC. In *The Art of War*, Sun Tzu proposes that all warfare is based on effective deceptive and tactical strategies. His recommendations for establishing tactical advantage have informed diverse arenas including historical and modern warfare, business negotiations, and game strategy.

Historians believe that Sun Tzu was a Chinese officer. His writings have influenced military scholars throughout history and have provided strategy for military groups around the world. Some consider *The Art of War* to be a book that intends to provide effective military strategy for those at a disadvantage in a conflict. However, this text is available to those on both sides of an altercation. In *The Art of War*, Sun Tzu emphasizes the importance of deception and infiltration of enemy forces and covers such topics as knowing the enemy, planning ahead, having contingency strategies, engaging an opponent, and effectively using spies. He outlines rules for military engagements, calculations for likelihood of victory, assessment of various outcomes, conservation warfare, maintaining strong alliances, recognizing opportunities and limiting the enemies opportunities, knowing your enemy and yourself, understanding the nature of the conflict, remaining fluid and changing strategies as needed, effectively moving through enemy territory, maintaining focus, and maintaining sources of intelligence about the enemy.

Most of the philosophy in *The Art of War* is not indicated in U.S. tactics of warfare, likely to its detriment. However, U.S. military leaders should be at least aware of the tactics because opponents will likely use them, and such an understanding could inform how to engage enemies more effectively on the battlefield. An understanding of the cultural, historical, and psychological elements of an opponent would similarly inform conflicts in ways that the U.S. military frequently overlooks. Some scholars point to Sun Tzu's writings to explain why the United States lost the Vietnam War. Basically, the U.S. military did not understand the people they were fighting. The Vietnamese used Sun Tzu's principles and won a war in which they never won a battle on the field. They used strategy and infiltrations to undermine, confuse, and psychologically cripple an enemy that arguably had superior firepower and forces. They built their approach around strategy rather than strength, and this discrepancy is arguably still a weakness of American forces today.

Sun Tzu's writings elaborate effective strategies for large armies as well as individual guerrillas. Sun Tzu emphasizes maneuverability over battlefield victories. Use of diplomacy, political strategy, and combat formations are all equally important to win a victory. Groups that focus only on physical combat are vulnerable to an enemy that employs all three. To win a war, the focus must be on defeating the opponents' strategies and alliances, not simply their soldiers. The goal is to limit the opponents' options while maximizing one's own, rather than direct attack and defeat.

Sun Tzu emphasizes that to be successful in an engagement, one must not only engage in successful deception but also recognize the deceptive attempts of an opponent. War is about intelligent strategy rather than the strength of an army. Those who know their enemy are more likely to deceive and detect deception. In such a vein, fighting with a friend can be more subtle, strategic, and effective than taking wild shots at a stranger. Sun Tzu also emphasizes that successful competitors must have the objective of understanding their own strengths and weaknesses, as well as the strengths and weaknesses of the opponent. Successful strategists use their strengths and cover their weaknesses; they endeavor to appear weak when strong and appear strong when weak; and they attack opponents' weaknesses, evade their strengths, and know when to engage.

Though it might appear extreme to liken war with corporations or game play, Sun Tzu's advice is readily and successfully applied to business negotiations and athletic competitions. His tenets, such as lead by example, approach or retreat as needed, treat allies well, use diplomacy rather than confrontation to win arguments, break resistance subtly, provide predominantly honest signals, and negotiate behind the scenes can all enhance success in the business world or on the athletic field. Additionally, competitive success relies on knowing opponents, being detail oriented, keeping competitors close, waiting for and recognizing opportunities, giving opponents a place to retreat, and evading rather than engaging as needed. In this sense, applying warfare strategy has informed business and athletic success.

See also: Benefits of Lying; Espionage; Fake News; Politics; Propaganda; Prisoner's Dilemma; Recursive Awareness; Signaling Theory; Tactical Deception; Theory of Mind.

Further Reading
Griffith, S. B. (trans.) (1963). *The Art of War*. Oxford University Press.
Jackson, E. (2014, May 23). Sun Tzu's 31 best pieces of leadership advice. *Forbes*. Retrieved from https://www.forbes.com/sites/ericjackson/2014/05/23/sun-tzus-33-best-pieces-of-leadership-advice/?sh=7fb89935e5ef
McCready, D. M. (2003 May–Jun). Learning from Sun Tzu. *Military Review*. Retrieved from https://www.hsdl.org/?view&did=717890

Astroturfing

Astroturfing is a concept that was coined in the 1980s that refers to a practice where political candidates or large corporations spread information to persuade others that there is public support for their message or products. Though this practice is not new, it has become more and more common in the internet age. Corporations or political parties that engage in astroturfing may use one of several techniques. They may use front groups or sockpuppets, or they may pay individuals to provide positive reviews on a public platform. They may also engage in similar tactics to disparage a competitor. In an effort to curb astroturfing, U.S. legislation has been put into place requiring that incentives for reviews be made public.

Astroturfers tend to mimic grassroots organizations. Their goal is to spread information and misinformation to influence widespread attitudes and garner public support. Astroturfers may use software to mask their identity and may be funded by corporations or government agents to create and shape public opinion. For example, one individual may create several profiles to create the appearance of a greater base of support for an organization or message. The use of astroturfing allows for a small subsection of a movement to create and exaggerate their position. Since most people tend to be highly influenced by the beliefs of their peers, perceiving widespread support for an issue may be more influential than presentation of accurate information. Planting seemingly widespread opinions about an issue can therefore influence others. Even if individuals doubt some of the opinions online, they are still influenced.

Astroturfing can be used at different levels. It can take the form of positive reviews for a product or support for a political candidate, or it can be used to alter perceptions about social issues. With widespread reliance on social media, blogs, and product reviews, astroturfing can convince consumers that a product is better or worse than it really is. In this sense, astroturfing can be likened to false advertising. Because of this, the Federal Trade Commission has made it illegal for companies to pay individuals to endorse products without disclosing that they are being compensated.

Researchers from the University of Texas at San Antonio define the emergence of online astroturfing as coordinated campaigns where information supporting a specific issue is spread on online platforms. These campaigns use deception to create the appearance of widespread support for issues or products. Those who seek information on the internet may be influenced or perceive issues differently based on the astroturf information. These researchers found that astroturfing was most commonly used in business and in politics. Influencing public opinion translates to making sales or getting votes. Some companies label such endeavors as public relations with the goal of presenting a positive public image and discrediting critics. Companies may pay employees, for example, to submit favorable reviews of a product or unfavorable reviews of competitors' products. If the information seems to be coming from an array of unbiased individuals, it tends to be more effective and more persuasive.

Dr. Charles Cho and colleagues from the John Molson School of Business demonstrated the effect of astroturfing in a study examining the issue of climate change. In their research, they found that exposure to astroturf websites created by large corporate polluters confused consumers about issues surrounding climate change. The websites used misinformation, skewed information, and gave the appearance of educated opinions on the topic, which led users to question the impact and existence of climate change and humans' role in the phenomenon. This effect held even when researchers told users who funded the site. Beliefs and expectations are significantly impacted even when the source was identified as biased.

Astroturfing exaggerates the amount of public support for an issue in an attempt to sway others and to drive or prevent change. Due to its impact on public opinion, regulations have been put into place around the world in an attempt to discourage the practice. In the United States, astroturfing is prohibited, with fines and jail time for those who misrepresent an endorsement. In the European Union, the media is required to disclose the sponsor for a presentation, and a corporation is not allowed to impersonate a consumer. Despite legal regulations to discourage astroturfing, it is still estimated that about one-third of online reviews are fake and can significantly skew public perception.

See also: Advertising; Alternative Facts; Catfishing; Competition; Corruption; Fake News; Manipulation; Phishing; Politics; Propaganda; Social Media; Sockpuppets; Trolling.

Further Reading

Cho, C. H., Martens, M. L., Kim, H., & Rodrigue, M. (2011). Astroturfing global warming: It isn't always greener on the other side of the fence. *Journal of Business Ethics, 104*(4), 571–587.

Lee, C. W. (2010). The roots of astroturfing. *Contexts, 9*(1), 73–75.

Zhang, J., Carpenter, D., & Ko, M. (2013). Online astroturfing: A theoretical perspective. *Proceedings of the Nineteenth Americas Conference on Information Systems, Chicago, Illinois, August 15–17*, 1–7.

Autism Spectrum Disorder

Autism spectrum disorder (ASD) refers to a range of disorders, varying in level of disability, characterized by specific patterns of behavior. These behaviors typically revolve around difficulties in communication and social interaction. Most individuals with autism display a deficit with theory of mind, or the ability to represent another person's mental experiences. That is, they struggle to take in another person's perspective or to think about what another person may be thinking or feeling. Given these deficits, individuals with ASD tend to struggle with detecting deceitful behavior and tend to show a truth bias where they assume others are being honest. Individuals with autism also typically do not engage in deceptive behavior to influence or manipulate others' beliefs, and they struggle with producing socially appropriate lies, such as keeping secrets, surprising others, telling jokes, or competing in games, which impact their social interactions.

Results from a variety of research studies show that children with ASD do not tend to spontaneously engage in deceptive behaviors, are less likely to successfully deceive others when needed for a game paradigm, and have difficulty identifying when others are lying to them, as compared to same-age controls. They show an inability to use social cues, such as eye gaze, gestures, or vocal pitch, to detect deception. Even adults with symptoms of ASD struggle to detect even transparent lies.

In social situations, an inability to lie convincingly or to identify when being lied to makes children more susceptible to bullying. In turn, being a victim of bullying directly correlates to overall anxiety levels and the likelihood of engaging in self-injurious behaviors. Children with ASD are less likely to build connections with others and more likely to violate social display rules and unintentionally offend others. For example, children with autism are less likely to tell polite lies or to lie to protect someone's feelings. They are also more likely to be manipulated or taken advantage of because they struggle with negotiation and tend to be trusting of others, since they assume others are telling the truth.

Behavioral interventions can be used to treat some of these symptoms of ASD. For example, behavioral skills training can teach children with high-functioning autism to recognize deceptive comments and to respond accordingly. Children can be coached about the signs of deception and given specific training for situations where lying may be the socially appropriate course of action. They can be rewarded for identifying deceptive statements and for telling socially appropriate lies, reinforcing the skill. While typically developing children start to realize others may have a different perspective and naturally start to detect deception by age three and to lie by age four, children with ASD do not seem to develop these skills on their own. Thus, for children with autism, deception and deception detection must be a learned skill rather than a naturally emerging ability. Using training, feedback, and reward, Dr. Najdowski and Dr. Tarbox from The Center for Autism and Related Disorders have been able to teach children with ASD to detect lies, to use a polite lie when receiving a disappointing gift, and to respond in a socially appropriate way when asked about someone else's appearance.

Though high functioning individuals with ASD can be taught to lie to protect the feelings of others, to be socially appropriate, or to conceal a transgression, they struggle to maintain the lie with subsequent statements or when asked follow-up questions. Since they struggle with perspective-taking, they tend to be unable to create a convincing fabrication that will successfully mislead others. They remain unaware of what cues others are using to detect deception or may provide conflicting reports that undermine their false story. They also tend to forget to control nonverbal behaviors that may reveal their dishonesty, such as looking toward a hiding spot, smiling, or displaying conflicting verbal and nonverbal statements, making intervention strategies successful only at the surface level.

See also: Age Differences; Detecting Deception; Development of Deception; Nonverbal Behavior; Polite Lies; Prosocial Lying; Recursive Awareness; Theory of Mind; Transparent Lies and the Illusion of Transparency; Truth-Default Theory.

Further Reading

Bergstrom, R., Najdowski, A. C., Alvarado, M., & Tarbox, J. (2016). Teaching children with autism to tell socially appropriate lies. *Journal of Applied Behavior Analysis, 49*(2), 405–410.

Li, A. S., Kelley, E. A., Evans, A. D., & Lee, K. (2011). Exploring the ability to deceive in children with autism spectrum disorders. *Journal of Autism and Developmental Disorders, 41*, 185–195.

Ranick, J., Persicke, A., Tarbox, J., & Kornack, J. A. (2013). Teaching children with autism to detect and respond to deceptive statements. *Research in Autism Spectrum Disorders, 7*, 503–508.

Williams, D. M., Nicholson, T., Grainger, C., Lind, S. E., & Carruthers, P. (2018). Can you spot a liar? Deception, mindreading, and the case of autism spectrum disorder. *Autism Research*. Retrieved from https://www.ncbi.nlm.nih.gov/pubmed/29701910

Yang, Y., Tian, Y., Fang, J., Lu, H., Wei, K., & Yi, L. (2017). Trust and deception in children with autism spectrum disorders: A social learning perspective. *Journal of Autism and Developmental Disorders, 47*, 615–625.

B

Bait and Switch

The bait and switch strategy refers to the deceptive marketing practice of advertising an exceptionally good bargain but then delivering a product that is inferior to, or more expensive than, the one advertised. Once consumers have taken the bait and traveled to the store, they are more likely to buy the more expensive alternative if the one that was advertised is not available. Bait and switch is a form of false advertising and is regulated through the Federal Trade Commission. However, retailers may simply include a caveat in their marketing such as "while supplies last" or "limited stock available" to protect themselves against accusations of false advertising. That is, the very first customer might get the good deal, but for any additional customers the product is out of stock.

Bait and switch works by capturing customers' attention and engaging their interest in a product. Once customers have invested the mental energy to make a decision to purchase, they are more likely to follow through, even if the original deal is unavailable. If a secondary option is also presented as a good deal, even if it is not as good as the one that brought them to the store, they may not even realize that they were a victim of a scam. For consumers to protect themselves from being victims of the bait and switch scam, they must carefully read the fine print of an advertisement and be savvy consumers. If an offer seems too good to be true, consumers may benefit from calling the business prior to a visit to ensure that the product is in stock. If the product is then unexpectedly out of stock when the consumer arrives, the company can be reported to the Federal Trade Commission for using bait and switch practices. The Federal Trade Commission laws stipulate that companies may not mislead consumers regarding promised features or prices in any advertising.

Being an informed consumer may decrease the likelihood of being a victim of a bait and switch scam. Unrealistically good deals are likely scams. Retailers need to make money to stay in business, so selling items at a loss is not a realistic business practice. An advertisement that is confusing or contains a lot of fine print can also signal a bait and switch scam. Another red flag may be if the salesperson immediately offers or promotes a different product or another deal that was not in the advertisement.

The bait and switch strategy is frequently used with high-priced items like electronics, automobiles, or real estate. Sellers may bait customers with high discounts on limited items or with advertisements such as 0 percent financing (caveat: for those who qualify), though almost no customers will actually qualify for that rate. When making large purchases, therefore, it is important to read the terms and conditions, compare the item with those from other sellers, curb impulsive tendencies to buy the backup replacement item, and look at online reviews about the seller. There may be extenuating circumstances that explain the low price such as a going-out-of-business sale or special promotions, but an exceptionally good deal should cause a consumer to take notice and proceed with caution.

Dr. Marie Marchand and colleagues from the University of Provence demonstrated how the bait and switch tactic works. This tactic influences behavior in three steps. First, individuals are baited and make a decision, such as to buy a product. Second, a barrier is presented. Third, a secondary option is offered. Because individuals have already made the decision to purchase, whether it was stressful or rewarding, they are then more likely to continue even with a less rewarding secondary option. To demonstrate, these researchers asked university students to participate in an experiment for which they would be reimbursed. One minute later, the students were informed that the researchers had enough participants and they were not needed. However, they were given the option of engaging in a different experiment that was unpaid. Seventy percent of participants agreed to participate in the unpaid study in comparison to 35 percent who were invited without the initial bait. The bait and switch strategy explains this increase in behavior. The students had made a decision to engage in a task. When that decision was blocked, they were likely to continue and engage in a less-rewarding secondary task to maintain the consistency of the decision.

See also: Advertising; Benefits of Lying; Cognitive Dissonance; Fine Print; Fraud; Media; Scams.

Further Reading

Joule, R.-V., Gouillous, F., & Weber, F. (1989). The lure: A new compliance procedure. *Journal of Social Psychology, 129,* 741–749.

Marchand, M., Joule, R.-V., & Gueguen, N. (2015). The lure technique: Replication and refinement in a field setting. *Psychological Reports: Sociocultural Issues in Psychology, 116*(1), 275–279.

Smith, K. (2019). *Bait and switch advertising scams—Definition, Examples & Laws.* Retrieved from https://www.moneycrashers.com/bait-and-switch-advertising-definition-laws/

Bald-Faced Lies

A bald-faced lie is a claim that is clearly a lie and easily contradicted with obvious evidence. They are called bald-faced lies because liars do not attempt to cover up their lies or disguise them as the truth. These bald-faced claims tend not to be reflective of reality and are generally self-important, impudent, and disrespectful of others. Because they are obvious deceptions, they are usually easy to detect and disprove. However, some bald-faced liars are so confident in their claims that they may sound convincing to a willing listener or confuse the listener, or they may result in self-deception.

Examples of bald-faced lies can include childish lies such as one who claims not to have eaten the chocolate cake despite having a face smeared with chocolate.

A child may also claim, "I didn't do it!" when caught making a mess or being naughty. However, bald-faced lies can also appear in marketing and politics. In marketing, advertisers may use bald-faced lies to sell a product. These lies are typically humorous and the claims so extraordinary that the consumer knows they are not literal. In politics, bald-faced lies are less humorous and are used to attempt to persuade the public. Fact-checkers, for example, have accused Donald Trump of engaging in bald-faced lies when he made claims that were easily disproved. For example, he claimed that the crowds at his inauguration were the largest ever when the data clearly contradicted his statement. Because his lies are said with such confidence, listeners may believe him, particularly if the lies align with what they want to hear. Logic or reason could reveal the lie, but sometimes these lies are effective because logic is not applied. Additionally, bald-faced liars may self-deceive and believe their own lies, even when they are contradicted by evidence. Bluster and confidence can dupe oneself or a willing listener.

Some bald-faced lies are told for prosocial means. Dr. Bella DePaulo and colleague Dr. Kathy Bell found that participants in a research study were likely to lie when honesty would hurt another person's feelings. Researchers asked participants in their study to view artwork and rate which two pieces they liked the most and which two they liked the least. Participants committed their answers in writing and wrote what they liked or disliked about the art. Then a confederate (someone secretly working with the experimenter) entered and discussed the paintings with the participant. As part of the study, the confederate claimed to have painted one of the paintings that the participants liked the least or one of the paintings that they liked the most. The participants were forthcoming and honest about endorsing which painting they liked the most when the confederate claimed to have painted it. However, when confronted with the confederate who painted the one the participant liked the least, only about 40 percent admitted to not liking it. Furthermore, 16 percent of the participants went as far to tell a bald-faced lie and explicitly claimed that they liked the painting, even though they had demonstrably rated it as their least favorite.

For those participants who chose not to tell a bald-faced lie, most still engaged in deception. For example, when asked to discuss what they liked and disliked about the painting, the participants were more likely to find aspects that they liked when the artist was present. Thus, they were still engaging in dishonesty by omitting information but covered their deception by finding aspects that they did like to emphasize in the discussion. When the artist was not present, the same pattern did not emerge. In this way, the participants could assuage their guilt about lying because they told aspects of the truth and allowed the listener to draw their own conclusions.

In most instances, such as in this experiment, bald-faced lies are relatively rare. Most liars are more savvy and integrate subtle lies with omissions and aspects of the truth to emphasize aspects to which they want the listener to pay attention. To rationalize their lies, most liars mislead in a more subtle fashion than actual bald-faced lies. Omitting pertinent information or emphasizing those aspects that are more socially acceptable are more common traits of effective lying than bald statements that commit a liar to the lie.

See also: Advertising; Black Lies; Blue Lies; Categories of Deception; Charlatans; Fact-Check; Fake News; Gaslighting; Machiavellianism; Narcissism; Omission, Lies of; Politics; Puffery.

Further Reading

Biziou-van-Pol, L., Haene, J., Novaro, A., Liberman, A. O., & Capraro, V. (2015). Does telling white lies signal pro-social preferences? *Judgment and Decision Making, 10*(6), 538–548.

DePaulo, B. M., & Bell, K. L. (1996). Truth and investment: Lies are told to those who care. *Journal of Personality and Social Psychology, 71*, 703–716.

Sorensen, R. (2007). Bald-faced lies! Lying without the intent to deceive. *Pacific Philosophical Quarterly, 88*, 251–364.

Barefaced Lie (See Bald-Faced Lies)

Behavior Analysis Interview

The Behavior Analysis Interview (BAI) is a standard interview procedure developed by John E. Reid and Associates in 2001, which is used by police when interviewing suspects, witnesses, and victims prior to an in-depth interrogation. The goal of the BAI is to determine whether or not an individual is withholding information regarding the situation under investigation. In a series of provoking questions, verbal and nonverbal responses are observed to identify individuals who should be questioned further and individuals who are likely innocent. During the BAI, the interviewer is particularly interested in information that reveals inconsistencies, insights, or association with the issue under investigation. Since interrogation can have the side effect of eliciting false confessions, one goal of the BAI is to rule out innocent suspects prior to interrogation procedures, and not to determine ultimate guilt. In one successful research study, 91 percent of guilty suspects and 80 percent of innocent suspects were categorized correctly when interviewed using BAI procedures.

The BAI consists of 15 standardized questions that are designed to elicit different responses depending on whether or not the respondent has information about the situation under investigation. Both verbal responses and nonverbal behaviors are analyzed when responding to questions, such as,

- "What is your understanding of the purpose of this interview?"
- "Did you commit the crime?"
- "Do you know who committed the crime?"
- "Who would have had the best opportunity to commit the crime if they wanted to?"

Questions are divided into background questions, investigative questions, and behavior-provoking questions.

An underlying assumption of the BAI is that innocent individuals have a tendency to provide more details and propose more ideas when questioned about a situation, while guilty individuals are less verbose. For example, following a crime, innocent individuals demonstrate more curiosity and tend to give longer, more detailed responses reflecting their innate curiosity of figuring out what must have happened, since they do not know. This curiosity tends to be strongest when the crime is directly related to the individual's experiences, such as the crime having occurred in their workplace or neighborhood; when they are informed about the crime and have had time to think about what may have happened; and when they are motivated to help the police.

Alternatively, proponents of the BAI believe that guilty individuals will show less curiosity and tend to provide less information overall. The main goal of guilty individuals is to conceal their guilt rather than to figure out what happened, because they already know. Thus, guilty people tend to give shorter verbal responses, and they are more evasive when asked about the purpose of the interview, less helpful in naming possible suspects, and less likely to divulge other information. Guilty suspects also tend to express more confidence in being exonerated.

Nonverbal behaviors are also of particular interest during this interview process. Some specific nonverbal behaviors that are examined are rate of speech, response latency and length of response, facial expressions, head movements, posture changes, foot and leg movements, and direction of eye gaze. Though these individual behaviors naturally vary between individuals and cannot conclusively indicate guilt or innocence, changes in these behaviors during the interview corresponding with particular questions can reveal increased anxiety or emotional arousal, providing the interviewer with information about which questions are salient or provoking to the interviewee.

Proponents of the BAI propose that innocent individuals tend to move their hands and shift their posture more, and they sit more forward in their chairs, with uncrossed arms and legs, than guilty suspects. They are less guarded in their movements and smile and nod more. Innocent suspects also use more words per response on average than guilty individuals. Again, since there are individual differences in all of these behaviors, comparison between suspects' behaviors during the behavior-provoking questions and their behaviors during the background and investigative questions is key.

Critics of the BAI point out that innocent individuals may be upset and anxious due to the situation and may appear guilty under the guidelines of the BAI. They may show nervous behaviors, evade eye contact, or fidget, especially if there are severe consequences for being found guilty. Upon reviewing over 100 scientific studies on deception, results conflicted with the assumptions of the BAI. For example, experienced liars tended to increase eye contact and decrease movements to improve their credibility. They also tried to align with the interviewer and were more helpful when providing other leads and information. Dr. Aldert Vrij and colleagues actually found that liars tended to be more helpful and more relaxed than those who were telling the truth, and truth-tellers appeared to be more evasive when discussing the purpose of the interview and demonstrated more nervous behaviors.

When used appropriately by a trained interviewer, the Behavior Analysis Interview may help experienced interviewers rule our innocent suspects. Due to the inconsistency in laboratory studies, the BAI should only be used for the initial survey of suspects but not for ultimately determining guilt or innocence. Experienced liars may be able to manipulate their verbal and nonverbal responses to more accurately mimic an innocent individual, and innocent individuals may be nervous or unguarded, making the BAI less conclusive.

See also: Brokaw Hazard; Coercion; Concealed Information Test; Control Questions Test; Detecting Deception; Eye Gaze; False Confessions; Motivational Impairment Effect; Nonverbal Behavior; Polygraph Tests; Reid Technique; Sherlock Holmes Effect; Vrij, Aldert.

Further Reading

Blair, J. P. (2008). The Behavioural Analysis Interview: Clarifying the practice, theory and understanding of its use and effectiveness. *International Journal of Police Science and Management, 10*(1), 101–118.

REID. (2014). *The Reid behavior analysis interview.* Retrieved from https://reid.com /resources/investigator-tips/the-reid-behavior-analysis-interview

Vrij, A., Mann, S., & Fisher, R. P. (2006). An empirical test of the behavior analysis interview. *Law and Human Behavior, 30*(3), 329–345.

Bending the Truth

Bending the truth is a subtle type of deception where one makes a statement that is not entirely true with the specific purpose of creating a false impression in others. Typically, one bends the truth in order to be more persuasive, to avoid embarrassment, or to conform to social norms or expectations rather than for malicious reasons. When bending the truth, one may add or eliminate details to elicit a specific response from the listener, to make oneself seem more impressive, or to avoid social censure. Though bending the truth is not usually as socially condemned as outright lying, it can still lead to reputation damage as well as self-deception.

When one bends the truth, listeners often are aware that the story is exaggerated or that details are being fabricated. In these situations, bending the truth simply leads to a more entertaining or impressive story. Common examples are the size of the fish one catches on a fishing trip, the skills of one's performance in a competition, or one's feelings toward another person. Bending the truth may consist of simply rounding up when reporting how much one earns or won or rounding down about how much one spent or lost. However, with repeated tellings, individuals may fall victim to their own lies and start to believe their own exaggerations or minimizations. Repeatedly bending the truth causes a skewing of reality, and the more practice one has bending the truth, the more common the behavior tends to become.

In the short term, bending the truth may have positive outcomes such as increases in attention, respect, and social acceptance. However, being dishonest, even subtly dishonest, tends to result in increases in anxiety and depression, as well as decreases in self-esteem. Repeatedly bending the truth leads to less personal sensitivity to lying behavior, which contributes to increased lying overall. Thus, bending the truth can have compounded consequences.

Though people tend to bend the truth to gain attention, bending the truth can also be used when attempting to avoid negative interactions in relationships, when trying to secure a job during an interview or business negotiation, or when attempting to convince others of one's worth, such as in a political campaign. Those who deceive by bending the truth are able to maintain a conscious self-assessment of not being an outright liar. There is a kernel of truth in their statements, the essence of the statement is honest, if exaggerated, and typically, the liar does not intend to do harm. However, repeated use of the behavior can damage one's credibility, and those with whom they have repeated interactions may start to question the veracity and accuracy of even honest statements.

In the modern day, use of social media is correlated with increased frequency of bending the truth. Some incidents of bending the truth are not premeditated, such as when recounting memories or adventures with friends. Other types can be purposeful and strategic to gain an advantage, such as editing an experience before posting online. Presenting a doctored image of oneself and one's achievements requires a slight bending of reality, which has a corresponding detrimental effect on personal esteem and the esteem of others. Feeling the need to alter images or achievements decreases individuals' abilities to accept themselves as they are and makes others feel inferior when they compare themselves to an altered version of reality. Posting inaccurate information on social media can also cause a cascade effect where the information is spread and altered to such an extent that what started as an exaggerated truth becomes an outright lie.

Bending the truth may be used to avoid hurting another person's feelings or to divert arguments. These subtle deceptions may be used to persuade children to eat healthy or stay safe. They may also be used to buffer another person's self-esteem. However, relying on such embellishments to avoid honest interactions can lead to long-term difficulties; thus such behaviors should be used sparingly, if at all. Protracted exaggerations lead to reputation damage and justified suspicion from others, which can make future interactions more difficult and undermine intimacy and trust within relationships.

See also: Alternative Facts; Consequences of Lying; Costs of Lying; Exaggeration; False Memory; Half-Truths; Lying to Children; Minimization; Omission, Lies of; Politics; Prosocial Lying; Romantic Relationships; Self-Deception; Social Media; White Lies.

Further Reading

Campbell, T., & Anderson, R. (2012). Truth bending: Why politicians are such comfortable liars. *Behavioral Economics & Psychology*. Retrieved from https://advanced -hindsight.com/blog/truthbending/

Seglin, J. L. (1998). The right thing; Bosses beware when bending the truth. *The New York Times*. Retrieved from https://www.nytimes.com/1998/12/20/business/the-right -thing-bosses-beware-when-bending-the-truth.html

Benefits of Lying

Lying behavior is very common in social situations and has many beneficial effects. People lie to friends, family, children, parents, strangers, and even to themselves. Most simplistically, people lie because it helps them get what they

Strategies of Successful Bluffers

Arguably, there are circumstances where successfully deceiving others has its benefits. There are times when it is imperative to appear more confident than one actually is or spin a tale to protect feelings or maintain relationships. Additionally, a specific type of deception, known as bluffing, particularly emerges in athletic or other competitive events. Those who can bluff effectively can manipulate the behavior of those around them, providing a heightened chance of success for the bluffer.

Some key skills are needed to be a successful bluffer. One must have impeccable timing, confidence, behavioral control, and awareness of one's audience. To build these skills, one needs to think about body language, vocal tone, emotional expressions, and paraverbal behaviors ahead of time. The anxiety elicited by telling a lie may make liars more conscious of all of these aspects, which makes their lies less convincing. Practicing the lie can help but may also make it wooden and unemotional, necessitating a balance between practice and easiness to remain convincing. Successful bluffers stay relaxed. They do not turn away, fidget, or tense up. They keep their message consistent and stick to the truth as closely as possible.

The most successful bluffers have a clear goal and plan ahead. Those who try to make up lies on the spot are more likely to give away indications of lying. A clear, well-planned-out lie allows bluffers to keep their stories consistent and convincing, and prevents the need for constructing information in the moment that may be inconsistent or suspect. Successful bluffers also incorporate as much truth as possible into their bluffs. If most of the story is truthful, listeners are less likely to suspect dishonesty. Furthermore, even if the audience senses that something is amiss, they will not know which part of the story is not true.

Another common strategy is to distract or minimize the lie. Successful bluffers do not emphasize the bluff. They expect to be believed, provide few details, and then change the subject. Successful bluffers practice, know their own tells, and take measures to compensate, such as maintaining animated facial expressions to prevent expressions of disgust, anger, or anxiety from leaking out. Rather than simply suppressing such facial expressions, they camouflage them with an alternative expression.

Successful bluffers also get to know their opponents. Successful athletes, for example, will study their opponents to learn their tells to be able to better predict their moves in play and to more effectively mislead or misdirect them. If opponents are also familiar with the bluffer, however, it may be more difficult to successfully bluff because the opponent will be more likely to be able to read the buffer's tells. Thus, successful bluffers must think about their audience to know what the others might expect and what they may be most likely to believe.

Finally, the most effective bluffers are honest most of the time, and therefore, those around them have no reason to harbor suspicion. To be an effective liar or effective bluffer, lies should be rare and unexpected. This also allows successful bluffers to keep track of their lies because they are not mixed in with a tangled web of deceit.

want. In that way, lying can be naturally reinforcing, and the more the liars benefit from lying, the more likely they are to lie again. Lies help individuals maintain relationships, avoid awkward social situations, and avoid punishments. Individuals also lie to save face, garner respect, or protect their own mental health.

Dr. Robert Feldman and colleagues from the University of Massachusetts at Amherst found that college students who were good at being deceptive were the most popular with their peers. These students lied during conversations with strangers approximately 3 times every 10 minutes. Such rates of lying cause the behavior to become automatic, and many people start to become unaware of the lies that they are telling. Dr. Feldman also found that individuals who were effective at self-deception suffered fewer depressive symptoms than those who were honest with themselves. Thus, those with a healthy balance of protective self-deception may be more mentally stable than those who are honest with themselves about their own flaws and weaknesses. Dr. Feldman found that accepting lies can also buffer self-esteem. Accepting compliments or positive feedback, even if it is dishonest, feels good and increases confidence. In general, use of deceptive tact, or social grace, seems to be valued more highly than honesty in many social settings.

Dr. Brian Gunia from Johns Hopkins University and Emma Levine from the University of Chicago Booth School of Business found that intentions may matter more than strict honesty. Telling a lie that has someone else's self-interest in mind may actually be more beneficial than telling the truth when attempting to build trusting relationships. These prosocial lies can benefit other individuals, build self-esteem, and serve as motivators. Lies may also be called for when there is limited time to make changes. Supporting choices when there is no alternative for change may help buffer self-esteem and confidence. Avoiding the blunt truth in new relationships can also be beneficial. Honesty can be particularly damaging if the individuals do not have an established trusting relationship. Being honest with family or friends, alternatively, can have much more beneficial outcomes than lying because trust has already been established. So, though honesty is important for trusting relationships, many are built on deception.

Another benefit of lying includes increasing productivity by avoiding unnecessary social interactions. Lying may be a simple way to deter others in a socially appropriate way by claiming a prior commitment. White lies can also motivate others, increase their confidence, and help keep them on track. Lying may help individuals negotiate more effectively and promote cooperative alliances or avoid punishment for transgressions. And lying to oneself can help protect self-esteem and decrease feelings of depression.

The benefits of lying revolve around gaining personal benefits and avoiding costs that would occur if one told the truth. Most individuals are more likely to tell unfair lies to strangers and more altruistic lies to friends. Furthermore, lying is actually a sign of healthy cognitive growth. Dr. Shanna Williams from McGill University and colleagues found that children who tell prosocial lies actually have higher skills in working memory and better cognitive control. Thus, lying seems to be a by-product of healthy brain development. These children frequently tell prosocial lies rather than antisocial lies. Such prosocial lying provides behavioral evidence that children have developed theory of mind, empathy, compassion, and the ability to see the consequences of their statements. Such behavior also shows they are able to inhibit the truth, produce a plausible lie, and monitor the listener, all highly developed cognitive skills necessary to interact in the social world.

See also: Butler Lies; Consequences of Lying; Costs of Lying; Lying to Children; Motives for Lying; Polite Lies; Prosocial Lying; Self-Deception; Tactical Deception; Theory of Mind; White Lies.

Further Reading

Crow, S. (2018, March 26). This is why lying is good for you: A little fib never hurt anyone—In fact, lying may be good for you. *Bestlife*. Retrieved from https://bestlifeonline .com/lying-health-benefits/

Feldman, R. S., Tomasian, J. C., & Coats, E. J. (1999). Nonverbal deception abilities and adolescents' social competence: Adolescents with higher social skills are better liars. *Journal of Nonverbal Behavior, 23*, 237–249.

Gunia, B. C., & Levine, E. E. (2019). Deception as competence: The effect of occupational stereotypes on the perception and proliferation of deception. *Organizational Behavior and Human Decision Processes, 152*, 122–137.

Rose, L. (2005, October 24). Lying is good for you. *Forbes*. Retrieved from https://www .forbes.com/2005/10/19/lying-dishonesty-psychology_cx_lr_comm05_1024lie .html?sh=7ca41de2107c

Shortsleeve, C. (2018, October 2). Honesty isn't always the best policy in relationships. Here's when experts say it might be better to lie. *Time*. Retrieved from https:// time.com/5406989/when-better-to-lie-than-tell-truth/

Williams, S., Moore, K., Crossman, A. M., & Talwar, V. (2016). The role of executive functions in theory of mind in children's prosocial lie-telling. *Journal of Experimental Child Psychology, 141*, 256–266.

Betrayal

Betrayal refers to sharing private information, intentionally or unintentionally. Betrayal can include breaching an agreement, being unfaithful, sharing secrets, or other violations of trust. Betrayal involves violating either unspoken or established expectations. Betrayal most frequently occurs in close relationships such as friendships, romantic relationships, or established groups, such as political organizations. Because betrayal involves sharing private information, the individual engaging in betrayal has to be close enough to be privy to such information. Thus, betrayal is a particularly harmful type of deceit because it involves a violation within a personal relationship. If enemies engaged in similar behaviors, it would not be considered betrayal because such behaviors would not violate expectations.

Common types of betrayal include exposing private information, spreading rumors, having an affair, lying, and not providing assistance when needed. The extent of the betrayal depends on the depth of trust being violated and the amount of harm done. Betrayal can lead to feelings of hurt within a relationship, PTSD-like symptoms, hyper-arousal and hyper-reactivity, avoidance of the betrayer, distress, self-doubt, and difficulty in trusting others. Individuals who are victims of betrayal report feeling humiliated, traumatized, and ashamed. Since betrayal depends on the violation of a trusting bond, psychological distress occurs even though there may not be a physical wound.

Healthy relationships consist of trust and support, but even healthy relationships may experience moments of betrayal. Stress, temptations, and different preferences can lead to behaviors that may jeopardize the stability of the relationship and cause situations where forgiveness may be needed to maintain the relationship. The extent of forgiveness following a betrayal may depend on how one perceives and explains the deceptive act, how emotionally provoking the behavior was, the quality of the relationship, and future goals. Reactions can range from understanding and forgiveness to retribution and revenge.

Forgiveness includes behaviors, cognitive interpretations, and emotional reactions. For couples who have high commitment levels, long-term reconciliations are more positive, particularly for behaviors and cognitive interpretations. Individuals in committed relationships report more immediate negative emotional reactions, but long-term emotions tend to be more positive. Couples in relationships characterized by low commitment showed overall lower forgiveness after a betrayal. Thus, more highly committed couples were more forgiving despite the fact that they experienced more negative emotions at the time of the betrayal. The stronger negative emotions may be due to violations of higher expectations and greater forgiveness may occur due to an interest in maintaining the relationship.

Romantic betrayals are one of the most common types of betrayal. These types of betrayal can take many forms. Romantic betrayals can be sharing confidences, not being supportive of a partner, being sexually unfaithful, engaging in physical abuse, or seeking a divorce. Regardless of the type of betrayal, psychological effects tend to result. Those who are the victims of significant acts of betrayal typically experience emotional distress, anxiety, depression, anger, jealousy, and decreased self-esteem, at least initially. They may experience psychosomatic problems, such as headaches, stomachaches, or elevated blood pressure, and may engage in self-destructive behaviors such as alcohol consumption or drug use. Though many people may experience various levels of betrayal, not everyone reacts in the same manner. Some individuals blame themselves for the betrayal, while others blame their partners. In most cases, placing the blame on the betrayer leads to fewer long-term psychological and health problems.

Unsurprisingly, betrayal threatens the stability of relationships and can affect how an individual views future relationships. Since trust is important for a stable relationship, its violation is likely to end a relationship. However, since time and energy have been invested into a partner, some couples do decide to try to work on and maintain their relationship after a betrayal such as sexual infidelity. Couples may decide to stay together due to the amount of time invested in the relationship or their children, or they may be motivated to make the relationship work. However, to successfully overcome betrayal, both partners must be invested in working to repair the relationship. Counseling is typically needed to regain trust, and the individuals must engage in proactive repair. Honesty, openness, communication, and commitment are needed to recreate stability and support within a relationship.

See also: Categories of Deception; Catfishing; Consequences of Lying; Dating; Infidelity; Motives for Lying; Online Dating; Romantic Relationships.

Further Reading

Couch, L. L., Baughman, K. R., & Derow, M. R. (2017). The aftermath of romantic betrayal: What's love got to do with it? *Current Psychology: A Journal for Diverse Perspectives on Diverse Psychological Issues, 36*(3), 504–515.

Finkel, E. J., Rusbult, C. E., Kumashiro, M., & Hannon, P. A. (2002). Dealing with betrayal in close relationships: Does commitment promote forgiveness? *Journal of Personality and Social Psychology, 82*(6), 956–974.

Patrick, W. L. (2017, June 10). How some couple stay together even after an affair: A personal choice to put grace over justice. *Psychology Today*. Retrieved from https://www.psychologytoday.com/us/blog/why-bad-looks-good/201706/how-some-couples-stay-together-even-after-affair

Rachman, S. (2010). Betrayal: A psychological analysis. *Behaviour Research and Therapy, 48*, 304–311.

Black Lies

Black lies, sometimes referred to as real lies, refer to selfish lies told for personal gain. These lies benefit the teller and take something from the one who is being deceived. An example of a black lie would be selling someone an electronic device or used car that one knows is defective. The liar receives money and the receiver loses out. Black lies are typically antisocial and are the lies condemned as immoral across cultures. They are told for malicious, self-serving reasons and are complete fabrications of information. They are manipulative, deceitful, premeditated, and devious.

Black lies are frequently called high-stakes lies in research because there is risk of loss of reputation or likelihood of punishment if the lie is detected. Thus, before engaging in black lies, these liars are likely to assess the likelihood that they will get away with the lie, the amount that can be gained from the lie, the likely punishments they will receive if caught in the lie, and the cost of losing the relationship with the target should the lie be detected. Black lies are more frequently told when the chances of detection are small, the potential for gain is high, and the liar does not have a close relationship with the target. Individuals caught in black lies typically sustain damage to their reputations, may lose relationships, or may incur legal punishments. They tend to face more consequences than those who are caught telling other types of lies. Those who are caught engaging in prosocial lies, white lies, or exaggerations do not tend to face these same consequences.

People are motivated to lie for a variety of reasons and tend to assess different types of lies as more or less devious. When motivations for lying were examined, differences emerged between motivations to engage in prosocial lies, white lies, and antisocial black lies. Prosocial liars and white liars tend to be motivated by smoothing over social interactions or avoiding hurting the feelings of others. Black liars, alternatively, use lies to secure an advantage over others, and they are less empathetic of others' feelings or perceptions. Most individuals endorse understanding and forgiveness of white lies and condone their use more readily. Most individuals do not support black lies and consider such lies as unethical and antisocial, across development and across cultures. Permissibility of these lies varies in relation to the extent of self-focus and potential harm. The more harmful the lie, the more likely raters will rate it as unethical. Using black lies to increase self-esteem or to increase social standing tends to be less negatively rated than using them to gain an advantage over others, such as to get money or a reward.

Individuals with personality traits that fall within those highlighted by the Dark Triad, specifically Machiavellianism, narcissism, and psychopathy, are more likely to endorse using lies, particularly black lies. Those having high scores on scales of Machiavellianism show less guilt when telling lies and are more comfortable telling high-stakes black lies, compared to individuals who score low on these traits. Those scoring high on scales of narcissism, psychopathy, and Machiavellianism are likely to endorse malevolent intentions with potential negative consequences as acceptable. These individuals were more likely to see lies as an acceptable and justifiable means to attain a goal, even when they use them for personal gain. Interestingly, with age, lying behavior wanes, as do scores of narcissistic personality traits.

See also: Antisocial Personality Disorder; Bald-Faced Lies; Blue Lies; Categories of Deception; Commission, Lies of; Dark Triad; Fabrication; Gaslighting; Instrumental Lies; Lying; Machiavellianism; Manipulation; Motives for Lying; Narcissism; Sex Differences in Lying Behavior; Tactical Deception; White Lies.

Further Reading
Biziou-van-Pol, L., Haene, J., Novaro, A., Liberman, A. O., & Capraro, V. (2015). Does telling white lies signal pro-social preferences? *Judgment and Decision Making, 10*(6), 538–548.

Bryant, E. (2008). Real lies, white lies, and gray lies: Towards a typology of deception. *Kaleidoscope: A Graduate Journal of Qualitative Communication Research, 7,* 23–48.

Dreber, A., & Johannesson, M. (2008). Gender differences in deception. *Economic Letters, 99*(1), 197–199.

Rose, C., & Wilson, M. S. (2014). Perceptions of everyday deceptions: Individual differences in narcissism and psychopathy associated with black and white untruths. In A. Besser (Ed.), *Handbook of the Psychology of Narcissism* (pp. 229–248). Nova Science Publications.

Blue Lies

Blue lies are a specific type of lie that are told to benefit a group, rather than an individual. Blue lies are used to maintain relationships and to bond rather than for purposes of individual gain. Blue lies are a type of prosocial lie that are not as selfless as altruistic lies, which are told to help others, nor are they as selfish as black lies, which both benefit the liar and harm others. Instead, blue lies benefit the group to which one belongs. Thus, blue lies are self-serving because they serve the individual who is part of the group, but they can also help others because they benefit the group as a whole. Such lies function to make the group more cohesive and facilitate social connection. However, blue lies also tend to widen the divide between groups. Group members who are unified by blue lies are likely to justify, excuse, or deny the deceptive behavior of someone within the group to maintain the social relationships and to strengthen the group bonds.

Just as we see an increase in white lies over development, blue lies similarly increase as a means of protecting others. Individuals tell blue lies as a means of maintaining social norms, conforming to group etiquette, and strengthening relationships. By age 11, children are likely to tell blue lies to support the group that they identify with even if there is little benefit for themselves. They may tell blue lies to protect their sports teams, their friends, their classmates, or any other group to which they belong. Furthermore, this tendency increases with age. In adulthood, adults tell blue lies to protect their families, teams, communities, and other groups to which they identify. An excellent example of the power of the group on telling and accepting lies is political parties. Those who strongly identify with a political party are likely to tell and accept lies that support their group, even if they do not personally benefit from the lie and even if there is no evidence to support the claims.

Donald Trump provided an interesting example of the power of blue lies throughout his presidency because, though he engaged in bald-faced lying, such lies did not seem to undermine his level of support. If one examines the content of his lies, most were told as a means of strengthening or unifying the Republican Party. These blue lies strengthened rather than weakened the bonds between members of the group, and thus individuals within that party may have felt supported and became more committed as a result of accepting the lies rather than turning against the liar or contradicting the lies.

Since blue lies benefit groups, they tend to be more accepted by and acceptable to group members. There is a strong tendency to want to believe blue lies because they are told to benefit the group to which one belongs, and therefore, individuals can be convinced by these lies even when there is little or no empirical evidence. For example, those who deny climate change or claim that the earth is flat are not interested in the truth. They are more interested in believing the blue lies told by group members and conforming to and supporting their group. This solidarity strengthens the group and pits them against the opposition. The phenomenon of blue lies demonstrates an individual's desire to be loyal, to cooperate, and to build trusting relationships with those around them. Blue lies also demonstrate the ease with which a group can dehumanize or discredit those outside of the group, regardless of evidence.

In collectivist cultures, the development of blue lies is particularly salient. For example, research by Dr. Kang Lee and his colleagues' shows Chinese children are more willing to lie to benefit the group than to benefit themselves. This demonstrates to some extent why lying behavior is so prevalent in many aspects of adult life. Most adults, particularly those from collectivist cultures, endorse lying to protect their group members even if they do not endorse lying to protect themselves. Moreover, since blue lies tend to benefit the group as well as the individual, they may be the most common and accepted of all.

See also: Bald-Faced Lies; Black Lies; Categories of Deception; Cognitive Dissonance; Cultural Differences; Development of Deception; Motives for Lying; Prosocial Lying; Self-Deception; White Lies.

Further Reading

Fu, G., Evans, A. D., Wang, L., & Lee, K. (2008). Lying in the name of the collective good: A developmental study. *Developmental Science, 11*(4), 495–503.

Smith, J. A. (2017). How the science of "Blue Lies" may explain Trump's support. *Scientific American*. Retrieved from https://blogs.scientificamerican.com/guest-blog/how-the-science-of-blue-lies-may-explain-trumps-support/

Bluffs

A bluff is a form of deception in which individuals make confident, though false, claims in order to intimidate or deceive others. Bluffs can emerge in the animal kingdom, in conversations, or in competitions. For example, in nature, animals who are injured and have no hope of winning an altercation may instinctually bluff and act aggressively to intimidate opponents and prevent them from engaging in a fight. If opponents believe the bluff, they will back down. Alternatively, birds may feign injury to draw a predator away from their nests, only giving up on the ruse once the danger is over. In conversations, individuals may claim to be stronger, smarter, or faster than others, particularly in situations where it is not likely that they will be asked to prove their claims. Through such bluffs, they may gain position, power, or resources.

In competitions, bluffs are used to intimidate or to gain competitive advantage over an opponent. Bluffs are particularly common in poker. Players may bluff and bet money as if they are holding cards of high value in order to intimidate other players into dropping out. Successful bluffs may allow individuals to deceive others well enough to escape detection, which allows them to continue to bluff in the future. Individuals can also bluff in a variety of situations such as in business negotiations, job interviews, or police interrogations in an attempt to gain an advantage.

To call someone's bluff is to force them to carry out the implied behavior or otherwise prove their claim, such as by showing their cards or providing proof of achievements or threatened behavior. For example, individuals may challenge or threaten others and insinuate a consequence of which they are unable to follow through. If another person calls their bluff, then they are challenged to carry out the threat or to otherwise prove that they can back up their claims. The hazard of calling a bluff lies in situations where the person can actually follow through and proves not to have been bluffing. However, frequently bluffers may back down, likely with damage to their reputation.

When bluffing occurs in a competitive game setting, it is typically not considered to be unethical. A bluff in a game situation is expected and is a common strategy that players may use to gain the upper hand. It is common in poker or in competitive sports where players may feign their next moves to distract or trick opponents. Part of the game strategy is to learn to recognize when opponents are telling the truth and when they are bluffing. This may require calling their bluffs on occasion and risking defeat to learn how to better determine whether or not they are telling the truth in the future.

In police interrogations, bluffs create more of an ethical dilemma. Officers may resort to a bluff tactic to convince suspects to reveal more information than they intended. In such a situation, interrogators may imply that they have more evidence than they actually do or have more witnesses or information to trick a suspect into revealing information. Dr. Jennifer T. Perillo and Dr. Saul M. Kassin from John Jay College of Criminal Justice in New York demonstrated that, though the use of bluffs does increase the number of confessions by guilty suspects, it also tends to increase false confessions. The pressure of believing that interrogators have evidence may confuse, intimidate, or make suspects feel more vulnerable, leading to confessions of crimes, even by innocent individuals, to gain a less severe punishment. If the bluff is convincing, suspects may start to doubt their own perceptions, internalize guilt, and feel trapped. Thus, the use of bluffs needs to be ethically evaluated in situations where there is an imbalance of power.

See also: Benefits of Lying; Black Lies; Categories of Deception; Competition; Ethics; False Confessions; False Memory; Polygraph Tests; Tactical Deception; White Lies.

Further Reading

Patomaki, J., Yan, J., & Laakasuo, M. (2016). Machiavelli as a poker mate—A naturalistic behavioural study on strategic deception. *Personality and Individual Differences, 98*, 266–271.

Perillo, J. T., & Kassin, S. M. (2011). Inside interrogation: The lie, the bluff, and false confessions. *Law and Human Behavior, 35*(4), 327–337.

Bold-Faced Lies (See Bald-Faced Lies)

Borderline Personality Disorder

Borderline personality disorder (BPD) is a psychological disorder in which individuals have difficulty in regulating their emotions, presenting a coherent and stable identity, and regulating social interactions. They are likely to feel higher rates of helplessness and dependence and lower levels of control, and they are more likely to engage in deception to try to get what they want without considering how their behavior may affect others. They tend to be manipulative and attempt to influence others with their words or actions. They also tend to be inconsistent in their own opinions, likely resulting from an unstable identity. They tend to fear abandonment, have unstable relationships, have a distorted view of reality, and are impulsive and moody. Individuals with BPD frequently display comorbidity with other psychological problems. Additionally, individuals with BPD frequently display pathological lying without any signs of guilt.

Dr. Scott Snyder worked with individuals presenting with borderline personality disorder and observed a greater likelihood of these individuals purposefully withholding information to manipulate others. Dr. Snyder suggested that it is frequently difficult to determine whether such deceptions are purposeful or if they are a by-product of a distorted view of reality. Given the presentation of the symptoms, such lies may function to maintain the individual's self-esteem or as a mechanism of acting out fantasies. Individuals with BPD may use lies to buffer their sense of self or to elevate how they view themselves. They may use lying behavior to protect themselves or because they believe it is necessary, given the way they are interpreting the situation. Patients with BPD tend to struggle with understanding the beliefs of others and may project their own beliefs on to those around them. They may also lack impulse control and lie without thinking of the consequences and with little concern for the impact of their lies on others.

Dr. Eugenia Mandal and Dr. Dagna Kocur from the University of Silesia in Poland interviewed 125 therapists who work with patients with borderline personality disorder and found that 88 percent of the therapists reported that patients with BPD are more likely than healthy controls to engage in attempts at manipulation. These patients were likely to make threats or to plead with the therapist to get their way. The most common behaviors reported were telling lies or attempting to induce guilt in the therapist to gain sympathy or benefits. In Dr. Mandal's study, though almost all of the therapists noted that their patients were likely to use manipulation, the patients themselves denied such attempts. The patients were either unaware of their manipulative attempts or unwilling to admit to them.

Some specific examples of manipulation commonly used by patients with BPD include attempting to take over sessions, demanding special accommodations, demanding promises or implying that promises had been made, attempting to impose conditions, threatening the therapist with self-destructive behaviors, omitting information, attempting to make a positive impression, or expressing contradictory opinions. One difficulty in studying individuals with BPD is that most deny manipulation attempts, and it is difficult to determine whether such attempts are premeditated or unconscious. Since they have an unclear sense of themselves, their behavior may be unintentionally inconsistent rather than purposefully manipulative. If this is the case, then increasing the individuals' sense of themselves and self-insight may be key in treating the disorder.

Researchers from the University of Turin, Italy, examined the connection between theory of mind and BPD. One reason that individuals with BPD may have difficulty with social interactions is that they show difficulties in taking in others' perspectives. This is a theory of mind deficit that causes the individual to have difficulty in understanding the beliefs or emotions of others. In a host of research studies, individuals with BPD had more difficulty in recognizing and interpreting negative emotional expressions of a social partner. Furthermore, when asked to explain the emotions or beliefs of characters in a short video, individuals with BPD showed difficulties in interpreting the emotions and likely beliefs of the characters, particularly for complex, realistic social interactions. Individuals with borderline traits seem to misinterpret what other people are experiencing. When patients with BPD were asked to interpret the thoughts of others, they demonstrated difficulty in distinguishing the mental states of others as distinct from their own thoughts and feelings. BPD individuals are also more likely to demonstrate suspicious or hostile attribution biases, which means they are more likely to interpret ambiguous social interactions as hostile and react accordingly.

See also: Antisocial Personality Disorder; Compulsive Lying; Delusions; Emotional Effects; Instrumental Lies; Manipulation; Self-Deception; Theory of Mind.

Further Reading

Colle, L., Gabbatore, I., Riberi, E., Borroz, E., Bosco, F. M., & Keller, R. (2019). Mind-reading abilities and borderline personality disorder: A comprehensive assessment using the Theory of Mind Assessment Scale. *Psychiatry Research, 272*, 609–617.

Mandal, E., & Kocur, D. (2013). Psychological masculinity, femininity and tactics of manipulation in patients with borderline personality disorder. *Archives of Psychiatry and Psychotherapy, 1*, 45–53.

Snyder, S. (1986). Pseudologia Fantastica in the borderline patient. *The American Journal of Psychiatry, 143*(10), 1287–1289.

Brokaw Hazard

The Brokaw Hazard refers to the difficulty of accurately detecting deception when engaging with unfamiliar social partners. Having an understanding of the cues that signal deception does not take into account the individual differences for such behaviors. Dr. Paul Ekman coined the term in 1985, naming it after renowned news anchor Tom Brokaw, who expressed that he used verbal cues to detect deception during interviews. Mr. Brokaw found that convoluted answers to direct questions were a relatively accurate indicator of attempts to deceive. However, Dr. Ekman points out that the issue then becomes that some honest people may naturally have a convoluted conversation style. Thus, individual differences in behaviors may cause some individuals to be perceived as liars although they are actually telling the truth, even when empirically supported methods to evaluate veracity are applied.

If an individual is not acquainted with a social partner and thus not familiar with their individual idiosyncrasies, they are at risk of falling victim to the Brokaw Hazard. Individuals vary in the way they respond to stress, emotional arousal, excitement, and nervousness or anxiety. Vocal pitch changes, pauses, speech errors, and mannerisms that have been empirically demonstrated as being associated with deception may be normal for some individuals, even when they are telling the truth. Alternatively, practiced liars may be able to control such indicators and pass for someone who is telling the truth. Dr. Ekman cautions that there are no cues to deceit that are reliable for all people. Most people may react in specific ways when lying, but such behaviors are not conclusive of lying for everyone. Being familiar with an individual's typical speech patterns and mannerisms may decrease the likelihood of falling victim to the Brokaw Hazard.

To avoid the Brokaw Hazard, one must base judgments on changes in behavior rather than one-time behavior. Such comparisons may be made within an interview or interrogation by asking individuals to respond to a broad range of questions. Verbal and nonverbal patterns can then be established in order to create a basis for comparison. First-time interactions are the most vulnerable to errors as well as high-stress interactions, making the Brokaw Hazard particularly applicable to interrogations and suspect interviews. Distinguishing between anxiety due to guilt and anxiety due to the fear of not being believed is difficult, if not impossible. Basing decisions of guilt on signals of arousal, particularly without a basis of comparison, therefore makes one particularly prone to making a mistake and falling victim to the Brokaw Hazard. The hazard can be decreased by having a thorough understanding of the individual's typical mannerisms and ways of communicating and by making judgments on changes in behavior rather than on behavior in isolation.

For most interrogation techniques, an interviewer must first obtain a measure of baseline behavior. Baseline behavior is behavior that is typical for that specific individual. To identify deceptive cues such as higher vocal pitch or changes in eye contact, one must first know how an individual typically communicates. Everyone has personal idiosyncrasies, and if these idiosyncrasies are mistaken for deceptive attempts, the Brokaw Hazard has occurred. Furthermore, as illustrated by the Othello Error, individuals who are suspected of lying may actually show increase in behaviors typically associated with lying, creating a negative feedback loop. One suspected of lying demonstrates increased arousal that increases behaviors typically associated with liars, which is then used as proof of lying.

The Brokaw Hazard emerges because behavioral, verbal, and nonverbal cues vary among people. There are no reliable cues of deception that apply to all people in every situation. Thus, when attempting to detect deception, interviewers or other individuals must be careful not to draw incorrect conclusions about innocent individuals simply based on superficial cues. Alternatively, one must be aware that savvy liars may not show cues of deceit, making their deceptive statements likely to be read as honest, further convoluting detection efforts. Tom Brokaw may have had some success in reading deception during interviews given his years of experience, but researchers caution that his methodology cannot be applied broadly or conclusively, particularly in highly arousing situations.

See also: Behavior Analysis Interview; Concealed Information Test; Control Questions Test; Detecting Deception; Ekman, Paul; Emotional Effects; Language; Meyer, Pamela; Motivational Impairment Effect; Nonverbal Behavior; Othello Error; Polygraph Tests; Vocal Changes When Lying.

Further Reading

Dunn, S. (2020). What is the Brokaw Hazard? *Behavior, Motivation, Property, & Life*. Retrieved from https://studunnsdl.wordpress.com/2020/01/17/what-is-the-brokaw-hazard/

Ekman, P. (1985). *Telling Lies: Clues to Deceit in the Marketplace, Politics, and Marriage*. Norton.

Bullshit (*See Careless Liars*)

Butler Lies

A butler lie is a polite lie dictated by social norms as a means to maintain good manners, particularly used to avoid or end social interactions. Both parties may recognize a butler lie as untrue but it serves to maintain the relationship and smooth over social interactions. Butler lies can help individuals to exit conversations or to avoid starting a conversation without offending the partner. In historic times, butlers served as a buffer between an individual and a guest. If instructed, the butler could provide a social barrier by stating that his employer was otherwise engaged or unavailable, protecting the employer's time while maintaining a polite and civil interaction. In modern times, most people do not have butlers and must provide their own excuses to avoid interactions. Additionally, butler lies have become more frequent to maintain boundaries as modern technology creates the means for greater and greater availability.

Prior to mobile phones, to avoid phone interruptions, individuals could retroactively tell a simple butler lie and claim they were not at home. Now, with mobile phones, it becomes more difficult to avoid these social interruptions. Individuals may occasionally claim poor service or a bad connection to end a call, but it is more difficult to avoid the disruption. Avoiding others sounds socially inappropriate, but in the technological age, a need has arisen to protect productivity from constant distractions. Technology has made individuals ever available for interruptions and many fall victim to email, text, and message overload. Because of this ever-present availability, butler lies are now most commonly sent electronically and are used to avoid or terminate conversations while maintaining relationships. These polite lies have become the social norm to preserve relationships in an ever-accessible age. Butler lies are used particularly as ways to end conversations so that one can move on to other tasks or to avoid interruptions in order to get other things accomplished.

Not only do new platforms for electronic communication, such as email, text messaging, instant messaging, direct messaging, Snapchat, and Instagram, make individuals more and more accessible but also research shows that employees, students, and professionals expect prompt responses to emails and perceive a slight when emails go unanswered for even short periods. Smartphone users send thousands of texts, and instant messaging is on mobile devices that individuals carry with them. Thus, instant responses have become the norm and are frequently expected. Unsurprisingly, such on-demand expectations can be detrimental to productivity. The possibility of interruptions also makes individuals less able to focus on tasks and can be detrimental to psychological health. Butler lies are a simple methodology to provide individuals a smooth exit strategy to protect time and sanity. The average individual now spends more time and effort managing availability and protecting time than ever before.

The most common butler lie presented over instant messaging platforms is simply telling the conversation partner that one has to go, when in fact one is really just ready to end the conversation. Other common lies include providing a specific excuse to end the conversation such that one is headed out, ready to eat, or going to bed. Alternatively, butler liars may just avoid a conversation and later express that they were away from the computer, had a dead battery, did not see the message, or were asleep. The conversation partner does typically not challenge such lies even if they are not believable and they allow individuals to smoothly exit or avoid conversations without causing rifts in the relationship. To combat constant interruptions, some instant messaging platforms allow users to mark themselves as "away" as a means of deterring or providing an excuse to delay a response. When examined, butler lies in electronic messaging were most common when exiting a conversation or explaining why there was a delay in response.

Butler lies are told more readily to individuals with whom one communicates frequently, demonstrating their use in maintaining relationships. When analyzed, researchers such as Dr. Jeremy Birnholtz and colleagues from Northwestern University found that 2 percent of the instant messages analyzed consisted of butler lies. Furthermore, these researchers revealed that almost all instant messengers interviewed used butler lies, and all users rated them as an appropriate way to end online conversations, even if they are obviously untrue.

See also: Benefits of Lying; Categories of Deception; Motives for Lying; Polite Lies; Prevalence of Lying; Prosocial Lying; Social Media; White Lies.

Further Reading

Birnholtz, J., Reynolds, L., Smith, M. E., & Hancock, J. (2013). "Everyone has to do it": A joint action approach to managing social inattention. *Computers in Human Behavior, 29*, 2230–2238.

Hancock, J., Birnholtz, J., Bazarova, N., Guillory, J., Perlin, J., & Amos, B. (2009). Butler lies: Awareness, deception, and design. *Computer Mediated Communication, 1*, 517–526.

C

Camouflage

Deception can be viewed as an evolutionary adaptation that functions at a basic level to allow species to survive. For humans, deception tends to be verbal statements or nonverbal cues intended to mislead others in order to gain an advantage or avoid punishment, but deception can take many forms. In plants and other animals, deception can emerge through camouflage. Though naturally occurring camouflage does not include conscious attempts to deceive, it still can be categorized as deception because it misleads others. Camouflage evolved because those organisms who blended more closely into their environments were less likely to be eaten by predators. Blending into one's surroundings may also allow organisms to hunt more effectively. Both of these benefits of camouflage allow organisms to survive more readily. Survival then allows for increased time to reproduce to pass on those physical traits. In this way, camouflage is selected via natural selection. Those individuals within a species that have the physical markings that allow them to survive reproduce at greater rates, increasing the number of those with particular color patterns in the species.

There are four basic types of camouflage. The first type of camouflage is coloration that matches the background. Lizards, frogs, hares, and owls, for example, can have coloring that matches their typical environment. The second type of camouflage is patterned coloration that helps an animal be less noticeable within their environment. Stripes, spots, or patterns allow some animals to blend in better and create less of a stark contrast to the surrounding environment, such as that seen in zebras, cheetahs, and snakes. The third type of camouflage is disguise. Insects such as walking sticks camouflage themselves by appearing to be something else that is common in the environment. Finally, mimicry is a type of camouflage in which animals or insects look like another animal or insect that is toxic in order to deter predators, such as in butterflies or moths that mimic their toxic relatives.

The peppered moth provides an excellent example of the benefits of camouflage. The peppered moth species has natural variation in wing color, ranging from very light to very dark. Individual moths vary in how peppered, or spotted, their wings appear. In an unpolluted environment, moths with lighter wings tend to match the white birch or lichen-covered trees on which they rest during the day. These lighter moths tend to survive better in such environments and pass on the light wing color trait to their populous offspring. Darker winged moths tend to stand out against the light trees and are more likely to be eaten by predator birds. During the Industrial Revolution at the turn of the twentieth century, pollution killed the lichen and darkened the trees. Soon the lighter moths no longer were camouflaged when they rested on the trunks during the day. The rarer dark moths then reaped the benefits of being camouflaged on the dark trees, leading to a rapid evolution of the species. Within a few generations, the lighter moths were quickly picked off by predator birds, and the black moths now survived to reproduce and pass on the darker wing color. Environmental efforts to clean up the environment then led to another shift in wing color, demonstrating the importance of camouflage in effectively misleading predators to ensure survival and reproduction.

Though camouflage is frequently not conscious, some evidence shows that the moths and other animals select resting places that more closely match their own coloring or pattern. Other species also take advantage of their own coloring that emerged via natural selection. For example, different types of fish, lizards, and octopi can change color to blend into their background to decrease their susceptibility to predators. Other species use camouflage to blend in when hunting. Crocodiles, for example, lie motionless for extended periods, blending into logs and driftwood until prey comes close enough to attack and consume.

Dozens of species have naturally developed camouflage as a by-product of natural selection pressures. Humans have adapted the use of camouflage in a purposeful fashion to aid attempts in war. Purposefully camouflaged military uniforms blend into the environment in which an altercation will likely take place. Tan camouflage is used in desert warfare, green camouflage is used in forest or jungle environments, and blue camouflage for warfare is used at sea. Whether naturally occurring or used purposefully, camouflage can be an effective means of deception to promote survival.

See also: Bluffs; Deception in Animals; Espionage; Evolution of Deception; Mimicry; Signaling Theory.

Further Reading

Behrens, R. R. (2002). *False Colors: Art, Design, and Modern Camouflage*. Bobolink Books.

Bond, C. F. (1988). The evolution of deception. *Journal of Nonverbal Behavior, 12*(4), 295–307.

Stevens, M., & Merilaita, S. (2011). *Animal Camouflage: Mechanisms and Function*. Cambridge University Press.

Careless Liars

Careless liars are those who lie as a means of impressing others. Their lies are often not premeditated, and they make up lies in the spur of the moment as a means of contributing to a conversation. Most careless liars do not try to conceal their lies and often contradict themselves with subsequent lies, sometimes within the same interaction. These liars tell lies about experiences and achievements simply to gain attention, to sound impressive, or in order to have something to contribute. They are likely to pretend that they know more than they do, answer questions even if they do not know what they are talking about, and deny their lies if confronted. They are unlikely to change their behavior and seem unable to recognize or acknowledge that they are not being truthful.

In conversations, careless liars seem to always have something to add, claim to have any experience being discussed, and act as if they know everything. They do not seem to put much thought into their lies but simply use them to keep a conversation moving, to keep attention on themselves, and in an attempt to give a favorable impression to others. Careless liars tend to tell lies that revolve around nonsensical, trivial, or insincere things. Typically individuals who engage in careless lies are simply attempting to provide listeners with an overall impression, such as trying to seem impressive, knowledgeable, or important. Unsurprisingly, this strategy usually has the opposite effect, and their habitual lying does not tend to lead to a long-term favorable impression. Though they may seem interesting initially and may make a good first impression, others quickly pick up on the inconsistencies and lack of genuineness, and this positive impression is frequently not maintained. Very quickly their behavior comes across as bragging and starts to irritate those around them. Interestingly, however, careless liars tend to be relatively unconcerned with whether or not what they are saying is accurate or believed, and they tend to perceive and remember social interactions more positively than is warranted.

For most careless liars, lying has become a habit. They use careless lies to cover up their own inadequacies and use them to buffer their own self-esteem in an attempt to be popular with others. Because their lies are not very well thought out, however, they often must make up new lies to cover up the other lies that they told. Even when confronted, they are likely to assert that they are telling the truth even when their twisted stories become ridiculous. They seem to operate under the assumption that if they tell the lie long enough, people will believe them. Furthermore, repeated assertions can lead to a situation where they may even start to believe themselves. Repeated telling of the same lies tends to lead to situations where the lies grow more and more impressive and where the individual starts to convolute which parts are actually true and which parts are made up.

In contrast to pathological liars or those with antisocial personality disorder, careless liars do not seem to have a lack of empathy or a need to control or manipulate others. These lies tend to be more innocent and result from low self-esteem and a corresponding need to try to impress others or to feel better about themselves. An inability to accept and tell the truth about oneself, however, tends to have the opposite effect. Instead of feeling better about themselves, telling careless lies reinforces the feeling that they are not acceptable the way they are, necessitating even more lies, perpetuating a negative feedback loop. If careless liars continue with the behavior, it can develop into compulsive lying.

There are several avenues through which careless liars can change the behavior. Though most careless liars struggle to recognize and control the pattern of lies, having trusted friends who can identify the lies as they happen may help them decrease the behavior. Building a solid sense of high self-esteem may also decrease the reliance on feeling the need to lie to cover up for insecurities. Self-acceptance and strong friendships can help careless liars become more honest with themselves and with others; however, careless liars tend to have a hard time forming those genuine relationships because of their tendency to lie.

See also: Antisocial Personality Disorder; Categories of Deception; Compulsive Lying; Emotional Effects; Fibs; Puffery; Self-Deception.

Further Reading
Carson, T. L. (2006). The definition of lying. *Nous, 40*(2), 284–306.
Frankfurt, H. G. (2005). *On Bullshit.* Princeton University Press.
Muzinic, L., Kozaric-Kovacic, D., & Marinic, I. (2016). Psychiatric aspects of normal and pathological lying. *International Journal of Law and Psychiatry, 46*, 88–93.

Categories of Deception

Lies can take many different forms. There are lies of commission, in which a liar says something that is not true; lies of omission, where an individual leaves out pertinent information or purposefully does not correct misperceptions; and lies of influence, in which a liar provides unrelated true information to avoid or cover a lie. Lies of influence may include answering a direct question with unrelated information to mislead, misdirect, and influence the listener.

Dr. Bella DePaulo, one of the predominant researchers who studies why, when, how, and to whom people lie, analyzed hundreds of lies to examine the categories of deception. Dr. DePaulo specifically examined the content, orientation, and form of lies. She identified five categories of lying behavior. Cognitive lies include lies about feelings and opinions; achievement lies include lies about knowledge, achievements, and failings; action lies are lies about plans and activities; explanation lies are lies about why someone is behaving a particular way; and personal lies are about facts, personal details, and personal possessions.

Dr. DePaulo revealed that the prevalence of these types of lies vary within populations. The most common lies in college populations, for example, are cognitive lies about feelings and opinions. College students profess to care about activities and others more than they actually do; they lie to protect other's feelings, and they exaggerate how they feel about situations. College populations tend to profess support for friends even if they secretly disagree and lie to be socially appropriate.

Achievement, action, and explanation lies are also common within college-aged groups. Achievement lies tend to revolve about knowledge and achievements and include things such as bragging about past accomplishments, professing more knowledge than one actually has, lying about course achievements, or lying about body weight or personal accomplishments. College-aged individuals also lie about their actions. Common action lies include denial of cheating on romantic partners, lying about where they have been and activities they have engaged in, and about the time spent studying or engaging in prosocial activities. Lies centered on explanations account for 10 percent of lies in undergraduate populations. These lies may focus on fabricating excuses for being late, blaming others for unpopular decisions, or professing ignorance after committing a transgression. Personal lies about facts, family details, and personal possessions were the least commonplace in college-aged groups. College students only occasionally lie about their family or about their belongings in an attempt to influence the perception of peers.

Within these categories of lies, many different types of lies emerge. Additionally, within each category the magnitude and potential harmfulness of the lies vary. Lies of varying magnitude include prosocial lies, white lies, polite lies, butler lies, noble lies, fibs, broken promises, fabrications, exaggerations, plagiarism, boasts, bluffs, bald-faced lies, careless lies, and antisocial lies. Most everyday lies are white lies told to protect the feelings of others, smooth over social interactions, or get attention. These lies may include providing excuses to avoid a social gathering or event or to extricate oneself from a conversation. These lies are likely tactful and socially sanctioned and told to protect reputation or self-esteem. Such lies may bolster social standing, garner respect from peers, or create a sense of intimacy between individuals via gossip or rumors.

Dr. Kay Bussey found that antisocial lies are most commonly told in childhood to conceal misdeeds or avoid punishments, and these lies tend to decrease over the life span. By adolescence, lies to parents about friends, money, activities, drugs, dates, and sex become more common, particularly if there are strict guidelines to which the adolescents are expected to adhere. Adolescents tend to lie less frequently when given autonomy and support to make their own decisions. By the end of adolescence and into young adulthood, individuals more commonly use white lies to make excuses for performance or behavior, to explain absenteeism, or to cover up a true opinion. Adults lie the least and tend to lie to smooth social interactions or avoid hurting others. Most liars do not regret their lies, and most report that they would lie again if confronted with similar situations. Most of lying behavior is to present a better image of oneself to others, to make a divergent viewpoint less extreme, or to smooth over conflicts. Though antisocial lies may be highlighted in most research works, they are much less common than prosocial lies and are a rarer category of deception.

See also: Age Differences; Bald-Faced Lies; Betrayal; Black Lies; Blue Lies; Bluffs; Butler Lies; Careless Liars; Commission, Lies of; Defamation; DePaulo, Bella; Exaggeration; Fake News; Fibs; Fraud; Lying at Work; Lying to Children; Lying to Parents; Noble Lies; Omission, Lies of; Paternalistic Lies; Prevalence of Lying; Prosocial Lying; Sex Differences in Lying Behavior; White Lies.

Further Reading

Andreae, M. (n.d.). Different types of lies. *Science of People*. Retrieved from https://www.scienceofpeople.com/different-types-lies/

Bussey, K. (1999). Children's categorization and evaluation of different types of lies and truths. *Child Development, 70*(6), 1338–1347.

Chiu, S., Hong, F., & Chiu, S. (2016). Undergraduates' day-to-day lying behaviors: Implications, targets, and psychological characteristics. *Social Behavior and Personality, 44*(8), 1329–1338.

DePaulo, B. M. (2004). The many faces of lies. In A. G. Miller (Ed.), *The Social Psychology of Good and Evil* (pp. 303–326). Guilford.

Ekman, P. (1997). Deception, lying, and demeanor. In D. F. Halpern & A. E. Voiskounsky (Eds.), *States of Mind: American and Post-Soviet Perspectives on Contemporary Issues in Psychology* (pp. 93–105). Oxford University Press.

Serota, K. B., & Levine, T. R. (2015). A few prolific liars: Variation in the prevalence of lying. *Journal of Language and Social Psychology, 34*(2), 138–157.

Catfishing

Catfishing is a term for the creation of a false social media profile that deceives other individuals on an online platform. Catfish attempt to deceive other people in order to start romantic relationships, solicit money, gather information, or otherwise facilitate deceptive online interactions. The term has become popular recently in response to Nev Schulman's MTV series, where he helps people investigate online partners who are suspected of being dishonest. In his series, *Catfish: The TV Show*, Nev and his cohost, Max Joseph, explore the ramifications of falling victim to a catfish and the motives that drive people to create and maintain false online profiles and relationships.

Some of the motivations that have been found to drive catfish include the desire to explore gender and sexual identities in an anonymous way, to hide true identities due to low self-esteem, to convince online partners to send money, to engage in illegal relationships with minors, to catch criminals, or to bully or seek revenge on a known individual. Using any of these motivations, the catfish creates a false profile and engages in an online relationship with others online. A catfish typically uses pictures of other individuals and creates a new identity to attract and fool others. Once the catfish has established a relationship, he or she may solicit money, information, or sexually explicit material. Due to the anonymity of the internet, catfish may never be caught unless the person being catfished becomes suspicious of the inconsistencies or refusals to meet in person.

Catfishing can be dangerous, particularly for vulnerable or young individuals. Catfish may be sexual predators who use an online platform to find targets or to convince minors to meet in person. Catfishing in teen populations has also been used for bullying. Catfish can build a sense of trust to gain information and then use that information to damage another's reputation offline. Catfishing has become more common and has recently been documented as contributing to suicide attempts in teenagers.

Because of the incidence of catfishing and the increased likelihood of deception attempts online, use of social media can be risky. However, despite this risk, most users report that social media sites, such as online dating apps, allow them to find good matches and make healthy connections. In addition, users report that the anonymity of the online environment allows them to be themselves and to control their experiences. Furthermore, connecting with those similar to oneself on online platforms allows for better social health and less depression, particularly for youth who have difficulty fitting in with their peer group. A problem emerges because 80 percent of users admit to lying in their profiles. These lies range from lying about personal attributes to committing fraud, identity theft, or aggressive acts of cyber bullying. Such instances can be damaging for mental health. Thus, a healthy skepticism of online messages and personas is needed to protect oneself against catfish or any other phishing attempts.

Internet users must be wary of invitations from strangers or from individuals who refuse to video chat or meet in person. Profiles that are too good to be true should be treated with doubt. Examination of dating profiles may illuminate the risk associated with catfishing attempts and serve to educate users so they can protect themselves against catfish. Examining the photographs for evidence of photoshop or engaging in video chats can increase the confidence that the user is not a catfish. Carefully guarding one's own private and financial information can also decrease the negative outcomes of being the victim of a catfish.

Most individuals on online dating platforms are likely to exaggerate or accentuate their own qualities in an attempt to appear more attractive to potential online dating partners. However, most of these individuals do not go to such an extreme to be categorized as a catfish. For relationships to transition offline, the deceptions cannot be so extreme that they are noticeable when meeting in person. Perceiving that an online dating partner has lied after meeting face-to-face decreases the attraction and likelihood of a future relationship. For this reason, most catfish must avoid meeting face-to-face or via video chat because their deception would be revealed, and the relationship would likely end.

See also: Clickbait; Dating; Online Dating; Phishing; Romantic Relationships; Social Media; Sockpuppets; Trolling.

Further Reading

Jarecki, A., Schulman, A., Bishop, B., Metzler, D., Joost, H., Karshis, J., Steffens, J. L., Smerling, M., Eisen, M., Schulman, N., Bonilla, G., Leidner, N. E., Forman, T., & Maroney, J. (Producers) (2020). *Catfish: The TV Show* [Television broadcast]. Catfish Picture Company.

Lauckner, C., Truszczynski, N., Lambert, D., Kottamasu, V., Meherally, S., Schipani-McLaughlin, A. M., Taylor, E., & Hansen, N. (2019). "Catfishing," cyberbullying, and coercion: An exploration of the risks associated with dating app use among rural sexual minority males. *Journal of Gay and Lesbian Mental Health*.https://doi.org/10.1080/19359705.2019.1587729.

Sharabi, L. L., & Caughlin, J. P. (2019). Deception in online dating: Significance and implications for the first offline date. *New Media and Society, 21*(1), 229–247.

Chadwick, Cassie

Cassie Chadwick was a Canadian con artist who was born Elizabeth Bigley, but who transitioned through at least eight other pseudonyms throughout her life. She was born in Ontario in 1857 and became one of the most notorious con women in history. Her greatest hoax was pretending to be Andrew Carnegie's illegitimate daughter to defraud American and Canadian banks of millions of dollars.

Cassie Chadwick's deceptive behavior started early when she forged her first documents around the age of 13. With these documents, she fooled a local bank in Woodstock, Ontario, into thinking that her uncle had passed away and left her some money. Using the forged notification, the bank agreed to give her an advance on the money, and she used the credit to make several purchases. Though she was caught and charged with forgery, she was released due to her age. About 10 years later, she engaged in a similar scam, this time for the more substantial amount of $15,000. She fabricated an inheritance and created business cards billing herself as an heiress. To profit from the scam, she wrote checks for expensive items and asked for cash back. She used some of this cash to pay other debts to maintain a reputation of being trustworthy, and most establishments were willing to forward her money on viewing her business card. Once she was caught, she escaped to Cleveland, Ohio, and changed her name.

In Cleveland, she took out a loan using her sister's home as collateral and used the funds to establish herself as a clairvoyant. She then met and married Dr. Wallace S. Springsteen in 1882. Her marriage to Dr. Springsteen lasted 12 days, just long enough for her to profit from the collateral of her husband's furniture and home. Once she was discovered, she changed her name again, moved to Pennsylvania, and claimed to be a sick niece of a Civil War general. She used the story to collect loans to ostensibly make her way back to Cleveland. After collecting the money, she fled and sent word back of her own death to avoid repaying the loans. In 1886, she reestablished herself as a clairvoyant and worked her way through two more husbands. Her second husband left her an inheritance after his death, and her third husband claimed she had hypnotic powers. Using her charm and the persona of a soft-spoken innocent woman, she forged promissory notes and had her husband cash them to the extent of $40,000. When she was caught, she was jailed, but she used her wiles to convince the parole board to sign papers for an early release.

After her release, she married a wealthy doctor and went on a spending spree. When her husband objected to her spending his money, she took out loans against a fabricated future inheritance. Her loans involved deals with up to 20 banks. Initially she used subsequent loans to pay off previous loans to build a sense of good credit. She then started taking larger loans and ultimately swindled upward of $17 million in today's currency.

For her biggest and final con, Ms. Chadwick conned a lawyer into believing she was Andrew Carnegie's illegitimate daughter and heiress. She achieved this by asking the lawyer to accompany her to Andrew Carnegie's home as a chaperone and then asked him to wait outside while she went in. When inside, she actually just chatted with the housekeeper under the pretense of getting a reference check for a house cleaner she wanted to hire. Upon leaving, however, she insinuated to the lawyer that she was Andrew Carnegie's illegitimate daughter by arranging for him to glimpse forged promissory notes for exorbitant amounts. She implied that Carnegie felt a sense of responsibility for her well-being and thus kept her well funded. She asked for his silence on her parentage knowing that he would not likely keep the secret.

When this misinformation leaked, banks offered their services, and Ms. Chadwick took out loans totaling over $50 million in today's currency. Banks believed that she would receive $400 million upon Carnegie's death, so they had faith that they would be repaid. Because of the sensitivity of her story, no one asked Mr. Carnegie about its veracity. She racked up massive debt over the course of six years, and only after she had taken out millions in loans did her story start being questioned. When Mr. Carnegie was finally asked, he denied all knowledge of her, and when he viewed the forged papers, he pointed out both spelling and punctuation errors that illustrated their poor quality. Ms. Chadwick was subsequently arrested, and her con led to major upset and bankruptcy within the banking community. She was ultimately found guilty of fraud and conspiracy and was imprisoned. In prison, her health deteriorated, and she died within two years.

See also: Charlatans; Fraud; Hoax; Hwang Woo-Suk: Impersonator; Loch Ness Monster; Scams.

Further Reading

Abbott, K. (2012). The high priestess of fraudulent finance. *Smithsonian Magazine.* Retrieved from https://www.smithsonianmag.com/history/the-high-priestess-of-fraudulent-finance-45/

Crosbie, J. S. (1975). *The Incredible Mrs. Chadwick.* McGraw-Hill.

Docevski, B. (2016). The turbulent life of Cassie Chadwick—The imposter who claimed to be Carnegie's illegitimate daughter. *The Vintage News.* Retrieved from https://www.thevintagenews.com/2016/11/22/the-turbulent-life-of-cassie-chadwick-the-impostor-who-claimed-to-be-carnegies-illegitimate-daughter/

Charlatans

A charlatan is a fraud or an individual who falsely claims to have special abilities or skills. Charlatans typically use deceptive tactics to take advantage of others to gain personal benefits or advantages. A charlatan may feign medical expertise, be a charmingly suave salesperson, or claim special status or expertise. The charlatan then uses these claimed skills to swindle others. Historically, charlatans traveled from town to town taking advantage of uneducated, naive townspeople, dating back to the Dark Ages. In the nineteenth century, charlatans were common throughout the Western United States, where traveling medical shows swindled money out of unsuspecting people by selling faux medical elixirs and miracle cures for every ailment. Along with fortune-tellers and rigged gambling games, charlatans provided simple explanations and false cures for complex problems to fool people out of their money. Then they would disappear to the next town before being discovered.

In modern times, research on charlatans has become particularly focused on organizations. Though traditionally charlatans engaged in elaborate independent hoaxes or attempts to con people to get ahead, such behaviors are now used more subtly in modern work environments. Charlatans use deceptive behaviors to get ahead of peers, secure undeserved promotions, or get away without doing their jobs. The behaviors of these organizational charlatans can be detrimental to an organization because they undermine other employees and lead to unqualified individuals being in positions of authority.

Organizational charlatans rise through corporations by masquerading as competent employees, particularly when in positions where there is no close oversight. These employees tend to have high social intelligence and engage in presenting a good impression to those in positions of power. They take credit for the work of others, take measures to enhance their perceived performance, and lobby for higher status and higher wages within organizations. Skillful charlatans are more likely to be hired and promoted and likely to receive better assignments than their peers. They are also likely to receive positive performance evaluations despite inadequate actual performance. Ultimately, organizational charlatans can damage the morale of the group or organization, particularly if others are doing their work and not receiving due credit.

Dr. John Parnell from Texas A&M University and Dr. Mark Singer from Middle Tennessee State University developed an instrument to measure the false performance frequently perpetuated by organizational charlatans in the United

States. They discovered that organizational charlatans predominantly engage in impression management. When interviewed, these charlatans were more likely to endorse items such as "it is more important to look busy than actually be busy," "it is important to impress the right people at work," "it is important to maintain a positive image," and "it is important to know what your organization wants from you so you can tailor your work to those needs" than their more honest peers. They showed evidence of being overall more concerned with appearances than actual performance. However, since they maintain that appearance in front of the right people, they are frequently rewarded more than those who are actually endeavoring to do good work without thought to who witnesses their efforts.

Dr. Gbolahan Gbadamosi from the University of Worcester and his colleagues from Botswana and Swaziland extended this research in non-Western settings. They also found that organizational charlatans can undermine employee commitment and level of trust within an organization. To maximize employee commitment and quality, it is important to identify charlatans. These researchers predict that charlatan behavior will most likely emerge when employees do not have trust in the management. Their data implied that managers who cultivate a high level of trust are less likely to have employees who engage in charlatan behavior. Once an employee begins engaging in and benefiting from such behavior, it tends to spread throughout the organization and leads to a widespread decline in performance as well as a decline in company morale. Employees who observed that charlatans are not punished or that charlatans are rewarded tend to have diminished trust in the organization, which tends to lead to increases in charlatan behavior cross-culturally.

See also: Chadwick, Cassie; Competition; Corruption; Fraud; Hoax; Impersonator; Instrumental Lies; Lying at Work; Motives for Lying; Social Intelligence.

Further Reading

Gbadamosi, G., Ndaba, J., & Oni, F. (2007). Predicting charlatan behavior in a non-Western setting: Lack of trust or absence of commitment? *Journal of Management Development, 26*(8), 753–769.

Parnell, J. A., & Singer, M. G. (2001). The organizational charlatan scale: Developing an instrument to measure false performance. *The Journal of Management Development, 20*(5), 441–455.

Cheating (See Academic Cheating; Infidelity)

Clandestine Operations (See Diversionary Tactics; Espionage)

Clickbait

Clickbait is a modern marketing strategy in which attention-grabbing headlines are used to attract the attention of internet users. A clickbait headline tends to contain information that is sensationalized or controversial in order to sway users to click on the link. Since the number of clicks on a link frequently directly correlates with sponsorship and advertising money, it has become a common online strategy. Clickbait can also be used for phishing attacks to get users to open links in order to spread malicious files or to gain user information. Clickbait is a form of fraud and frequently takes users to sites unrelated or only tangentially related to the headline presented. In order to be categorized as clickbait, the linked article or webpage must be misrepresented by the headline. Clickbait headlines usually include exaggerations, shocking statements, or outright lies to gain attention. Clickbait is a blatant form of deception where the propagator manipulates the reader to get more clicks, which leads to more money from advertisers.

Clickbait in its most innocuous form is a waste of time for viewers. Frequently if users click on a clickbait link, they end up clicking through multiple pages, each laden with ads, in an attempt to get the promised story. Though clickbait can be effective, it ultimately undermines an audience's trust. Failing to get the promised story or information quickly makes a reader suspicious of that particular company. So, though clickbait may work in the short term, it is not a successful long-term strategy for media outlets. However, many still use it because novice readers do click. Many readers are fighting back by leaving comments that lay out the deception or the ultimate payoff so that other readers do not have to click through the entire story.

Clickbait titles are designed to manipulate emotions and create anticipation, which is rewarding at a neurological level. The titles used tend to be hyperbolic and salient to grab attention and elicit curiosity, which makes them hard to resist. Clickbait titles are frequently extremely polarized to capture the interest of viewers from both sides of an issue. Use of superlatives attract attention, and titles typically refer to something epic, amazing, and mind-blowing or create a cliff-hanger, and readers must click to assuage the cognitive dissonance created by wanting to know more. Readers frequently find themselves enticed and are then trapped into clicking through a series of pages that are slow to provide the promised information or provide information that is useless, manipulative, or inaccurate.

Even when individuals recognize that clickbait articles are not accurate news sources, many still click on an article out of curiosity, boredom, or simply for entertainment. However, the harmful aspect of such sites is that they can also be used as an avenue for phishing attacks, hackers, fake news, or propagation of false information. The site may gather information that can be used to gain access to accounts or media profiles. Clickbait may also contain information that sways voters, causes scandals, or muddies actual news.

Due to its effectiveness, some legitimate news sites also use clickbait headlines to get attention for actual news stories. News outlets may post controversial or even inaccurate headlines to grab the attention of the reader. The information from the headlines is then rejected and disproven in the actual article. However, this strategy tends to spread fake news because many users do not read beyond the headline and are left with the impression of the false information from the headline.

Clickbait has been found to be particularly effective if it elicits a strong emotion such as anger. Angry posts are spread through shares at triple the rate of posts that convey other emotions. If viewers are already angry about an issue, they are even more likely to click on a link that conveys information that agrees with their sentiments. Clickbait is not a new phenomenon. Newspaper boys in the 1800s were aware that claiming a controversial news story would elicit more buyers. An individual's curiosity and eagerness to be informed, particularly of scandalous information, can be used to generate a profit at the reader's expense. This is an effective technique, and a savvy audience has to suppress the urge to give in to such manipulative attempts. Understanding the tactic does not negate its effects but may allow a reader to be aware they are being influenced.

See also: Advertising; Bait and Switch; Catfishing; Cognitive Dissonance; Doublespeak; Fake News; Fraud; Hoax; Manipulation; Neuroscience; Phishing; Red Herring; Social Media.

Further Reading

Dewey, A. (2017). The dangers of clickbait and fake news. *The Communicator*. Retrieved from https://chscommunicator.com/54916/opinion/2017/06/the-dangers-of-clickbait -and-fake-news/

Escher, A., & Ha, A. (2016). WTF is click bait? *TechCrunch*. Retrieved from https:// techcrunch.com/2016/09/25/wtf-is-clickbait/

Gardiner, B. (2015). You'll be outraged at how easy it was to get you to click on this headline. *Wired*. Retrieved from https://www.wired.com/2015/12/psychology-of-clickbait/

Coercion

Coercion involves manipulating another person's behavior through threats, force, brainwashing, or pressure. Coercive tactics include threats to one's physical well-being or the safety of loved ones, psychological control via brainwashing or gaslighting, or manipulation of the emotions of others. Coercion can include blackmail, assault, or other threats to achieve cooperation. Coercion can be physical or psychological. Physical coercion achieves obedience through direct force, while psychological coercion is more likely to include deception and manipulation tactics. One engaging in coercion may use real or fabricated threats in legal proceedings, in personal or professional relationships, or for personal gain.

Dr. Laura Fallon and Dr. Brent Snook from Memorial University of New-foundland examined coercive tactics in witness and suspect interviews. They found that study participants could identify the presence of threats and overt coercion in typical police tactics. Observers identified overt pressure and threats during interviews, which resulted in increased stress for the witnesses. However, the same observers were not as good at identifying covert coercion. Thus, covert coercion is likely more effective and less well regulated and controlled than overt coercion.

Research suggests that psychological coercion can lead to false confessions in interrogation situations. However, most people in the court system endorsed the belief that psychological coercion is necessary during interrogation. This covert form of coercion can include behaviors such as minimizing the importance of a confession or exaggerating the seriousness of the offense. These behaviors can increase false confession rates if suspects or witnesses give false information to please the interviewer, without understanding the severity of the confession, or if suspects provide false confessions because they are scared of more severe consequences should they not comply. In either case, coercion undermines the accuracy of the legal process.

Coercion can also be common within personal relationships, such as friendships or romantic relationships. Dr. Amy Katz and her colleagues from Indiana University School of Medicine and Purdue University found that 22 percent of females and 8 percent of males in a rural high school study had experienced sexual coercion at least once. Sexual coercion in the study included experiencing forced sexual activities including kissing, touching, or intercourse with a dating partner. Females were much more likely to experience sexual coercion than males, but both genders experienced other types of coercion and reported the experience of feeling controlled by their partners. Furthermore, Dr. Tiara Willie and her colleagues from Brown University demonstrated that sexual coercion was correlated with higher rates of teen pregnancies and lower scores on parenting measures. Overall, sexual coercion was correlated with decreased contraception use, lower confidence, and poorer mental health.

Researchers from the University of Essex and The State University of New York, Dr. Veronica Lamarche and Dr. Mark Seery, identified personality traits and situational factors correlated with coercive behavior in romantic relationships. Individuals who score high on the trait of narcissism and low on measures of self-esteem are more likely to use control tactics and sexual coercion, particularly following an experience of feeling rejected by others. Examinations of instances of sexual coercion revealed that perpetrators manipulated emotions and made the partner feel guilty about refusing sex, or they made threats to end the relationship if the partner did not comply with their expectations. They also threatened to undermine the other individual's reputation, family well-being, or living situation, or they engaged in physical abuse or rape.

Those who suffer from low self-esteem may be particularly vulnerable to coercion. Feeling a sense of low self-esteem makes one more sensitive to rejection and more likely to comply with demands in order to maintain intimacy with a partner. Narcissists, alternatively, tend to be more aggressive when they feel rejected, and they are less likely to feel empathy toward others. Thus, if a partner denies sex, they may endorse the belief that the partner should be punished. These individuals are much more likely to endorse the use of sexual coercion to get what they want. Dr. Lamarche and Dr. Seery report that men with low self-esteem who rate high on the personality trait of narcissism were the most likely to endorse sexual coercion after being rejected. This collection of traits and experiences may interact and lead to increases in the likelihood of sexual assault.

See also: Dating; False Confessions; Gaslighting; Manipulation; Narcissism; Personality; Romantic Relationships.

Further Reading

Fallon, L., & Snook, B. (2020). Beyond common sense and human experience: Lay perceptions of witness coercion. *Criminal Justice and Behavior, 47*(2), 208–221.

Katz, M. P. H., Hensel, D. J., Hunt, A. L., Javan, L. S., Hensley, M. M., & Ott, M. A. (2019). Only yes means yes: Sexual coercion in rural adolescent relationships. *Journal of Adolescent Health, 65*, 423–435.

Lamarche, V. M., & Seery, M. D. (2019). Come on, give it to me baby: Self-esteem, narcissism, and endorsing sexual coercion following social rejection. *Personality and
Individual Differences, 149*, 315–325.

Willie, T. C., Alexander, K. A., Amutah-Onukagha, N., & Kershaw, T. (2019). Effects of
reproductive coercion on young couples' parenting behaviors and child development: A dyadic perspective. *Journal of Family Psychology, 33*(6), 682–689.

Cognitive Changes while Lying

When considering cognitive processes that are involved with deception, researchers Dr. Anja Leue and Dr. Andre Beauducel from the University of Kiel and the
University of Bonn in Germany recognize that deception, whether it is creating
false information or concealing true information, creates greater cognitive
demand, or cognitive load, and takes more mental effort than simply telling the
truth. In a meta-analysis study, they demonstrated that there are cognitive differences between when people are engaging in deception and when they are behaving in a nondeceptive manner, and such differences may be key in identifying
liars. When lying, response times and brain activity predictably vary as compared
to when someone is telling the truth.

Increased demands on cognitive processing when lying impact response times
as compared to when being honest. An unpremeditated lie makes response times
slower because liars must create plausible lies, monitor whether or not the lies are
believed, keep their stories consistent, suppress the truth, and suppress behaviors
that may reveal that they are lying. Alternatively, if lies are prepared and rehearsed
ahead of time, the response may actually be faster than honest responses. Thus,
very quick or very slow responses reflect the differences in cognitive processing
required for deception as compared to honest responses.

The increases in mental effort required to create plausible lies in real time create predictable changes in brain activity as well, particularly in the parietal lobe.
When concealing information, there are smaller P3 amplitudes measured in the
parietal cortex. This is thought to be because when individuals must conceal
information during a response, there are greater demands on cognitive resources.
More resources must be directed to suppressing knowledge, leaving fewer
resources available to process new stimuli. The amplitude within the parietal cortex also varies predictably when an individual is confronted with known or
unknown stimuli. Unknown stimuli evoke less positive amplitudes, while known
or relevant stimuli provoke more positive amplitudes. Such differences may delineate between situations where suspects recognize stimuli and situations where
they do not. Furthermore, deception behavior in legal scenarios tended to evoke
larger effect sizes than deception in other contexts, particularly when mock crime
scenarios were used rather than simply asking a participant to imagine and then
lie about criminal behaviors.

Though there are demonstrated differences in cognitive functioning correlated
with deception, contexts of deception vary widely. Deception may occur in interpersonal relationships, legal contexts, or as part of a game. In each scenario, the
consequences of being caught vary substantially as do the levels of arousal

associated with the deception. The resulting cognitive changes seem to correlate with the severity of the possible consequences and level of arousal. For example, deception in social environments may lead to discomfort or embarrassment, but lying in a legal situation can lead to substantial fines or incarceration. Lying in game situations or in personal interactions, furthermore, may be simply to get ahead in a game or skim over personal information. The severity of the perceived consequences directly affects the cognitive changes associated with the lie. More high-stakes consequences induce greater cognitive load and arousal.

Though lying does produce predictable differences in cognitive arousal, Dr. Bram Van Bockstaele and his colleagues from Ghent University demonstrated that people who practice lying can actually decrease the cognitive effort involved. In their research, individuals who were trained to lie and those who lied more frequently were able to lie more easily and with less cognitive effort. Participants who were trained to tell the truth, alternatively, found lying more difficult over time, and subsequent lies required more cognitive effort. In their study, the participants who were given the opportunity to lie more frequently showed quicker response times on the lie trials. At the same time, their responses on the truth trials became slower. Alternatively, those who were given the opportunity to tell the truth more frequently became faster at responding when telling the truth, and when asked to lie, producing a response became more difficult and onerous. In these cases, practiced liars did not experience increased mental effort when lying. Therefore, detecting a practiced liar may be more difficult even with developed tools to detect deception. One application of this research in legal settings may be to induce suspects to practice telling the truth by including a higher rate of verifiable questions during an interview or interrogation. If the suspects respond truthfully to most questions, their ability to lie may be affected, and they may find that it takes more mental effort to lie on the incriminating questions.

See also: Cognitive Dissonance; Cognitive Distortion; Detecting Deception; Emotional Effects; Memory; Mental Effort; Models of Lying; Neuroscience; Physiology; Reaction Time.

Further Reading

Leue, A., & Beauducel, A. (2019). A meta-analysis of the P3 amplitude in tasks requiring deception in legal and social contexts. *Brain and Cognition, 135,* 1–16.

Van Bockstaele, B., Verschuere, B., Moens, T., Suchotzki, K., Debey, E., & Spruyt, A. (2012). Learning to lie: Effects of practice on the cognitive cost of lying. *Frontiers in Psychology, 3,* 526. https://doi.org/10.3389/fpsyg.2012.00526

Walczyk, J. J., Harris, L. L., Duck, T. K., & Mulay, D. (2014). A social-cognitive framework for understanding serious lies: Activation-decision-construction-action theory. *New Ideas in Psychology, 34,* 22–36.

Cognitive Dissonance

Cognitive dissonance occurs when one's thoughts and behaviors do not align. The experience of cognitive dissonance is an uncomfortable emotional sensation that often motivates individuals to change either their thoughts or their behaviors to regain an equilibrium and alleviate the discomfort. In many instances, changing behavior takes effort, so individuals may simply adjust the way they think or what they believe to regain an equilibrium. Engaging in deceptive behavior frequently stimulates cognitive dissonance. Most individuals have been socialized to believe that lying is wrong, so when they engage in lying behavior, they suffer from cognitive dissonance. At that point, the individuals must change their behavior and admit to lying or they must change their attitude about lying. Either of these actions will resolve the discomfort felt from having conflicting behaviors and thoughts.

In many cases, to resolve the uncomfortable feeling of cognitive dissonance, instead of changing or admitting to the behavior, individuals will rationalize their lies, which leads to changes in their thoughts, attitudes, or values. For example, undergraduate students' attitudes toward cheating were positively correlated with their previous cheating behavior. Those who had cheated in the past were more likely to have rational reasons in support of cheating. Rationalizations included claiming that the test was unfair, that they did not have the time to study, and that the class did not matter or asserting that everyone cheats. Those who had not cheated had strong beliefs about being honest. Interestingly, however, those who were induced to cheat during the study showed a shift in their attitudes and became more similar to the cheaters. This change in attitude also made it more likely that those individuals would cheat again when given the opportunity. Therefore, resolving the cognitive dissonance by rationalizing rather than changing behaviors had long-term effects on their future behaviors.

Cognitive dissonance mechanisms can also lead to self-deception, particularly when individuals feel guilty about deceiving others. For those who engage in malingering or inventing or exaggerating symptoms of a disorder in order to achieve external rewards, cognitive dissonance may cause them to internalize the symptoms. Reporting fake symptoms causes a sense of cognitive dissonance, and thus, individuals may convince themselves that they are actually experiencing the symptoms in order to resolve the psychological discomfort. In this case, individuals may come to experience the symptoms that they were initially only faking. Self-deception is less likely to happen if there is a strong external reward for the deceptive behavior. If an individual has a strong external reason to engage in a behavior that is at a mismatch with their beliefs, they can blame the incentive for the behavior rather than struggling to make their thoughts and actions consistent.

The more uncomfortable someone feels about the deceptive attempts, the more likely they will internalize and start to believe their own deceptions. For example, malingering frequently starts as a conscious process with particular aims and ends up as an unconscious case of deceiving the self. High levels of cognitive dissonance also lead to suppressed immune system functioning, making people more susceptible to disease. Though there are individual differences, some people are sensitive to cognitive dissonance and more likely than others to suffer from physical effects of cognitive stress, creating an interesting psychological-biological feedback loop.

Cognitive dissonance occurs frequently because most people are relatively inconsistent. Though most people may like to believe that their thoughts guide their actions, the reverse is probably more often the case. Individuals frequently react without thinking things through and then retroactively align their thoughts, values, and attitudes with their behavior. When an individual is experiencing cognitive dissonance, there are measurable changes in physiology. They become more aroused and more motivated, and individuals describe the sensation as uncomfortable. Resolution of the dissonance is needed to alleviate the discomfort.

Dr. Madan Palsane demonstrated that individuals who engaged in behaviors that cause cognitive dissonance, that is, behaviors out of line with their stated beliefs, had higher stress levels and reported higher levels of discomfort, arousal, and restlessness. They were also more motivated to restore homeostasis. These individuals also had overall lower self-esteem, greater levels of stress, and more physical and mental disease. Furthermore, if participants were given false information about their own health, they often started to experience the symptoms as a method of aligning their experience with their beliefs to resolve dissonance. Believing false information about psychological or physical health actually altered the way they viewed the experience. In such cases, individuals highly overinterpreted ambiguous sensations to align with what they believed they should be experiencing, and these effects lasted for several days.

See also: Alternative Facts; Cognitive Distortion; Instrumental Lies; Malingering; Physiology; Self-Deception.

Further Reading

Merckelbach, H., & Merten, T. (2012). A note on cognitive dissonance and malingering. *The Clinical Neuropsychologist, 26*(7), 1217–1229.

Palsane, M. N. (2005). Self-incongruent behavior, stress, and disease. *National Academy of Psychology, India, 50*(4), 283–297.

Storch, E. A., & Storch, J. B. (2003). Academic dishonesty and attitudes towards academic dishonest acts: Support for cognitive dissonance theory. *Psychological Reports, 92*, 174–176.

Cognitive Distortion

Most people want to think of themselves as honest and ethical, yet they may frequently act in deceptive and unethical ways. In order to deal with the cognitive dissonance, or the emotional discomfort, that occurs after unethical behavior, memory researchers have demonstrated that people distort their own memories to reduce discomfort associated with lying or deceiving others. In this manner, lying about a situation actually changes how people remember an event, and individuals tend to have less clear memories about misdeeds than about other behaviors. Furthermore, since individuals distort the memories of their deceptive actions, they are more likely to have an inaccurate assessment of their own levels of honesty, and most rate themselves as more honest than they actually are.

Cognitive distortion, or the modification of what one remembers about an event, may allow a dishonest individual to maintain a positive self-image and to reduce psychological discomfort even after acting in an unethical way. Dr. Maryam Kouchaki from Northwestern University and Dr. Francesca Gino from Harvard University demonstrated that individuals tend to forget behaviors that make them feel guilty or uncomfortable. Over time, memories of dishonest behaviors tend to become less detailed and less vivid than ethical or neutral actions.

In general, Dr. Kouchaki and Dr. Gino have shown that individuals experience a sense of discomfort when they engage in immoral behaviors. These behaviors cause a sense of cognitive dissonance that needs to be resolved to reduce negative emotionality. To reduce the feelings of discomfort, individuals essentially experience unethical amnesia. Dr. Kouchaki and Dr. Gino provide evidence that memory for details of immoral actions tends to fade more quickly than those for moral or neutral actions. Thus, changes in memory following an unethical behavior may actually act as a mechanism to reduce psychological distress. This reduction in accuracy of memory occurs because individuals actively suppress details about the deceptive behavior due to feelings of guilt or distress. Since memories that are not reinforced tend to fade more quickly, memories that are suppressed fade. Though such mechanisms may serve to maintain self-esteem and self-concept, they may also cause individuals to engage in more dishonest behavior because the negative effects are alleviated.

Cognitive researchers have long demonstrated that memory is not static. Memories are altered after each retrieval, rehearsal, and reconsolidation. This makes them extremely open to modification. Suggestions, new information, impressions, emotions, suppression, and purposeful deception can alter what one remembers. For example, a story about an event may subtly or radically change with repeated tellings, even if the storyteller is not intending to deceive. When repeating information, one may add new details, and the new information becomes integrated into the memory of the event. Prior or future experiences can also change how one interprets, remembers, or retells events.

In most cases, individuals may never become aware that their memories have become distorted. However, in some situations, such as with confrontations with the legal system, determining what actually happened may be necessary. Because illegal behaviors likely cause a sense of cognitive dissonance, memories of such actions can become easily distorted. For example, research with sexual offenders shows that they tend to engage in significant cognitive distortion and self-deception. Their distorted memories of their own behaviors may allow them to minimize the seriousness of their actions, place the blame on others, and misinterpret their victims' role in the situation. Those motivated to perpetuate sexually abusive acts must find a way to rationalize and overcome the societal inhibitions that would prevent them from following their urges. Thus, offenders demonstrate a tendency to gather information in a biased way and to have distorted reasoning to support their actions. Molesters may selectively interpret information as sexual interest, such as smiling, touching, and hugging, and discount the innocence and context in which these behaviors occur.

Dr. Robert Wright and Dr. Sandra Schneider from the University of South Florida found that convicted molesters commonly voiced distorted views to explain their offenses. These self-deceptions and misperceptions allow the perpetrators to feel better about their actions. The molesters may blame the victim, the situation, or others in the environment. They distort the events preceding the offense to explain, provide excuses for, or minimize the impact of their behaviors. These self-deceptions and cognitive distortions reduce the cognitive dissonance that results from molesting children because perpetrators have rationalized and distorted their perceptions to make the offense seem more acceptable.

With the heightened use of social media, photographs, and video recording, memories of events may become less susceptible to distortion because there is a concrete record to consult. Looking back at photographs or videos of experiences may help reinforce what actually took place and prevent the distortion that can otherwise occur. However, such recordings still only provide one viewpoint of situations and allow room for individual interpretations, perceptions, and distortions.

See also: Coercion; Cognitive Dissonance; Denial; Ethics; Exaggeration; False Memory; Gaslighting; Manipulation; Memory; Reality Monitoring; Self-Deception.

Further Reading

Kouchaki, M., & Gino, F. (2016). Memories of unethical actions become obfuscated over time. *PNAS, 113*(22), 6166–6171.

Wright, R. C., & Schneider, S. L. (2008). Motivated self-deception in child molesters. *Journal of Child Sexual Abuse, 8*(1), 89–111.

Cognitive Load (See Mental Effort)

Collusion (See Conspiracy Theories)

Commission, Lies of

Different types of deception vary in level of intentionality. Deception by commission means that one is engaging in behavior or making verbal statements designed to actively and intentionally mislead others. Lying by commission means that one tells a lie or provides false information to purposefully confuse, mislead, or influence others. This is in counterpoint to lies by omission in which an individual leaves out information or allows other people to draw erroneous conclusions without actively influencing, enhancing, or correcting their beliefs.

Lies of commission are typically told to gain an advantage or to get out of trouble. For example, children may actively blame a sibling when accused of a transgression or straight out deny taking a cookie. Lying by commission is typically more intentionally driven and more purposeful than lying by omission. When one attempts to merely suppress or withhold information, it may be easier for others to detect the omission. When one provides extraneous information via commission, however, others may not even notice that they have been deceived, particularly if the liar is subtle, stays close to the truth, and is consistent.

As shown in many previous deception research studies with children, those who provide misleading information rather than just attempt to neutralize their responses, generally, are more effective deceivers. The most successful deception by children occurs when they shift their strategies, provide misleading verbal and nonverbal cues, and actively engage their partner in the task. Those who withdraw or attempt to suppress information tend to be less effective at deceiving others. The ability to fabricate believable information is likely a product of increased insight into the partner's intentions and increased insight into how a partner may be interpreting one's own intentions, as well as increased confidence in one's own abilities to keep critical information private.

In a competitive card game paradigm with an adult partner, Dr. Rachelle Smith from Husson University and Dr. Peter LaFreniere from the University of Maine demonstrated that children from ages four to eight began to use commission to increase the effectiveness of their deceptive attempts, at least within a game paradigm. While younger children tended to attempt to suppress or omit information, with age, children began to use commission as a more effective tactical strategy. These children provided false cues such as purposefully looking at the wrong answer, verbalizing misinformation, and engaging in misleading body movements to effectively mislead an adult opponent. By age eight, children demonstrated quite mature deceptive skills and could articulate how their verbal and nonverbal behaviors would influence the beliefs of an adult partner. Not only did they provide misinformation, but they were also able to articulate how they mixed deceptive attempts with true information so that an adult partner could not determine which cues were accurate and which were commissions. Additionally, the children were able to draw from the cues of the partner to make more accurate assessments of the adult's future behavior. This progression of understanding the opponent's intentions and expectations translated to an increase in success over the three age groups with 11 percent of the four-year-olds, 49 percent of the six-year-olds, and 76 percent of the eight-year-olds successfully deceiving a partner at the task.

Aside from their accepted use in some competitive games, lies by commission are typically thought to be more vindictive and less ethical than other types of deceptive behavior. Such lies tend to be self-serving and are used to gain an advantage or avoid punishment. They differ from exaggerations or lies of omission because they are intentional misrepresentations of reality that serve to influence others to one's own advantage, and it is much more difficult to claim innocence when caught in such a lie.

See also: Bald-Faced Lies; Black Lies; Blue Lies; Categories of Deception; Competition; Diversionary Tactics; Ethics; Exaggerations; Fabrication; Instrumental Lies; Recursive Awareness; Tactical Deception; Theory of Mind.

Further Reading

Feldman, R. S., Jenkins, L., & Popoola, O. (1979). Detection of deception in adults and children via facial expressions. *Child Development, 50*, 350–355.

Gosselin, P., Warren, M., & Diotte, M. (2002). Motivation to hide emotion and children's understanding of the distinction between real and apparent emotions. *Journal of Genetic Psychology, 163*(4), 479–495.

LaFreniere, P. J. (1988). The ontogeny of tactical deception in humans. In R. Byrne & A. Whiten (Eds.), *Evolution of Social Intelligence* (pp. 238–252). Oxford University Press.

Saarni, C. (1984). An observational study of children's attempts to monitor their expressive behavior. *Child Development, 55*(4), 1504–1513.

Smith, R. M., & LaFreniere, P. J. (2013). Development of tactical deception from 4 to 8 years of age. *British Journal of Developmental Psychology, 31*, 30–41.

Comparison Question Test (See Control Questions Test)

Competition

Research has demonstrated that deceptive behavior and competition are mutually reinforcing. Competition can intensify incentives for deceptive behavior and can alter perception with regard to when it is appropriate to lie. When facing a competitor, deceptive behavior is more accepted and viewed as less immoral than when facing someone outside of a competitive context. The higher the competitive pressure, the more likely that deception will emerge. Competitive situations can emerge within the context of sports, personal partnerships, business, and politics. The extent of competition can be influenced by past experiences, self-esteem, and even levels of neurotransmitters in the brain. Some level of competition can be healthy; however, excessive competition tends to degrade self-esteem and increase the occurrence of unethical conduct.

In competitive situations, such as in sports competitions, deceptive behavior is common and typically termed friendly competition. However, the extent and quality of deception is correlated with previous experiences with the competitive partner. Deceptive behaviors tend to emerge more when one is facing a rival or opponent with whom one's interactions have been poor or which lack mutual respect. Competitors learn about their opponents from past exchanges, and the quality of such exchanges informs the extent of their future deceptive behavior. In sports, competition is generally socially acceptable, but competition can have more negative effects in other realms, such as in personal or business relationships.

Dr. Nick Feltovich, a professor of economics from Monash University, found evidence that individuals who discover that a personal or professional partner is attempting to deceive them are more likely to engage in competitive and deceptive behavior themselves. Getting caught lying to a romantic or professional partner tends to undermine how one is viewed by oneself and by others. However, reactive deception, such as deception as a response to others who engaged in deceptive behavior first, tends to be less damaging to one's sense of oneself and more socially acceptable. Essentially, competition or social norms of deception give one justification to engage in such behavior without censure.

In marketing, researchers such as Dr. Gokham Aydogan and his colleagues from Arizona State University report that competitive business environments can increase immoral, deceptive, and illegal behavior. Not only are marketing professionals intrinsically motivated by increased sales, but they may also be extrinsically motivated if other companies are engaging in competitive behaviors. Simply being exposed to such competitors may create a social norm that is more accepting of deception. Such trends in behaviors have been observed in marketing, sports, politics, and business. When deceptive behaviors emerge, they create a new norm that makes identification and punishment of deceptive individuals more difficult to implement.

Dr. Aydogan and colleagues examined the influence of the neuropeptide oxytocin on lying behavior. Oxytocin is typically thought to increase affiliative behavior and conformity, but Dr. Aydogan found it to increase deception in competitive environments. Individuals exposed to oxytocin were more likely to conform and cooperate with the in-group in cooperative environments, but administration of oxytocin in competitive environments increased deception. Essentially, after administration of oxytocin, individuals were more likely to adhere or conform to the behavior of their social partners. If their social partners were cooperative, they were more likely to cooperate, and if their social partners were competitive, they were more likely to engage in competitive behaviors. Thus, deceptive and competitive behavior seems to be partially regulated by neurotransmitters. Also, deceptive behavior is moderated by the expectations or social norms within a group. If there is an expectation of deceptive or competitive behavior in a social group, then individuals are much more likely to lie. However, if there is a group norm of honesty and cooperation, individuals are less likely to violate the social norm and engage in deceptive behavior.

The impact of group exceptions explains situations, such as political campaigns, where there can be a general degradation of honesty once an environment of dishonesty is created. Once one side of a campaign begins to engage in dishonest claims or smear campaigns, it becomes much easier for other candidates to engage in similar behaviors with less detriment to their own self-image, since they are conforming to the new social norm. Similar arguments could be made for sports competitions or marketing campaigns, and intervention measures may be more successful if they focus on changing the norm of unethical conduct. Once such behaviors are deemed less acceptable, individuals are less likely to engage in deceptive and competitive behaviors.

See also: Advertising; Cognitive Dissonance; Cognitive Distortion; Ethics; Neuroscience; Physiology; Politics; Prisoner's Dilemma; Propaganda; Social Media; Tactical Deception.

Further Reading

Aydogan, G., Jobst, A., D'Ardenne, K., Muller, N., & Kocher, M. G. (2017). The detrimental effects of oxytocin-induced conformity on dishonesty in competition. *Psychological Science, 28*(6), 751–759.

Feltovich, N. (2019). The interaction between competition and unethical behaviour. *Experimental Economics: A Journal of the Economic Science Association, 22*(1), 101–130.

Compulsive Lying

Compulsive lying, or pathological lying, describes an individual who engages in chronic lying behavior, and such behavior can be a symptom of several psychological disorders. Other terms for this condition include pseudologia fantastica and mythomania. While many people occasionally tell small lies to smooth social transactions or to avoid hurting the feelings of others, compulsive or pathological liars tell lies for no apparent reason, possibly simply out of habit. It is unclear whether compulsive liars intend to lie or if the individuals actually believe their lies, at least in the moment.

Compulsive liars tell extraordinary lies about unbelievable experiences in which they are the hero or martyr, and they come to believe the lies they tell. Most compulsive liars are convincing and charming, particularly to those who do not know them well. They tend to be great storytellers and hold their audience enthralled in their fantastic accounts of experiences. They usually are in no hurry to get to the point and are calm and confident. Most lies are continuous and are not for any specific personal gain. They also do not seem to show remorse or embarrassment when discovered, especially given that many of the lies may be unbelievable. Instead, they deny lying and may respond emotionally if their audience expresses disbelief. Their stories may also morph over repeated telling.

Frequently, compulsive liars are convincing even though their claims are extreme. For example, Judge Patrick Couwenberg of California falsely reported that he was part of the CIA and held a master's degree in psychology. Furthermore, he claimed to have been awarded the Purple Heart for his injuries from the Vietnam War and that he still had shrapnel lodged in his body. Upon investigation, it was discovered that he was never part of a CIA operation, did not earn a degree in psychology, and had never been to Vietnam. When evaluated, a psychiatrist deemed that Judge Couwenberg had pseudologia fantastica. It is likely that he had told the stories so frequently that he came to believe them and did not even remember that he was lying.

Compulsive lying is similar to lying that is seen in fantasy play in childhood. Though this type of play is beneficial for children's cognitive and social development, when it persists into adulthood, it crosses over into abnormal behavior. Compulsive liars seem to engage in more wishful thinking and depart from reality more readily than white or intentional liars. Most compulsive lies are unplanned, and though the liar may admit to their falseness when pressed, most do not self-assess and appear to believe the lies as they are telling them.

Compulsive lying may be a symptom of other disorders, such as borderline personality disorder, malingering, factitious disorders, or narcissistic personality disorder, but it is not always associated with another diagnosis. For many individuals who engage in compulsive lying, they may be otherwise successful and respected. Their lies tend to make them look more successful or more intelligent than they actually are and are frequently exaggerations and ego-boosting deviations from the truth. These lies may only become a problem when discovered, and these individuals may need to change social groups frequently to recoup respect and esteem; such behaviors tend to interfere with the development of healthy long-term relationships.

It is likely that compulsive liars may only seek treatment if this lying gets them in trouble with the law or damages valued relationships. Otherwise, many compulsive liars do not believe that their lying is a problem. Their lies may stem from anxiety, depression, or low self-esteem, so therapy or medicine may help alleviate the cause and allow the individual to work toward being more truthful. Medication can also help the individual control the behavior, though more research is needed to determine the underlying neurological dysfunction that accompanies the disorder. Interestingly, though compulsive liars may have difficulty controlling their lies, they tend to otherwise have good judgement. They can be successful and articulate and tend to be charming. However, difficulties arise if they are called upon to tell the truth, such as if their testimony is needed for a court case. Since their lies tend to be obvious and extraordinary and change over time, their testimony cannot be trusted. If they are unable to control their lies, they cannot be held in contempt of court, but they may confuse the proceedings.

The question remains of whether or not these individuals have conscious control over their lying behavior. When specifically probed, compulsive liars frequently admit that their report is not entirely accurate. Thus, at least in retrospect and when directed, they can identify the inaccurate aspects of their reports. However, their behavior may not be conscious or controlled when it is occurring, and they may be unable to prevent themselves from embellishing and exaggerating.

See also: Antisocial Personality Disorder; Careless Liars; Delusions; Detecting Deception; Exaggeration; Malingering; Perjury; Reality Monitoring; Self-Deception.

Further Reading

Dike, C. C., Baranoski, M., & Griffith, E. E. H. (2005). Pathological lying revisited. *The Journal of the American Academy of Psychiatry and the Law, 33*(3), 342–349.

Dimitrakopoulos, S., Sakadaki, E., & Ploumpidis, D. (2014). Pseudologia fantastica a deux: Review and case study. *Psychiatriki, 25*, 192–199.

Con Artist (*See* Impersonator; Scams)

Con Man (*See* Impersonator; Scams)

Concealed Information Test

The Concealed Information Test (CIT), also known as the Guilty Knowledge Test, can be administered during a polygraph session in order to determine whether the individual being interviewed is attempting to conceal information. During the interview, the examiner poses multiple choice questions that relate to the situation under investigation. The possible multiple choice answers include one that is accurate and others that are plausible, given the circumstances. Innocent suspects who have no inside knowledge about the crime would not know the correct answer and thus would show no differential physiological or emotional response to that answer compared to the incorrect answers. Guilty suspects, however, know the correct answer and tend to show physiological changes when confronted with that choice. For example, when presented with the correct answer, they may have changes in breathing, changes in blood pressure, and changes in electrodermal and brain activity, even if they are controlling their verbal and nonverbal behaviors. Based on their physiological reactions to the multiple choice answers, the interviewer can gauge whether or not the individual has knowledge that an innocent respondent would not have.

For example, when interviewing suspects about a home robbery, an impartial interviewer who does not know the details of the crime may pose the following question and answers: "Where did the robber enter the house? Repeat these possible areas of entry after me: 1. Garage door; 2. Basement window; 3. Back porch; 4. Front door (correct answer); 5. Dining room window." A suspect who knows where the house was entered typically has a differential response to the correct answer. A suspect who does not know where the house was entered would not show such a change in physiology because all of the answers are plausible. In preliminary research studies, use of the Concealed Information Test allowed researchers to determine guilt 84 percent of the time and confirm innocence in 94 percent of the trials. Even if an innocent suspect is highly anxious or aroused, the lack of change of physiology when presented with the correct answer helps determine their innocence, unlike other interview procedures that use overall arousal as a sign of guilt.

Despite its effectiveness, the CIT is the least commonly used test of any psychophysiological detection method, even though it has stronger theoretical validation than all of the other methods combined. Some investigators claim that it is too difficult to administer because questions have to be created specific to the situation in question. However, proponents of the CIT argue that it has been scientifically verified; is less intrusive than other measures; is relatively quick to set up, conduct, and score; and is less likely to result in false positives. CIT is, however, a recognition test, not a deception test. The CIT can only be used if information about the crime has not been made public and new items must be created for each crime scene. An investigator must gather information at the crime scene, determine what the suspect claims not to know, construct questions, and have the test administered by someone who is blind to the circumstances of the crime so that the interviewer cannot influence the suspect during the test.

Additionally, a physiological response to the correct answers does not prove that suspects are guilty of the crimes. A response simply shows that they have more knowledge about the events than they are reporting. Though there are some guilty participants who can fool the test, it is much less likely that an innocent subject will be found guilty or that a false confession will be elicited. Suspects cannot have stable responses to the correct answers if they do not know that information.

In one mock-crime study led by Dr. Shinji Hira of Fukuyama University, researchers used the CIT to test participants immediately following a staged crime, one month later, and one year later. At each point, results from the CIT correctly identified all participants as either guilty or not guilty. For delayed interviews, environmental surroundings tended to be forgotten and thus were less helpful in determining guilt or innocence. However, details directly related to the crime, such as what was stolen, where it happened, and how it was done, were still key in detecting guilty knowledge. Researchers also demonstrated that guilty participants had more extreme responses to questions about information they were specifically instructed to conceal than they did to irrelevant or neutral stimuli in a mock-crime scenario.

Another significant use of the CIT can be to gather unknown information about a crime from a known perpetrator. By constructing questions about the crime and listing all possible answers, a researcher can gather information based on the suspect's responses. For example, in 1988, when the U.S. Customs Service believed that a ship was transporting illegal drugs, they interviewed the crew about where the drugs were stored. By providing possible hiding places and monitoring the crews' responses to the alternatives presented, they were able to narrow down where the 4,800 pounds of cocaine were hidden.

See also: Behavior Analysis Interview; Control Questions Test; Detecting Deception; Motivational Impairment Effect; Nonverbal Behavior; Polygraph Tests; Reid Technique.

Further Reading

Ben-Shakhar, G., & Elaad, E. (2003). The validity of psychophysiological detection of information with the guilty knowledge test: A meta-analytic review. *Journal of Applied Psychology, 88*(1), 131–151.

Carmel, D., Dayan, E., Naveh, A., Raveh, O., & Ben-Shakhar, G. (2003). Estimating the validity of the guilty knowledge test from simulated experiments: The external validity of mock crime studies. *Journal of Experimental Psychology: Applied, 9*(4), 261–269.

Hahm, J., Ji, H. K., Jeong, J. Y., Oh, D. H., Kim, S. H., Sim, K., & Lee, J. (2009). Detection of concealed information: Combining a virtual mock crime with a P200-based guilty knowledge test. *Cyber Psychology & Behavior, 12*(3), 269–275.

Hira, S., Sasaki, M., Matsuda, T., Furumitsu, I., & Furedy, J. J. (2002). A year after the commission of a mock crime, the P300 amplitudes, but not reaction time, are sensitive guilty knowledge test indicators. *Psychophysiology, 39*, S42.

Krapohl, D. J., McCloughan, J. B., & Senter, S. M. (2009). How to use the concealed information test. *Polygraph, 38*(1), 34–49.

MacLaren, V. V. (2001). A quantitative review of the guilty knowledge test. *Journal of Applied Psychology, 86*(4), 674–683.

Confabulation (See False Memory)

Conscience

One's conscience is thought to be responsible for the feelings of remorse following a thought or behavior that is misaligned with one's moral beliefs. Such discordant behavior creates a sense of cognitive dissonance, and to alleviate the discomfort, one needs to either change one's behavior or alter one's beliefs. Conscience has been studied through religious, secular, and philosophic lenses and is typically intertwined with deceptive behaviors and moral development.

Over childhood, children develop through two types of morality. The first type of morality is that of constraints which predominates until age seven or eight. Using this type of morality, children lack reasoning and simply conform to adult expectations. The more mature morality is that of cooperation or reciprocity. As this develops, conscience emerges, and behaviors are self-evaluated rather than externally controlled. Conscience emerges as children internalize cultural and social rules, and by adulthood, self-recrimination and self-assessment predominate over external punishments. Parents can encourage the development of a strong conscience by communicating a clear moral code and using consistent rewards and punishments for behavior. Children raised in this manner tend to engage in more moral thinking and moral behavior. Alternatively, children, raised in environments where the social norm is to deceive, learn it is acceptable to engage in deception and feel less remorse. In this way, conscience seems to be guided by social norms and expectations rather than an idealized sense of right and wrong.

For this reason, despite the guidance of conscience, many individuals still engage in deceptive and dishonest behaviors. Some even rate not feeling guilty after engaging in such behaviors. One reason for this seeming lack of conscience is that individuals tend to justify deceptive behaviors through disengagement. Disengagement is the process of making immoral actions acceptable by justifying them to oneself. Such rationalization alleviates the discomfort that may emerge when behaviors do not match one's personal moral code. Furthermore, practice with such rationalization makes it easier to do again in the future, to the extent that discomfort may not even be entertained because one has already rationalized their actions. One easy rationalization is that everyone lies or everyone cheats. By believing the social norm is dishonesty, an individual can feel less discomfort because they feel they are engaging in socially sanctioned behaviors.

The justifications that individuals make to excuse their own dishonest behaviors actually mirror those that criminals use to justify their crimes. Individuals who have low levels of empathy, who lack a clear sense of their own moral values, and who have an external locus of control are all more likely to engage in moral disengagement, where they excuse their own immoral behaviors through justification or rationalization. They become more lenient in their attitudes toward deception and less likely to feel pangs of conscience when engaging in such behaviors. Those who resist temptation to cheat or engage in immoral behavior, alternatively, are likely to continue to resist temptation.

Dr. Lisa Shu and her colleagues from Harvard University found that increasing the saliency of morality by having individuals sign an honor code, discuss moral values, or view others engaging in moral acts significantly reduced the likelihood of immoral behaviors when given an opportunity, and increased moral behavior and engagement. Activating the conscience via such means made it more likely that individuals would avoid dishonesty and more likely that they would feel discomfort after engaging in deceptive behaviors. Activation of one's conscience also makes it more difficult to disregard or justify one's own dishonest acts. Alternatively, engaging in immoral acts, witnessing immoral acts, or acting without thinking all increase the likelihood of engaging in future immoral acts. In a sense, individuals seem to be able to turn their conscience on and off with experience, situation, and effort. Those interested in increasing honesty and ethical behavior in particular situations should increase the salience of morality via cues in the environment.

Conscientious behavior is particularly needed in business. Negotiations, for example, tend to encourage deceptive behavior because individuals typically strive to increase their own benefits. Most also expect others to engage in deceptions during negotiations, making the behavior easier to justify. Whether the negotiation is thought to be competitive or cooperative can have an effect on whether one's conscience will deem deceptive behaviors as acceptable. Thus, implicit expectations about a situation can influence whether or not one's conscience is activated and whether there are ready justifications for engaging in immoral behaviors. If there are external reasons for engaging in such behaviors or if deception is the social norm in a particular situation, then engaging in deception does not create a sense of remorse or discomfort. Thus, for conscience to work effectively, the situation must be characterized by moral and ethical behavior to set up the expectation for such behaviors.

See also: Cognitive Dissonance; Locus of Control; Machiavellianism; Self-Deception; Tactical Deception.

Further Reading

Boehm, L., & Nass, M. L. (1962). Social class differences in conscience development. *Child Development, 33*, 565–574.

Gasper, J. P., & Chen, C. C. (2016). The unconscious conscience: Implicit processes and deception in negotiation. *Negotiation Journal, 32*(3), 213–229.

Shu, L. L., Gino, F., & Bazerman, M. H. (2011). Dishonest deed, clear conscience: When cheating leads to moral disengagement and motivated forgetting. *Personality and Social Psychology Bulletin, 37*(3), 330–349.

Consequences of Lying

Successful deception can have many benefits, which explains why it is so ubiquitous. Since lies tend to help one gain an advantage, good liars may be more successful in business and personal relationships than those who are honest. However, for those caught in a lie, costs can range from loss of reputation to loss of relationships or to even legal action. And even successful deception may have costs. Liars tend to suffer more from feelings of guilt and mental and physical health problems and have difficulty in sustaining relationships and building true intimacy, and many are not able to get too close to those around them because their lies may be discovered.

The professed benefits of lying range from prosocial to malicious. Individuals can use lies to smooth over social interactions, maintain harmony in relationships, prevent hurt feelings, enhance how they are perceived by others, gain an advantage over others, or procure material gain. Those who tell prosocial lies, or lies that benefit another person or prevent hurting another person's feelings, actually tend to be rated as more trustworthy than people who tell the truth. People who engage in prosocial lying typically build and maintain larger social networks than those who lie for other reasons or those who tell the truth. Those who lie to improve what others think about them tend to be motivated by low self-esteem. Such liars

Strategies for Being More Honest in Day-to-Day Interactions

Sometimes telling a white lie may seem easier than telling the truth. However, engaging in deceptive behavior has behavioral, physical, and social ramifications, and can quickly become a habit. For those interested in engaging in more truthful behavior, there are several strategies to build a habit of honesty. The first step is to pay attention to when and how often one lies. Most lies are unimportant or told to be polite. Before attempting to curb these lies, individuals should just start paying attention to when and how often they occur. Once people have a sense of when they lie, they can start to practice curbing the behavior or planning out socially acceptable alternatives to the lie. If they are lying to please a particular person or to avoid a particular reaction, they may need to change the dynamic of the relationship in order to change the lying behavior.

To increase honesty, it is most important that individuals are honest with themselves. Sometimes individuals lie in an attempt to save face or to convince themselves of something. Being honest with oneself about wants, likes, or personality traits is the first step in being honest with others. Knowing oneself is also helpful when making commitments. Most people make time for things that are important to them so one should take the time to determine which commitments are priorities. One may also buy time to consider an invitation or a response by pausing to check one's schedule first and thinking it through before responding.

In many situations people lie without thinking. To increase honesty, one should admit to lies as soon as they are noticed. Accidental liars can simply tell others that they misspoke or did not want to hurt feelings. Such honesty may go a long way to untangle a web of white lies, especially for those trying to break a lying habit. Most people will respect others who admit when they made a mistake. Such honesty is refreshing and tends to contribute to strong, trusting relationships. In turn, however, one must be gracious when others admit to lies or provide honesty in return.

For habitual liars, it may be easiest to practice within inconsequential situations. Individuals may start by telling the truth about preferences and desires. Then they can work up to telling the truth about more substantial opinions or needs. When practicing telling the truth, individuals should pause and consider an answer before answering questions. For habitual liars, the first instinct may be to lie to smooth over the social interaction. One should take the time to consider one's words and find a tactful way to be honest.

Focusing on being more honest can go a long way in curbing lying behavior. An important distinction is that successful honesty does not necessitate that one always tells the brutal truth. Instead, one should work toward fewer exaggerations about day-to-day experiences, stop giving excuses, and construe the truth as constructively as possible. Being truthful tends to have direct correlations with increased relationship satisfaction and increased physical and mental health. Those who are honest report fewer stressors and stress-related complaints. They also grow to value their own opinions and feel less need to provide excuses, which buffers their mental health and self-esteem.

do not feel as though they are competent or impressive and lie to keep their deficits hidden from others. Such lies may serve to increase social standing or perceived competence. Those who lie to gain an advantage over others reap the rewards of power or material gain.

However, even individuals who reap the benefits of these different types of lies tend to suffer the consequences. Prosocial liars are rated as more trustworthy in the short term, but telling lies to others to buffer self-esteem or to prevent hurt feelings can cause them to continue with a behavior or make poor decisions. A truth teller may cause hurt feelings in the moment, but then others have the true information on which to base future decisions. Those who engage in prosocial lying may eventually be less trusted because they give bad advice. Those who engage in lying to cover up for low self-esteem also tend to suffer long-term consequences, even if their lies are not discovered. Lying about one's own abilities tends to perpetuate the need to lie to maintain the ruse. It is psychologically healthier to admit to a weakness and to work to improve one's own abilities than to lie to maintain a reputation. Such liars tend to suffer even greater losses of self-esteem as they learn that they must lie to be effective. In fact, those who score high on scales of deception suffer from increasingly poor self-esteem, physical health, and mental health; higher stress levels; more diseases; and higher levels of reported chronic illnesses, even if they are successful in their deceptions.

The above consequences occur even when the liar is not discovered. However, consequences can also occur if the liar is revealed. When a lie is discovered, the victims typically have emotional and cognitive responses. They may be upset and lose trust in the person who lied. They may be more suspicious, avoid the person, or want revenge, depending on the type of lie. Liars also may attempt to use additional lies to cover up for their behavior and tend to experience uneasiness and dread. They also find that when they tell the truth, others are still suspicious. Once individuals gain a reputation as a liar, they may struggle to get others to trust any future claims. Liars may also be ostracized, disrespected, or held legally responsible for their lies.

Those who engage in lying for material gain or to gain an advantage become more and more likely to engage in additional deception over time. Furthermore, those around them become more likely to lie as well. Since such lying typically provides a benefit for the liar, they are rewarded for the behavior in the short term. They also tend to rationalize their behavior, making it easier to lie in the future since they have already found justification for such inauthentic communications. Maintaining more lies, however, is cognitively depleting, increases the risk of discovery, and decreases self-esteem, which may lead to additional lying. Thus, though lying may have short-term benefits, in the long term it tends to be detrimental to physical and psychological health and creates a negative feedback cycle for relationships and future lying behavior.

See also: Benefits of Lying; Black Lies; Cognitive Dissonance; Commission, Lies of; Conscience; Instrumental Lies; Lying; Prosocial Lying; Self-Deception.

Further Reading

Arcimowicz, B., Cantarero, K., & Soroko, E. (2015). Motivation and consequences of lying. A qualitative analysis of everyday living. *Qualitative Social Research, 16*(3). Retrieved from https://www.qualitative-research.net/index.php/fqs/article/view/2311/3892

Palsane, M. N. (2005). Self-incongruent behavior, stress, and disease. *National Academy of Psychology, India, 50*(4), 283–297.

Wiltermuth, S. S., Newman, D. T., & Raj, M. (2015). The consequences of dishonesty. *Society for Personality and Social Psychology*. Retrieved from http://www.spsp.org/news-center/blog/the-consequences-of-dishonesty

Conspiracies (See Conspiracy Theories)

Conspiracy Theories

Conspiracies are illegal, shared, premeditated deceptive attempts set in place to achieve a goal. Conspiracies typically refer to secret political plots to overthrow governments or widespread misinformation attempts to skew public opinion or cover up unlawful activities. However, there are several types of conspiracies. Civil conspiracies are acts by individuals who seek to mislead or defraud others in legal contexts. Criminal conspiracies are plans made to commit a crime. Political conspiracies result from groups who act to overthrow the political system. There are myriad conspiracies peppering history, frequently in the shape of coups to take over political power. However, conspiracy theories, or unjustified beliefs in premeditated deceptive attempts in which people believe deceptive actions were undertaken to shape public opinion, may be even more common.

A conspiracy theory is when a group or individual believes that a conspiracy is in progress or has taken place. Conspiracy theorists may ardently believe that an event was actually the work of a private or secret political movement or coordinated action, regardless of whether or not evidence exists to support such claims. In such cases, there may be more likely explanations, but conspiracy theorists believe that the incident is the work of a sinister secret group. Conspiracy theorists tend to be passionate in their beliefs, resist evidence that undermines their beliefs, and interpret any evidence as supporting their claims.

Though conspiracies do take place, conspiracy theories are more likely the byproduct of suspicion, paranoia, and psychological instability. Individuals with schizophrenia and other schizotypal disorders are likely to infer conspiracies from very fragmented evidence. Conspiracy theorists tend to ignore scientific or empirical evidence and rely on paranoia, signs, and projection to solidify and avow their beliefs. Some common conspiracy theories include the belief that aliens are housed in Area 51 or that Area 51 was used to stage the moon landing, that climate change is not occurring, and that vaccinations cause autism. There are ardent individuals who believe all of these things and cling to such beliefs despite contradictory empirical evidence.

Some individuals are more susceptible to believing in conspiracies than others. Researchers from New Mexico State University and Purdue University identified variables that made individuals likely to believe in conspiracy theories. Some of these variables included a sense of powerlessness, low self-esteem, low levels of trust, and an external locus of control. These individuals potentially believe in conspiracy theories as a simple way to understand complex events. Believing in a conspiracy theory also gives individuals a person or group to blame, which may alleviate anxiety about issues to which there is not a simple solution. Belief in conspiracy theories may also provide more concrete explanations for why things are happening as well as a target for aggressive feelings. Conspiracy theorists tend to distrust authority, have limited representation in leadership, and feel alienated by those in power.

Conspiracy theories tend to provide a sensationalized explanation of major events. Conspiracy theorists tend to make connections between events that are coincidental and provide structure to random information. At the same time, they disregard information that does not conform to their chosen beliefs. Perceiving situations and evidence in this manner allows an individual to create a sense of order and understanding, albeit incorrect or incomplete, of even complex situations.

The difficulty is in determining the difference between conspiracies and conspiracy theories. Conspiracies do occur, yet the wealth of conspiracy theories may lead one to overlook or discount actual conspiracies. A scandal, assassination, or terrorist attack could be the result of an actual conspiracy to undermine a reputation or a government. The amount of evidence for a belief may be one way to determine which are true and which are misguided beliefs. Thus, it may be more sound to think about conspiracy theories as unproven rather than untrue. For example, Watergate may have been a conspiracy theory until evidence was found to provide substantial proof. The sheer volume of conspiracy theories actually undermines the ability to identify actual conspiracies. One must be a perceptive and critical reader to delineate between conspiracy theories, such as Russia's involvement with spreading Coronavirus, and conspiracies with empirical backing, such as Russia's attempted interference with U.S. presidential elections. In the modern age, logical thinkers may likely discount actual scientifically corroborated conspiracies because they are so inundated with those spread by the uninformed populace.

Conspiracies tend to be logical and can be supported by empirical evidence. They are specific, goal-oriented, and covert, and many may be regarded as conspiracy theories until empirical evidence is found to support them. Conspiracy theories, alternatively, tend to rely on faith, and those who believe them find them to be irrefutable, even when contradictory evidence is revealed.

See also: *Art of War, The*; Cognitive Dissonance; Exaggeration; Fact-Check; Fake News; Hoax; Locus of Control; Politics; Propaganda; Red Herring.

Further Reading

Abalakina-Paap, M., Stephan, W. G., Craig, T., & Gregory, W. L. (1999). Beliefs in conspiracies. *Political Psychology, 20*(3), 637–647.

Dieguez, S., Wagner-Egger, P., & Gauvrit, N. (2015). Nothing happens by accident, or does it? A low prior for randomness does not explain belief in conspiracy theories. *Psychological Science, 26*(11), 1762–1770.

Locke, S. (2009). Conspiracy culture, blame culture, and rationalisation. *The Sociological Review, 57*(4), 567–585.

Control Questions Test

The most common test used during a polygraph session in the United States, Canada, and Israel is the Control Questions Test (CQT). The CQT is reportedly easier to implement than the Concealed Information Test (CIT), which is more commonly used in Japan. The CQT is used for criminal investigations and was historically used in employee screenings for businesses. In the CQT, an examiner compares an individual's physiological responses when responding to questions relevant to a crime or other nefarious act to responses when responding to control questions. This method of interview tends to be direct, such as asking a relevant question such as, "Did you commit the crime?" and a control question such as, "Have you ever committed a crime?" During the interview, the polygraph device monitors physiological changes to assess whether the individual is experiencing emotional arousal in response to a question or during a verbal response.

When given, examiners first allow suspects to describe what they know about the situation in question. During this description, the examiner composes questions to ask later in the interview. Once attached to the polygraph, the examiner asks relevant and control questions, and the physiological reactions are measured. Typically changes in breathing, electrodermal activity, and blood pressure are recorded, and the question set is repeated three of four times to establish consistency in reactions. The assumption is that guilty suspects should react more significantly to the questions relevant to the crime. For innocent suspects, however, the control questions should elicit greater physiological responses than questions about the current crime, with which they were uninvolved. If the pattern is inconsistent, the test is considered inconclusive.

Since the Control Question Test (CQT) relies on physiological responses, its validity is debated. For example, an innocent suspect who is unfamiliar with the interview process or who is worried about not being believed may show heightened physiological arousal to relevant questions, making the CQT vulnerable to false positives. Criminals may also have more practice in answering questions and controlling their emotional arousal and may be able to fool the experimenter.

Additionally, there is no definitive theory that demonstrates a specific physiological pattern that conclusively denotes deception. Response patterns during the test may signal emotional reactions, but do not conclusively indicate guilt. Any emotions such as surprise, anxiety, or stress may cause physiological changes. The veracity of the results also depends on the subjective judgment and interpretation of the examiner, rather than objective, standardized measures. Standardization is difficult given the subjective nature of the assessment, which allows potential bias of an examiner in an emotionally charged situation. Some accuse the CQT of being used to confirm suspicions rather than to objectively assess a suspect. Empirical tests demonstrate high rates of false negatives (finding guilty suspects innocent) and false positives (finding innocent suspects guilty), and the direct nature of the assessment can contribute to false confessions. The Concealed Information Test (CIT), alternatively, was designed around scientific principles; has empirically established validity, control, and reliability; and is much less likely to result in a false positive than the CQT. U.S. interrogators, however, report that it is more difficult to administer and thus it is not frequently used in the United States.

Dr. Michael Bradley and his colleagues from the University of New Brunswick examined the Control Questions Test and did show evidence of successful detection of deception, but only for individuals who score high on traits of Machiavellianism. Dr. Bradley surmised that those who score high on Machiavellianism were more likely to analyze the questions, realize which were crime relevant, and exude more effort in trying to conceal information. This effort translated into higher pulse rates and skin reactance measures. So, though those who score high on measures of Machiavellianism tend to be convincing liars because they engage in detailed assessment of the situation; this difference in their attention and effort is measurable by the CQT. Guilty suspects who scored low on traits of Machiavellianism were less likely to be detected by the CQT.

See also: Concealed Information Test; Detecting Deception; False Confessions; Machiavellianism; Motivational Impairment Effect; Othello Error; Physiology; Polygraph Tests.

Further Reading

Ben-Shakhar, G. (2002). A critical review of the control questions test (CQT). In M. Kleiner (Ed.), *Handbook of Polygraph Testing* (pp. 103–126). Academic Press.

Ben-Shakhar, G., & Elaad, E. (2003). The validity of psychophysiological detection of information with the guilty knowledge test: A meta-analytic review. *Journal of Applied Psychology, 88*(1), 131–151.

Bradley, M. T., & Klohn, K. I. (1987). Machiavellianism, the control question test and the detection of deception. *Perceptual and Motor Skills, 64*, 747–757.

Carmel, D., Dayan, E., Naveh, A., Raveh, O., & Ben-Shakhar, G. (2003). Estimating the validity of the guilty knowledge test from simulated experiments: The external validity of mock crime studies. *Journal of Experimental Psychology: Applied, 9*(4), 261–269.

Corruption

Corruption refers to deceptive behavior typically perpetuated by those in positions of power. Corruption can include bribery, falsification, and manipulation, and frequently results in personal gain. Corruption exists in the political arena as well as in the legal system and in corporations. In politics, corruption can take the form of using one's power for personal gain. In the legal system, it can include taking bribes or using one's position to manipulate consequences. In corporations, it can range from using power for personal gain to embezzlement on a grand scale.

Corruption undermines economic growth and stability and is more likely to occur in systems where there is a great imbalance in power, inequality, lack of education, high desire for personal gain with low commitment to society, and in cultures where dishonesty is accepted. To combat corruption, direct penalties; high transparency from those in power; and an equitable distribution of wealth, power, and control is needed.

Some companies and countries tend to have higher levels of corruption than others. The Corruption Perception Index was created in 1995 to identify corruption so it could be addressed worldwide. The United States was ranked 23rd in 2019 with Denmark, Finland, Sweden, New Zealand, and Switzerland leading the rankings for least corruption, and Somalia, South Sudan, and Venezuela ranking among the most corrupt. However, labeling countries as a means of decreasing corruption had the reverse effect for highly corrupt countries. Once identified, these countries became more isolated, received less foreign investment, and the corruption became more extreme. Labeling the country as corrupt also created a self-fulfilling prophecy where the social norm of corruption allowed corruption to become more rather than less prevalent. Furthermore, when ousting corrupt leaders, frequently the climate of corruption was so widespread that the replacements were likely to be even more corrupt.

In an effort to reduce corruption, Dr. Norman Bishara and Dr. Cindy Schipani from the University of Michigan identified a framework to govern and prevent corruption. Their framework includes identifying, preventing, detecting, and eradicating corruption. Ultimately, changes must be made internally in corrupt countries or corporations to address the ethical challenges. In order to identify and prevent corruption, leaders must be proactive and have oversight by ethical committees. The committee could be charged to anticipate areas that could be easily exploited and to anticipate loopholes. Once potential corruption has been identified, the next step is to have mechanisms to detect and eradicate it. Finally, countries or companies must commit to learn from mistakes and anticipate and prevent future corruption.

A governance that is transparent and open contributes to a culture of ethical behavior. Alternatively, leaders who engage in corrupt behavior model such behavior to shareholders, employees, or citizens, increasing those behaviors at every level. Having leaders who avoid such behavior creates the opposite model for all involved. The struggle is in finding leaders who want to prevent corruption. Leaders must give up personal gain in order to benefit the country or company as a whole. Companies known for not engaging in corrupt behavior tend to have higher long-term gains and greater overall value, increasing the incentive to have an ethical approach.

Dr. Ori Weisel and Dr. Shaul Shalvi from the University of Nottingham and Princeton University propose that collaborative and cooperative environments can play a role in emerging corruption. When engaging in cooperative tasks in which the group can benefit from deception, corruption is more likely to arise. As the cooperators align with one another, they engage in corrupt collaboration to more effectively compete with outsiders. Because the whole in-group benefits, it is easier to justify the corrupt activities, and cognitive dissonance is alleviated. Dr. Weisel and Dr. Shalvi demonstrated that in a cooperative task with mutually beneficial outcomes, corruption tended to emerge. However, when completing a comparable task alone or when the behaviors were not mutually beneficial, corruption levels dropped. Corruption may not be entirely self-serving because most people do not engage in corrupt behaviors to benefit themselves alone. The phenomenon emerges when corrupt and deceptive behaviors benefit the group. This becomes particularly detrimental because those who engage in corrupt behaviors tend to be those in power. The behaviors benefit themselves and others in power, creating further harm to those who do not have power. Thus, more equal distribution of power and resources could undermine corruption.

Cross-cultural differences in corruption emerge quite readily. Activities considered to be corrupt also differ cross-culturally. In collaborative countries that put stronger emphasis on building relationships, engaging in behavior for one's own benefit may be considered corrupt. In individualistic countries, engaging in selfish behavior may be the norm, even at the expense of colleagues or friends. Differences in ethical norms between cultures may pose a problem for identifying and combating corruption. In this sense, fighting corruption cross-culturally involves the finesse of understanding the culture in order to understand the implications of the actions.

See also: Advertising; Cognitive Dissonance; Doublespeak; Ethics; Fake News; Machiavellianism; Manipulation; Paternalistic Lies; Politics; Propaganda; Red Herring.

Further Reading

Bishara, N. D., & Schipani, C. A. (2009). Strengthening the ties that bind: Preventing corruption in the executive suite. *Journal of Business Ethics, 88*, 765–780.

Cleveland, M., Favo, C. M., Frecka, T. J., & Owens, C. L. (2009). Trends in the international fight against bribery and corruption. *Journal of Business Ethics, 90*, 199–244.

Hooker, J. (2009). Corruption from a cross-cultural perspective. *Cross Cultural and Strategic Management, 16*(3), 251–267.

Warren, D. E., & Laufer, W. S. (2010). Are corruption indices is self-fulfilling prophecy? A social labeling perspective of corruption. *Journal of Business Ethics, 88*, 841–849.

Weisel, O., & Shalvi, S. (2015). The collaborative roots of corruption. *Proceedings of the National Academy of Sciences, 112*(34), 10651–10656.

Costs of Lying

Though lying is very common in day-to-day social interactions, there are many costs associated with being dishonest. Individuals may reap short-term benefits from low-stakes or high-stakes lies, but the long-term costs of lying may negate the short-term benefits. Most people lie at one time or another. Though not everyone tells big lies, most people tell white lies or butler lies on occasion, and some individuals are more prolific liars. Most individuals lie to impress others, to appear more interesting, or to avoid social embarrassment or discomfort. Individuals use lies to gain an advantage, create a favorable impression, maintain an upper hand, or avoid conflict. Many engage in self-deception and create excuses or rationalize behaviors to eliminate the feeling of discomfort.

According to social workers Linda Bloom and Charlie Bloom, even white lies can have a detrimental effect. Telling lies undermines trust, respect, and intimacy within relationships. Most individuals report feelings of guilt and anxiety following dishonesty, which leads to decreases in mental and physical health. Those who lie also tend to mistrust others more than those who typically tell the truth and feel less comfortable in social situations. Telling lies also reinforces feelings of being ill-equipped to deal with the consequences of the truth and lowers feelings of self-efficacy.

Telling strangers or acquaintances that one is fine even when one is not, or thanking them for an unwanted gift, likely has limited negative ramifications. Lying to an intimate partner or a close friend, however, can have longer term consequences and undermine trust in the relationship. Marriage and family therapist Darlene Lancer proposes that keeping secrets and telling lies tend to block intimacy with a partner. If one cannot be genuine, then one is prevented from having a real connection. Lying to partners or friends tends to elicit feelings of guilt, anxiety, and discomfort. One may start avoiding activities or conversations with the other because of the lie. Liars may feel incapable of telling the truth or unable to be vulnerable, or they may feel shame, which causes them to hide parts of themselves.

Being unable to share oneself with the other thus creates a feedback loop, leading to greater feelings of inadequacy. These feelings may also cause individuals to become irritable, aggressive, or judgmental in relationships. Such resentment can cause further damage to the connection. Liars are also frequently suspicious of others and expect others to lie in return. Lies in such circumstances can also be hurtful when the truth comes out. Partners or friends may feel a sense of betrayal.

In a study completed at the University of Massachusetts, researchers revealed that over half of the adults in the study lied at least once within a 10-minute conversation. Furthermore, those people who lied told an average of 3 lies during the 10 minutes. They found that most people lied to friends, siblings, and spouses about things that were not important. They also found that people lie on their resumes, their dating profiles, and during interpersonal conversations. One of the biggest costs of lying that emerged was damage to one's reputation. Being caught exaggerating or lying gives a negative impression to others. Telling lies in business or in relationships tends to create a fabricated version of reality, which prevents individuals from confronting problems or managing issues. Rather than tackling issues straight on, individuals rationalize or cover them up. Being honest in relationships or in business allows individuals to be present and proactive in their relationships and business deals.

Lying in the workplace also undermines trust. It is difficult to create a productive work environment if employees cannot trust one another or cannot trust the leaders of the company. Admitting to mistakes allows for personal growth in a way that covering up or lying about mistakes does not. Routinely engaging in lying behavior also has an impact on an individual's own self-esteem. As self-esteem decreases, individuals feel even less able to be honest.

For those who curb their lying behavior, there are immediate physical and mental benefits. In a research study at the University of Notre Dame, Dr. Anita Kelly asked participants to practice telling the truth in all social interactions over the course of two and a half months. By the end of the study, the participants had significant physical and mental health improvements. Those who stopped lying had 56 percent fewer physical complaints and endorsed having fewer headaches and fewer digestive problems. Additionally, they had 54 percent fewer mental health complaints like anxiety and stress. Refraining from lying also increased ratings of relationship satisfaction, which had positive impacts on overall health and self-esteem.

See also: Benefits of Lying; Betrayal; Butler Lies; Cognitive Dissonance; Consequences of Lying; Corruption; Emotional Effects; Instrumental Lies; Prevalence of Lying; Romantic Relationships; Self-Deception; White Lies.

Further Reading

Bloom, L., & Bloom, C. (2019). The cost of a lie: Watch out for rationalizations. *Psychology Today*. Retrieved from https://www.psychologytoday.com/us/blog/stronger-the-broken-places/201903/the-cost-lie

Campbell, R. (2014). The surprisingly large cost of telling small lies. *The New York Times*. Retrieved from https://boss.blogs.nytimes.com/2014/03/11/the-surprisingly-large-cost-of-telling-small-lies/

Lancer, D. (2018). The cost of secrets and lies. *Psych Central*. Retrieved from https://psychcentral.com/lib/the-cost-of-secrets-and-lies/

Covert Operations (See Diversionary Tactics; Espionage)

Cover-Ups (See Espionage)

Cultural Differences

All cultures discourage lying behavior, yet individuals from all cultures lie. Thus, culture does not determine lying behavior, but there is evidence to show that culture does guide what individuals tend to lie about. For example, individuals in collectivist cultures, such as China and Korea, are more likely to lie to protect the group while individuals from individualistic cultures, such as the United States and Canada, are more likely to lie to protect one's rights, interests, and enhance one's own reputation. Individuals from China rate lying to help the group or a friend or to increase modesty as more appropriate than lying to promote one's own interests. Individuals from the United States or Canada, however, were more likely to endorse lying to protect one's own reputation.

When asked whether or not it would be appropriate to lie for a friend, Koreans, on average, viewed lying for a friend less negatively and were more likely to provide reasons to explain why it would be morally justified to lie in such a situation. Americans were more likely to provide reasons to justify why they should tell the truth. Koreans focused more on "for a friend" while Americans focused on "lying." Since Korean culture tends to view relationships more strongly than Americans do, this finding reflects the relationship-oriented, collectivist thinking.

Similar results were found when comparing Canadian and Chinese children who were asked to make recommendations for storybook characters who faced situations where they had to choose between lying or telling the truth. Both groups of children were able to distinguish between lies and truth, and older children endorsed lying more readily than younger children across cultures. However, which lies were viewed as acceptable varied by culture. Chinese children rated individuals who lied about their own good deeds as more acceptable and appropriately modest than those who told the truth and bragged about their own good deeds. Canadian children rated those who told the truth about good deeds as being self-confident and having better self-esteem. Chinese children, alternatively, rated lies told to help a group more positively and truths that hurt the group more negatively. Canadian children were more likely to focus on the benefits to the individual rather than the group in both circumstances.

Though the content of lies tends to vary by culture, the ability to detect lies seems to be consistent, at least within cultural groups. Research on the ability to detect deceptive behavior across cultural lines has conflicting findings. When Americans, Jordanians, and Indians were asked to lie and tell the truth, individuals from all three groups were able to detect liars with equal accuracy across all the groups as long as they had access to both audio and visual components of the speaker. These findings indicate that the behaviors that surround lying are common across cultures. Increased arousal and increased demands on cognitive processing likely give rise to the same behaviors regardless of language or culture. However, there was some evidence that individuals were more willing to give other cultural groups the benefit of the doubt and were more likely to believe them. Racial judgments followed a similar pattern. For example, in a research study by Dr. E. Paige Lloyd and colleagues from Miami University, white participants judged that Black participants were telling the truth more often than white participants. In both circumstances, this bias may be due to motivation to avoid appearing prejudiced. White participants were more likely to focus their eye gaze on the response box that indicated lying when the targets were Black even though they were more likely to select truth as their final response. Thus, actual behavior and beliefs may differ from what are reported in lab studies.

Other research demonstrates that raters may misinterpret differences in behavioral norms as indicative of deception. Thus attempting to detect lying via nonverbal behavior may be more difficult cross-culturally. Different cultures show different behavioral norms when interacting with authority or with the opposite sex, differences in typical emotional expression, and differences in social etiquette. If two cultures have different behavioral norms, viewing the other culture leads to violations of expectations, which leads to decisions of deviance, which may lead to the assessment of deception. For example, Arabs are more likely to make eye contact, sit closer, and speak more loudly than do typical Americans. Such behavior may be misinterpreted as deceptive when rated by Americans since it does not fit conversation norms. Japanese students, additionally, smile more and thus may be perceived as attempting to cover up a lie when rated by American observers. Education about differences in cultural norms can help alleviate the bias and can help increase cross-cultural accuracy.

See also: Age Differences; Detecting Deception; Facial Cues; Nonverbal Behavior; Truth-Default Theory.

Further Reading

Bond, C. F., Jr., & Atoum, A. O. (2000). International deception. *Personality and Social Psychology Bulletin, 26*(3), 385–395.

Castillo, P. A., Tyson, G., & Mallard, D. (2014). Investigation of accuracy and bias in cross-cultural lie detection. *Applied Psychology in Criminal Justice, 10*(1), 66–82.

Choi, H. J., Park, H. S., & Oh, J. Y. (2011). Cultural differences in how individuals explain their lying and truth-telling tendencies. *International Journal of Intercultural Relations, 35*, 749–766.

Fu, G., Xu, F., Cameron, C. A., Heyman, G., & Lee, K. (2007). Cross-cultural differences in children's choices, categorizations, and evaluations of truths and lies. *Developmental Psychology, 43*(2), 278–293.

Lloyd, E. P., Hugenberg, K., McConnell, A. R., Kunstman, J. W., & Deska, J. C. (2017). Black and White lies: Race-based biases in deception judgments. *Psychological Science, 28*(8), 1125–1136.

Taylor, P. J., Larner, S., Conchie, S. M., & Ven Der Zee, S. (2015). Cross-cultural deception detection. In P. A. Granhag, A. Vrji, & B. Verschuere (Eds.), *Detecting Deception: Current Challenges and Cognitive Approaches* (pp. 175–201). Wiley.

D

Dark Triad

The Dark Triad refers to three distinct personality traits that tend to co-occur, specifically narcissism, Machiavellianism, and psychopathy. Individuals who score high on any of these traits are more likely than average to engage in malicious and non-prosocial behaviors. Individuals who score high for all of these traits tend to have more problems conforming to societal norms and laws and difficulty sustaining healthy relationships due to their manipulative tendencies. Many make friends easily but have difficulty in sustaining these relationships. These individuals also tend to be disagreeable and have a lack of conscientiousness about the feelings and needs of others.

Narcissism refers to an inflated sense of self-importance with a lack of empathy for others and persistent attention-seeking behaviors. Those who score high on scales of narcissism tend to be reactive and aggressive if threatened or when they experience rejection. Machiavellianism describes individuals who use manipulation and deception to achieve goals and who lack a sense of empathy or moral behavior. These individuals tend to be antisocial and use manipulation and covert aggression to achieve their goals and improve their own status. Psychopathy typically refers to individuals who consistently demonstrate antisocial, impulsive, and uncaring behaviors. These individuals are likely to misbehave due to impulsivity and boredom and to seek stimulation.

Of the three, narcissism and psychopathy have strong genetic components. Machiavellianism is most open to environmental influence, though it also shows some genetic heritability. Those with Dark Triad traits tend to be successful in the short term, likely accounting for the propensity for the traits to be maintained in society. Additionally, males are much more likely to exhibit these traits than females, though women are expressing more of these traits now than in previous generations.

In research on the Dark Triad, typical behavior patterns emerged. Individuals who scored high on narcissism tended to deceive others for financial or personal gain or as an attempt to increase reputation or status. Those high on traits of Machiavellianism and psychopathy were likely to deceive others without any particular goal. Since all three traits are linked to greater rates of deceptive attempts, they may have all evolved as a means to gain the advantage in a competitive environment. In fact, those scoring high on psychopathy were found to use deception for aggressive and exploitative goals, while Machiavellianism was correlated with strategic lies, and narcissists were more likely to lie about their own appearance and level of power.

Additional research, such as that by Nicole Azizli from Adler Graduate Professional School and her colleagues from The University of Western Ontario, examined the potential connection between Dark Triad traits and likelihood of misconduct and high-stakes deception. Assessment of individuals who scored high on these traits revealed that there were significant correlations among almost all variables studied. Individuals who demonstrate Dark Triad traits were significantly more likely to engage in antisocial and criminal activity, violent behavior and sexual misconduct, substance abuse, harassment, theft, and driving under the influence. Additionally, misconduct was most closely correlated with psychopathy traits, while Machiavellianism was most predictive of high-stakes deception, involving deceit that involves substantial risk if the liar were caught. This may consist of losing money, being arrested, or academic expulsion.

Individuals with these personality traits are more likely to engage in deception across a variety of situations. When looking at manipulative behaviors online, researchers studied phishing attempts made by individuals with Dark Triad traits. Those with Machiavellian tendencies were more likely to put effort into manipulating others through specific email efforts, or spear phishing. Researchers were also interested in examining whether individuals with these traits are more likely to be victims of deceptive attempts. In one study on phishing, Dr. Shelby R. Curtis and colleagues predicted that these individuals who tend to be low on agreeableness would be less likely to be victims because of higher suspicious tendencies. However, they found that individuals who ranked high on measures of narcissism had an inflated sense of self-confidence and thus were more likely to be victims of phishing. They tended to be more impulsive and overconfident in their ability to detect deception and thus were less cautious. They were particularly vulnerable when targeted by phishing attempts from narcissistic phishers.

See also: Antisocial Personality Disorder; Coercion; Commission, Lies of; Compulsive Lying; Detecting Deception; Fraud; Gaslighting; Intelligence; Machiavellianism; Manipulation; Narcissism; Personality; Phishing, Sex Differences in Lying Behavior.

Further Reading

Azizli, N., Atkinson, B. E., Baughman, H. M., Chin, K., Vernon, P. A., Harris, E., & Veselka, L. (2016). Lie and crimes: Dark Triad, misconduct, and high-stakes deception. *Personality and Individuals Differences, 89*, 34–39.

Curtis, S. R., Rajivan, P., Jones, D. N., & Gonzalez, C. (2018). Phishing attempts among the Dark Triad: Patterns of attack and vulnerability. *Computers in Human Behavior, 87*, 174–182.

Jakobwitz, S., & Egan, V. (2006, January). The Dark Triad and normal personality traits. *Personality and Individual Differences, 40*(2), 331–339.

Jonason, P. K., Lyons, M., Baughman, H. M., & Vernon, P. A. (2014). What a tangled web we weave: The Dark Triad traits and deception. *Personality and Individual Differences, 70*, 117–119.

Dating

First impressions are important, and they are particularly important when an individual has high expectations or a desire for a dating relationship. When encountering a potential sexual partner, many individuals are likely to strive to make a good first impression, even if that means stretching the truth or outright lying. Drs. Gurit Birnbaum and Mor Iluz from Herzliya Interdisciplinary Center and Dr. Harry Reis from the University of Rochester demonstrated that lying is particularly common at the beginning of dating relationships, though the type of relationship pursued frequently determines the likelihood of deception. Those interested in short-term relationships tend to lie more readily to engage and interest a partner. Those interested in long-term relationships tend to be more honest.

Dr. Birnbaum and colleagues found that when participants were presented with potential attractive dating partners in a research paradigm, both sexes were more likely to engage in deception. Both sexes endeavored to appear more attractive, to increase the amount of perceived similarity between themselves and the potential partner, and both were likely to embellish or lie in an attempt to make a positive impression on the other. When participants were asked to express attitudes about different topics, they were more likely to change their own attitudes in order to match the attitudes of the partner. These same efforts did not emerge when interacting with a less attractive partner or a partner who did not hold dating appeal.

Dr. Wade Rowatt from Baylor University and his colleagues found participants were more likely to lie about their personal appearances, attitudes, financial status, prior relationships, personality traits, and intelligence when the prospective date was more attractive. Individuals interested in a new dating partner minimized their past dating and sexual experiences, particularly at the beginning of the relationship. When confronted with an attractive potential partner, both men and women were more likely to report fewer previous partners than they initially reported on a questionnaire. When sexually motivated, individuals were more likely to lie to appear more attractive and to present good first impressions.

These efforts are frequently counterproductive. At some point, individuals must show their authentic selves to build true intimacy. If the authentic self varies greatly from the ideal presented initially, this can lead to rejection. Alternatively, those who initially engage in an honest and authentic way tend to develop stronger relationships than those who start with deception. This creates competing motivations. When encountering a potential romantic partner, both men and women endorse wanting to be accepted for who they are, but they also endeavor to present themselves in a more ideal way to increase the chance of interest. This dishonesty tends to emerge from personal insecurities and fear of rejection.

Dr. Dory Hollander, author of *101 Lies Men Tell Women and Why Women Believe Them*, examined how lies are used to manipulate and control dating partners. She particularly focused on men's lies in relationships. She acknowledged that deception is used to flirt, evade uncomfortable topics, preserve harmony, avoid confrontation, and mollify the feelings of a dating partner. In her research, Dr. Hollander found that men initially use lies to attract romantic partners and then continue to lie to get their way, to buffer their partner's self-esteem, and to avoid confrontation. Men emphasize (or lie about) commitment, interest, and success to attract others. They also use lies to distance themselves when no longer interested in the relationship. Women are vulnerable to these lies because the lies bolster self-esteem, feel good, and typically correlate with what they want to hear.

Research by Dr. Rosanna Guadagno from the University of Alabama and her colleagues from Ohio State University at Newark also found that men were more likely to exaggerate their personal qualities when interacting with a potential date. Men tend to emphasize their positive characteristics more at their first meeting online than when meeting face-to-face. Though men tend to lie more in dating relationships, neither sex is free from deceptive attempts. Men lie to protect their reputations, their self-image, or to avoid punishment. Women lie to increase intimacy or to protect their partner. In dating relationships, therefore, men are more likely to lie about their personal qualities and women are more likely to exaggerate the connection or quality of intimacy within the relationship.

See also: Evolution of Deception; Exaggeration; Manipulation; Online Dating; Romantic Relationships; Sex Differences in Lying Behavior; Social Media.

Further Reading

Birnbaum, G. E., Iluz, M., & Reis, H. T. (2020). Making the right first impression: Sexual priming encourages attitude change and self-presentation lies during encounters with potential partners. *Journal of Experimental Psychology, 86*. https://doi.org/10.1016/j.jesp.2019.103904

Bleske-Rechek, A., & Buss, D. M. (2006). Sexual strategies pursued and mate attraction tactics deployed. *Personality and Individual Differences, 40*(6), 1299–1311.

Guadagno, R. E., Okdie, B. M., & Kruse, S. A. (2012). Dating deception: Gender, online dating, and exaggerated self-presentation. *Computers in Human Behavior, 28*(2), 642–647.

Hollander, D. (1995). *101 Lies Men Tell Women and Why Women Believe Them*. Harper Collins.

Rowatt, W. C., Cunningham, M. R., & Druen, P. B. (1999). Lying to get a date: The effect of facial physical attractiveness on the willingness to deceive prospective dating partners. *Journal of Social and Personal Relationships, 16*(2), 209–223.

Deceiver Stereotype

The deceiver stereotype refers to the commonly held belief that dishonest people engage in specific behaviors that reveal dishonesty. Some stereotypical beliefs are that liars will fidget more, will avert their eye gaze or look up to the right, will be more likely to stutter, will pause more frequently while speaking, and will make more elaborate hand gestures. In addition, older adults are stereotypically considered more trustworthy than younger individuals, by both younger and older raters. Though there are some relatively accurate nonverbal indicators of deception, many of the stereotypical behaviors are not actually correlated with deception. Furthermore, contrary to expectations, older adults may be dishonest. These stereotypical beliefs are learned and strengthened over the life span as individuals develop an understanding of cultural display rules and societal expectations.

Some actual nonverbal indicators of deception include more pauses and more stalling for time when answering unexpected questions; tighter vocal cords, which cause higher-pitched speech; less elaborate responses to questions; and decreased use of personal pronouns. Though some of these behaviors are part of the deceiver stereotype, there are many other behaviors that observers relate with deception that do not hold up in psychological research, and some directly contradict the stereotype. Participants in psychological research incorrectly endorse the stereotype that liars will speak more slowly, will smile less, will avert their gaze, and will fidget more due to nervousness.

In direct contradiction to these stereotypic behaviors, liars are more likely to sustain eye contact in an attempt to be more convincing and to monitor whether or not their story is being believed. They also tend to show decreased subtle movements of the arms and legs during deceptive attempts and engage in less fidgeting. This decrease is likely due to the perception that fidgeting is an indication of deception, so savvy liars control these behaviors to give the impression of sincerity. The increased cognitive demands of lying may also be taxing and leave less attention and energy for nonverbal behaviors, which also results in the decreased movements. In any case, this lack of movement could actually give a cue to deception, if the observer is aware that the fidgeting stereotype is incorrect.

To test the extent of the deceiver stereotype, Dr. Aldert Vrij from the University of Portsmouth and his colleagues observed behavior during deception and analyzed beliefs about behavior during deception. They found that increased rigidity emerged during attempts to deceive. That is, liars tended to control hand and leg movements during deceptive attempts. They also found that, when the liars were asked to assess their own behavior, they were unaware of the decrease in movements and actually believed that their movements increased during the lying attempts. Additionally, more motivated liars showed the greatest decrease in movement.

To examine whether or not this stereotype could be overcome, Dr. Vrij explained to the subjects the tendency to decrease subtle movements during deception. Knowledge of the behavioral tendency was not enough to overcome the behavior. After understanding that a decrease in subtle movements tends to occur during deception, participants increased larger gestures and head movements, likely in an attempt to compensate. However, they still demonstrated decreased subtle movements. It may be the case that subtle hand, finger, leg, and foot movements are outside of conscious control. Compensating for the decline in subtle movements with purposeful big gestures and head movements may in fact just make the liar conform to the fidgeting stereotype.

Despite evidence that some nonverbal behaviors are actually correlated with deception while other behaviors are merely a stereotype, many individuals continue to endorse the stereotypes. This becomes a particular issue in the legal system. Practiced liars are aware of the stereotypes and will likely manipulate these behaviors to appear more honest. Thus, having a bias toward looking for these behaviors tends to be a relatively ineffective tool for identifying liars. Not only are the behaviors not correlated with deception but also someone who is lying will carefully not show them. Alternatively, individuals who are not lying may show behaviors that conform to the stereotype, whether due to anxiety or because they are not trying to mislead the examiner, interrogator, or lawyer. Therefore, a careful analysis of one's misconceptions is necessary for accurate lie detection skills.

See also: Brokaw Hazard; Detecting Deception; Language; Motivational Impairment Effect; Nonverbal Behavior; Othello Error; Reality Monitoring; Vrij, Aldert.

Further Reading

Slessor, G., Phillips, L. H., Bull, R., Venturini, C., Bonny, E. J., & Rokaszewicz, A. (2012). Investigating the "deceiver stereotype": Do older adults associate averted gaze with deception? *The Journal of Gerontology, Series B: Psychological Sciences and Social Sciences, 67*(2), 178–183.

Vrij, A., Semin, G. R., & Bull, R. (1996). Insight into behavior displayed during deception. *Human Communication Research, 22*(4), 544–562.

Deception in Animals

Deception in animals varies by level of intentionality. Animals may deceive through mimicry or camouflage, behavioral instincts, conditioned behavior, or through deliberate tactical attempts. Deception, as it is understood in human societies, is of this last category. Deliberate deception requires theory of mind ability or the understanding that one's behaviors can influence the thoughts and behaviors of another. This self-awareness and other-awareness is thought to be a uniquely human ability, so there is a question as to whether other species can intentionally deceive. However, research does show that the animal kingdom is rife with other types of deception.

Many species mimic other species to gain a competitive advantage. These mimicking behaviors deceive other species into providing food or avoiding predatory behavior. Camouflage provides similar benefits. Coloring that allows an animal to blend in increases the likelihood of survival. Instinctual behaviors such as a cat freezing to lure in prey similarly increase survival rates. Mimicry, camouflage, and instinctual behaviors are shaped over evolutionary time. Those individuals who naturally look or act in a particular way are more likely to survive and reproduce, shaping the instinctual behaviors of the species over time. Behaviors such as feigning a broken wing to lure predators away from a nest, hiding from a predator, or feigning death to avoid attack all increase survival and perpetuate passing on those traits. All such deceptions increase survival, but are not considered a result of conscious choice.

The next level of deception involves learned behaviors. Some behaviors lead to rewarding outcomes and animals learn to associate such behavior with reward, leading to an increase in the behavior in the future. Though this is a higher-level deceptive ability, it still does not require any understanding of the mental experience of others. Animals can learn to hide food to prevent it being eaten by others or engage in behaviors to secure a reward, without any understanding or conscious intention to deceive. The behaviors are merely a method to gain a reward or avoid a punishment. Such deception can be carried out without any understanding of one's ability to influence the mental states of others.

The final level of deception, true higher-order deception, involves the ability to think about the emotions, intentions, and thoughts of others and selectively act to influence those thoughts. This requires the ability to think hypothetically about future possibilities and to select an action that will most effectively achieve one's goal. This type of deception necessitates intentionality and flexibility to change strategies as needed. Most research to date has not found such ability to be widespread in any other species aside from humans.

Most deceptive attempts in other species can be explained by simple behavioral conditioning. For example, dogs may learn to wait until their owners are out of the room before climbing on forbidden furniture. Though they may be appearing to engage in higher-order deception, a simpler explanation is that they have learned the connection between the behavior and punishment (when the owner is present) and the behavior and reward (when the owner is away). Rather than ascribing understanding of mental states, it is more likely behavioral conditioning is at play.

In non-human primates, there are some anecdotes of higher-order deception. In such circumstances, the deception is undertaken to achieve a goal such as food or power and thus may also be explained as learned behaviors that lead to reward. For example, Dr. David Premack and Dr. Guy Woodruff demonstrated that one chimpanzee in their research, Sarah, used a form of tactical deception when faced with a villainous trainer. After several trials in which the trainer deceived Sarah after she helped him with a task, she started to feign ignorance, refused to assist him, or would indicate incorrect information. Another primate who demonstrated simple skills in tactical deception was Koko, a gorilla who was taught sign language. Koko was noted to use sign language to deflect blame to her kitten for her own naughty behavior.

In both of these examples, the primates seem to be using tactical displays to influence the beliefs of a partner, though such behaviors may also be explained by learning principles. Previous behavior was either rewarded or punished, increasing or decreasing its subsequent frequency. They may mislead others or feign ignorance but the behavior can be explained by learning principles rather than an understanding of theory of mind, an ability still primarily thought to be unique to humans.

See also: Camouflage; Evolution of Deception; Instrumental Lies; Primates; Recursive Awareness; Signaling Theory; Tactical Deception; Theory of Mind.

Further Reading

Courtland, S. D. (2015). Detecting animal deception. *Journal of Mind and Behavior, 36*(3–4), 121–138.

Hall, K., & Brosnan, S. F. (2017). Cooperation and deception in primates. *Infant Behavior & Development, 48*(Part A), 38–44.

Heberlein, M. T. E., Manser, M. B., & Turner, D. C. (2017). Deceptive-like behaviour in dogs (Canis familiaris). *Animal Cognition, 20*(3), 511–520.

LaFreniere, P. J. (1988). The ontogeny of tactical deception in humans. In R. Byrne & A. Whiten (Eds.), *Evolution of Social Intelligence* (pp. 238–252). Oxford University Press.

Mitchell, R. W. (1986). A framework for discussing deception. In R. W. Mitchell & N. S. Thompson (Eds.), *Deception: Perspectives on Human and Nonhuman Deceit* (pp. 3–40). State University of New York Press.

Oesch, N. (2016). Deception as a derived function of language. *Frontiers in Psychology, 7*, 1–7.

Premack, D., & Woodruff, G. (1978). Does the chimpanzee have a theory of mind? *Behavioral and Brain Sciences, 1*(4), 515–526.

Deception in Research

Many research studies contain an element of deception in order to ensure that the results are unbiased and not due to expectation alone. The impact of such deception is an imperative field of study to ensure that research is not causing lasting harm to participants. History is rife with examples of unethical deception in research, such as Milgram's Obedience Experiments in the 1960s, and the Tuskegee Syphilis Study that ran from the 1930s through the 1970s. Such studies prompted the creation of the modern Institutional Review Board (IRB) in the mid-1970s, which serves to ensure that researchers follow ethical guidelines and do not cause harm to participants. Despite progress and advances in ethical understanding, the use of deception in research is still an actively debated topic across the sciences.

The use of deception in research peaked in the 1970s with over 75 percent of research studies using deception as part of the research paradigm. Use of deception has declined due to oversight of the IRB, but deception is still an inherent part of many research studies. To engage in deceptive research under the IRB, researchers must demonstrate that the use of deception is the only way to achieve the research goals, that the research makes significant contributions to knowledge, and that the deception will not cause physical, emotional, or psychological harm to the participants. Additionally, the deception must be revealed and the participants debriefed as soon as possible. Despite these guidelines, some institutions still ban the use of deception and cite ethical concerns about how deception may negatively impact the participant's view of themselves, the institution, or research in general.

Dr. Marcella Boynton and her colleagues propose that there are two types of deception used in research, indirect and direct, and note that deception varies in severity. Indirect deception generally proceeds with the knowledge of the participant, who agrees to complete the study without knowing the true purpose. This type of deception is typically not detrimental to participants because they have willingly agreed to the conditions. Direct deception is when researchers deliberately mislead the participants without their knowledge. Researchers may provide misinformation, create staged interactions with confederates, or provide false feedback. These participants typically are not able to make an informed decision about participating in such research and may suffer psychological discomfort as a result. Though participants are allowed to withdraw from a study at any time, many do not because they feel uncomfortable due to the imbalance of power between themselves and the researchers.

Severe deceptions are those that impact the participant's view of the self, such as challenging their self-concept or self-confidence. Mild deceptions are those that create beliefs about things peripheral to the participant's self, such as disguising the purpose of the study. Mild deceptions may include retroactively asking the participant to remember details of the study, though they were not previously informed that it was a study on memory. Such deceptions are not typically detrimental or impactful beyond the scope of the session. Severe deceptions, however, may cause lasting impacts on a participant's self-concept that exist beyond the study. Due to these predictable influences, use of severe deception is much more difficult to justify and less likely to receive IRB support.

Dr. Boynton and colleagues examined three potentially harmful aspects of deception: task deception, false feedback, and level of professionalism. The first, task deception, refers to misinforming the participant about what is actually being measured in the study. False feedback is feedback during the study that causes participants to believe something inaccurate about themselves or their own performance. Level of professionalism refers to the interpersonal interactions and how well they are handled during a debriefing session. Dr. Boyton demonstrates that false feedback and unprofessional behavior lead to the greatest decrease in trust in research. However, effective debriefing mitigates these effects. They found that false feedback and task deception posed little psychological harm to participants in research and that basic debriefing, or explaining the purpose after the fact, was enough to ameliorate the negative effects. The most impactful negative aspect of deceptive research lies in the professionalism of the researcher. Unprofessional research behavior had the most substantial impact on the perceptions of the participants. This behavior influenced the level of trust and the mood of the participant, but these effects were also reversed with debriefing and explanation. Thus, effective debriefing and professionalism in the debriefing session seem to be effective in reducing negative effects of deception within a research paradigm.

See also: Consequences of Lying; Emotional Effects; Ethics; Hwang Woo-Suk; Instrumental Lies; Milgram's Obedience Experiments; Motives for Lying; Reaction Time; Tuskegee Syphilis Study.

Further Reading

Boynton, M. H., Portnoy, D. B., & Johnson, B. T. (2013). Exploring the ethics and psychological impact of deception in psychological research. *IRB: Ethics & Human Research, 35*(2), 7–13.

Kimmel, A. J., Smith, N. C., & Klein, J. G. (2011). Ethical decision making and research deception in the behavioral sciences: An application of social contract theory. *Ethics & Behavior, 21*(3), 222–251.

Defamation

Defamation is a type of deception that involves publishing or communicating false information about someone else, which has negative implications for the person's reputation or which exposes him or her to ridicule or contempt. Methods of defamation include slander and libel. Slander is verbal defamation, whereas libel tends to occur in writing or in print. Slander can be difficult to prove and punish, because it relies on remembering what was said and finding witnesses to corroborate one's story. Because memory for events can be fallible, it also relies on how people perceived the situation and the intention behind the statements. However, defamation by slander can be punished if an individual can prove another person spread false claims about things such as the person committing a crime, having a sexually transmitted disease, or being unfit for a profession and the negative consequences can be demonstrated. Libel, on the other hand, is more explicit because the false information has been recorded in text, and thus, it can be much easier to provide evidence of the defamation and to demonstrate the negative effects.

To be considered defamation, the inaccurate or deceptive information must be shared with others who have the power to impact the future opportunities of the individual in question. Defamation does not occur if the information is presented as an opinion, is a fair comment, is spread with consent of the individual in question, has no actual impact on reputation, or is true. Defamation convictions can result in jail time and fines if there is substantial proof that the information caused measurable reputation or career damage. For example, if an individual was falsely accused of a crime that resulted in the loss of a job or harassment by the press, they could sue the accuser for defamation.

If charged with defamation, there are several possible defenses. The accused individual can strive to justify the information, prove that the information written or said is true, demonstrate that it is an understandable opinion based on facts, or demonstrate that it was voiced during a conversation that was protected by privilege, such as information provided as evidence in a court case or without malicious intent.

Defamation has become more pervasive and arguably more impactful in the internet age. False information can be spread rapidly and be widespread. Someone engaging in defamation can damage an individual's or a business's reputation very quickly on a global scale. In the United States, where citizens have a right to free speech, it becomes a question of finding the balance between one's own free speech and another's right to protect his or her own reputation. Defamation law, therefore, is designed to protect reputation while still allowing individuals to express opinions. The law requires the media, for example, to provide evidence for claims that may be damaging to the reputation of individuals or companies. There are also regulations in place to identify and punish sockpuppets, phishers, or false advertisers to decrease the amount of defamation online. For example, companies may create sockpuppets, or fake online consumers, to undermine their competitor's reputations by fabricating poor reviews for services or products. Due to the level of anonymity via the internet, such behaviors are difficult to detect and prevent, which makes it even more difficult to police defamation behavior and more difficult for consumers to know which reviews to believe. Furthermore, fake news sites often mix truth with fiction, which makes parsing apart true and false information even more difficult.

Though defamation has become more widespread since the advent of the internet, it is definitely not a new behavior. There are examples of defamation from the time of the formation of the United States of America. It was common practice for political competitors to publish false news stories about one another to undermine each other's reputations. Many of these were published under pseudonyms and rarely were retractions printed. In this way, political leaders could sway the public's perception of their competitors.

Defamation is still prevalent as a political tool to undermine the competition within political campaigns. Defamation can take the form of comments during debates, offensive tweets, or attack campaign advertisements. To combat the possibility of defamation from these ads, political candidates are required to state that the information presented within their materials is their opinion and divulge by whom it was funded. Many candidates engage in defamation but avoid punishment by carefully selecting information for attack ads that is objectively true, though presented out of context. Such ads can be very effective because they spread fear and doubt about the opposition, which can only be overcome by effortful research to see if the claims are an accurate assessment of the candidate.

See also: Advertising; Betrayal; Fact-Check; Fake News; Instrumental Lies; Memory; Politics; Sockpuppets; Trolling.

Further Reading

McPherson, F. M. (1984). Defamation and privilege. *Bulletin of the British Psychological Society, 37*, 411–412.

Sanders, A. K., & Olsen, N. C. (2012). Re-defining defamation: psychological sense of community in the age of the Internet. *Communication Law & Policy, 17*, 355–384.

Delusions

Delusions are irrational beliefs that are unwavering even in the face of contradictory or rational arguments. Delusions are frequently a symptom of psychological disorders such as schizophrenia or mania. Individuals who experience delusions do express information that is not true, but they likely do not intend to engage in deception. Individuals experiencing delusions have a loss of contact with reality and believe what they say, even if it is not rational.

Delusions have several common themes. One common theme is that others are attempting to control or persecute the individual. Another is that the individual has exceptional abilities or feels exceptionally unique as compared to other people. Delusions tend to be rather radical ideas that are firmly believed, irrational, and unchangeable even when the individual is confronted with contradictory evidence or logical argument. Delusions differ from mistaken beliefs that are based on insufficient or biased information and even differ from irrational beliefs that are shared by a region or culture. For example, religious beliefs cannot be rationally explained or empirically supported, but they are not considered delusions because groups share them as an ideology or dogma.

Individuals who are experiencing delusions engage in deception without the intention to deceive. Their assertions may be subjectively, if not objectively, true. In clinical or legal cases, being able to distinguish delusions from purposeful attempts to deceive and from rational beliefs is necessary. During polygraph testing, individuals experiencing delusions may believe they are telling the truth even if it is not reflective of reality. Thus, polygraph tests may conclude that individuals experiencing delusions are telling the truth, even if their claims are not possible or not based in reality. In such cases, interviewers would need to exercise caution because polygraph results would be ineffective in distinguishing reality from delusions.

Psychologists propose different causes of delusions. One approach to viewing delusions is that they serve an adaptive function. For example, the psychodynamic perspective views delusions as manifestations of unacceptable beliefs that are repressed from consciousness to protect oneself. The delusions serve as a form of self-deception that allows the individual to reduce anxiety by masking the truth. Viewed from this perspective, delusions are protective of the psyche and mask pain or distress that the individual is not ready to consciously regulate. This theory would predict that resolving the source or the stress would eliminate the delusions. Thus, the most common treatments for delusions include psychotherapy, cognitive-behavioral therapy, and group therapy.

Another view is that delusions are entirely pathological and stem from disordered cognitive processes. From this breakdown of typical cognitive processing, deficits may emerge in theory of mind processing ability, or in logical reasoning skills. If connections in the brain are damaged or disrupted in some way, the individual may experience a disordered perception of reality. This view would suggest medications would be most effective in reestablishing the typical connections in the brain. Therefore, medication to stabilize mood and block receptor sites is also used when treating individuals who are experiencing delusions. Interestingly, however, medication alone is not very effective at treating delusions. Medical treatments tend to be more effective when they are coupled with therapy. This suggests that there is likely a connection between the different perspectives about what causes delusions.

Since individuals who suffer from delusions are already expressing information that is not true, Dr. Catherine Kaylor-Hughes and her colleagues from the University of Nottingham were interested in determining if it is possible to distinguish between unintentional delusions and intentional deceit in such individuals. Using fMRI technology, they found that even individuals who have delusions show similar brain functioning as healthy controls when they engage in voluntary deceptive attempts. Even though these individuals experience false beliefs, their purposeful deceits created frontal lobe activation similar to that in individuals without delusions. Individuals with delusions also demonstrated longer response times when constructing lies, similar to healthy controls. Thus, conscious, purposeful deception seems to occur in a similar manner in those with delusions as in healthy individuals.

See also: Cognitive Distortion; Conspiracy Theories; Gaslighting; Munchausen Syndrome; Neuroscience; Self-Deception; Theory of Mind.

Further Reading

Kaylor-Hughes, C. J., Lankappa, S. T., Fung, R., Hope-Urwin, A. E., Wilkinson, I. D., & Spence, S. A. (2011). The functional anatomical distinction between truth telling and deception is preserved among people with schizophrenia. *Criminal Behaviour and Mental Health, 21*, 8–20.

Langleben, D. D., Dattilio, F. M., & Guthiei, T. G. (2006). True lies: Delusions and lie-detection technology. *The Journal of Psychiatry & Law, 34*, 351–370.

McKay, R., Langdon, R., & Coltheart, M. (2005). "Sleights of mind": Delusions, defenses, and self-deception. *Cognitive Neuropsychiatry, 10*(4), 305–326.

Dementia

The use of deception when interacting with patients who have chronic and degenerative disorders, particularly those that cause cognitive degeneration, is a controversial topic in the medical field. In such cases, it may be argued that deception may increase quality of life, decrease anxiety, and promote feelings of safety. For example, health care providers routinely engage in deception when working with patients who have different types of dementia. Since health care ethics and codes of conduct strictly sanction honesty, the common use of deception when working with dementia patients creates an ethical dilemma.

Dr. Daniel Sokol argues that deception can be morally acceptable on rare occasions, such as in some instances of dementia. Dr. Sokol developed a deception flowchart to help doctors make more informed decisions about when to violate their oath of honesty. He recognizes that dishonesty in the doctor-patient professional relationship can undermine trust and autonomy and should be avoided. However, small deceptions may prevent substantial psychological harm. His flowchart asks doctors to consciously consider whether their statements are deceptive. If they are engaging in deception, he then challenges them to examine the justifications for deception, the likelihood of success, the alternatives, and the possible objections. Finally, they must assess whether their justifications outweigh the objections, whether the action would be defendable at a hearing of peers, and whether a reasonable patient would consent to the deception. If not, he encourages physicians to find an alternative or to tell the truth.

Dr. Ruth Elvish and her colleagues from Newcastle University and Newcastle General Hospital in the United Kingdom examined typical lies used with patients who suffer from dementia. The most common include going along with misperceptions, withholding the truth, and telling outright lies. In a survey, 96 percent of health care providers endorsed using deception when caring for individuals with dementia, particularly when such lies were judged to be in the best interest of the patient. These providers report using deception to manage behavior and to only tell the parts of the truth that will further the goals of treatment. Rationalization for lying behavior included not upsetting the patient, keeping them calm and comfortable, or eliciting cooperation. Health care workers note that honesty may cause stress, whereas going along with a misperception or lying may provide a therapeutic or calming effect. For example, dementia patients may repeatedly ask for their spouse, and health care providers may opt to lie and say the spouse will return later rather than repeatedly reminding the patient that their spouse has passed away. A third option that circumvents the ethical debate is to redirect conversations to avoid lying or telling the truth. The drawback of redirection is that patients may grow frustrated or feel like they are not being heard or that their questions are not being answered.

Though white lies may be beneficial in direct care with dementia patients, Dr. Elvish's research revealed that some physicians also engage in deception when diagnosing the disease. Given the lack of a cure, physicians claim that labeling the disease may not change treatment options. The majority of the physicians surveyed admitted they were more likely to soften the diagnosis rather than outright conceal it. Some tell patients they have preliminary signs or early-stage dementia rather than disclosing that they have a progressed form of the disease. This makes the patient more amenable to treatment since they have more hope and motivation. However, knowledge about one's own diagnosis is necessary to make plans and set affairs in order. A delayed or softened diagnosis could delay decisions to a point where the individual is no longer capable of making legal and medical decisions, which makes this type of deception more of an ethical concern.

Despite the findings that nurses and physicians are likely to lie to dementia patients, family members tend to overwhelmingly endorse full disclosure to allow for processing and coping as a family. However, in later stages of the disease, families also struggle with daily challenges and may lie to the afflicted family member in an attempt to alleviate distress. They may omit information, go along with mistaken beliefs, or tell outright lies to prevent agitation. Though these lies are usually intended to comfort, individuals with dementia who become aware that others are deceiving them find the behavior demeaning and patronizing. Negative emotions may permeate those relationships even as the disorder progresses.

Despite widespread admittance of deceptive behavior from health care workers, therapists, and family members, deception with patients with any disorder may have deleterious effects. If the patient becomes aware of the deception, loss of trust and increased stress may result. Furthermore, lies may also serve to increase confusion, patients may feel like their concerns are being ignored, and family members may experience feelings of guilt.

See also: Emotional Effects; Ethics; Minimization; Motives for Lying; Parkinson's Disease; Placebo Effect; Prosocial Lying.

Further Reading

Elvish, R., James, I., & Milne, D. (2010). Lying in dementia care: An example of a culture that deceives in people's best interests. *Aging & Mental Health, 14*(3), 255–262.

Seaman, A. T., & Stone, A. M. (2017). Little while lies: Interrogating the (un)acceptability of deception in the context of dementia. *Qualitative Health Research, 27*(1), 60–73.

Sokol, D. K. (2007, May 12). Can deceiving patients be morally acceptable? *The British Medical Journal, 334*, 984–986.

Denial

Denial occurs when an individual claims not to have engaged in a behavior or to have no knowledge about an event. Individuals may use denial to deceive by pretending they know nothing about a situation when they actually do have information, or they may even fabricate false information to contradict what actually happened. Within deception research, denial is defined as the endeavor to hide true information from others, typically by withholding information from a social partner. In this common sense, denial is an intentional behavior meant to mislead others. However, in a psychological sense, individuals are said to be suffering from denial when they are unable to admit the truth even to themselves. In such cases, denial is a defense mechanism, and individuals may not even realize that they are engaging in self-deception.

Though an individual may engage in intentional denial for various reasons such as to avoid punishment, as a result of coercion, or to gain an advantage, the act of engaging in denial can actually shape one's memory about an event. When Dr. Henry Otgaar and colleagues from Maastricht University in the Netherlands asked participants to deny information about an event that they witnessed in a video, the participants actually showed more difficulty in remembering the true information in later sessions. In this sense, these researchers demonstrated that denial can contribute to memory impairment for the denied information. When asked to try to actually remember what they witnessed, many of the participants omitted the information that they had previously denied and remembered details that they had fabricated.

In a similar study, participants were asked to engage in denial by feigning amnesia about an event. Drs. Kim Van Oorsouw and Harald Merckelbach from Maastricht

University found that individuals who feigned amnesia remembered the event less clearly than those who did not suppress the information. When later asked to try to remember the event, those who had previously feigned amnesia remembered less, made more errors on forced recall questions, and had a poorer memory performance than the honest control group. These findings have implications for the legal system in cases where guilty individuals deny knowledge about an event. Such denial may actually impact memory for an event or may even induce false memories, particularly in younger suspects. The likely mechanism for this memory impairment is lack of rehearsal. Denied information is not rehearsed while fabricated information is, which influences how much and how efficiently it is remembered later.

In some cases, denial is not an intentional form of deception. In the field of psychology, denial refers to a defense mechanism that is unconsciously used when reality is too upsetting. When individuals engage in denial, they unconsciously block anxiety-provoking thoughts or memories. Individuals who are experiencing denial downplay reality, refuse to believe evidence, or forget that an event happened. Individuals may experience denial after being confronted with upsetting news, when grieving, or after a traumatic event. Individuals may ignore evidence, entirely deny a situation, or may minimize the severity of the situation in order to not become overwhelmed. For example, if an individual was an unwitting participant in criminal activity, they may refuse to believe what happened, minimize their contribution, or minimize the severity of the situation. They may deny their own responsibility, misremember their own involvement, or strive to justify their behavior. However, as demonstrated in the previous research studies on conscious denial, such denial may shape the way individuals remember the event even after the danger or emotional upset has passed. Psychological denial frequently stems from an unwillingness to accept that bad things happen to good people, to avoid feelings of guilt for behavior, and to avoid punishment, or it is a self-protective mechanism. Such denial is a form of self-deception. Individuals engage in denial to protect themselves from others as well as from themselves.

See also: Cognitive Dissonance; Cognitive Distortion; Commission, Lies of; Delusions; False Memory; Minimization; Omission, Lies of; Reality Monitoring; Self-Deception.

Further Reading

Otgaar, H., Howe, M. L., Memon, A., & Wang, J. (2014). The development of differential mnemonic effects of false denials and forced confabulations. *Behavioral Sciences & the Law, 32*(6), 718–731.

Otgaar, H., Romeo, T., Ramakers, N., & Howe, M. L. (2017). Forgetting having denied: The "amnesic" consequences of denial. *Memory & Cognition, 46*, 520–529.

Van Oorsouw, K., & Merckelbach, H. (2004). Simulating amnesia and memories of a mock crime. *Psychology, Crime & Law, 12*(3), 261–271.

DePaulo, Bella

Bella DePaulo, PhD, is an expert on the social psychology of lying. Dr. DePaulo's work on deception and lie detection revolves around the most common lies that occur in ordinary social interactions. Her work spans more than three decades, and she has explored why people lie, to whom they lie, the ability to detect lies, and how normal people can become extraordinary liars. Dr. DePaulo has published multiple books such as *The Psychology of Lying and Detecting Lies* and *Behind the Door to Deceit: Understanding the Biggest Liars in Our Lives* and research articles such as "Liking and Lying" and "Lying in Everyday Life" over her career.

Dr. DePaulo's research reveals that individuals lie on average between one to two times a day, with fluctuations over the life span and between genders. However, most of these lies are not indicative of crime or negative intentionality. Dr. DePaulo reveals that most liars use lies to smooth social interaction, buffer the self-esteem of social partners, or to create favorable impressions. Dr. DePaulo's early research at the University of Virginia also demonstrated that individuals are more likely to lie to people they like. She found that undergraduate participants were more likely to tell prosocial lies to enhance interpersonal connections in order to impress or please people they were interested in getting to know. However, once a solid relationship was established, she found that individuals were more inclined toward honesty.

Dr. DePaulo also explored the use of nonverbal behavior to manipulate the perception of others. As with lies, simulated nonverbal behaviors such as smiling or nodding are frequently used to present a more likable or favorable impression to others. However, although nonverbal behaviors can be manipulated, they are not entirely under one's voluntary control. Facial expressions and physical movements can occur quickly and are hardwired into our emotional system. So, one may attempt to suppress or manipulate them, but some information may leak out or be beyond the individual's awareness. Furthermore, since people cannot observe their own behaviors, they may not always be aware of how their behaviors may be perceived, making nonverbal behaviors a means of detecting deception.

Dr. DePaulo undertook a massive literature review to examine the best methods of detecting deception. In her research, she explored the work of primary researchers such as Drs. Ekman, Friesen, Zuckerman, Buller, and Burgoon, among others. Upon analyzing over 100 studies, she found that motivated liars tend to be more tense and less forthcoming, share fewer details, and show more personal detachment than those who are telling the truth. However, most other behaviors show no discernible or consistent differences. Furthermore, the signs of lying are generally only apparent when an individual is particularly motivated and when the lies are about personal transgressions.

Since most common lies are not extremely provoking or arousing, Dr. DePaulo noted that most lies may be difficult or impossible to detect. Lies used to create favorable impressions or to smooth social interactions, which have very few consequences if detected, do not tend to be particularly arousing, so many will not show signs of lying. Only when liars feel particularly guilty or apprehensive about their lies will emotional cues be apparent. Dr. DePaulo identified that the cues to deception can be faint and difficult to detect. Such cues will be stronger when the liar is highly motivated, and thus highly aroused; does not have time to prepare; or is caught unaware. Unfortunately, high arousal can also make truth-tellers appear to be more nervous and hesitant, even if they are not attempting to deceive. Thus, conclusions must be carefully drawn in highly arousing situations.

See also: Categories of Deception; Detecting Deception; Ekman, Paul; Eye Gaze; Motivational Impairment Effect; Nonverbal Behavior; Polygraph Tests; Prosocial Lying; Sex Differences in Lying Behavior; White Lies.

Further Reading

Bell, K. L., & DePaulo, B. M. (1996). Liking and lying. *Basic and Applied Social Psychology, 18*(3), 243–266.

DePaulo, B. M. (1992). Nonverbal behavior and self-presentation. *Psychological Bulletin, 111*(2), 203–243.

DePaulo, B. M. (2009). *Behind the Door to Deceit: Understanding the Biggest Liars in Our Lives.* CreateSpace Independent Publishing.

DePaulo, B. M. (2018). *The Psychology of Lying and Detecting Lies.* CreateSpace Independent Publishing.

DePaulo, B. M., & Bond, C. F., Jr. (2012). Beyond accuracy: Bigger, broader ways to think about deceit. *Journal of Applied Research in Memory and Cognition, 1,* 120–121.

DePaulo, B. M., Kashy, D. A., Kirkendol, S. E., & Wyer, M. M. (1996). Lying in everyday life. *Journal of Personality and Social Psychology, 70*(5), 979–995.

DePaulo, B. M., Lindsay, J. J., Malone, B. E., Muhlenbruck, L., Charlton, K., & Cooper, H. (2003). Cues to deception. *Psychological Bulletin, 129*(1), 74–118.

Detecting Deception

The ability to detect when someone else is lying is a skill that has been extensively studied. This ability tends to improve with age and experience. However, even most adults are not especially proficient at detecting lies told by other adults. Researcher Rachel Adelson reviewed 253 studies on lie detection and found that the overall accuracy for detecting lies is about 53 percent, which hovers right around chance. Though lying is correlated with a range of facial expressions, body language, and linguistics behaviors, most people do not have the skills or practice to detect them in real time to make accurate assessments of honesty.

Cues to deception are wide ranging and include verbal, nonverbal, and paraverbal behaviors, as well as physiological changes. In verbal statements, liars tend to use fewer first-person pronouns, less complexity in their speech, more repeated words or phrases, and fewer details in their answers. Nonverbal cues of deception include such things as pursed lips, fewer gestures, more nervous behaviors, emotional expressions that are inconsistent with the content of the verbal report, and averted or sustained eye contact. Paraverbal cues include slower speech rate, longer response latency, greater use of fillers, and increased vocal pitch. Physiological changes include increased heart rate and sweating, higher anxiety and blood pressure, and higher arousal. Though there are many cues, they are hard to detect in real time, especially if an observer is not familiar with a deceiver's typical mannerisms. Detecting deception from those one knows well may be easier because these changes in behavior will be more noticeable.

One reason that detecting deception in day-to-day interactions may be so difficult is that most people have a truth bias and are inclined to believe social partners. Only in situations where suspicions have been aroused would one expect or

Signals that Someone Is Lying to You

Research shows that most individuals are not adept at detecting lies. Most lies are pro-social and help smooth social interactions, so it is frequently beneficial to let them pass uncontested. For those who endeavor to detect lies, however, there are several signals that indicate lying behavior. These include verbal, paraverbal, and nonverbal cues. Furthermore, individuals can lie by omission, which means they leave information out, or by commission, which means they add something that is not true.

Though there are no foolproof behaviors that absolutely indicate lying, one way to increase one's accuracy in lie detection is to pay attention to a partner's typical pattern of communication. Knowing someone's typical cadence, speed, and mannerisms may be key to detecting abnormalities that may emerge during lying behavior. An abnormal increase in vocal pitch; abnormalities in eye gaze, eye contact, and body movements; and atypical pauses, stutters, and phrases all indicate increased anxiety and may indicate an active attempt to deceive. Inconsistencies between the verbal message and their facial expression also provide a clue of deception. Frequently, liars shake their head when telling a lie or present fleeting facial expressions of disgust, anger, or glee. Lies may be revealed when the expressed emotion does not match the content of the verbal message, an inconsistency that is usually ignored or goes unnoticed.

Practiced liars may be harder to detect. A practiced liar will frequently mix in truthful information with lies. Even if a lie is suspected, it is difficult to determine which parts are true and which parts are fabricated. Experienced liars are also aware of the stereotype that liars will avoid eye contact and fidget, and thus many control these behaviors to increase the perception of honesty.

To actively catch even a practiced liar, one technique is to ask questions about the content of the suspected lie. Describing true events is easier and tends to lead to more detailed statements than descriptions of fabricated events. Liars' statements and descriptions tend to be less detailed and shorter than those of truth-tellers. Furthermore, it takes more effort to come up with a plausible fabricated answer than it does to tell the truth. Surprise questions may reveal lying behavior because it will take the liar longer to respond as compared to answering predictable questions or telling the truth. Basically, fabricating a plausible response to a surprising question takes more time than an honest answer about something that actually happened.

In general, psychological research points to several indicators that can be helpful when trying to determine if someone is lying. Since experienced liars are likely to control their body language, a detector must use both verbal and nonverbal cues to detect lying. Some characteristics that can be indicators are vague, short responses to questions, stalling for time or delays in responses to questions, inability to provide consistent details when probed, and behaviors that indicate anxiety such as fidgeting or playing with one's hair or face. Other indicators are mismatches between verbal and nonverbal reports. There may be a mismatch between the emotional tone of the statement and the emotion expressed by the speaker. Additionally, liars are frequently inconsistent or brief in their report, especially when asked to provide details or to tell their story in an unrehearsed order.

be wary of a lie. However, even in those circumstances, most people still can only correctly identify lies about half the time. Drs. Paul Ekman and Maureen O'Sullivan investigated individual differences in lie detection. In line with their previous research, most participants could detect deception about 54 percent of the time, or at chance levels. However, Dr. Ekman and Dr. O'Sullivan did identify some people (50 of 20,000 tested) who were more accurate at perceiving lies.

Dr. Ekman called these individuals wizards of deception detection. One thing that Dr. Ekman's truth wizards had in common is that they were exceptionally astute at observing nonverbal and paraverbal behaviors and identifying the mismatch between verbal content and nonverbal behavior.

Though lying is universally discouraged, everyone lies. Most lies are social lubricants to maintain cohesion and to protect feelings. These prosocial lies are arguably beneficial; thus, it may not be in an individual's best interest to detect them, likely contributing to our evolved difficulty in lie detection. However, in legal situations, the ability to detect lies becomes necessary. For these situations, interviewers and interrogators have developed strategies to reveal deception. Some common techniques used include polygraph tests such as the Concealed Information Test, the Behavior Analysis Interview, and the Control Questions Test.

During interviews or interrogations, interviewers can increase lie detection accuracy using these tests. Interviewers also use techniques such as asking for more information, asking unexpected questions, and asking suspects to tell what happened in the reverse order or while completing a competing task. These additions should be relatively simple for someone who is telling the truth. For a liar, the greater effort in coming up with additional information, particularly when surprised or when completing another task, impairs their ability to maintain convincing deception or consistency in their reports. Using such techniques as unexpected questions, pauses, and cognitive loading can improve lie detection accuracy from chance levels to 70 percent accuracy.

See also: Age Differences; Behavior Analysis Interview; Concealed Information Test; Control Questions Test; Development of Deception; Ekman, Paul; Evolution of Deception; Language; Meyer, Pamela; Microexpressions; Motivational Impairment Effect; Nonverbal Behavior; Othello Error; Physiology; Polygraph Tests; Reality Monitoring; Reid Technique; Social Intelligence; Theory of Mind; Truth-Default Theory; Vocal Changes when Lying; Vrij, Aldert; Wizard's Project.

Further Reading

Adelson, R. (2004, July/August). Detecting deception: Some research links lying with such facial and bodily cues as increased pupil size and lip pressing but not with blinking or posture. *Monitor on Psychology, 35*(7), 70–72.

Burgoon, J. K. (2016). Deception detection accuracy. In C. R. Berger & M. E. Roloff (Eds.), *The International Encyclopedia of Interpersonal Communication* (pp. 1–6). John Wiley & Sons.

Ekman, P., O'Sullivan, M., & Frank, M. G. (1999). A few can catch a liar. *Psychological Science, 10*(3), 263–266.

Von Hippel, W., Baker, E., Wilson, R., Brin, L., & Page, L. (2016). Detecting deceptive behavior after the fact. *British Journal of Social Psychology, 55*, 195–205.

Vrij, A., Fisher, R., & Blank, H. (2015). A cognitive approach to lie detection: A meta-analysis. Legal and criminological psychology. *The British Psychological Society, 22*, 1–21.

Development of Deception

Successful deception is a complicated endeavor that requires cognitive maturation, practice, attention, and skill. Successful liars must recognize the possibility for deception, construct a plausible alternative to reality, plan ahead, remember their lies, consider the perspectives of others, manipulate language skills, and demonstrate emotional control. Thus, lying behavior requires memory, executive functioning skills, prefrontal cortex development to modulate emotional signals and think about consequences, inhibitory control to suppress true information, and a mature theory of mind to understand the perspective of a social partner.

To lie effectively, individuals must take the listener's point of view into consideration and accurately judge the listener's expectations, feelings, and beliefs. Effective deception also requires that the liar be able to inhibit true information and present false information in a coherent, consistent, and believable fashion. Not only does the initial lie need to be believable but also subsequent information provided must be consistent with the initial lie.

Children's first experience with lying may be through secrets and pretend play. By age three, children begin to experiment with primary lies. Primary lies are untrue statements that do not take into account that the listener is privy to the truth. Around age four, secondary lies emerge. Secondary lies do take the listener's perspective into consideration and thus are more effective deceptive attempts, even if they are tenuous and break down under scrutiny. Both primary and secondary lies are commonly used for selfish purposes, such as to avoid punishment after a transgression. By age seven or eight, children begin to tell tertiary lies. These lies not only take the listener's perspective into account but are also supported by consistent follow-up information and hold up more readily under inquiry. At this age, children also start to show the use of prosocial lies and may lie to protect the feelings of others. Starting around age nine, children start to tell blue lies, or lies that combine selfish and prosocial purposes. They select lies that benefit themselves and the group.

Though many parents may show concern when their child starts to lie, such behavior actually indicates healthy cognitive development and emerging theory of mind ability. Parents may also unwittingly encourage lying behavior through pressures to conform to social norms. Children are taught cultural display rules, they start to understand the expectations within families and social groups, and this understanding guides their lying behavior. For example, children are often encouraged to be polite even if it means being dishonest. Thus, parents provide contradictory expectations, and children are told lying is wrong, but they must pretend to enjoy even unwanted gifts. Young children are more likely to be honest than polite, but by school age, children tend to engage in polite lies and start to evaluate those who tell polite lies more positively than those who tell the truth.

Psychological researcher Dr. Carolyn Saarni examined children's ability to moderate their emotional expressions as needed in social situations. Dr. Saarni demonstrated that socially appropriate lies increase over the ages of four to nine. She used a disappointing gift paradigm that has been widely replicated to look at children's ability to engage in socially appropriate lies. She found that when children received a disappointing gift as part of the research paradigm, their ability to accept it in socially appropriate ways increased with age. Older children were more likely to say thank you and express feigned pleasure than the younger children in the study. Not only does the ability to lie effectively improve with age but the way individuals think about lying also changes over the life span. Throughout childhood, children understand the difference between lies and the truth. They also can identify different types of lies and start to rate polite lies less negatively with age. Adolescents and adults draw an even greater distinction between polite, or prosocial, and other types of lies.

As deceptive behavior emerges, children tend to start to use it strategically. In a research study by Dr. Rachelle Smith from Husson University and Dr. Peter LaFreniere from the University of Maine, when children were encouraged to conceal information in a game paradigm, there were distinct differences in deceptive success over childhood. Three- and four-year-olds demonstrated difficulty in moderating their behaviors, facial expressions, and verbal statements and were relatively unsuccessful at deceiving an adult. Five- and six-year-olds were better at moderating their verbal reports but still tended to leak information through their facial expressions and body posture (e.g., looking at or orienting to the correct answer). Seven- and eight-year-olds showed the most success at deception. Not only were they able to conceal information, but they were also able to provide fabricated misinformation to confuse the adult. These differences correlate with maturation of theory of mind and continue to become more nuanced over adolescence and adulthood with cognitive maturation and practice.

See also: Age Differences; Blue Lies; Instrumental Lies; Intelligence; Polite Lies; Prosocial Lying; Reality Monitoring; Recursive Awareness; Saarni, Carolyn; Tactical Deception; Theory of Mind; White Lies.

Further Reading

Chandler, M., Fritz, A., & Hala, S. (1989). Small-scale deceit: Deception as a marker of two-, three-, and four-year-olds' early theories of mind. *Child Development, 60*, 1263–1277.

Cheung, H., Siu, T. C., & Chen, L. (2015). The roles of liar intention, lie content, and theory of mind in children's evaluation of lies. *Journal of Experimental Child Psychology, 132*, 1–13.

Ekman, P. (2018, August 27). *Learning to lie* [Blog]. Retrieved from https://www.paulekman.com/blog/why-kids-learning-to-lie/

Evans, A. D., & Lee, K. (2013). Emergence of lying in very young children. *Developmental Psychology, 49*(10), 1958–1963.

Lavoie, J., Nagar, P. M., & Talwar, V. (2017). From Kantian to Machiavellian deceivers: Development of children's reasoning and self-reported use of secrets and lies. *Childhood, 24*(2), 197–211.

Lewis, M., Stanger, C., & Sullivan, M. W. (1989). Deception in 3-year-olds. *Developmental Psychology, 25*(3), 439–443.

Saarni, C. (1984). A observational study of children's attempts to monitor their expressive behavior. *Child Development, 55*(4), 1504–1513.

Smith, R. M., & LaFreniere, P. J. (2013). Development of tactical deception from 4 to 8 years of age. *British Journal of Developmental Psychology, 31*, 30–41.

Talwar, V., Gordon, H. M., & Lee, K. (2007). Lying in the elementary school years: Verbal deception and its relation to second-order belief understanding. *Developmental Psychology, 43*(3), 804–810.

Xu, F., Bao, X., Fu, G., & Talwar, V. (2010, March/April). Lying and truth-telling in children: From concept to action. *Child Development, 81*(2), 581–596.

Disappointing Gift Task (See Saarni, Carolyn)

Diversionary Tactics

Diversionary tactics describe a tactical deception strategy in which one diverts attention away from an issue, question, or event rather than addressing it. One skilled at using diversionary tactics can redirect an opponent's attention and distract them from their original goal without alerting the opponent that distraction has taken place. Diversionary tactics can be used to avoid interpersonal arguments or disagreements, to avoid combat, or to avoid giving away information. They are key elements of sports competitions, political debates, and interviews and can be used for evasion and in covert or clandestine operations. Diversionary tactics may include implying a false future behavior, changing the subject, answering a direct question with another question, shifting the blame to something outside one's control, or creating an emergency to be addressed to get out of a conversation. Frequently a diversionary tactic introduces another salient issue to pull attention away from the subject at hand.

An extreme example of a diversionary tactic is gaslighting. Gaslighting is the purposeful distortion of reality to shape the perception of another person. For example, a man found to be cheating on his wife may insist she is imagining things and evade the accusations, even in the face of hard evidence. One who is gaslighting may alter events, deny that something actually happened, or use manipulation to divert attention away from what actually occurred. Usually one who uses gaslighting strategies gives off an overwhelming sense of confidence in their assertions, which plants a seed of doubt in the accuser. In this way, one who is a victim of gaslighting ends up with a distorted sense of reality and starts to question their own understanding of what has actually happened. Gaslighting efforts use diversions to create confusion and distract the accuser from the issue.

Diversionary tactics are often used in politics. The use of diversions can be used to shift the public's attention to inconsequential issues while more substantial or controversial issues are quietly carried out in the background. Diversions can be achieved by highlighting inconsequential issues in news stories to cover up more controversial issues that are more quietly addressed outside of the public eye. If more controversial issues are published, those savvy at diversionary tactics then use fear, anger, polarization, deflection, superiority, blame, and emotions to confuse and distract attention from the actual issue. Strong negotiators or politicians are adept at diverting attention away from issues that threaten or undermine their position, frequently so smoothly that the observers do not notice that the issues are not addressed.

Diversionary tactics may be used during acts of evasion. In evasion, an individual may dodge, deceive, or use tricks to avoid the topic or a responsibility. An evasion may consist of making honest statements that are designed to mislead the listener in order to create a diversion. Evasions can include sidestepping a discussion, answering a direct question with an indirect challenge or alternate question, attacking the conversation partner, or changing the subject. These tactics are particularly used by political candidates who want to maintain a positive reputation in public support by equivocating and not taking a strong stance on controversial issues. Diverting the public's attention away from the question, challenging the question, providing a vague answer, never actually providing an answer, or sidestepping the question may all be effective diversionary tactics to maintain popularity without outright lying. When used skillfully, most listeners do not even realize that the initial question was never answered.

Covert and clandestine operations predominantly use diversionary tactics to maintain secrecy. Covert operations are military operations in which individuals go undercover to infiltrate an enemy or to persuade a population. The key for covert operations is that the public remains unaware of those who sponsor the operation, and thus, diversionary tactics are needed to divert attention away from the issue or to cover up the root of the issue. Clandestine operations tend to be performed in secret; thus, the public's attention must be diverted away in these cases as well.

Diversionary tactics are also used in athletics. In competitive situations, one may feign or otherwise create a diversion that misleads the opponent about intentions. Though in this context, such diversions are usually quickly revealed, it may be too late for the opponent to mount a defense. Diversionary tactics range from acceptable tactics, such as in competitive sports, to more nefarious tactics, as in political issues, espionage, or gaslighting efforts.

See also: Doublespeak; Equivocation; Espionage; Gaslighting; Manipulation; Politics; Red Herring; Tactical Deception.

Further Reading

Mitchell, S. M., & Prins, B. C. (2004). Rivalry and diversionary uses of force. *The Journal of Conflict Resolution, 48*(6), 937–961.

Well, P. (1998). Equivocation theory and news interviews. *Journal of Language and Social Psychology, 17*(1), 36–51.

Door-in-the-Face Tactic (See Reverse Psychology)

Double Agents (See Espionage)

Doublespeak

The term "doublespeak" refers to the use of euphemisms that are intended to mislead or deceive others. Some euphemisms are understood by select groups and are used to refer to ideas or concepts pertinent to that group; some become part of the general lexicon, and others peak and fade away. In general, doublespeak euphemisms mean the opposite of what is stated, and they are frequently used to make the truth sound less severe or more acceptable. The concept originally stems from George Orwell's novel *1984* in which the government uses contradictory terms to distort reality, cloud the truth, and manipulate the populace.

Doublespeak can be used as an innocuous way of expressing potentially offensive ideas in inoffensive ways. For example, couples may profess to sleeping together when the intention behind the message is that they did more than sleep. Other types of doublespeak are less innocuous and have a greater intention to deceive. These consist of deliberately disguising the actual meaning behind a phrase to make it sound more socially appropriate, politically correct, or to cultivate support. For example, managers may present layoffs as career change opportunities. The intention is to achieve buy-in from the public or even from the individual in question and to smooth over social awkwardness or bad press.

Professor Ralph Slovenko provides a slew of examples in his commentary on euphemisms. For example, pacification is doublespeak for mass destruction of a village or group of people. Ethnic cleansing is a persuasive way to gain support for mass exterminations of ethnic groups or genocide. Enhanced interrogation is used to cover up the use of torture, and termination is a nice way of describing killing an enemy. In all of these examples, doublespeak is used to avoid using true, yet distasteful, terms. And though euphemisms are not necessarily intended to mislead, doublespeak euphemisms typically are of that nature. In the political or business realm, many move into doublespeak territory in order to engender public support or cover up the truth.

Marketing managers may use doublespeak to manipulate the consumer or to mask their ultimate intentions. For example, salary cuts may be termed as efforts to reduce costs. To the general consumer or investor, efforts to reduce costs sounds like a positive initiative, but it is not positive for the individuals who now receive lower pay. Doublespeak may also be used by politicians to confuse unpopular messages. They may describe undesirable events in desirable terms to make them sound good to uncritical people. Prisoners of war may be referred to as detainees. A preemptive strike is a nice way of covering up the fact that a unit engaged in an unprovoked attack.

Though many may be inclined to be suspicious of doublespeak in politics, war, and media, it may also be present in research, medical care, and therapy. Some companies may brand their medications or research trials with names that leave a positive impression on the user or participant. Even the term "clinical trial" is a nice way to phrase an experiment to garner greater public buy-in and participation. The lack of mention of the experimental nature of the engagement may underplay the nature of the experience and encourage belief in beneficial effects. In actuality, most participants will not benefit from experimental medicines, contrary to how the research and consent forms make it sound. Dr. Mark Hochhauser, from the North Memorial Health Care IRB, points out that terms such as "study medications" instead of experimental drugs and "therapeutic studies" rather than medical experiments are essentially doublespeak that engender consumer, IRB, and even government support. The terms are designed to sound beneficial and may interfere with the informed consent process required for research.

Though some phrases of doublespeak are widely understood and culturally endorsed methods of communicating embarrassing or offensive information in inoffensive or politically correct ways, other uses of doublespeak can potentially do more damage. Doublespeak in military, government, and from others in positions of power can confuse, mislead, or manipulate a population. Doublespeak is a deceptive method of communication that obfuscates the truth to the benefit of the speaker.

See also: Black Lies; Butler Lies; Detecting Deception; Diversionary Tactics; Gaslighting; Half-Truths; Manipulation; Politics; Propaganda.

Further Reading

Hochhauser, M. (2002). "Therapeutic misconception" and "recruiting doublespeak" in the informed consent process. *Ethics & Human Research, 24*(1), 11–12.

Orwell, G. (1948). *Nineteen Eighty-Four.* Secker & Warburg.

Slovenko, R. (2006). Euphemisms. *The Journal of Psychiatry & Law, 33*, 533–548.

E

Ekman, Paul

Paul Ekman, PhD, is a foundational researcher in the field of deception. Dr. Ekman has studied topics such as the development of deception, the link between emotions and deception, microexpressions, verbal deception, nonverbal behaviors of deception, masking deception, signs of lying, deceptive motivations, the universality of emotional expression, and the difficulty humans have detecting lies.

The original purpose of Dr. Ekman's work was to more accurately identify individuals at risk for suicide who deny depression or suicidal thoughts. To do this, he minutely examined emotional expressions, particularly those that emerge during attempts to deceive. He thought facial expressions, especially those expressions that are difficult to control, might be key in detecting concealed emotions. He developed the facial action coding system (FACS), which is a system used to measure the facial movements that make up universal facial expressions. He specifically identified microexpressions, or the unconscious and uncontrolled aspects of facial expressions. Since these microexpressions are not under conscious control, they are useful in identifying emotions that an individual may be attempting to conceal during deceptive attempts.

Through his work with facial expressions, Dr. Ekman contributed effective guidelines for detecting deception, as fictionalized in the 2009–2011 TV series *Lie to Me*. Dr. Ekman demonstrates that successfully detecting hidden emotions relies on assessing nonverbal behavior, particularly of the body, mouth, and eyes. Dr. Ekman cautions that detection of hidden or inconsistent emotions does not automatically indicate deception. Individuals may conceal emotions for prosocial, antisocial, or unrelated reasons. However, liars frequently do attempt to control or manipulate their own emotional expressions to be more convincing to others.

Dr. Ekman identified different categories of cues that contribute to exposing lying behavior. He proposes thinking cues and feeling cues. Thinking cues revolve around keeping lies consistent and believable. Liars may speak more slowly as they are thinking about the lies they are telling. Feeling cues, however, may be even more prevalent. Liars who are worried about being detected may show disgust or fearful emotional expressions and body language. Their voices tend to raise in pitch, and they tend to speak more loudly and more quickly and have more pauses, more speech errors, and more indirect speech. Additionally, some liars experience positive emotions associated with tricking someone or getting away with a lie. They may demonstrate gleeful expressions that are inconsistent with the content of their speech. Alternatively, a controlled, blank facial expression may reveal attempts to conceal true emotions. The more at stake and the more motivated an individual is to convince a listener, the more likely these feeling cues will emerge. Low-stakes lies may not be sufficient to evoke the emotional arousal that would cause such emotional cues to emerge.

According to Dr. Ekman, there are several reasons that people are such bad lie detectors. For one, there is typically a lack of feedback about the accuracy of lie detection. Even if people suspect that another person is lying, they may never know whether or not they were accurate. People also tend to rely too heavily on the verbal message and ignore discrepancies between the verbal and nonverbal message or the emotions being expressed. Furthermore, most people want to believe others and have a truth bias. They are likely to take a smile at face value and allow compliments and commissions to ease social encounters and to avoid awkward interactions. Thus, they tend to focus on the words and on the superficial, posed facial expressions rather than looking deeper and analyzing the veracity of the message. Dr. Ekman proposes that most people use lies for prosocial means. Thus, the ability to detect deception is usually neither necessary nor beneficial. Believing lies told to smooth social interactions and protect feelings has mutual benefits for the liar and the receiver; thus, humans have not evolved to be adept lie detectors.

In his longitudinal research study called the Wizard's Project, Dr. Ekman, along with Dr. Maureen O'Sullivan looked at the typical ability to detect lies about emotions, opinions, and crimes. Most people scored at chance levels for all types of lies. There were some people who had a particular ability of detecting lies about emotions while others were good at detecting lies about opinions or crimes. Only a select few individuals, subsequently termed Truth Wizards, were able to detect lies across all modalities. Training programs based on what was learned from these wizards can radically improve an average individual's ability to detect lies. Focus on emotional inconsistencies and microexpressions are key in identifying those who are attempting to deceive.

See also: Detecting Deception; Development of Deception; Language; Lying; Microexpressions; Nonverbal Behavior; Prosocial Lying; Self-Deception; Vocal Changes when Lying; Wizard's Project.

Further Reading

DePaulo, B. M., Lindsay, J. J., Malone, B. E., Muhlenbruck, L., Charlton, K., & Cooper, H. (2003). Cues to deception. *Psychological Bulletin, 129*(1), 74–118.

Ekman, P. (1988). Lying and nonverbal behavior: Theoretical issues and new findings. *Journal of Nonverbal Behavior, 12*(3), 163–175.

Ekman, P. (1991). Invited article: Face, voice, and body in detecting deceit. *Journal of Nonverbal Behavior, 15*(2), 125–135.

Ekman, P. (1997). Deception, lying, and demeanor. In D. F. Halpern & A. E. Voiskounsky (Eds.), *States of Mind: American and Post-Soviet Perspectives on Contemporary Issues in Psychology* (pp. 93–105). Oxford University Press.

Ekman, P. (2017, August 1). *My six discoveries: One scientist. Six discoveries. Fifty-five years in the making: 1955–2010*. Retrieved from https://www.paulekman.com /blog/my-six-discoveries/

Ekman, P., O'Sullivan, M. O., & Frank, M. G. (1999). A few can catch a liar. *Psychological Science, 10*(3), 263–266.

Paul Ekman Group. (2018). *Dr. Paul Ekman*. Retrieved from https://www.paulekman
.com/about/paul-ekman/

Embellishment (See Exaggeration)

Emotional Effects

Deception is inherently connected with emotions. Attempts to deceive directly impact an individual's emotional experiences and emotional health, and experienced emotions impact one's ability to deceive others. In general, deceptive attempts increase brain and nervous system arousal, blood pressure, breathing, and attention and trigger emotional reactions. In most cases, deceptive attempts activate more negative emotional reactions, such as anger, sadness, and disgust, than are experienced when telling the truth. Deception may also trigger experiences of delight, known as duping delight, particularly if individuals feel like they are getting away with the ruse.

During lie detector tests, these marked changes in level of arousal are what are used to determine whether someone is experiencing an emotional reaction that might reveal lying behavior. However, emotions may be triggered for reasons other than lying as well. A confrontation or telling others the truth, particularly a truth to which others may not respond well, may also trigger an emotional response. Thus, changes in emotion cannot rule out honesty, but such changes may indicate the part of a conversation that is particularly salient or important.

Since emotions may reveal lying, learning to control one's own emotions may allow people to be better deceivers. Liars can use emotion to make their lies seem more realistic. Crying, for example, may elicit sympathy and allow lies to be accepted more readily. However, cranial nerves connect the facial muscles directly to the limbic system, a part of the brain that is not under conscious control. Thus, initial, unpremeditated facial expressions tend to be more truthful than those that are posed after conscious reflection, and the mismatch may reveal deceptive attempts.

True emotional expressions tend to be brief, difficult to control, and difficult to create in the absence of genuine emotion. Recognizing flashes of emotional expressions that do not match the content of the speech or that are immediately covered up may be a key to detecting liars. In general, individuals who use emotional expressions to judge whether or not someone else is lying do better at detecting deception, particularly for high-stakes lies.

Deceivers may attempt to simulate, mask, or neutralize true emotional reactions. Simulated emotions are emotional expressions that are not felt, and most find that they are difficult to fake convincingly. For example, producing tears without feeling sadness is a difficult skill. Masked emotions occur when individuals cover up one emotional expression with another. This complicates the emotional display and may keep information from leaking through. Neutral expressions are when one attempts to keep the face neutral even while feeling an emotion.

How Lying Affects Health

In day-to-day life, little white lies may help smooth over social interactions, help one get out of conversations or commitments, and protect self-esteem, all while preserving social relationships. Due to these benefits, white lies are very common in face-to-face, phone, text, and email communications. However, research shows that even white lies drain mental and physical resources and have a cumulative negative effect on psychological, physical, and relationship health.

Lying triggers the production of stress hormones, which cause an increase in heart rate and blood pressure. These hormones have a negative impact on immune system functioning. Lying behavior, even white lies, contributes to tension headaches, body aches, back pain, sore throats, stomachaches, fatigue, and sleep problems. If the lie causes feelings of guilt, additional physical effects can include digestive problems, upset stomach, and nausea. Lying about aspects of oneself can be particularly damaging. Individuals who feel the need to hide details about life experiences, sexual orientation, or medical conditions experience more stress, are less healthy, and are more prone to degenerative diseases and stress-related disorders than those who can be open about such issues.

Frequent lying also contributes to low self-esteem, anxiety, and depression. Lying tends to increase when one feels incompetent, guilty, or inadequate for a task. Lying also increases when feeling defensive, cornered, or unconfident. Lying in these situations can create a negative feedback cycle in which one must continue to lie to cover up insecurities, which leads to feeling even more insecure, which then culminates in an even greater need to lie. Lying to cover up true thoughts, opinions, or desires leads to decreased self-esteem, increased anxiety, and feelings of isolation due to lack of true intimacy.

Lying also tends to have an impact on one's own perspective and relationships. Rather than admitting to a lie, many people will attempt to justify, cover, defend, or blame others. This can cause trust issues, increase feelings of insecurity, lower self-esteem, and cause misunderstandings. To resolve discomfort, individuals may convince themselves that the other person was at fault, treat the other more kindly out of a sense of guilt, engage in self-deception, or avoid the other person. All of these strategies have negative effects on relationship health.

Research shows that those who practice telling the truth grow more confident in their own opinions. Those who avoid exaggerations and excuses and who find constructive ways to be honest start to feel that their opinions are valid, acceptable, and worthwhile. Those who practice telling the truth, own up to mistakes and deficiencies, and engage in fewer exaggerations tend to be healthier, have better relationships and higher self-esteem, and suffer from less anxiety and depression. People who practice telling the truth, even in difficult situations, experience a sense of freedom and strength, even if there are negative consequences. Additionally, in the most difficult situations, declining to respond or providing parts of the truth does not result in the same negative health effects as straight out lying.

Secrets or lies may be used to maintain a position of power, protect reputation, protect feelings, or maintain a competitive advantage. However, secrets and lies also make individuals feel more tired and tasks more effortful; they are distracting, and they inhibit the immune system. Alternatively, practicing honest communication has physical and psychological health benefits.

This is perhaps the most difficult to do successfully because true emotions are difficult to control.

Lying tends to correlate with a broad spectrum of emotions including envy, anger, anxiety, or sadness. Feeling envious increases the likelihood that people will lie to those who they envy. Anger also increases the likelihood of deception.

Angry individuals focused on retaliation may perceive less risk and less trust in the social partner, leading to more deceptive attempts. Anxiety results from uncertainty, and those who feel anxiety are more likely to use deception as a protective technique. Those feeling anxious tend to perceive more threat and react by lying to protect themselves or to maintain control.

Those who are feeling sad are less likely to use deception. The same is true for those who are feeling happy. Happiness may allow for or result from the feeling that one can be honest and that a conversation or interaction is going well, and deception is not needed to influence the outcome. Feeling happy also tends to be contagious, and others in the dialog may also feel happier, increasing their likelihood of cooperation and honesty. Experiencing feelings of gratitude has a similar effect. Expressions of gratitude may inform social partners that there will be a positive outcome to the interaction and deception is not necessary.

Emotions can increase or decrease lying behavior, but controlling one's lies also has an effect on one's emotions. Dr. Anita Kelly, from the University of Notre Dame, asked participants not to lie over the course of two and a half months. Those participants had significant physical and mental health improvements. Those who stopped lying had 56 percent fewer physical complaints and 54 percent fewer mental health complaints, such as anxiety and stress. Refraining from lying also increased ratings of relationship satisfaction, which has positive impacts on overall physical and mental health.

See also: Consequences of Lying; Detecting Deception; Ekman, Paul; Microexpressions; Physiology; Prosocial Lying; Vocal Changes when Lying; Wizard's Project.

Further Reading

Methasani, R., Gaspar, J. P., & Barry, B. (2017). Feeling and deceiving: A review and theoretical model of emotions and deception in negotiation. *Negotiation and Conflict Management Research, 10*(3), 158–178.

Ofen, N., Whitfield-Gabrieli, S., Chai, X. J., Schwarzlose, R. F., & Gabrieli, J. D. (2016). Neural correlates of deception: Lying about past events and personal beliefs. *Social Cognitive and Affective Neuroscience, 12*(1), 116–127.

Polage, D. (2017). The effect of telling lies on belief in the truth. *Europe's Journal of Psychology, 13*(4), 633–644.

Proverbio, A. M., Vanutelli, M. E., & Adorni, R. (2013). Can you catch a liar? How negative emotions affect brain responses when lying or telling the truth. *PLoS ONE, 8*(3), 1–12.

Shaw, H., & Lyons, M. (2017). Lie detection accuracy—The role of age and the use of emotions as a reliable cue. *Journal of Police and Criminal Psychology, 32*, 300–304.

Wu, S., Cai, W., Zou, H., & Jin, S. (2017). The effect of senders' perceived ability to control emotion on raters' deception judgments. *Social Psychology, 48*(2), 61–70.

Equivocation

Equivocation is when speakers use ambiguity or words that have multiple meanings to compose a logical but misleading argument to get their way, mask the truth, or confuse or deceive a listener. An equivocation is usually a technically honest statement that distracts or obscures the truth rather than providing clarity. In that way, equivocations help speakers deceive or mislead others without actually lying. Equivocations are very common in everyday communication and are used to maintain social harmony, smooth over discordance, facilitate diplomacy and cooperation, and maintain the perception of positive character. They are a type of deception used to distract, evade, or divert attention from the issue at hand. For example, politicians may use equivocation to avoid committing to an issue. They may provide an impassioned claim that an issue is important when pressed without actually committing to doing anything about it. Their statements convince listeners that they are committed, but in actuality, no promises are made.

Equivocations are an example of a logical fallacy. Those who use them may rely upon the double meanings or vagueness of words to avoid an issue or to give a false impression. For example, one may admit to committing a transgression a few times, drawing on the ambiguity of the term "a few" to disguise how frequently the behavior actually occurred. Equivocations may also include contradictions, inconsistencies, or purposeful misunderstandings to disguise meaning. Dr. Janet Bavelas and her colleagues from the University of Victoria propose that equivocations likely emerge when a speaker must choose between two unpopular replies to answer a question or when there is risk of hurting or alienating another person or group. They are used in personal conversations, interviews, and political speeches.

In political speeches, public officials use equivocations to avoid answering direct questions. Their answers, instead, skirt around the issue, introduce ambiguity, or change the subject. In this way, savvy politicians can avoid giving their true opinion on controversial topics in order to avoid alienating the group of voters on the opposite side of an issue. Skilled equivocators can answer a question similar to the one that was asked or can use words from the question asked to answer a related question, and listeners may not even be aware that the question was not actually addressed. Such politicians can maintain their approval ratings and preserve credibility even while not committing to either side of an issue. Listeners can infer whichever answer they want due to the deliberate vagueness of the answer provided.

In personal relationships, equivocations tend to be used in situations where individuals feel trapped between hurting someone's feelings or telling a lie. Equivocating allows for a third option in which the individual can avoid lying and avoid being hurtful as a way of avoiding two evil alternatives. Avoidance does not increase clarity of communication but merely extricates one from a situation. For example, if one receives an unattractive gift, one must either lie or risk hurting the giver's feelings. An equivocation is a third choice in which one can avoid lying while omitting the full truth. Claiming that the gift is unique and thoughtful may be true, and one can avoid adding that it is also ugly.

Equivocations also commonly emerge in reference letters and interviews. Frequently letter writers will equivocate by emphasizing positive qualities and omitting or reframing negative qualities. Letter readers have to get good at recognizing what is not being said to get a full view of the candidate. During interviews, similarly, candidates may equivocate when answering questions. Candidates may claim they have experience for a particular skill while not mentioning that the experience was limited, unsupervised, or unrelated to the task at hand.

The use of equivocations can help individuals conform to social norms and expectations without technically lying. Skilled listeners may be able to decode equivocations through attending to the tone of voice, noticing what is not said, and critically thinking about whether a question was actually answered. Being aware of the times equivocations are commonly used, such as during interviews, in recommendation letters, and during political speeches, may also cue a listener in on when to assess statements more carefully.

See also: Detecting Deception; Diversionary Tactics; Doublespeak; Minimization; Omission, Lies of; Politics; Red Herring.

Further Reading
Alhuthali, M. (2018). Equivocation in political discourse: How do we know when it is happening? *International Journal of English Linguistics, 8*, 69.
Bavelas, J. B., Black, A., Bryson, L., & Mullett, J. (1988). Political equivocation: A situational explanation. *Journal of Language and Social Psychology, 7*(2), 137–145.
Bello, R. (2005). Situational formality, personality, and avoidance-avoidance conflict as causes of interpersonal equivocation. *Southern Communication Journal, 70*, 285–299.
Williams, M. L. (1975). Equivocation: Character insurance. *Human Communication Research, 1*(3), 265–270.

Erotomania

Erotomania is a delusional disorder in which individuals have a strong belief that another person is in love with them. The other person is most frequently unattainable and may be high status, married, imaginary, or even deceased. The delusion may take over the person's everyday life, and they may see messages from their target in ambiguous everyday stimuli. Such beliefs may lead to stalking behaviors and may be resistant to treatment. Unlike other types of deceptive behavior, the individual suffering from erotomania is likely not intending to deceive themselves or others. Their belief is delusional and sincere.

These delusional fantasies are equally common in women and men and tend to start after puberty. The fantasies tend to involve individuals who represent idealized love and attraction, and the individuals who engage in such fantasies tend to be isolated and inexperienced with real relationships. The target of the fantasy may align with the individual's romantic ideal, and the individual may interpret stimuli such as smiles, glances, or expressions as more meaningful than they are intended to be. As the belief solidifies, the individual then interprets any stimuli in ways that support their delusions.

Most individuals who suffer from erotomania have low self-esteem and feelings of incompetence and loneliness that are coupled with a traumatic emotional loss or stress that triggers the onset of the delusion. Frequently, physicians or therapists are the targets of the delusion because they behave in kind, caring, and attentive ways that are misinterpreted as stemming from personal romantic interest. Such delusions may protect the individual from feelings of incompetence, rejection, or loneliness, so they are stressful for the individual to confront or negate. They also tend to prevent the individual from developing healthy personal relationships with others because so much of their time and attention is focused on the unattainable ideal.

Frequently, those who are suffering from erotomania are preoccupied with the person whom they believe is in love with them. To an observer, there may be no evidence of a relationship, but the individual suffering from the disorder is thoroughly enmeshed in self-deception and may constantly talk about the person who they believe loves them. If the individual is a celebrity, the sufferer may obsess over any media they can find about the person. They are also likely to send letters and gifts and try to contact the person. They may feel jealous if the other person appears to be giving attention to someone else and may believe that any comments or actions are a message meant personally for them. These individuals can frequently become so obsessed with and so preoccupied with the other individual that it is detrimental to other parts of their lives.

Treatment for erotomania typically involves both therapy and medication. Erotomania is frequently associated with other disorders such as bipolar disorder and delusional disorders, so treating those disorders may alleviate the symptoms. Antipsychotics to reduce the experience of delusions may also allow the individual to benefit from therapy. Left untreated, the symptoms may resolve themselves or may escalate to the point where the individual engages in aggressive behaviors toward their target or toward themselves. In general, however, patients are not likely to be dangerous or harass their targets but are more likely to suffer in isolation.

See also: Cognitive Distortion; Delusions; Self-Deception.

Further Reading

Kennedy, N., McDonough, M., Kelly, B., & Berrius, G. E. (2002). Erotomania revisited: Clinical course and treatment. *Comprehensive Psychiatry, 43*(1), 1–6.

Seeman, M. V. (2016). Erotomania and recommendations for treatment. *Psychiatric Quarterly, 87*, 355–364.

Espionage

Espionage is the overarching term for deception in the form of spying by governments or corporations to gain military, political, or economic advantages. Espionage can be used in clandestine and covert operations, for cover-ups, in secret societies, in smuggling operations, and during attempts at treason and may result in double agents.

Espionage is a method of obtaining information or intelligence in a clandestine, or secret, way, typically to gain an advantage over an enemy or competitor. Those engaging in espionage, known as spies, may infiltrate an enemy and be accepted as one of their own. Such methods may reveal weaknesses of an enemy, provide insight into their goals or methods, and provide information about their plans. Spies may also plant disinformation with an enemy to sabotage their plans or redirect their goals. Because acts of espionage can so radically undermine military efforts, the Espionage Act was passed in the United States in 1917 in an attempt to prevent individuals from sharing classified information with enemies of the United States that might disrupt military efforts.

Clandestine operations are those in which espionage or other covert activities are completed without the knowledge of the general population. These operations may have the goal of gathering information about a competitor or enemy, eliminating threats, or stealing technology. Yet, throughout the duration of the operation, everything is completed in secret and without public awareness. Covert operations differ from clandestine operations because the covert operation does not necessarily go unnoticed, but the sponsors of the activity are concealed. Covert operations may result in very noticeable consequences, but the general public is not aware of who committed the behaviors or may blame the wrong group for the measures. Covert groups may include secret societies or secret organizations that hide their true activities, even while maintaining a public facade.

Cover-ups occur when clandestine or covert operations are mistakenly revealed. In such cases, all information regarding the event may be suppressed and alternative explanations are provided to mislead the public. Because governments do have a tendency to cover up actions that would undermine their credibility and integrity, some individuals have grown suspicious and are likely to see cover-ups in any government-related activity. These conspiracy theorists are likely to see cover-ups for a variety of unexplained phenomena including Area 51, the 9/11 attack, and even the Coronavirus pandemic.

Double agents are those individuals who engage in espionage for two competing groups, without the knowledge of the groups involved. Each group believes that the operative is in their own employment and is working to further their goals, even while the individual manipulates one or both to the individual's own benefit. Those who are detected can be charged with treason, which is the act of betraying one's own country.

An example of a double agent who was charged with treason is Benedict Arnold. Benedict Arnold was a military officer during the Revolutionary War. His acts of treason are so well known in American history that his name has become used to describe an individual who engages in an act of betrayal. During the Revolutionary War, Benedict Arnold provided the British with information about American troops and plans. In 1780, when Arnold was given an opportunity to take command of West Point, he sent detailed information to British troops with an offer to surrender West Point for 20,000 pounds. When Benedict Arnold's espionage was discovered, he fled to the British troops and served in the British army until he left for England in 1781. Today, research from the Defense Personnel Security Research Center identified that almost 90 percent of American spies between 1947 and 2001 who committed treason were white males who had at least a high school education. Most were married and were born in the United States. Well over 60 percent were under the age of 29. Most were motivated by money, and about 20 percent were motivated by being disgruntled. Those who tend to engage in treason have personality traits that include psychopathy and narcissism.

Espionage is illegal in most nations, though the benefits acquired by its use may be so great that governments take the risk of training and employing spies. Gathering information is particularly important in times of war, and intelligence agents, or spies, may be employed by governments to gain a competitive advantage. The theme of espionage is so popular that many fictional books and movies revolve around it. The digital age has had massive influences on espionage. The ability to collect information about competitors has grown exponentially. Cyber espionage can allow spies to collect information via the internet rather than through physically infiltrating an enemy or creating a contact.

See also: *Art of War, The*; Benefits of Lying; Camouflage; Conspiracy Theories; Diversionary Tactics; Fake News; Instrumental Lies; Motives for Lying; Narcissism; Personality; Politics; Propaganda; Sockpuppets; Tactical Deception.

Further Reading

Herbig, K. L., & Wiskoff, M. F. (2002). *Espionage Against the United States by American Citizens 1947–2001*. Defense Personnel Security Research Center.

O'Toole, G. J. A. (1988). *The Encyclopedia of American Intelligence and Espionage: From the Revolutionary War to the Present*. Facts on File.

Wilder, U. M. (2017). Why spy now? The psychology of espionage and leaking in the digital age. *Studies in Intelligence, 61*(2), 1–17.

Ethics

Ethics refers to the principles that guide appropriate moral behavior. Ethics revolve around making choices that are not only good for oneself but also good for greater society. Ethics can include acting with integrity, honesty, loyalty, and respect for oneself and others. The field of ethics examines the consequences of choices and determines what behaviors are acceptable within society and culture. Ethical behavior comes into play in personal choices, within relationships, and within organizations. Ethics can be overarching, guiding, unspoken expectations of a culture or explicit, systematized rules of an organization.

The social contract theory is the idea that individuals within civilized society need to create ethical rules by which everyone abides. Such rules may be unspoken, or explicit, agreements that individuals will follow ethical rules of behavior. Social contract theory is a way that individuals can guide their own moral behavior independent of divine law. The theory proposes that following social contracts can maintain harmony, and rational individuals can decide which behaviors are acceptable and which should be avoided and can guide their own behavior accordingly. In such a state, irrational and immoral individuals may be at an advantage, and thus formalized laws and punishments are regularly articulated and enforced. Social contract theory dates back to philosophers such as Hobbes, Rousseau, and Kant and has been carried through time through moral and political philosophy.

Because unspoken rules of ethical behavior are not necessarily enforceable, such rules are often documented and made explicit in codes of ethics for various professions to serve as a guide for appropriate behaviors. The American Psychological Association (APA) code of ethics outlines the ethical standards that must be followed to ensure ethical practice and research. Within psychology, violation of the code of ethics can lead to loss of licensure. The goal of the code of ethics is to protect the rights of patients and clients and ensure that practitioners behave with integrity. The code of ethics commands that psychologists, or other practitioners who work under the guide of the code, help others while not causing additional harm. It instructs that each practitioner should maintain the confidentiality of their clients and be honest with those around them. Clinicians are required to work to be competent and unbiased and must treat others with respect. The APA standards cover those engaged in research with human subjects as well as practicing psychologists. Different professions have similar codes such as the American Medical Association (AMA) code of ethics and the American Dental Association (ADA) code of ethics. Each revolve around similar topics to ensure honesty and integrity in health care professions. Furthermore, most professions have similarly established codes, such as those in carpentry, construction, and automotive services.

Typically, honesty is considered to be more ethical than deception. However, deception may occasionally be ethical depending on one's goals and the consequences of both honest and dishonest behavior. Within science, for example, ethics outline the rules by which one may treat participants in a study. Ethical research requires informed consent, prevention of harm, and debriefing. Since research studies frequently must deceive subjects about the purpose of the experiment, researchers must struggle to make sure the deception is ethical, causes no harm, and is revealed and explained after the experiment. The Institutional Review Board (IRB) put into place in the 1970s attempts to ensure that research is ethical and will not cause harm. Researchers in the United States must secure IRB approval before studies can be carried out.

Ethical leaders tend to be rated as more effective, ethical groups are more productive, and ethical individuals have better reputations. Having a reputation of honesty leads to greater trust, increased influence over others, and more effective problem resolution. However, though honesty is valued, everyone lies. People lie to themselves, to those with whom they have personal relationships, in the workplace, and in scientific research. The question is whether or not such lies can ever be beneficial. Since those who lie do have the opportunity to take advantage of others, honesty frequently becomes a matter of ethics. Honesty is a choice that tends to have long-term benefits, while dishonesty may have more short-term benefits.

There are instances where individuals may perceive a lie or deception as an ethical course of action. Telling lies to boost others' confidence, to induce hope, or to prevent panic may have long-term benefits. There are unspoken social contracts for situations in which one would actually be encouraged to lie. Saying thank you for well-intended gifts, complimenting a bride's appearance on her wedding day, or encouraging a child even if you think they will fail are all common lies that are socially acceptable. Telling the truth in such situations may actually cause more negative consequences.

See also: Benefits of Lying; Conscience; Deception in Research; Lying to Children; Noble Lies; Paternalistic Lies.

Further Reading

American Psychological Association. (2010). *Ethical Principles of Psychologists and Code of Conduct*. American Psychological Association.

D'Agostino, F., Gaus, G., & Thrasher, J. (2017, May 31). *Contemporary approaches to the social contract*. Stanford Encyclopedia of Philosophy. Retrieved from https://plato.stanford.edu/archives/sum2021/entries/contractarianism-contemporary/.

Euphemisms (See Doublespeak)

Evasion (See Diversionary Tactics; Equivocation)

Evolution of Deception

The field of evolutionary psychology proposes that the ability to lie effectively has been selected through the process of natural selection, as has the ability to detect deceptive attempts. Because effective deception can lead to personal profits, the most skillful liars arguably reap the most benefits from those around them. However, once individuals become effective at lying, those who are naturally good at detecting deception have an advantage because they are less likely to be fooled by others. Over evolutionary time, these skillful detectors are less likely to be taken advantage of and thus more likely to secure benefits for themselves. Once effective detectors emerge, deceivers must become more clever to maintain the advantage. Once deceivers develop more subtle skills, only detectors who can detect these deceptive attempts maintain an advantage. In this way, more and more subtle deception and more acute detection skills have recursively driven each other over evolutionary time, ultimately leading to the skilled deceivers and detectors currently present in the human species.

Through this process of natural selection, humans have evolved a remarkable ability to deceive and to detect deception. While most people do engage in deceptive behavior, most individuals do not capitalize on their ability to detect when others are lying. Instead, most people actually ignore their instincts in order to facilitate social cohesion. In this sense, most individuals have a truth bias, particularly for people they trust. They want to believe others and typically are willing to give others the benefit of the doubt, even in the face of an obvious lie. Individuals override their emotional and instinctual response due to a desire to maintain relationships and smooth over social interactions. Training programs that teach individuals to pay attention to their gut instincts and emotional arousal levels can radically improve individuals' detection abilities.

Evolutionary psychologists such as Dr. Peter LaFreniere have long understood that strategic management of verbal and nonverbal cues can facilitate or reveal deception. Cues such as facial expressions, intonation, and word choice can be manipulated to honestly or deceptively communicate intentions, beliefs, and future behavior. Furthermore, manipulating such cues can be advantageous in competitive situations. Such tactical deception can involve active use of verbal or nonverbal communications to mislead others. Tactical deception can also be achieved by withholding information or suppressing nonverbal cues. The skill and ability to use such cues provides a competitive advantage that has led to more and more delicate and precise control of verbal and nonverbal communications.

In humans, increasingly effective attempts at deception have evolved in part with increasing social cognitive skills. One such social skill is theory of mind, or the understanding that others have alternative representations of the world that may be true or false and that may differ from one's own. Another skill that has evolved is recursive awareness, which is the ability to understand that one's non-verbal or verbal cues can influence the beliefs and behaviors of observers and that cues provided by others can influence one's own beliefs and behaviors. Thus, the use of purposeful false signals has been selected because they can effectively influence others, yet individuals must maintain awareness that others may be providing false signals as well. Individuals must remain savvy about detecting false signals from others while wielding false signals of their own. This delicate balance results from the evolutionary arms race between more and more effective manipulation of signals and increasing abilities to detect such attempts.

The ability to deceive effectively has evolved to such an extent that social structures are regularly put into place to regulate and prevent such behaviors. For example, most cultures have laws to prohibit and punish deception, particularly in business, and most have law enforcement structures in place to catch, regulate, and punish those who engage in deceptive attempts. Furthermore, organized religions openly and clearly denounce deception as a means of controlling this innate behavior. Overall, deception can be a beneficial means of maintaining a competitive advantage with friends or adversaries and achieving one's goals. However, to maintain trusting relationships, one must at least provide the appearance of honesty. Those who are too honest may be taken advantage of and those who are too deceptive may be punished, so individuals must ride a fine line between maintaining an advantage and maintaining a good reputation to effectively survive and reproduce.

See also: Detecting Deception; Development of Deception; Ekman, Paul; Recursive Awareness; Social Intelligence; Tactical Deception; Theory of Mind; Truth-Default Theory.

Further Reading

Bond, C. F. (1988). The evolution of deception. *Journal of Nonverbal Behavior, 12*(4), 295–307.

Dawkins, R., & Krebs, J. R. (1978). Animal signals: Information or manipulation? In J. R. Krebs & N. B. Davies (Eds.), *Behavioral Ecology* (pp. 282–309). Blackwell Scientific Publishers.

LaFreniere, P. J. (1988). The ontogeny of tactical deception in humans. In R. Byrne & A. Whiten (Eds.), *Evolution of Social Intelligence* (pp. 238–252). Oxford University Press.

LaFreniere, P. J. (1996). Co-operation as a conditional strategy among peers: Influence of social ecology and kin relations. *International Journal of Behavioral Development, 19*(1), 39–52.

Schultz, T. R., & Cloghesy, K., (1981). Development of recursive awareness of intention. *Developmental Psychology, 17*(4), 465–471.

Smith, R. M., & LaFreniere, P. J. (2009). Development of children's ability to infer intentions from nonverbal cues. *Journal of Social, Evolutionary, and Cultural Psychology, 3*(4), 315–327.

Wellman, H. M., Cross, D., & Watson, J. (2001). Meta-analysis of theory-of-mind development: The truth about false belief. *Child Development, 72*(3), 655–684.

Exaggeration

An exaggeration is a statement that serves to describe a situation, ability, or event as better or worse than it actually was. Exaggerations usually serve to emphasize the importance of an event to others or to garner attention, sympathy, or approval. Exaggerations are commonly boasts of one's own achievements or overelaborations of one's own struggles. Exaggerations can range from simply embellishing the truth to telling outright lies. This type of deception can be tricky to detect, especially if the exaggerations are subtle, because they tend to be built on truth and contain a mixture of true and untrue statements. Frequently, exaggerations may increase over time, and even the liar may begin to believe his or her own claims.

Individuals may use exaggerations in conversation to such a degree that conversation partners can easily determine that the claims are not literal truth but simply a dramatized communication of what actually happened. These exaggerations can be used for entertainment value or to emphasize the emotions associated with an event. In such a situation, they may not even be categorized as deception because all conversation partners realize that the claims are not literal. Interestingly, however, in these situations, individuals frequently use the word "literally" in tandem with their exaggeration, altering its meaning. If one was extremely excited, for example, he/she may claim to have literally died. Obviously, such a statement is not literally true but serves to convey the intensity of emotion felt in an attempt to describe the extent of one's excitement.

In many situations, exaggerations are innocuous and serve to enhance communication. However, exaggerations can also be used to avoid responsibilities, such as exaggerating an injury, or as deceptive ploys to magnify situations into dramatic events. They may also be used when attempting to manipulate others' perceptions of what actually happened, to disparage an enemy, or to puff up a friend. In these circumstances, exaggerations can detract from effective communication and can serve as actual deceptive attempts. Thus in such conversations, it is imperative that a listener critically evaluate the source, be aware of potential biases, and seek corroborating evidence for extreme claims.

Tendency toward exaggeration can also serve to signal or exacerbate psychological or physical disorders. For example, Dr. Ryan Martin and Dr. Eric Dahlen, from the University of Southern Mississippi, demonstrated that exaggerating, catastrophizing, or engaging in self-blame about one's likelihood of failure may reinforce states of depression or anxiety. Alternatively, consistently exaggerating one's own ability can signal or reinforce narcissistic or grandiose personality disorders. Exaggerating the number of times an offense has occurred may increase anger toward another person or oneself. Exaggerating the likelihood of something happening can also lead to paranoia, anxiety, or catastrophic beliefs and heightened worry.

In medical or clinical situations, patients may exaggerate the severity of their symptoms in an effort to secure treatment, gain sympathy, or avoid responsibilities or for financial gain. Personality tests such as the MMPI-2 and tests of malingering have been developed in an attempt to discriminate between exaggerations and actual symptoms in neuropsychological cases. Additionally, exaggerating symptoms can lead to increased physiological sensitivity. Thus, exaggerating symptoms can actually cause one to feel the symptoms more intensely and make them persist longer.

Though exaggerations can be used to enhance entertainment, garner attention, and increase communication, they can also be used to mislead, manipulate, and deceive. The tendency to exaggerate can increase over time and with practice. Thus, learning to recognize and control one's own exaggerations can ultimately contribute to a more honest reputation, better mental and physical health, and greater relationship satisfaction.

See also: Consequences of Lying; Delusions; Gaslighting; Malingering; Narcissism; Puffery; Self-Deception; White Lies.

Further Reading

Frazier, T. W., Youngstrom, E. A., Naugle, R. I., Haggerty, K. A., & Busch, R. M. (2007). The latent structure of cognitive symptom exaggeration on the Victoria Symptom Validity Test. *Archives of Clinical Neuropsychology, 22*(2), 197–211.

Martin, R. C., & Dahlen, E. R. (2005). Cognitive emotion regulation in the prediction of depression, anxiety, and anger. *Personality and Individual Differences, 39*(7), 1249–1260.

Eye Gaze

There is a common belief that liars have a tendency to avoid eye contact when lying. However, due to this commonly held belief, experienced liars may purposefully maintain eye contact in an attempt to improve their credibility. Thus, research shows that extended, purposeful eye contact is actually a better indicator of lying behavior than gaze aversion, at least for adults. Since eye gaze tends to be manipulated so readily by liars, other nonverbal behaviors, such as hand and feet fidgeting, and paraverbal behaviors, such as vocal pitch, emerge as more reliable indicators of deception.

To examine whether adults associate eye contact with honesty, Dr. Gillian Slessor and her colleagues asked participants of varying ages to rate the truthfulness of statements made by individuals who maintained direct eye gaze and those who showed varying degrees of gaze aversion. Prior to the study, most participants indicated that liars would be more likely to avert their gaze when lying. In line with this belief, during the study, participants were likely to rate the speaker who maintained eye gaze as more honest. Alternatively, participants rated speakers who averted their eye gaze as dishonest.

When examined more closely, analysis revealed that there were differences based on the age of the rater. Younger adults tended to use eye contact more readily and were more extreme in their appraisals of eye gaze behavior in their assessments than older adults. Thus, younger adults tended to make judgments in line with the deceiver stereotype and associated direct gaze with honesty and averted gaze with dishonesty. Older adults were less sensitive and less reactive to gaze direction, possibly because they spent more time looking at the mouths of the speakers rather than at the eyes.

Older adults become increasingly vulnerable to fraud and exploitation. A decreasing ability to detect cues of deception may be one explanation for this. Older adults in Dr. Slessor's study were less sensitive to subtle differences in gaze aversion and were less likely to use eye gaze to infer intention. Older adults focused on the mouth when engaging in a conversation and missed the signs of deception that younger adults rely on to detect deceptive attempts. Interestingly, both age groups were likely to rate older speakers as more honest, regardless of eye gaze aversion, demonstrating a bias for believing that older adults are less likely to lie.

When examining adult liars, most individuals purposefully increased eye contact when lying, possibly to appear more convincing. Additionally, adult liars tend to closely assess their audiences as they attempt to manipulate beliefs. Thus, adult liars may have increased eye contact because they are assessing whether the listener is believing their lies. This eye contact is deliberate and tends to last a fraction longer than normal, nondeliberate eye contact. In a study by Dr. Samantha Mann and colleagues, liars made more deliberate eye contact than truth-tellers. Furthermore, adults who reported that gaze aversion is a sign of lying were the most likely to maintain eye contact when attempting to deceive others. Since young children are less aware of the stereotype and are less likely to assess their listener when lying, their behaviors tend to be less guarded. Children were, thus, the most likely to noticeably avert their gaze when lying.

There are circumstances when even adult liars will avert their gaze, in line with the deceiver stereotype. If an adult liar feels ashamed about their lie, they are more likely to avert their gaze. They may also avert their gaze if they are thinking. This may occur if they did not have time in advance to prepare and practice the lie. Gaze aversion may also be particularly noticeable when lying about feelings rather than about facts.

A meta-analysis of the research on the relationship between eye contact and deception reveals that eye gaze is not a reliable measure to detect deceit. Since liars tend to be particularly concerned about convincing others, they are more likely to monitor their words and behaviors as well as whether or not the listener seems to be believing their words. Thus, despite the common belief that deceivers may look away when attempting to deceive, they, in fact, often increase deliberate eye contact. This research is particularly important because most people still think gaze aversion is linked to lying. For example, when researchers in Britain asked police how they could tell when a suspect is lying, 73 percent of the police officers reported that liars will avert their gaze, despite the research that shows that experienced liars will purposefully maintain eye contact.

See also: Age Differences; Deceiver Stereotype; Detecting Deception; Nonverbal Behavior; Theory of Mind; Transparent Lies and the Illusion of Transparency; Vocal Changes when Lying.

Further Reading

Mann, S., Vrij, A., Leal, S., Granhag, P. A., Warmelink, L., & Forrester, D. (2012). Windows to the soul? Deliberate eye contact as a cue to deceit. *Journal of Nonverbal Behavior, 36*, 205–215.

McCarthy, A., & Lee, K. (2009). Children's knowledge of deceptive gaze cues and its relation to their actual lying behavior. *Journal of Experimental Child Psychology, 103*(2), 117–134.

Slessor, G., Phillips, L. H., Bull, R., Venturini, C., Bonny, E. J., & Rokaszewicz, A. (2012). Investigating the "deceiver stereotype": Do older adults associate averted gaze with deception? *The Journal of Gerontology, Series B: Psychological Sciences and Social Sciences, 67*(2), 178–183.

F

Fabrication

Fabrication is a general term that refers to any statement or assertion where information that misleads others is constructed. Fabrication goes beyond simply suppressing or altering true information in order to deceive and refers to active and effortful construction of false information. Fabrications can be for pleasure, for prosocial or selfish means, or to manipulate others. To be effective, information that is fabricated must be presented smoothly in a realistic and unremarkable way, must be consistent with the other information presented, and must be believable. Fabrication can also refer to the creation of false findings in a scientific study. In science, fabrications refer to creating or misinterpreting data to achieve the results one was hoping to find.

Dr. Melanie Sauerland and colleagues from the Netherlands found that 80 percent of research participants fabricated information when reporting on past transgressions. Such fabrications seemed to be self-protective and served to make the individual appear more socially appropriate. To investigate how such fabrications affect memory and future behavior, Dr. Sauerland invited participants to complete a survey about previous transgressions. As part of the design, she asked participants to respond truthfully on some statements and to fabricate answers on other specific items. In a follow-up session, the investigators interviewed the participants about their responses. However, the researchers altered some of the responses. When asked to explain their answers more fully at a later time, participants did not notice that their original answers had been changed for those items that they had originally fabricated. They did notice when their true responses were altered, however. Furthermore when asked to complete the questionnaires again, participants were likely to shift their answers to more closely align with the altered responses, showing that they misremembered their fabrications over time.

These findings may be particularly important in the realm of police interrogations. If police alter the responses given by suspects on subsequent interviews, it may actually change how suspects remember the events. Restating, reemphasizing, or altering a suspect's original claims may make them more likely to cognitively restructure their own memory to align with the altered claims.

Fabrication has also been shown to contribute to self-deception. When an individual fabricates information repeatedly, it is actually strengthened in memory and becomes easier to recall and to believe. Also, excessive fabrication can lead to an inability to remember what one said or more confusion when recounting or trying to accurately remember events later. So, to use fabrication effectively for one's own gain, one must remember what one said and keep those fabricated details consistent overtime, frequently at the detriment to one's memory for the actual event.

The wealth of research in this area demonstrates that fabrication, in tandem with denial, can have a significant impact on memory. Individuals, motivated to deny involvement with an event, suppress their memory of what actually occurred. Adding fabrication to provide an alternative explanation of what occurred takes effort, and the fabricated information becomes more fully ingrained into memory than the true events that are being suppressed. So, not only does denial suppress the efficiency of subsequent recall but also fabricating information may permanently alter memory about an event. During interviews, suspects may be internally or externally motivated to fabricate details about how an event may have occurred, and such fabrications may further shape their memory. Fabrications tend to lead to more commission errors, and suspects remember details about an event that did not actually occur and fabricated information is incorporated into the individual's memory about the event. This false information may interfere with the true account or memory of the event, leading to both omission and commission errors when they later try to accurately describe what happened. Those who deny involvement tend to remember less, but those who fabricate information remember incorrectly.

This increase in commission errors may be because fabrication increases activation of the left dorsolateral and right anterior prefrontal cortex, both of which are responsible for executive functioning. Research by Dr. Nobuhito Abe and his colleagues from Tohoku University demonstrated that during fabrication, the ventromedial prefrontal cortex and amygdala also showed increased activation. Both of these areas are active during emotional processing, which may explain why they are active during the arousal of deception. These areas are also involved with conforming to socially appropriate expectations as well as decision-making. These increases in brain activity require more cognitive effort and may cause greater cognitive processing of fabrications than true statements. Such increases in processing may lead to more solidification in memory and greater likelihood of remembering the fabricated events later.

See also: Commission, Lies of; Denial; Ethics; False Memory; Fraud; Hwang Woo-Suk; Loch Ness Monster; Memory; Neuroscience; Omission, Lies of; Reality Monitoring.

Further Reading

Abe, N., Suzuki, M., Mori, E., Itoh, M., & Fujii, T. (2007). Deceiving others: Distinct your responses of the prefrontal cortex and amygdala in simple fabrication and deception with social interactions. *Journal of Cognitive Neuroscience, 19*(2), 287–295.

Otgaar, H., & Baker, A. (2018). When lying changes memory for the truth. *Memory, 26*(1), 2–14.

Sauerland, M., Schell-Leugers, J. M., & Sagana, A. (2015). Fabrication put suspects at risk: Blindness to changes in transgression-related statements. *Applied Cognitive Psychology, 29*, 544–551.

Facial Cues

Verbal, nonverbal, and paraverbal cues have all been examined as effective means of detecting deception. Just as there are correlations between word choices, vocal pitch, and body movements and lying behavior, there are also indicators within facial cues that signal deceptive attempts. Dr. Paul Ekman presented microexpressions as a way to glimpse a speaker's true emotional state. Microexpressions are brief, true facial expressions that are beyond cognitive control. These expressions, when at a mismatch with verbal statements, can reveal hidden emotions that may reveal deception. Dr. Ekman analyzed expressions and behaviors in addition to microexpressions and determined that monitoring the social partner's face, especially the eyes, is a prominent means of seeking information with respect to the partner's intentions. Though deceptive attempts may also show indicators in body movements, the bulk of the information seems to be in the face itself, which is why detecting deception in conversations that are not face-to-face is exceedingly difficult. Because most socially savvy individuals are aware that others are watching their face for veracity cues, however, these are also the cues that tend to be the most controlled.

One facial cue that can be particularly indicative of desires, intentions, or beliefs is eye gaze. Dr. Simon Baron-Cohen from the University of Cambridge, as well as a wealth of other researchers, demonstrated that by preschool age, children begin to use eye gaze to infer mental states. Children learn to monitor duration and frequency of eye gaze to make inferences about the desires or thoughts of others and can rely on such cues to infer intentions, even when faced with contradictory verbal cues. Children also use emotional expressions to determine intentions. For example, Dr. Peter LaFreniere from the University of Maine and Dr. Rachelle Smith from Husson University, examined children's ability to use eye gaze and facial expressions in a competitive game scenario. Dr. LaFreniere and Dr. Smith engaged children in competitive games in which children needed to notice facial cues to compete successfully. In an initial paradigm, Dr. LaFreniere smiled slightly whenever he was providing the child with misinformation. By age six, children solved the contingency task when the experimenter smiled while lying, demonstrating that children could use facial cues to infer intentions and make decisions. Children were able to alter their behavior based on this assessment and commented on the sneaky experimenter who was trying to trick them.

In everyday conversations, individuals tend to readily use facial cues, as well as vocal, verbal, and paraverbal cues, to understand the intentions behind conversations. Most individuals use facial expressions to accentuate, negate, or otherwise convey information beyond the actual verbal content of their speech. Conversation partners must read the intonations and intentions of an eyebrow raise or smirk to fully understand and respond to requests and communications. When deception is intended, the liar must carefully conceal such signals. Savvy liars tend to maintain eye contact to avoid appearing dishonest or anxious and tend to present socially acceptable emotional expressions to convince their conversation partner. A savvy detector must carefully note the mismatch between the verbal statement and the emotional expression or the mismatch between the initial microexpression and the following emotional expression in order to detect that something is awry. Frequently, liars will have a flash of anger, disgust, or glee that is not consistent with their words. They may also smile assuredly in an attempt to convince listeners even when it is not needed for the content of their speech.

Increases in arousal due to the deceptive attempts may also cause flushing, sweating, or increases in blinking behavior. Knowing a social partner well can help a listener note such differences in visual displays. Furthermore, since true emotions are difficult to fabricate, a careful observer may note when the speaker's facial expression is not genuine. For example, a social smile that does not reach the eyes may indicate that the speaker is not truly feeling the emotion he or she professes. To effectively use facial cues to recognize deception, it is important for the observer to have a baseline. Knowing an individual's typical mannerisms is necessary in order for one to notice aberrations.

See also: Detecting Deception; Ekman, Paul; Emotional Effects; Eye Gaze; Language; Microexpressions; Nonverbal Behavior.

Further Reading

Baron-Cohen, S. (2005). The empathizing system: A revision of the 1994 model of the mindreading system. In B. J. Ellis & D. F. Bjorklund (Eds.), *Origins of the Social Mind: Evolutionary Psychology and Child Development* (pp. 468–492). Guilford.

Freire, A., Eskritt, M., & Lee, K. (2004). Are eyes windows to a deceiver's soul? Children's use of another's eye gaze cues in a deceptive situation. *Developmental Psychology, 40*(6), 1093–1104.

LaFreniere, P. J. (1998, August). *Card sharks and poker faces: Links between developmental research on deception and evolutionary models.* Paper presented at the International Society for Human Ethology, Vancouver, BC.

Schultz, T. R., & Cloghesy, K. (1981). Development of recursive awareness of intention. *Developmental Psychology, 17*(4), 465–471.

Smith, R. M., & LaFreniere, P. J. (2013). Development of tactical deception from 4 to 8 years of age. *British Journal of Developmental Psychology, 31*, 30–41.

Wellman, H. M., Cross, D., & Watson, J. (2001). Meta-analysis of theory-of-mind development: The truth about false belief. *Child Development, 72*(3), 655–684.

Fact-Check

Fact-check refers to the need for consumers to verify the facts presented in modern media news. The need to fact-check information has become an increasing concern due to deceptive websites spreading fake news. At times, even legitimate news sources pick up false stories in an attempt to stay current, given the speed at which information now travels. Unfortunately, checking the facts can be difficult, and it assumes that there is reliable unbiased truth to be found. The threat that the public may fact-check does reduce the amount of deliberate misinformation provided in legitimate news sources. To maintain their reputation, legitimate news sources have a responsibility to be as accurate and unbiased as possible. However, much of the onus is on the news consumer. Readers must engage in critical thinking, compare reports, and look at the source of the information for cues to its veracity.

Illegitimate news stories are generally attention grabbing and enticing. Thus, they catch the reader's attention and, even if later rejected, continue to have an influence on future beliefs and behaviors because they are easily pulled into consciousness or into memory. Thus, misinformation can continue to influence an individual's thought process even if fact-checking later reveals that the information is incorrect. One example of this is the false report that vaccines are linked with autism. Though this report has been repeatedly and empirically rejected, it continues to influence people's beliefs and behavior. So, while fact-checking has become increasingly important, it does not alleviate the problem of being exposed to misinformation.

Psychological researchers find that providing specifics and details when refuting false information tends to be more effective at combating continued belief in the false information. The details provide more information that can be pulled into mind when thinking about the issue. Refuting false information seems to be most effective when the incorrect information is repeated and directly addressed. This activates the false information and the new information in the mind at the same time, allowing the true information to overwrite the false information.

The practice of fact-checking is particularly prominent in the political arena. This retroactive response to public statements attempts to clarify misinformation presented by the media or political candidates. There are many organizations that engage in fact-checking such as FactCheck.org and Snopes.com. Since much news is spread through social media, individuals must have a method to know which reports can be believed. Engaging in fact-checking, sharing findings, or even seeking out fact-check sources requires proactive effort by the consumer. Specific characteristics make some individuals more likely to engage in fact-checking than others.

Dr. Michelle Amazeen and her colleagues from Boston University and the University of Colorado Boulder found that individuals tend to share fact-checks that align with their own attitudes and that fact-checking increases with age. Analysis of the 2016 U.S. presidential election revealed that Democrats were more likely to seek out fact-checking as compared to Republicans. Additionally, those who seek out more news and who are more interested in politics are also more likely to seek or share results of a fact-check. Fact-checkers profess an interest in educating audiences but frequently also include persuasive messages to shape the attitudes of the reader to more closely align with their own beliefs.

Dr. Brendan Nyhan and colleagues used the 2016 U.S. presidential election to more closely study the effects of political fact-checks. Interestingly, they found that exposure to fact-checks of Donald Trump's statements did improve participants' factual understanding of events. However, improved accuracy of such information had no effect on their attitudes toward Trump. They concluded that facts-checks can improve perceptions but have little effect on the attitudes that influence vote choice. Individuals may simply disregard facts that contradict their beliefs about their preferred candidate and seek out data to support their beliefs. Though participants were able to state more accurate information, such information had no impact on their attitudes toward their favorite candidate, particularly for Republicans. Given that Donald Trump is infamous for making extreme exaggerations, it may be the case that his supporters have already rationalized this behavior in order to continue to support him. The fact-checks are not likely to impact political stance, at least in those with strong attachments to their party or candidate.

See also: Alternative Facts; Blue Lies; Cognitive Dissonance; Detecting Deception; Fake News; Mental Effort; Politics; Propaganda.

Further Reading

Amazeen, M. S., Vargo, C. J., & Hopp, T. (2019). Reinforcing attitudes in a gatewatching news era: Individual-level antecedents to sharing fact-checks on social media. *Communication Monographs, 86*(1), 112–132.

Ecker, U. K. H., O'Reilly, Z., Reid, J. S., & Chang, E. P. (2020). The effectiveness of short-format refutational fact-checks. *British Journal of Psychology, 111*(1), 36–54.

Nyhan, B., Porter, E., Reifler, J., & Wood, T. J. (2019). Taking fact-checks literally but not seriously? The effects of journalistic fact-checking on factual beliefs and candidate favorability. *Communication Monographs, 86*(1), 112–132.

Factitious Disorders (See Munchausen Syndrome)

Fake News

Fake news refers to information that is published in the media that is not based on empirical evidence. These false news stories are frequently used to attract attention, attract advertisers, improve ratings, or increase revenue or used as propaganda to further a specific agenda. Fake news is typically intentional and has the agenda of creating financial or political gain. Though false news stories are sometimes loosely based on actual events, some are entirely fabricated and sensationalized to generate interest. Sometimes fake news stories start on social media and are picked up by mainstream media by journalists who do not take the time to check the sources. Many fake news stories are published anonymously, which increases the difficulty of validating the information or prosecuting the perpetrator. Once the news stories gain traction with the public, the misinformation becomes difficult to negate.

There are several examples of fake news stories that are still perpetuated despite contradictory evidence from scientific research. For example, vaccination research has discredited the link between vaccinations and a range of developmental disorders, but many consumers are still influenced by the fake news stories that erroneously claimed there was a link. Fake news regarding diet fads and political scandals also have long-term detrimental effects on behavior and beliefs, even in the face of contradictory evidence. Since fake news tends to be sensationalized and emotionally provoking, most people, particularly those with lower levels of cognitive ability, are not likely to adjust their judgments even if information is explicitly contradicted or sources are invalidated. When researchers from Ghent University examined the effect of exposure to fake news, they found that individuals who make judgments based on fake news have difficulty moderating their beliefs even after contradictory information is presented.

This difficulty in moderating beliefs is likely because emotionally laden impressions are resistant to change even in light of logical data. Furthermore, expectations and beliefs affect how new information is processed. Those with lower cognitive ability are more likely to be swayed by their emotional reactions, to disregard logical arguments, and to maintain their initial assessments even in the light of new information. Those with lower cognitive ability are less likely to

How to Spot Fake News

Fake news refers to information that is shared as fact even though it is not based on empirical data. Fake news may be based on opinion, be purposefully misleading, or be based on inaccurate or incomplete data analysis. Though the concept of fake news is not new, online platforms and social media make the dissemination of fake news more concerning than ever before. Simply skimming through an online platform exposes individuals to a wealth of unsolicited information. Attention-grabbing headlines and pop-up news stories can skew readers' views of events, and many may not even be aware they are being influenced. Furthermore, online algorithms tailor the fake news stories to which users are exposed, strengthening and skewing their beliefs without exposing them to counterpoints or information actually based in fact.

Due to the ubiquitous nature of fake news, it is becoming more and more difficult to be an educated consumer of information. Over the past decade, unvalidated media sources have become more widespread in U.S. society, yet consumers have not necessarily developed correlating media literacy. Readers interested in protecting themselves against being influenced by fake information must take steps to become educated readers. Critical thinking and social awareness need to be applied constantly to filter empirically based information from sensationalized interpretations of data. Educated readers must consider the source; understand the biases of which the source is likely guilty; find corroborating expert sources; and be mindful of their own biases. Anonymous articles should be treated with the most suspicion because the reader cannot assess the credibility and expertise of the source.

An educated reader must also read more than just headlines. Since internet users may find themselves inundated with incessant information, it is easy to fall into the trap of just skimming the heading information. Unfortunately, headlines are frequently worded to be controversial in order to spark enough interest for a reader to click on the link to read the full story. When reading the actual article, the information in the title is frequently negated. But if readers do not read beyond the headlines, they are left with incorrect impressions of the information.

To become a more savvy consumer of information, remember that when a news article sounds sensational, revolutionary, or surprising, it is good practice to find a corroborative source. Unfortunately, with the high rate of news publications on online outlets, a sensationalized news story may be picked up by several media outlets, without any actual validation of the information. Thus, finding an actual expert commenting on the information may be the best way to gauge the accuracy.

Being aware of one's own biases is another requirement to be an educated consumer of information. If information directly aligns with what one wants to believe, as may be the case given the algorithms designed to engage users, it is very easy to feel validated and not look further to verify information. Though how consumers engage with news has changed and continues to change, it is still safe to operate by the old adage that if it sounds too good to be true, it probably isn't.

critically evaluate their source initially, leading to more erroneous information being believed and perpetuated. Those with higher levels of cognitive ability tend to be less swayed by their initial erroneous impressions when provided with contradictory information. Thus, for a large segment of the population, fake news can lead to persistent, yet misinformed, beliefs.

Categories of fake news are widely varied. Fake news may take the form of articles with sensationalized titles that serve as clickbait. Fake news may be published propaganda aimed to convince the public to view a topic from a particular perspective. Fake news can stem from unethical journalism in which sources are paid, invalid, or created. Or, fake news can be spread by misleading headings that provide an incorrect assessment of a topic that could only be negated by carefully reading the article. Most fake news is presented by nonobjective news sources and it is difficult to combat given the anonymity of online sources and its pervasiveness on social media platforms.

Presidential elections frequently polarize the population in the United States and may perpetuate the spread of fake news with articles that make one candidate look more appealing while disparaging the other. Since supporters of both sides may start, perpetuate, or believe fake news stories, objective assessment of the candidates becomes relatively impossible. Additionally, the misinformation may change as it spreads, becoming more sensational and less representative of reality. Fake news is not new, but the term has been popularized in the modern era by Donald Trump, who tweeted about the prevalence of fake news during his presidency. During the 2016 presidential election, it became hard to distinguish between accurate and fake information perpetuated by both sides of the political debate. Furthermore, during the campaigns, fake news stories were noted to have had more readers than articles from genuine news outlets. As more individuals seek out news from social media platforms, more are misinformed by fake news stories that are more concerned with hits and sensationalism than accuracy.

Though fake news can spread more readily with online and social media platforms, it is not unique to modern times. Throughout history, individuals commonly published newspaper articles to slander opponents in war, political debates, or other altercations. Paintings depict warriors as noble and victorious even in battles that history shows they lost. Enemies are dehumanized by both sides in wartime to sway the beliefs of the general population. Regardless of the topic or era, fake news functions to rally support for initiatives or political candidates who may otherwise not be popular or to change the perception of an event to sway public behavior.

See also: Alternative Facts; Clickbait; Consequences of Lying; Defamation; Detecting Deception; Ethics; Fact-Check; Intelligence; Machiavellianism; Propaganda.

Further Reading

De keersmaecker, J., & Rotes, A. (2017). 'Fake news': Incorrect, but hard to correct. The role of cognitive ability on the impact of false information on social impressions. *Intelligence, 65*, 107–110.

Mo Jang, S., Gang, T., Li, J. Q., Via, R., Huang, C., Kim, H., & Tang, J. (2018). A computational approach for examining the roots and spread patterns of fake news: Evolution tree analysis. *Computers in Human Behavior, 84*, 103–113.

False Confessions

False confessions are confessions elicited from innocent people for crimes they did not commit. Most research shows that lie detection is a difficult art, and the average person can only discriminate between a truth and a lie at about chance levels. During interrogations, one may assume people may deny committing a crime, even if they are guilty. However, one must also be aware that individuals may confess to a deed that they did not commit. This can be particularly harmful if an individual falsely confesses to a crime and thus is punished unfairly while the real perpetrator remains unpunished.

Many investigators demonstrate an investigator bias, meaning they are less likely to believe that statements made by suspects are true. While typical people have a truth bias and tend to take others at their word, investigators tend to be more suspicious and harder to convince. This may serve them well when talking with guilty suspects, but it can be detrimental when working with innocent suspects. This bias is especially damaging if the innocent suspects notice that the investigator does not believe them. It can also color the investigators' views if they have already made a foregone decision about the guilt of the suspect. Investigators may make direct accusations in order to obtain a confession. The directness of the accusation may serve to confuse, scare, or make the suspect anxious. Methods of interrogation are designed to break down suspects' claims of innocence and increase their willingness to confess. Interrogators isolate the individual in a small room and create feelings of helplessness and anxiety. These steps are exactly the measures that can induce even an innocent person to confess to a crime.

Psychological research has revealed that there are several types of false confessions. False confessions may be voluntary, coerced-compliant, or coerced-internalized. Voluntary false confessions are not the result of outside pressure and may be made in order to protect a guilty person, to get attention, or as a mode of self-punishment. The individuals know they are innocent but admit guilt voluntarily. Coerced-compliant false confessions, on the other hand, tend to be made as a result of external pressure. For example, these may occur when suspects do not think they can convince the investigator of their innocence. In this case, suspects may confess in order to receive a less severe punishment rather than maintaining their claims of innocence and risking full punitive action. The confession may be made to end the interrogation or to achieve a particular outcome, but the individuals still know they are innocent of the crime, even though they confess.

Finally, false confessions may be coerced-internalized. This type of confession is the result of a coercive interrogation during which the suspects actually come to believe that they are guilty. These suspects may be sleep deprived, exhausted, and confused and thus become more susceptible to outside influences and start to doubt their own innocence. Particularly when the interrogator is convinced about the suspect's guilt, the suspect may come to believe that they are guilty and that they must have blocked the crime from their own memory. Interrogators who use coercive tactics, including social factors, such as isolation and pressure; emotional factors, such as distress and fear; cognitive factors, such as expectations about consequences; situational factors, such as the nature of arrest and presence/absence of lawyer; and physiological factors, such as stress, arousal, and exhaustion, may be at much higher risk of obtaining a false confession. Additionally, unlike the coerced-compliant suspects, once the stress of the interrogation is over, these suspects still maintain the belief of their own guilt.

Dr. Julia Shaw from the University of Bedfordshire and colleagues empirically demonstrated that innocent adults could be convinced over the course of a few hours that they committed a crime during their teen years. In their study, 21 of the

30 participants who had not been associated with any crimes during their adolescence developed a false memory of an assault, an assault with a weapon, or a theft that ended with police contact, over the course of three one-hour sessions. Once the false memory was constructed, participants added details, elaborated on the experience, and reported confidence about their recollection of the event. This research illustrates the malleability of memory and the danger of making false accusations.

Despite the possibility of false confessions, research within typical prison populations and criminal cases shows that confessions that are later deemed false are typically quite rare. Only 0.04 percent of all FBI crime convictions were ultimately deemed to be false confessions. Furthermore, studies with inmates in Iceland found that fewer than 1 percent of current inmates claim that they gave false confessions and only about half of these were the result of an interrogation. In the United States, there have been approximately 125 proven instances of false confessions in the past 30 years. Since many false confessions are likely never revealed, conservative estimates of up to about 1,000 unidentified false confessions still make false confessions add up to less than 1 percent of criminal convictions.

Unfortunately, research shows that false confessions are indistinguishable from true confessions, and thus the possibility must be taken seriously. Use of interrogation tactics such as the Concealed Information Test, which was specifically designed to discriminate between those who have inside knowledge about a crime from those who do not, may strengthen the confidence an investigator can have in the veracity of a confession. Such procedures are not yet widespread in the United States but could be instrumental in increasing confidence in preventing false confessions.

See also: Behavior Analysis Interview; Coercion; Concealed Information Test; Control Questions Test; Detecting Deception; False Memory; Motivational Impairment Effect; Polygraph Tests; Reid Technique; Truth-Default Theory.

Further Reading

Blair, J. P. (2008). The behavioural analysis interview: Clarifying the practice, theory and understanding of its use and effectiveness. *International Journal of Police Science and Management, 10*(1), 101–118.

Bradford, D., & Goodman-Delahunty, J. (2008). Detecting deception in police investigations: Implications for false confessions. *Psychiatry, Psychology and Law, 15*(1), 105–118.

Kassin, S. M., & Wrightsman, L. S. (1985). Confession evidence. In S. M. Kassin & L. S. Wrightsman (Eds.), *The psychology of evidence and trial procedure* (pp. 67–94). Sage.

Shaw, J., & Porter, S. (2015). Constructing rich false memories of committing crime. *Psychological Science, 26*(3), 291–301.

False Memory

A false memory is a phenomenon in which an individual remembers something that never actually happened. These memories are a result of the fallibility of human memory and can occur when one attempts to deceive others, is inattentive, or is bombarded by too much information to remember things accurately. False memories can also develop as a result of police interrogations, therapy sessions, or intimate conversations.

Psychological research has consistently established that memory is fallible, and even individuals who strive to accurately represent events may have errors in perception. Such errors are then encoded into memory, and these inaccuracies are then "remembered." Given that even honest individuals can create false memories, liars may struggle even more to accurately remember events that they are attempting to misrepresent. Dr. Henry Otgaar and his colleagues from the University of London and the University of British Columbia demonstrated that liars tend to forget true details and misremember information to a greater extent than truth-tellers.

Lying places demands on cognitive resources since the liar must not only suppress the truth but also construct and maintain a plausible substitute. To come across as credible, liars must alter their verbal and nonverbal responses and construct or suppress information. These behaviors place a load on both cognitive processes and memory systems. In a simple memory experiment, participants who were asked to deny an experience were later less accurate in remembering what actually happened. Thus, individuals who lie about committing crimes may actually begin to misremember the actual events. If they should confess in the future, their memories of the crime may be compromised and inaccurate.

Similarly, individuals who were asked to fabricate details about an event also misremembered the true details. The added details became integrated into the individuals' memories of what actually happened, skewing their memories of the event. Though such confabulations likely have no detrimental impact when reminiscing about experiences, there may be huge implications for witnesses or suspects of a crime. Not only may witnesses or suspects lie, but they may also actually misremember what they saw, particularly if they were motivated to lie at the beginning. Even claiming not to remember impairs one's memory when motivated to make a report at a later time. Likely, those who claim not to remember do not rehearse the event, and thus, it is not committed to memory, whereas those who add details end up with a distorted memory of what happened.

Dr. Sigmund Freud proposed that individuals who experience traumatic events may repress the memories for an extended period of time. Later, when the individuals feel safe or during psychotherapy, these memories may be recovered, and the individuals may remember things that they had previously repressed. Once these memories are recovered, however, it may be difficult to determine if they are accurate or if they were influenced or created by the therapy process.

Dr. Julia Shaw and her colleagues from the University of Bedfordshire demonstrated this frailty of memory. Over the course of two weeks, they were able to successfully create vivid false memories in a group of healthy adults. By mingling true and false details about an event, the researchers were able to alter the participants' memories of what actually happened over the course of three interviews. By the end of three sessions, 70 percent of participants elaborated false memories about committing a crime as a teenager that never actually took place. By the end of the study, participants discussed their memories about the event and confidently reported details about an experience that never actually occurred.

Participants were especially susceptible when researchers used suggestive techniques and scenarios and included true details intermingled with the fabricated events. These are exactly the tactics used in therapy when attempting to help an individual recover lost memories as well as during police interrogations. Encouraging individuals to try to remember and providing them with accurate information along with suggested information can lead to the constructions of false memories that the individual then remembers as actually having happened.

Even the use of terms during an interview can radically change the perception and memory of an event. For example, when asked to estimate the speed of vehicles after watching a video of an accident, participants responded differently if the researcher asked how fast the cars were going when they *smashed* into each other than if asked how fast they were going when they *connected* with one another. The individuals who heard the question with the word "smashed" estimated that they were going faster and misremembered details such as damage and broken glass. Thus, misinformation provided after an event can radically change the perception and the memory of the event.

Research on the malleability of memory needs to be taken into consideration for both psychological treatment and criminal investigations. Therapists or interrogators who use techniques such as suggestive interview questions can permanently shift and shape individuals' memories of events, creating false recollections.

See also: Cognitive Changes while Lying; Consequences of Lying; Detecting Deception; Fabrication; Fake News; False Confessions; Gaslighting; Malingering; Mental Effort; Motives for Lying; Polygraph Tests; Reality Monitoring.

Further Reading

Engle, J., & O'Donohue, W. (2012). Pathways to false allegations of sexual assault. *Journal of Forensic Psychology Practice, 12*(2), 97–123.

Otgaar, H., & Baker, A. (2018). When lying changes memory for the truth. *Memory, 26*(1), 2–14.

Shaw, J., & Porter, S. (2015). Constructing rich false memories of committing crime. *Psychological Science, 26*(3), 291–301.

False Signals (See Signaling Theory)

Fibs

To fib is to tell an unimportant lie or to provide a relatively flimsy cover story. Fibs are typically associated with relatively trivial matters or events and are frequently not antisocial or nefarious, but rather relatively mundane or simple. Most fibs are not premeditated but are told in the spur of the moment to avoid a punishment or to gain an immediate advantage. Frequently, fibs are incomplete spontaneous lies that are not always convincing. Some fibs are told even when there is direct evidence to the contrary for the observer. For example, children may fib about eating their vegetables in order to get dessert even when their green beans are clearly still on their plate, under a napkin, or on the floor. They do not tend to be well-thought-out lies, and while they can be annoying, they do not usually have long-term negative consequences.

Though fibbing is typically connected with childish lies from childhood, there are many circumstances during which adults also fib. Parents may use fibs in order to get their children to cooperate or to avoid harsh truths. Even parents who endorse and enforce honesty occasionally fib to elicit desired behavior. Fibs may be used to get children to eat healthy food, go to bed on time, to explain the loss of a pet, or to profess love for a terrible gift. For parents who would like to avoid these fibs, which sometimes undermine trust in the parent-child relationships, alternatives include telling the child the truth, explaining why the parent may have told lies to others, or engaging in cooperative fantasy. If children observe their parents lying to others, it is beneficial for them to understand why lies were told (e.g., to protect someone's feelings) to keep a relatively consistent message about when it is okay to lie. Parents also find that engaging in fantasy play, such as creating a fantasy game that has the goal of cleaning up toys or completing a nighttime routine, can encourage the desired behaviors without resorting to telling fibs.

In some instances, small fibs may be used when telling the truth would cause hurt or anxiety. These are known as therapeutic fibs and could be used, for example, in the case of patients with dementia. The reasoning is that sometimes small fibs can have more therapeutic results than blatant honesty. An example provided by the Alzheimer's Association includes reducing caregiver distress by allowing or encouraging them to emphasize those details that will not cause the patient to be upset. In such cases small lies, or fibs, may be used to reduce stress and increase the level of comfort of the individual, which can overall benefit the patient. Rather than reminding the patient of lost loved ones or of their disease, fibs can be used to redirect attention or to distract the individual. When an Alzheimer's patient asks for a deceased spouse, for example, a caregiver may insinuate that they will be by later and substitute a different activity in the meantime. These fibs can be helpful, but care must be taken to otherwise interact with the patient as honestly as possible or else they may end up not feeling heard or lose trust in their caregiver if deception is suspected. Both of these instances would increase anxiety and distress rather than provide a therapeutic effect.

See also: Benefits of Lying; Categories of Deception; Dementia; Lying to Children; Lying to Parents; Prosocial Lying; White Lies.

Further Reading

Forte, T. (2010). When parents fib: When is it okay to tell a white lie? *Working Mother.* Retrieved from https://www.workingmother.com/2010/3/home/when-parents-fib

O'Sullivan, M. (2009). Why most people parse palters, fibs, lies, whoppers, and other deceptions poorly. In B. Harrington (Ed.), *Deception: From Ancient Empires to Internet Dating* (pp. 74–91). Stanford University Press.

Fifth Amendment

The Fifth Amendment to the U.S. Constitution allows defendants or witnesses to refuse to answer questions that they fear may be self-incriminating. Essentially, the Fifth Amendment allows suspects to remain silent until they have legal counsel and provides the right to not be impelled to serve as a witness for one's own behavior. The Fifth Amendment covers a number of other topics including double jeopardy, right to trial, due process, and eminent domain, but it is most commonly used in popular media when witnesses or defendants refuse to answer questions to avoid self-incrimination. Since lying under oath, or perjury, is a criminal offense, pleading the Fifth allows suspects to avoid deception in cases where honesty may go against their self-interest.

To make sure that suspects are aware of their right to remain silent, the Supreme Court decreed that individuals must be informed of their rights, particularly in inherently coercive situations, such as during arrest or during interrogation procedures. The Fifth Amendment is in place to help prevent those in power from exerting pressure through threats of punishment or other penalties to coerce suspects to self-incriminate. The goal of providing a right to remain silent is to increase the reliability of confessions. If suspects cannot be coerced to incriminate themselves, there are hopefully fewer false confessions.

In order to protect innocent suspects and the rights of all suspects and to insure integrity of confessions, interrogators are legally required to cease asking questions once suspects have asserted their Fifth Amendment rights. In cases where the Fifth Amendment right was violated, cases may be thrown out of court, making violation of such rights costly for accusers. The accuser must ensure that defendants understand their rights and know that they have the privilege against self-incrimination. Attorneys may not use the ignorance of a suspect to further their own case. If a suspect is incompetent or otherwise unable to comprehend their own rights, then they must be assigned council who can act in their best interest.

In cases of abuse, particularly child abuse, the Fifth Amendment right may create a problematic situation during therapeutic sessions for the abuser. In many therapeutic situations, in order for an abusive parent to be treated, he or she must admit to committing the abuse. Admitting to and taking responsibility for the abuse has been shown to relieve the burden from the child, who may feel responsible, and can also help restore family relationships. However, since psychologists are mandated reporters, requiring a client to admit to abuse creates a violation of their Fifth Amendment rights. In these situations, the courts may have ordered the abuser to participate in therapy, and since the therapist requires the abuser to admit their own guilt, they no longer have the right against self-incrimination. In some situations, the accused will not be released from therapy until they have admitted their guilt, creating a situation that may result in loss of custody and parental rights or even internal prosecution, regardless of whether the abuse actually occurred. The problem occurs when an accused parent is required to participate in treatment to maintain parental rights. Not cooperating with the treatment by not admitting the abuse may result in losing parental rights. However, cooperating and admitting the abuse may have similar ramifications, placing the parent in a no-win situation and violating their constitutional rights. In these situations, the court may feel the duty to protect the child over the interests of the parents, even though false positives may occur.

Unsurprisingly, in simulated jury situations, suspects who plead the Fifth are more likely to be suspected of being guilty. Thus, having the luxury to not implicate oneself may actually create the perception of guilt. Those suspects who plead the Fifth, regardless of their reasons, tend to sway the jury toward believing guilt is present. That suspicion of guilt may not be enough to return a guilty verdict, but it tends to provide an impression of guilt. In a study by Dr. Clyde Hendrick from Kent State University and David Shaffer from the University of Georgia, accused individuals were less likely to be viewed as guilty when they committed perjury and blatantly denied committing the offense than when they exercised their Fifth Amendment right. Furthermore, the more often they pleaded the Fifth Amendment, the guiltier they were suspected of being.

See also: Coercion; Consequences of Lying; False Confessions; Perjury; Polygraph Tests.

Further Reading

Hendrick, C., & Shaffer, D. R. (1975). Effect of pleading the Fifth Amendment on perceptions of guilt and morality. *Bulletin of the Psychonomic Society, 6*(5), 449–452.

Levine, M., & Doherty, E. (1991). The Fifth Amendment and therapeutic requirements to admit abuse. *Criminal Justice and Behavior, 18*(1), 98–112.

Minhas, H. M., & Westphal, A. (2016). Competency to waive Fifth Amendment rights during custodial interview. *The Journal of the American Academy of Psychiatry and the Law, 44*(1), 122–124.

Fine Print

Fine print is the small print at the bottom of an advertisement or contract that qualifies, explains, or contradicts the larger print. The use of fine print is a common advertising strategy that allows corporations to put forth a deceptive advertising message while maintaining claims of honesty. The larger, more eye-catching message may be attractive to consumers, and they are likely to overlook the small print at the bottom, which discloses the truth. The fine print may be tiny, in colors that blend in with the background, may only appear briefly for a television advertisement, or may be verbally stated at a fast rate of speech. Though the Federal Trade Commission (FTC) states that advertisements must be clear and that information must not be concealed or unreadable, consumers still need to use caution to ensure that they understand the terms and conditions that may not be apparent in the boldly stated advertisement.

Examples of information that may be included in the fine print of an advertisement include statements of exceptions to the stated offers, side effects for medications, conditions that must be met, time limits, or fees. Some organizations offer great low introductory rates for a limited time, and once that time limit passes, the rates go up, such as with cable service, banking loans, credit card interest rates, or any other services that have a monthly contract. Furthermore, the fine print may contain specifications about penalties if the consumer tries to end the service. In these situations, the changing rate structure or subsequent fees tend not to be highlighted in the advertisement, and the consumer may only notice the great introductory rate.

Businesses may also use a marketing strategy where an offer is presented that attracts customers, and only after customers commit does the company reveal fees, additional features that must be purchased, or exit penalties. For example, customers may initially be drawn in by a free prize but then end up spending money to maintain or receive the item, for installation or subscription, or are overcharged for shipping and handling of the item. Items may be sold at a very low price, such as razors, printers, or drills, but then the consumer must purchase high-priced blades, ink cartridges, or special batteries in order to use them. Many times, these accessories cost almost as much as purchasing new equipment. For example, inkjet cartridges cost about 90 percent of the cost of the printer, and 97 percent of consumers indicated that they did not know the cost when they originally purchased. The companies are not overtly deceiving the consumer because they are providing the prizes or offers that they claim to be. But only in the fine print can one possibly notice the caveats that come along with winning. This information is not overtly advertised, meaning that the consumer must be careful, ask questions, and seek out and read the fine print to not be deceived.

Standard-form contracts are becoming more common, and they typically list the terms in tiny font, or fine print. When purchasing things online, for example, consumers must agree to the terms and conditions, spelled out in fine print. This fine print also typically contains legalese and lengthy disclaimers. Unless consumers take the time to read the fine print carefully, they are at the mercy of the advertiser. Dr. Yannis Bakos and Florencia Marotta-Wurgler, JD from New York University, and their colleague, David Trossen, JD, tracked the online browsing behavior of almost 50,000 users of 90 online companies to determine how thoroughly online shoppers read the fine print or terms of service when making online purchases. Shockingly, they found that about 0.1 percent of users clicked on the fine print when shopping online and fewer than 0.1 percent read offers before clicking on the "I agree" option for terms of service. Furthermore, the 1 or 2 in 1,000 who clicked on the terms of service spent less than 30 seconds looking over the company's contract before agreeing to the terms. Given that many terms of service documents are multiple pages of fine print legalese, it is very likely that consumers neither read nor comprehend the fine print before agreeing to the terms.

Regardless of whether individuals read the fine print, they can still be held responsible for whatever conditions are outlined. Fine print in television ads may be a sentence or two, but in online purchases, these contracts can be long, hard to parse through, and too standardized for a typical consumer to understand. Such measures allow companies to protect their own interests and meet requirements set forth by the FTC, sometimes at the expense of the consumer.

See also: Advertising; Bait and Switch; Clickbait; Fraud; Media; Scams.

Further Reading

Bakos, Y., Marotta-Wurgler, F., & Trossen, D. R. (2014). Does anyone read the fine print? Consumer attention to standard form contracts. *Journal of Legal Studies, 43*(1), 9–40.

Garman, E. T., & Forgue, R. E. (2008). *Personal Finance* (9th ed.). Cengage Learning.

Foot-in-the-Door Phenomenon (See Reverse Psychology)

Fraud

Fraud is using dishonest means to unlawfully secure a reward, such as money or another benefit. Frequently those who engage in fraud claim to be someone they are not or to have accomplished something they have not. Someone committing fraud may engage in forgery, falsify documents, or engage in theft under false pretenses. Fraud frequently occurs in organizations when employees falsify receipts to steal money from the company or submit fraudulent insurance claims.

Because fraudulent insurance claims can cost companies billions of dollars each year, organizations are highly invested in detecting and preventing fraud. Dr. Danielle Warren from Rutgers Business School and her colleagues examined both field and laboratory research to investigate insurance fraud. They found that the best way to detect insurance fraud is through interviews with the claimant, rather than through background checks, witness interviews, or examination of physical evidence. Those attempting to engage in insurance fraud tend to engage in interpersonal avoidance and are likely to delay meetings with an investigator or avoid meeting face-to-face. Thus, repeated delays can signal a false claim. During interviews, claimants are also likely to confuse their story, have difficulty establishing and maintaining the timeline, and demonstrate misrepresentation. Dr. Warren found that the interview interaction and the tendency of the claimant to delay the interview are the best ways to determine fraud. Though there may be instances where an honest claimant may delay an interview, such behavior is much more common for one who is attempting to deceive.

Much research has gone into how to more consistently detect and prevent fraud. Dr. Sharon Leal from the University of Portsmouth and her colleagues examined factors that reduce fraud during insurance claims. The most impactful deterrent was to have individuals read out a statement promising that they will be truthful. Those individuals showed more honesty in their subsequent behavior than controls. Based on laboratory and field research, asking claimants to make a statement about their ethical beliefs at the beginning of an insurance claim form resulted in more honest behavior when filling out the form and in subsequent interviews. Though many forms already have such a declaration, it is frequently at the end of the document, which is too late to influence honesty when filling out the claim.

Another common type of fraud is phishing. Phishing is when individuals attempt to steal personal information, such as credit card numbers or passwords, to steal money or other rewards. Phishing schemes can include setting up fraudulent websites that look official. The ability of a user to detect when the sites are fraudulent is important to deter monetary loss. Websites that look professional may fool users. Many companies have employee training protocols to teach their employees how to identify and avoid such fraud. The ability to discriminate between legitimate websites and fraudulent websites is a priority. Understanding what type of information should be provided and what is suspicious is also a key to recognizing potential fraud. Many fraudulent websites include clues such as misspellings, grammatical errors, and inconsistent typeface or logos.

Susceptibility to fraud seems to change over the life span. Because technological advances heighten the risk of online fraudulent behavior, it has become increasingly important to protect oneself against attackers. Fraudulent attempts are quite prevalent via email distribution and malware links. Older adults have integrated internet use into their daily lives, yet most have less experience with computers and decreased sensitivity to deception. Since many older adults hold positions of power in organizations, their susceptibility to fraud can have pervasive ramifications. Dr. Natalie Ebner and her colleagues simulated a spear phishing attempt as part of a psychological research study. In Dr. Ebner's study, research participants received an email that they did not know was part of the study. The email contained a fraudulent link, and data were collected as to whether or not the individuals clicked on the link. The oldest individuals within the study, age 75–89 years, were most susceptible to falling victim to the fraud. Those between the ages of 62 and 74 were the next most susceptible group. These findings illuminate that older adults may need more education about signs of fraud to increase public health and to combat fraud.

See also: Age Differences; Categories of Deception; Catfishing; Chadwick, Cassie; Clickbait; Detecting Deception; Hoax; Impersonator; Perjury; Phishing.

Further Reading

Ebner, N. C., Ellis, D. M., Lin, T., Rocha, H. A., Yang, H., Dommaraju, S., Soliman, A., Woodard, D. L., Turner, G. R., Spreng, R. N., & Oliveira, D. S. (2020). Uncovering susceptibility risk to online deception in aging. *The Journals of Gerontology: Series B, 75*(3), 522–533.

Leal, S., Vrij, A., Nahari, G., & Mann, S. (2016). Please be honest and provide evidence: Deterrence of deception in an online insurance fraud context. *Applied Cognitive Psychology, 30*, 768–774.

Moreno-Fernandez, M. M., Blanco, F., Garaizar, P., & Matute, H. (2017). Fishing for phishers. Improving Internet users' sensitivity to visual deception cues to prevent electronic fraud. *Computers in Human Behavior, 69*, 421–436.

Warren, D. E., & Schweitzer, M. E. (2018). When lying does not pay: How experts detect insurance fraud. *Journal of Business Ethics, 150*, 711–726.

Fundamental Attribution Error (See Hypocrisy)

G

Gaslighting

Gaslighting is a form of deception in which an individual manipulates the perceptions of others to such an extent that they begin to doubt their own experiences and memories. Gaslighting could occur during interrogation proceedings when a confident examiner convinces suspects of their own guilt. Gaslighting may also occur in abusive relationships when an abuser makes a partner question his or her own sanity, experiences, or memory of an event. For example, some abusers deny the abuse or blame the victim, making the victims question their own role in the event as well as their own behavior.

The term "gaslighting" comes about from a 1938 play named *Gaslight* in which a husband convinces his wife she is misperceiving events and imagining things as he attempts to cover up a murder. The term was popularized in psychology in the late 1960s and has come to refer to attempts to alter others' perceptions of reality.

Some behaviors that align with gaslighting techniques include skewing descriptions of an event to make the abuser look less at blame, denying or contradicting the claims of a victim, verbally or physically demeaning a victim and isolating the person from outside influences, dismissing concerns, coercing the victim into agreement, and controlling and limiting the information the victim receives. Gaslighting is particularly successful when the individual is extremely confident in his or her claims, to the extent that it makes others question their own perceptions of the event, deteriorating their self-confidence and self-esteem. Gaslighting behaviors are an extreme form of manipulation that frequently accompany sociopathic or narcissistic personality traits.

Gaslighting can be observable in politics, personal relationships, and in workplaces. In American politics, for example, confident assertions from those in leadership, regardless of how blatantly false they are, may serve to confuse listeners and change the way that mass populations view reality, particularly after an event has occurred. News sources and fact-checkers must work furiously to discredit blatant claims that likely aim to convince the American population of things that are untrue in an attempt to further political careers and maintain power. Though these attempts are not new in politics, the modern technological age allows misinformation to spread more quickly than ever before, creating widespread cognitive dissonance and distortion.

Though it is possibly most common in the political arena, gaslighting can also occur in personal relationships or in the workplace. In romantic relationships, individuals may be coerced into blaming themselves for their partners' infidelity. Unfaithful partners may use gaslighting techniques to convince their spouses that the innocent spouse is at fault and that he or she drove the partner to be unfaithful. They may deny infidelity or convince their partners that they are being too suspicious, clingy, or unfair even if infidelity is actually occurring. In the workplace, employers may use gaslighting as a method to prevent employees from reporting misconduct. Employers may claim that the misconduct is typical or they may deliberately ignore, delay, mishandle, or cover up accusations. Someone who reports misconduct may be ostracized or set up to fail and targeted as unstable, or they may be praised for reporting the misconduct, but then no steps will be taken to alter the problem.

Gaslighting may not always be intentional, but it can still be damaging to personal or professional relationships, work environments, or within political systems. Those interested in recognizing gaslighting should be mindful of situations in which they find themselves being frequently accused of misperceiving situations or when their concerns are not taken seriously. One can also be mindful of situations where a social partner withholds information, refuses to listen, attempts to contradict or alter information about a situation, questions one's thinking or conclusions, trivializes one's feelings or experiences, points out flaws in one's character traits, frequently asks for apologies, or denies things previously stated. Keeping notes and putting conversations in writing can help protect an individual in a situation of gaslighting. Acknowledging that something is wrong and listening to one's gut instincts can be protective, as well as engaging a moderator for an unbiased assessment.

See also: Alternative Facts; Antisocial Personality Disorder; Blue Lies; Cognitive Dissonance; Cognitive Distortion; Fact-Check; Fake News; Manipulation; Narcissism; Personality; Polygraph Tests; Social Intelligence.

Further Reading

Ahern, K. (2018). Institutional betrayal and gaslighting. *Journal of Perinatal & Neonatal Nursing, 32*(1), 59–65.

DiGiulio, S. (2018, July 13). *What is gaslighting? And how do you know if it's happening to you?* Retrieved from https://www.nbcnews.com/better/health/what-gaslighting -how-do-you-know-if-it-s-happening-ncna890866

Greenberg, E. (2017, September 3). *Are you being "gaslighted" by the narcissist in your life: 7 signs that your partner is feeding your self-doubt on purpose.* Retrieved from https://www.psychologytoday.com/us/blog/understanding-narcissism/201709 /are-you-being-gaslighted-the-narcissist-in-your-life

Simon, G. (2011, November 8). *Gaslighting as a manipulation tactic: What it is, who does it, and why.* Retrieved from https://counsellingresource.com/features/2011/11/08 /gaslighting/

Sopel, J. (2018, July 25). *From 'alternative facts' to rewriting history in Trump's White House.* Retrieved from https://www.bbc.com/news/world-us-canada-44959300

Guilty Knowledge Test (See Concealed Information Test)

H

Half-Truths

Half-truths are statements that do not give a full account of the situation in question. Elements are omitted or concealed, and only those parts of the truth that are deemed safe to share are provided. Half-truths are frequently used to imply intentions while concealing true motives. Individuals may state their goals and even provide some reasoning, but they conceal other aspects that may not be socially acceptable or palatable given the situation. Half-truths can also be wielded through the manipulation of modifiers to imply information or distort meaning. One may profess to suspect something is true rather than to know firsthand in order to maintain deniability. Or one may profess to know something rather than to merely suspect in order to be more convincing. The general content of the statement stays the same, but the teller professes more or less conviction in order to more effectively claim or deny responsibility or adjust the statement to be more acceptable to this listener.

Dr. Ronny Turner from Colorado State University and colleagues examined 130 dyadic encounters to analyze the typical deceptive content within everyday communications. They classified about 62 percent of all statements in general interactions as containing some type of information that could be classified as deceptive. Only around 38 percent of interactions were characterized by total disclosure. Of the statements that were not entirely truthful, half-truths accounted for about one-third of all deceptive statements. In these common situations, the conversation partner used half-truths rather than outright lies and subtly and intentionally left out key pieces of information to regulate the social interaction, protect feelings, or garner cooperation. Another third of the deceptive responses were made up of diversionary responses. These statements gave information unrelated to the topic being discussed in order to divert the conversation away from uncomfortable topics and to distract the conversation partner. Unless a conversation partner has a particular goal, such diversionary strategies are effective in shifting the conversation to a new topic. The final third of deceptive responses were made up of outright lies. Other aspects of deception that made up smaller portions of the communications included exaggerations and secrets.

Half-truths can be very effective strategies of deception because elements of truth are mixed in with the deception, making the lies more difficult to detect. Since the speaker is not outright lying, the deceptive part of the statement seems more credible because it is included within a true statement. Speakers also have deniability if half-truths are caught. They can claim to have forgotten details or that they did not share all the information, or they claim that they misspoke.

Some refer to half-truths as bending the truth because there is partial truth in the statement. Half-truths may exaggerate or minimize details to engage in impression management. The basic content is true, but the details are manipulated to garner more respect or avoid starting a conflict. Half-truths are particularly common in adolescence as adolescents spend more time away from parents and become autonomous, cognitively capable individuals. When questioned by parents, adolescents may divulge information about where they went but omit information about whom they were with. Or they may report whom they were with, but neglect to mention all of the activities in which they engaged. Individuals tend to use half-truths when attempting to avoid conflict or tension, to manipulate the situation to their own benefit, to save face or avoid embarrassment in front of others, or to maintain relationships.

Though half-truths may serve to regulate social interactions, they still have overall negative implications for relationships. Not being entirely honest may smooth over a conversation in the short term, but long-term intimacy tends to be negatively affected. Furthermore, remembering which details were shared and which were not makes future conversations more complicated and less comfortable for the manipulator and may skew their memory about what actually occurred.

See also: Alternative Facts; Bending the Truth; Categories of Deception; Commission, Lies of; Detecting Deception; Diversionary Tactics; Exaggerations; Instrumental Lies; Lying to Parents; Manipulation; Minimization; Omission, Lies of; Politics; Prosocial Lying; Self-Deception.

Further Reading

Bryant, E. M. (2008). Real lies, white lies and gray lies: Towards a typology of deception. *Kaleidoscope: A Graduate Journal of Qualitative Communication Research, 7,* 23–48.

Turner, R. E., Edgley, C., & Olmstead, G. (1975). Information control in conversations: Honesty is not always the best policy. *Kansas Journal of Sociology, 11,* 69–89.

High-Stakes Lies (See Black Lies)

Hoax

A hoax is a story designed to mislead others, frequently large groups of others. Hoaxes are widespread fabrications that are similar to myths, legends, or cases of fraud. Hoaxes may start as jokes but then spread to more large-scale deceptions. Typically those who are the victim of a hoax do not realize they are being tricked. Throughout history, there have been scientific hoaxes, academic hoaxes, internet hoaxes, urban legends and myths, and alien hoaxes. Hoaxes may be for entertainment or may be used to gain a political advantage. Conspiracy theories may arise from hoaxes.

In an era of Photoshop, hoaxes can be perpetrated by creating false videos or photographs, or by altering documents, but there have been many hoaxes throughout history that used much less impressive technology. These hoaxes include those surrounding Area 51, crop circles, the Loch Ness monster, Lucy Lightfoot, psychic readings, and the Piltdown Man. Hoaxes can be perpetuated by the news, religious groups, extremist groups, scientists, or other individuals. Websites that engage in fact-checking such as Snopes.com attempt to reveal hoaxes.

In modern day, hoaxes can spread quickly throughout social media. Sometimes these false news stories appear to be legitimate. Cross-checking, looking at sources, or finding companion sources is required to identify whether or not the information is accurate. Interestingly, some revealed hoaxes remain in popular belief. Despite lack of evidence or evidence to the contrary, many believe that aliens linger in Area 51, that Loch Ness is populated by a monster, and that a tribe of half-man/half-apes lives somewhere in Africa. Frequently, hoaxes reign when information is lacking or when something is difficult to disprove. Belief in flying saucers, the paranormal, or time travel tends to catch the fancy, and many want to believe that such magic exists. Though many hoaxes are eventually revealed, it is difficult to eradicate them from the public consciousness. As such, many hoaxes tend to be perpetuated through generations.

One well-known historical hoax that still lingers in the public consciousness is that of the Loch Ness monster. Photographic "evidence" was created by Marmaduke Wetherell in 1934 and passed to the press by Dr. Robert Kenneth Wilson. Along with casts of footprints and periodic sightings, all of which have been discredited, the rumor of the monster still lingers in modern consciousness, and tourists still carefully watch in case they can catch a glimpse of something emerging from the water, showing the pervasiveness of a well-done hoax.

The Piltdown Man is another early hoax in which a paleontologist claimed to have found fossils of an unknown early species. He created the fossils by combining bones from an orangutan and a modern human. The excitement surrounding the discovery lingered for about 40 years until the fossils were exposed as a hoax.

In 1938, a radio broadcast of H. G. Wells' *The War of the Worlds* reportedly created panic as listeners believed they were listening to a real broadcast. The story was presented as a series of news bulletins, and newspapers reported that many Americans fell for the hoax and believed there was an alien invasion in progress. This report seems to consist of two hoaxes. There was the initial hoax of the program and then the follow-up hoax of the report of widespread panic. Later analysis shows that many people were not listening to the program, many who were listening recognized it as a radio play, and very few were convinced it was an actual news story. Yet, today the public consciousness is that many people fled their homes out of fear, a hoax perpetuated by news sources at the time that sensationalized the event.

Though many people believe in hoaxes, there have also been instances where empirically supported events were believed to be hoaxes. For example, segments of the population claim that the moon landing was a hoax, climate change is a hoax, and even COVID-19 is a hoax. All of these events have empirical support but some doubters are motivated by personal reasons, such as not wanting to change behaviors, and others have fallen victim to persuasive fake news sources that reject empirical science. Political groups may sow seeds of doubt to support their own platforms or to further their own agendas. For example, conservative political sponsors have published 90 percent of books discrediting or questioning climate change, and tobacco companies attempted to discredit the role of smoking in lung cancer.

See also: Conspiracy Theories; Fact-Check; Fake News; Fraud; Hwang Woo-Suk; Lightfoot, Lucy; Loch Ness Monster; Piltdown Man; Scams.

Further Reading

Darnton, J. (1994). Loch Ness: Fiction is stranger than truth. *The New York Times.* Retrieved from https://www.nytimes.com/1994/03/20/weekinreview/loch-ness-fiction-is-stranger -than-truth.html

Lewandowsky, S., Oberauer, K., & Gignac, G. E. (2013). NASA faked the moon landing— Therefore, (climate) science is a hoax: An Anatomy of the motivated rejection of science. *Psychological Science, 24*(5), 622–633.

Memmott, M. (2013). 75 years ago, 'War of the Worlds' started a panic. Or did it? *NPR.* Retrieved from https://www.npr.org/sections/thetwo-way/2013/10/30/241797346 /75-years-ago-war-of-the-worlds-started-a-panic-or-did-it

Pavid, K. (2016, August 10). Piltdown man hoax findings: Charles Dawson the likely fraudster. *Natural History Museum.* Retrieved from https://www.nhm.ac.uk /discover/news/2016/august/piltdown-man-charles-dawson-likely-fraudster.html

Honesty (See Ethics)

Hwang Woo-Suk

Hwang Woo-Suk was a South Korean professor and researcher who claimed to make revolutionary strides in stem cell research and human cloning. His work, which later became known as the Korean cloning scandal, was published in *Science* in 2004 and 2005. He reported successful creation of human embryonic stem cells by cloning. At the height of his popularity, Professor Hwang was featured on postage stamps, and posters of him with promotional text such as "the scientist who changed the world" could be found on public transportation throughout South Korea.

By 2006, it was revealed that much of his research had been fake, and his scientific publications were retracted. His scientific work was also plagued with unethical practices such as lying about the source of egg donations for his experimentation. Though he claimed to not know that his assistant had donated the eggs, it was later discovered that he personally accompanied her to the hospital for the extraction. His work was ultimately considered to be fraud, and it was discovered that the data had been intentionally fabricated for both of his revolutionary publications. He also embezzled almost three million dollars of his research funds and was charged with embezzlement.

In his 2005 article, Professor Hwang claimed to have cloned 11 human embryonic stem cell lines. Upon closer analysis, researchers discovered that the data had been fabricated. After this discovery, the 2004 article, in which Professor Hwang claimed to have established the first human embryonic stem cell line, was examined more closely, and DNA fingerprinting analyses on the samples revealed that the cell lines were not derived as Professor Hwang claimed. Examiners ultimately concluded that the analyses, data, and photographs of cells in the 2004 article had also been fabricated.

Fraud cases such as the Korean cloning scandal raise the issue of the problem of fabrication and exaggeration within scientific research. Given the lack of oversight of international research, this case provides evidence that inaccurate or fabricated scientific claims can be made and published without validation. Such acts call for improvements in scientific practice, communication, and oversight. Researchers Dr. Rhodri Saunders and Dr. Julian Savulescu from the University of Oxford suggest that improvement in practices could include such things as more rigorous education of science students, more monitoring and validation of research findings, stricter guidelines and oversight of tissue donation, and development of an international code of ethical practice. Lack of validation, oversight, and replication can lead to fraudulent claims of scientific findings that can mislead the scientific community at an international level.

Since research typically requires external funding, falsifying, plagiarizing, or withholding results can be motivated by the need to maintain sponsorship. A survey of researchers at the National Institute of Health revealed that 1.5 percent of the researchers admitted to falsifying, altering, or plagiarizing data. Publication in prestigious journals can secure and maintain funding, potentially increasing the pressure to exaggerate or creatively interpret research findings. Thus, deception in research publications is something that must be closely monitored, and education, guidelines, and funding practices may need reevaluation to maintain the structure and expectation of honesty in research.

See also: Academic Cheating; Deception in Research; Ethics; Fraud; Motives for Lying; Plagiarism.

Further Reading

Check, E., & Cyranoski, D. (2005). Korean scandal will have global fallout. *Nature, 438*, 1056–1057.

Hwang, W. S., Roh, S. I., Lee, B. C., Kang, S. K., Kwon, D. K., Kim, S., Kim, S. J., Park, S. W., Kwon, H. S., Lee, C. K., Lee, J.B., Kim, J. M., Ahn, C., Paek, S.H., Chang, S. S., Koo, J. J., Yoon, H. S., Hwang, J. H., Hwang, Y. Y., . . . Schatten, G. (2005). Patient-specific embryonic stem cells derived from human SCNT blastocysts. *Science, 308*, 1777–1783.

Hwang, W. S., Ryu, Y. J., Park, J. H., Park, E. S., Lee, E. G., Koo, J. M., Jeon, H. Y., Lee, B. C., Kang, S. K., Kim, S. J., Ahn, C., Hwang, J. H., Park, K. Y., Cibelli, J. B., & Moon, S. Y. (2004). Evidence of a pluripotent human embryonic stem cell line derived from a cloned blastocyst. *Science, 303*, 1669–1674.

Myung-hee, C. (2006). *Summary of the final report on Hwang's research allegation.* Retrieved from https://web.archive.org/web/20060117034101/http://www.snu.ac.kr:6060/sc_sne_b/news/1196178_3497.html

Saunders, R., & Savulescu, J. (2008). Research ethics and lessons from Hwanggate: What can we learn from the Korean cloning fraud? *Journal of Medical Ethics, 34*, 214–221.

Hypocrisy

Hypocrisy is the act of claiming to hold certain values but then engaging in contraindicated behaviors. One who engages in hypocrisy may publicly condemn others' behaviors while engaging in those same behaviors in private. In psychological research, between 90 and 100 percent of individuals admitted to engaging in hypocritical behavior. Not all hypocrisy is intentional. Some hypocritical behaviors are a by-product of self-deception. People in positions of power are most likely to engage in hypocritical behavior, but hypocritical behavior can be an issue in personal relationships as well.

Leaders may engage in hypocrisy as a result of attempting to set high ideals for a population or to maintain their reputation or social position. In such circumstances, leaders may set high expectations and purposefully condemn behaviors that are unpopular or immoral to maintain a public persona for garnering respect or power. However, it is much easier to set ideals and ethical standards than it is to consistently meet such standards. Thus, professing intentions and beliefs may represent a goal, whereas behavior may not always rise to expectations.

Hypocrisy can also result from self-deception. To maintain one's self-esteem or self-concept, one may publicly condemn certain behaviors or beliefs and yet find rationalizations or justifications after engaging in those exact behaviors in private. Individuals, for example, may publicly condemn infidelity but then be exposed for being unfaithful. To maintain a sense of consistency, these individuals need either to change their beliefs about infidelity or find excuses to justify the behavior. Justifications allow the individual to rationalize and minimize their own behavior to alleviate cognitive dissonance associated with the mismatch between their behavior and their professed beliefs.

Because of this tendency to rationalize one's own behaviors, people are often forgiving of lapses in their own behavior while harshly judging the behaviors of others. The fundamental attribution error describes this tendency to condemn others for their behaviors and blame the individual rather than the situation. For oneself, however, one is more likely to blame environmental influences for behaviors and less likely to take ownership of one's own immoral actions.

Dr. Honghong Tang, Dr. Shun Wang, and their colleagues from Beijing, China, found that individuals who are more concerned with the appearance of moral goodness and apparent fairness tend to engage in greater hypocrisy. These individuals are more likely to resort to self-deception and impression management to protect their own self-image. Those who are oriented toward behaving in prosocial ways and who are more concerned about increasing actual fairness rather than just the perception of fairness tend to engage in less hypocrisy. Research findings on hypocrisy also vary cross-culturally. People in collectivist cultures are less likely to engage in hypocrisy and are more likely to be prosocial and ethical in their behavior. Comparatively, people in individualistic cultures are more likely to attempt to maintain a more positive self-image by professing prosocial beliefs in public yet engaging in hypocritical behavior in private.

Hypocritical behavior is often hard to confront. When people engage in behaviors that do not align with their professed beliefs, they rationalize or justify the behavior and look upon it as an exception rather than a general trend. Therefore, confronting hypocritical behavior is frequently met with excuses or justifications. Individuals interested in confronting their own hypocritical behavior must look at situational effects as well as their own thought processes. Hypocritical behavior is often rewarding because if it goes undetected one receives benefits while still maintaining a positive public image. However, repeated hypocritical behavior can be damaging to one's own self-esteem and self-concept, as well as one's reputation if discovered.

Owning one's own failings and acknowledging deficits may be one way to exonerate oneself from negative effects of engaging in hypocritical behavior. Hypocrites who acknowledge their indiscretions tend to be perceived positively though they are committing the exact transgressions that they condemn. They are even viewed more positively than individuals who commit the transgressions without condemning them. Likely, this combination of beliefs and behavior communicates to others that the individual knows that the behaviors are immoral, and therefore, they are viewed positively for acknowledging that they made a mistake.

See also: Cognitive Dissonance; Ethics; Lying to Children; Machiavellianism; Minimization; Politics; Self-Deception.

Further Reading

Batson, C. D., Thompson, E. R., Seuferling, G., Whitney, H., & Strongman, J. A. (1999). Moral hypocrisy: Appearing moral to oneself without being so. *Journal of Personality and Social Psychology, 77*, 525–537.

Hertz, S. G., & Krettenauer, T. (2016). Does Moral identity effectively project Moral behavior?: A meta-analysis. *Review of General Psychology, 20*(2), 129–140.

Jordan, J. J., Sommers, R., Bloom, P., & Rand, D. G. (2017). Why do we hate hypocrites? Evidence for a theory of false signaling. *Psychological Science, 28*(3), 356–368.

Kris, A. O. (2005). The lure of hypocrisy. *Journal of the American Psychoanalytic Association, 53*(1), 7–22.

Lönnqvist, J.-E., Irlenbusch, B., & Walkowitz, G. (2014). Moral hypocrisy: Impression management or self-deception? *Journal of Experimental Social Psychology, 55*, 53–62.

Tang, H., Wang, S., Liang, Z., Sinnott-Armstrong, W., Su, S., & Liu, C. (2018). Are proselfs more deceptive and hypocritical? Social image concerns in appearing fair. *Frontiers in Psychology, 9*, 2268.

I

Identity Theft (See Impersonator; Scams)

Impersonator

An impersonator is an individual who pretends to be someone else. This facade can be covert or overt. For example, some individuals earn money by impersonating others for entertainment purposes. Celebrity impersonators dress and act like celebrities and earn a living entertaining others. In this circumstance, the impersonation is overt, and no one is fooled by the impersonator. Observers are aware that it is an act simply for fun. However, impersonators can also imitate others deceptively to gain an advantage. This type of impersonation frequently falls under criminal behavior and can include identity theft and fraud. Typically, these individuals have the objective of gaining a financial or social advantage at the expense of another and assume a false identity for means of deception.

History is peppered with all types of impersonators. There have been individuals who have attempted to impersonate specific individuals to gain an advantage, such as Anna Anderson who claimed to be the Grand Duchess Anastasia Romanov and Cassie Chadwick who claimed to be Andrew Carnegie's illegitimate daughter. Other individuals have claimed a false nationality, claimed to belong to a minority group to gain an advantage, or feigned expertise on a subject. In times of war, spies impersonate the enemy to gain access to information or individuals. Con artists use impersonation tactics to swindle their targets. Impersonators online may take over accounts, steal personal information, and use impersonation to target victims. These impostors use scams to get what they want. Some people pose as the IRS to try to solicit money or information, some may imitate tech support or pose as companies awarding prizes to try to get personal information, or some pose as friends asking for favors.

Con artists are particularly savvy at impersonation tactics. They try to inspire confidence and legitimacy to get what they want. They may use time pressure, scams, or charisma to cheat people out of money or information. Con artists steal up to $50 billion in the United States each year, and with modern technology, this number is rising. With the number of impersonators online, it is becoming more and more difficult to distinguish between legitimate offers and scams. Consumers must become more cautious to avoid being taken advantage of. Impersonators tend to work to elicit emotions so that the target is not thinking logically. They may do so by making limited time offers that require quick decisions, making offers that seem too good to be true, and posing as someone the target knows well.

Though impersonators typically engage in the behavior purposefully, there is a psychological phenomenon known as imposter syndrome in which an individual feels like an impersonator, even when they are not. This phenomenon typically affects high-achieving women or individuals from minority groups who do not feel as though they deserve the success that they have achieved. These individuals feel as though they are deceiving others and have a persistent fear that they will be exposed as a fraud. This is a common experience for new PhD graduates who believe that those around them have had more experience and are more intelligent and that they do not deserve the degree or jobs they have earned.

Those who are experiencing imposter syndrome tend to believe that their success is due to luck and that they are faking their professional standing. Frequently, such individuals feel guilty about their own success, particularly if they are in the minority for their field. They tend to have a hard time accepting compliments and do not feel qualified, even when they are an expert. Surprisingly, about 70 percent of individuals feel this way at some point during their professional career. Imposter syndrome occurs more often in individuals who have been overprotected as youth, have low self-esteem, are anxious or depressed, or have a high level of perfectionistic tendencies. These individuals are not imposters or impersonators; they just feel like they are. To overcome such feelings, it is important to identify the experience and recognize it as normal. Next, it is important to recognize and celebrate successes and be mindful of personal achievements and goals, as well as skills that still need improvement. Many of these individuals experience a sensation of "fake it 'til you make it," and it takes time to build up the repertoire of experience to feel legitimate.

See also: Anderson, Anna; Catfishing; Chadwick, Cassie; Charlatans; Clickbait; Espionage; Fraud; Hoax; Phishing; Scams.

Further Reading

Miller, A. (2013). Outsmarting con artists. *Monitor on Psychology*. American Psychological Association. Retrieved from https://www.apa.org/monitor/2013/02/con-artists

Sakulku, J., & Alexander, J. (2011). The imposter phenomenon. *International Journal of Behavioral Science, 6*(1), 73–92.

Imposter Syndrome (See Impersonator)

Infidelity

The most common definition of infidelity is engaging in sexual intercourse with someone other than one's committed partner. In the United States, about 20 percent of married individuals engage in sexual infidelity. Additionally, about 70 percent of unmarried individuals report committing or experiencing sexual infidelity in a past relationship. Infidelity is the most commonly reported reason for divorce, is correlated with domestic violence and homicide rates, and is one of the most difficult topics of conversation in couples therapy.

Infidelity can also refer to emotional engagement outside of a committed relationship. Emotional infidelity is having romantic feelings for another person and spending time with, sharing secrets, cuddling, or flirting with someone at the exclusion of one's partner. Dr. Amanda Guitar from State University of New York and her colleagues across the United States and Canada examined the different types of infidelity in long-term relationships. Though their study revealed that individuals view both sexual and emotional infidelity as problematic for relationships, evolutionary psychologist Dr. David Buss, from the University of Texas at Austin, discovered that men and women view the types of infidelity differently. On average, women are more concerned and distressed by emotional infidelity, whereas men are more upset by sexual infidelity.

These differences in attitudes toward infidelity are likely linked to differences in sex roles. Women tend to bear the brunt of child rearing, so they benefit from a stable, reliable partner. If their partner is emotionally unfaithful, it is likely he may leave and withdraw resources or provide resources to another partner. Men, alternatively, have more concerns about paternity. A partner's sexual infidelity is more distressing because it could result in cuckoldry. Accordingly, women are more likely to endorse forgiving or working through sexual infidelity, particularly if their partner is apologetic, but are less likely to forgive emotional infidelity. Men, on the other hand, are more likely to forgive or overlook emotional infidelity, but on discovering sexual infidelity, they tend to end the relationship.

Dr. Kayla Knopp and colleagues from the University of Denver found that individuals who engage in infidelity, experienced infidelity in a previous relationship, or suspected unfaithfulness were significantly more likely to experience those same behaviors in future relationships. Those who engage in sexual infidelity are three times more likely to engage in such activity in a subsequent relationship. Additionally, those whose partners cheated on them in a previous relationship were twice as likely to have a subsequent partner who also engaged in infidelity and four times as likely to suspect infidelity in future partners. Thus, knowing a partner's previous relationship practices may indicate likely future behavior.

Insecure individuals are more likely to lie, cheat, and engage in infidelity and more likely to detect cues of infidelity than secure individuals. Insecure individuals are more likely to be defensive, more careful, and observant of partner's behaviors due to heightened suspicion and negative experiences such as previous abuse or unfaithfulness. Insecure individuals are more likely to suffer from anxiety, are more worried about being abandoned, and are more likely to detect threats such as infidelity.

Those who rate high on traits of Machiavellianism are also more likely to engage in infidelity. These individuals are more likely to engage in sex to improve their social status, get revenge, and to buffer self-esteem. They use sex for gain rather than to build intimacy and are more likely to engage in infidelity for personal benefits. They are more likely to lie to a partner, engage in sex to gain power or avoid confrontation with a partner, and tend to engage in risky behaviors. They also engage in more deception in relationships, lack empathy for their partner's feelings, and have confidence that they will not be caught.

See also: Betrayal; Detecting Deception; Evolution of Deception; Machiavellianism; Personality; Romantic Relationships; Sex Differences in Lying Behavior.

Further Reading

Brewer, G., & Abell, L. (2015). Machiavellianism and sexual behavior: Motivations, deception and infidelity. *Personality and Individual Differences, 74,* 186–191.

Buss, D. M., Larsen, R. J., Westen, D., & Semmelroth, J. (1992). Sex differences in jealousy: Evolution, physiology, and psychology. *Psychological Science, 3*(4), 251–255.

Buss, D. M., Shackelford, T. K., Kirkpatrick, L. A., Choe, J. C., Lim, H. K., Hasegawa, M., Hasegawa, T., & Bennett, K. (1999). Jealousy and beliefs about infidelity: Tests of competing hypotheses in the United States, Korea, and Japan. *Personal Relationships, 6,* 125–150.

Ein-Dor, T., Perry-Paldi, A., Zohar-Cohen, K., Efrati, Y., & Hirschberger, G. (2017). It takes an insecure liar to catch a liar: The link between attachment insecurity, deception, and detection of deception. *Personality and Individual Differences, 113,* 81–87.

Guitar, A. E., Geher, G., Kruger, D. J., Garcia, J. R., Fisher, M. L., & Fitzgerald, C. J. (2017). Defining and distinguishing sexual and emotional infidelity. *Current Psychology, 36,* 434–446.

Knopp, K., Scott, S., Ritchie, L., Rhoades, G. K., Markman, H. J., & Stanley, S. M. (2017). Once a cheater, always a cheater? Serial infidelity across subsequent relationships. *Archives of Sexual Behavior, 46*(8), 2301–2311.

Instrumental Lies

Instrumental lies are those lies that are motivated by selfish concerns rather than regard for others. The use of instrumental lies tends to emerge early in development, and the first instrumental lies tend to be defensive rather than strategic. Young children tell instrumental lies when they attempt to deny their own behaviors to avoid punishments or to gain a material reward. Over development, instrumental lies become less frequent, though more strategic. Instrumental lies can be used to avoid consequences, secure benefits, persuade others, and change how one is perceived by others.

Dr. Jennifer Lavoie from McGill University and her colleagues asked parents to keep track of their children's lying behaviors. From this research, three main categories of lying behavior emerged. The first category was instrumental lies, which were lies most commonly told to avoid a task or obtain a reward. The second category was antisocial lies, which were lies used to avoid punishment, blame others, or protect the self. The final category was occasional and relational lies, which includes those lies that tend to be more socially acceptable or told for prosocial means.

The youngest children in Dr. Lavoie's study were the most likely to tell instrumental lies. These lies were spontaneous and defensive, used to gain a tangible reward or avoid punishment. They correlated with immature theory of mind abilities. As theory of mind abilities developed, children were likely to use more strategic instrumental and occasional lies. Children with underdeveloped theory of mind skills were also the ones who were most likely to tell antisocial lies. Overall, lying tends to decrease over healthy development, and occasional and prosocial lies emerge as more common than antisocial and instrumental lies. With age, there is also an emergence of relational lies, which serve to protect relationships with others, and identity lies, which serve to preserve one's own self-image. Some of these lies may be instrumental in the sense that the individuals are motivated to protect their relationships and image and to lie to achieve that goal.

Another common use of instrumental lies is as a bargaining tool when attempting to convince others to cooperate. Parents, for example, may use instrumental lies to encourage behavioral compliance. Such lies may include telling uncooperative children that the parent will leave without them or threatening a punishment or outcome that is unrealistic in order to garner cooperation. Instrumental lies may be told to encourage children to eat healthy food, to cooperate with chores or tasks, or to prevent spending money. In this sense, parents use lying behavior to achieve parenting goals.

Such intentional instrumental lies may also be used as bargaining techniques in the business world to achieve strategic business goals when negotiating. This instrumental deception may include lies, bluffs, and exaggerations about one's position or aim in order to convince others to concede, cooperate, or align with one's position. Using deception during negotiations can damage one's reputation if the deception is detected; therefore, many individuals, especially in high-stakes situations, will likely avoid such deception if possible.

See also: Age Differences; Bluffs; Categories of Deception; Development of Deception; Exaggeration; Lying; Lying to Children; Prosocial Lying; Theory of Mind.

Further Reading

Daly, J. A., & Wiemann, J. M. (2009). *Strategic Interpersonal Communication.* Psychology Press.

Heyman, G. D., Hsu, A. S., Fu, G., & Lee, K. (2013). Instrumental lying by parents in the US and China. *International Journal of Psychology, 48*(6), 1176–1184.

Koning, L., van Dijk, E., van Beest, I., & Steinel, W. (2010). An instrumental account of deception and reactions to deceit in bargaining. *Business Ethics Quarterly, 20*(1), 57–73.

Lavoie, J., Leduc, K., Arruda, C., Crossman, A. M., & Talwar, V. (2017). Developmental profiles of children's spontaneous lie-telling behavior. *Cognitive Development, 41*, 33–45.

Intelligence

General intelligence, or one's ability to learn, understand, and apply new information, is positively correlated with deceptive ability, although negatively correlated with deceptive attempts. Since effective deception relies on a diverse array of executive functions, those with superior cognitive abilities are more likely to be successful when attempting to deceive others. Specifically, higher scores on tests of verbal fluency and speed of processing positively correlate with effective deceptive behavior.

Individuals who are more intelligent may also feel more confident in their abilities to successfully manipulate the beliefs of others and thus show fewer signs of anxiety or self-consciousness during the deceptive attempt. They may also more readily recognize the benefits of deceptive behavior in specific situations and thus engage in more selective deception to achieve particular goals. However, although individuals with high scores on tests of intelligence are more effective at deceiving others, they do not tend to use deception as frequently as those who score lower on tests of intelligence. High scorers display more confidence when telling the truth and are more likely to have an internal locus of control, admit to errors, find tactful ways to address uncomfortable topics, or work to find honest solutions to problems.

Those individuals who score low on tests of intelligence are less effective at successfully deceiving others but are more likely to engage in deceptive attempts. In general, less intelligent individuals are more likely to look to others for guidance, directions, or support and are more likely to lie to conform to expectations. This is particularly salient in children who are under pressure from adults to meet expectations beyond their ability levels. These children learn to cover for deficits by lying about behavior, beliefs, and intentions or by cheating. Thus, while those who score higher on tests of intelligence are more likely to deceive successfully, lower scorers are more likely to feel as though they need to deceive.

Level of emotional intelligence is also highly correlated with deceptive behavior. Emotional intelligence is the specific ability to perceive, understand, and regulate one's own emotions as well as the emotions of others. High scores on measures of emotional intelligence are linked to better physical and emotional health, as well as academic and occupational success. High emotional intelligence is also correlated with increased ability to fake emotions and persist in deceptive displays. Thus, those who score high on measures of emotional intelligence and high on measures of cognitive intelligence have the highest ability to successfully deceive, though they tend to use deceptive attempts less frequently than those with low scores. Those who score low on measures of emotional intelligence are more likely to try to deceive others, even though their attempts tend to be less successful. Low scorers tend to be more vulnerable to the impact of negative emotions, experience more internalizing problems and stress, and are more likely to use deceptive attempts to regulate or avoid these negative emotions or interactions.

Though emotionally intelligent people have been found to be more influential liars due to an enhanced ability to regulate, display, and maintain emotional facial expressions, they actually tend to be less effective at detecting deception, particularly for emotionally-charged lies. Dr. Alysha Baker and colleagues from the Centre for the Advancement of Psychological Science and Law at the University of British Columbia examined the relationship between emotional intelligence and deception detection. They found that emotionally intelligent people tended to be overconfident in their assessments of sincerity and more likely to sympathize with emotional displays, even those displays that were later revealed to be deceptive. The emotional intelligence that sets these individuals apart actually clouded their decision-making process when judging the accuracy of emotionally charged pleas. Thus, those with a heightened ability to perceive and express emotions struggled to look past the emotional displays to detect deception, particularly for emotionally-charged lies.

See also: Detecting Deception; Emotional Effects; Facial Cues; Locus of Control; Personality.

Further Reading

Baker, A., ten Brinke, L., & Porter, S. (2012). Will get fooled again: Emotionally intelligent people are easily duped by high-stakes deceivers. *Legal and Criminological Psychology, 18*, 300–313.

Davis, S. K., & Nichols, R. (2016). Does emotional intelligence have a "dark" side? A review of the literature. *Personality and Social Psychology, 7*(1316), 1–10.

Sarzynska, J., Falkiewicz, M., Riegel, M., Babula, J., Margulies, D. S., Necka, E., Grabowska, A., & Szatkowska, I. (2017). More intelligent extraverts are more likely to deceive. *PLoS ONE, 12*(4), 1–17.

Schindler, W. J. (1975). *Locus of control and intelligence as predictors of overt lying behavior in nine through thirteen year old children not under and under expectancy pressure* (Unpublished doctoral dissertation). Kent State University, Kent, OH.

L

Language

Which words a liar chooses to use may be a key in decoding deception. Researchers have proposed several models of language use that may help detect deceptive attempts. Two such models include the Cognitive Strain Model and the Strategic Model. Furthermore, Dr. James W. Pennebaker, a social psychologist and professor of psychology at the University of Texas at Austin has revealed consistent differences in the content of deceptive statements as compared to honest reports using his Linguistic Inquiry and Word Count (LIWC) software. Deceptive statements tend to differ in pronoun use, use of emotion words, and use of words that indicate level of cognitive complexity.

The Cognitive Strain Model suggests that language is already a complex process, and anything that adds to our cognitive load will decrease the complexity of our speech. Thus, when people attempt to deceive others, the complexity of language decreases due to the increased cognitive load needed to create a false reality. In a host of psychological experiments, individuals who were instructed to lie used fewer descriptive words and more concrete verbs that revealed more simplistic thinking. The cognitive resources needed to lie convincingly took away from the resources needed to engage in complex linguistic communication.

Alternatively, the Strategic Model suggests the liars use complexity or simplicity in a strategic manner and vary their speech depending on what will be most effective in the given situation. Individuals in a psychological experiment decreased complexity when discussing alternative viewpoints but increased complexity when elaborating on the viewpoint about which they were lying. When attempting to deceive a naive individual, liars tended to use less complex language. When attempting to deceive a suspicious individual, however, liars used more complex language.

To examine lying in real-world scenarios, researchers analyzed past political speeches from John F. Kennedy and Richard Nixon. When lying, these politicians used more elaborative complexity but less logical reasoning. These same patterns were found when analyzing university students, providing evidence that the Strategic Model may be a better descriptor of the language of lying, at least when the liars have time to prepare their statements. Liars who have prepared their lies in advance rely less on immediate cognitive resources, whereas liars who must create their lies in real time may experience greater cognitive strain.

To analyze language use, Dr. Pennebaker developed the Linguistic Inquiry and Word Count (LIWC) software. The LIWC software is a text analysis program used to examine oral and written statements to search for differences in language use in honest versus deceptive communication. Use of the software revealed that deceptive attempts include very specific patterns that differ from honest accounts. Liars express more negative emotion words, particularly anger and denial, than truth-tellers. Liars also distance themselves more from the events being discussed by using fewer first-person pronouns and self-references than truth-tellers. Finally, liars refer less often to cognitive processes than truth-tellers and use fewer exclusionary words and more motion verbs, illustrating lower complexity in their speech. However, liars expressed the same level of certainty as truth-tellers. These findings were influenced by type of event, level of involvement, emotional intensity, level of interaction, and motivation. Overall, use of the LIWC software could significantly increase the ability to detect deception, simply based on analysis of language use.

In general, liars must carefully monitor their word choice to convey the most convincing message. Liars must choose their words carefully, conceal information they do not wish to convey, and make sure their verbal communication sounds smooth and natural to make their lie sound believable. Due to these concerns, spontaneous liars tend to be less willing to elaborate, less at ease, and less convincing than those who are telling the truth. These strategic and complicated needs influence the content of their reports, and although it may be difficult to detect in everyday conversation, computer programs can detect the aberrations in the content of the message. In line with the reality monitoring theory, descriptions of real events contain more perceptual and temporal events, whereas fabricated events are described in a more cognitive or conceptual way.

The capacity for complex language sets humans apart from any other species. Our ability to use language goes beyond what we need for simple, honest communication. Our tendency to lie may have been the driving force for the complexity of our language abilities. The need to decode deceptive attempts may have contributed to an evolutionary arms race that drove the complexity of cognition, language, emotions, and social capacities over time. This feedback loop likely re-enforces, directs, and shapes our cognitive abilities. Therefore, although we may perceive lying as a negative by-product of language, it likely contributed to the complexity of our modern language abilities. Deception research provides a unique vantage point to understand our cognitive potential.

See also: Detecting Deception; Evolution of Deception; Linguistic Inquiry and Word Count Analysis Program; Lying; Models of Lying; Motives for Lying; Nonverbal Behavior; Reaction Time; Reality Monitoring; Theory of Mind.

Further Reading

Dor, D. (2017). The role of the lie in the evolution of human language. *Language Sciences, 63*, 44–59.

Etcoff, N. L., Ekman, P., Magee, J. J., & Frank, M. G. (2000). Lie detection and language comprehension: People who can't understand words are better at picking up lies about emotions. *Nature, 405*, 139.

Hauch, V., Blandon-Gitlin, I., Massig, J., & Sporer, S. L. (2015). Are computers effective lie detectors? A meta-analysis of linguistic cues to deception. *Personality and Social Psychology Review, 19*(4), 307–342.

Newman, M. L., Pennebaker, J. W., Berry, D. S., & Richards, J. M. (2003). Lying words: Predicting deception from linguistic style. *Personality and Social Psychology Bulletin, 29*, 665–675.

Pennebaker, J. W., Francis, M. E., & Booth, R. J. (2001). *Linguistic Inquiry and Word Count: LIWC 2001*. Lawrence Erlbaum.

Repke, M. A., Conway, L. G., III, & Houck, S. C. (2018). The strategic manipulation of linguistic complexity: A test of two models of lying. *Journal of Language and Social Psychology, 37*(1), 74–92.

Libel (See Defamation)

Lie Detector Tests (See Polygraph Tests)

Liespotting (See Meyer, Pamela)

Lightfoot, Lucy

On June 13, 1831, at age 16, Lucy Lightfoot was seen tethering her horse at the gateway to St. Olave's Church on the Isle of Wight and entering the church. Lucy was reportedly enamored by a statue of Edward Estur, a knight of the Crusades, that was housed in the church. The legend claims that she spent a lot of time with his statue and spun wild stories about accompanying him on his adventures. On this day in June, a total eclipse of the sun as well as a violent thunderstorm drove Lucy to seek refuge at St. Olave's. Following the storm, her terrified horse was found still tethered to the gate, but Lucy was never seen again. For the next two years, her family searched for her, but no evidence of her whereabouts was found. However, when the effigy was examined, it was noted that a jewel from the dagger had gone missing.

Over 100 years later, Reverend James Evans, vicar of St. Olave's church, presented evidence unearthed by Reverend Samuel Trelawny back in 1865 that provided an explanation of Lucy's whereabouts. Reverend Evans presented documentation that Reverend Trelawny had discovered a manuscript dating back to the last Crusades. In the manuscript, three knights were credited for defeating Alexandria in 1365. One of the knights described in the manuscript was Edward Estur. In the description of his achievements, it was reported that he was accompanied by a beautiful girl from the Isle of Wight named Lucy Lightfoot. The document reported that Lucy Lightfoot was the one who presented the knight with a jewel that he always wore in his sword hilt.

Based on the information in this manuscript, investigators proposed that the electrical storm on the day of Lucy's disappearance may have induced a slip through time. This fantastical explanation caught public fancy and became the most prominent explanation of her disappearance. Upon the report of the discovery of the manuscripts, the story spread quickly, and it was published in numerous magazines and books. Such stories gave an explanation to locals about Lucy's disappearance. However, the manuscript that James Evans claimed was found was never seen by anyone else. Years later, Reverend Evans admitted to creating the hoax. As Vicar of St. Olave's, he claimed that the story was meant to be fanciful and to attract interest and raise funds for the church, but was taken far more seriously than intended.

Mark Wightman more recently investigated the story of Lucy Lightfoot's disappearance. With a little research, he discovered that there had not been a total eclipse over the island on the day of the disappearance as reported in the legend. Upon visiting the island, he found that the church and the effigy of Edward Estur were described accurately in the story. However, he saw no evidence of a damaged dagger that was featured in the legend. He ultimately began correspondence with Reverend Evans. Reverend Evans admitted that he had taken some historical reports and combined them with local legends to create an imaginative history. Reverend Evans' story had been written in such a convincing manner and peppered with historical facts that it made it convincing deceit. As research in deception shows, convoluting fact with fiction makes deceptive attempts much more believable. Having facts that can be verified makes the unverifiable details more convincing, even when they are unlikely.

Regardless of whether Reverend Evans intended to perpetrate this hoax, it was tied sparingly enough to reality to catch the imagination of the world. The legend of Lucy Lightfoot still inspires movies, music, and novels into the modern day.

See also: Hoax; Loch Ness Monster; Piltdown Man; Suspension of Disbelief.

Further Reading

The Legend of Lucy Lightfoot. Retrieved from http://www.insula.vecta.btinternet.co.uk/LucyLightfoot.html

Muller, A. J. (1999). For the love of Lucy. *In Front Magazine*. Retrieved from https://web.archive.org/web/20080313174321/http://www.r-l-p.co.uk/Lucy.html

Stares, C. (2015). Mystery of Lucy Lightfoot. *The Guardian*. Retrieved from https://www.theguardian.com/environment/2015/feb/10/country-diary-isle-of-wight

Wightman, M. (1988). *Lucy Lightfoot—Myths become legends*. Retrieved from http://www.iowrock.demon.co.uk/clearspot/lucy_mark.html

Linguistic Inquiry and Word Count Analysis Program

The Linguistic Inquiry and Word Count (LIWC) analysis program was developed by Dr. James W. Pennebaker, a social psychologist and professor of psychology at the University of Texas at Austin. The initial purpose of the program was to analyze spoken transcriptions, interviews, emails, speeches, or other communications to examine the connection between language use and health, behavior, and personality. The program categorizes word usage into different predetermined grammatical, psychological, and content categories. Using those categories, the program classifies the communications along psychological dimensions with the purpose of predicting behavioral outcomes. By creating a baseline of typical communication characteristics, the LIWC program can then use those base rates for comparison when analyzing individuals suspected of deception, with mental health issues, or other groups of interest.

Dr. Pennebaker's LIWC program has been used to analyze the language of Al-Qaeda leaders and political candidates with relatively high rates of predictive success. Dr. Pennebaker has found that the specific words individuals use when making a claim are predictive of future behavior regardless of the claim itself. His program has demonstrated the ability to identify deception better than a listener trained to detect deception.

The speech analysis includes a breakdown of the number of words, words per sentence, questions, unique words, first-person pronouns, second- and third-person pronouns, negations, assents, articles, prepositions, and numbers in a communication sample. The program identifies affective communications including those words that represent positive emotions and those that represent negative emotions. It analyzes cognitive processes such as words that refer to causation, insight, inhibition, and tentativeness. It also indicates words that refer to sensory and perceptual processes such as seeing, hearing, and feeling, as well as words that refer to social processes. These include words that refer to communication, friends, and family. It also identifies words that refer to time, space, and motion and provides data on words that reflect personal concerns such as those that refer to occupations, leisure activities, financial issues, physical issues, and physical state. Finally it shows the number of swear words and fillers.

Examination of honest statements provides a baseline for typical word usage for honest speakers. This baseline is then used to analyze the content of verbal statements from potentially deceptive speakers. Since its invention, the LIWC has been used to analyze verbal and written reports in order to detect deceptive statements of individuals ranging from political leaders to individuals who have created online dating profiles. In general, the LIWC revealed that when engaging in deceptive attempts, individuals tend to show lower cognitive complexity in their word choice and use fewer first-person pronouns. They tend to avoid statements that connect them to the content of the lie. They likely do this to distance themselves from the content of their story. They also use more negative descriptors of affect such as *hate*, *don't like*, and *bad*. The LIWC can detect significant differences of language use between honest speakers and deceptive speakers at higher rates than a human judge, including interrogation experts.

The topic of the conversation also plays a role. Communications that are about personal experiences tend to have different linguistic patterns than those about topics from which one is more detached. If someone is communicating a personal topic in which they are distancing themselves (using few self-references), avoiding responsibility, and using negative emotion words or words with lower cognitive complexity, this provides an indication that the communications are not honest. One of the keys for detecting deception, therefore, may be to attend to how a communication is phrased rather than its overall meaning, and analysis of word choice could be combined with analysis of nonverbal signals of deception for more accurate deception detection.

Use of the LIWC is based on the theory that one can learn a lot about others' motivations by attending to the words they use to communicate rather than the overall meaning of their statements. Even those skilled at lying may show leakage that is reflected in their word use. Linguistic styles such as use of pronouns, words reflecting emotions, and fillers that signal cognitive effort can be linked to particular motivations, including the motivation to deceive.

See also: Behavior Analysis Interview; Detecting Deception; Language; Nonverbal Behavior; Polygraph Tests; Reality Monitoring.

Further Reading

Chung, C. K., & Pennebaker, J. (2011). Linguistic inquiry and word count (LIWC): Pronounced "Luke,"… and other useful facts. In *Applied Natural Language Processing: Identification, Investigation and Resolution* (pp. 206–229). IGI Global. https://doi.org/10.4018/978-1-60960-741-8.ch012

Newman, M. L., Pennebaker, J. W., Berry, D. S., & Richards, J. M. (2003). Lying words: Predicting deception from linguistic styles. *Personality and Social Psychology Bulletin, 29*(5), 665–675.

Pennebaker, J. W., Francis, M. E., & Booth, R. J. (1999). *Linguistic inquiry and word count (LIWC)*. Erlbaum.

Loch Ness Monster

The Loch Ness Monster hoax was perpetuated by Marmaduke Wetherell, an actor, director, and hunter from Britain. Though the first rumors of a large beast along the shores of the Loch date back to AD 565, the hoax did not explode into popular awareness until the early 1900s when Mr. Wetherell spread the story. In the early 1930s, a road was built along Loch Ness, and the first modern sightings of a large animal in the lake were reported, echoing the ancient rumors. As more and more people claimed to see something in the lake, public interest grew, and rewards were posted for capture of the beast. Radio programs reported news and sightings, and hundreds of scouts and hunters arrived to hunt the beast.

As the legend of the monster grew, Mr. Wetherell was hired to find evidence of the beast. In his investigation, he reported finding large footprints of an animal that was projected to be a 20-foot-long sea serpent. He made plaster molds of the footprints and sent them to the Natural History Museum for inspection. His findings generated immediate interest, and tourists flocked to the area to try to catch sight of the creature. Upon analysis, the plaster molds were found to be made by a hippopotamus foot, and Mr. Wetherell's finding was publicly discredited by the newspapers. In response to such embarrassment, it seems that Mr. Wetherell conspired to create a photograph of the monster. He worked with conspirators to create a monster out of a plastic toy submarine and other materials and captured the grainy black-and-white photo of a sea serpent emerging from the lake that has since become one of the most viewed photographs of all time.

This photograph is popularly known as the "Surgeon's Photograph" because Mr. Wetherell had Colonel Robert Kenneth Wilson sell the photo to newspapers in 1934. Colonel Wilson's status as a physician gave credibility to the claim. Though skeptics insisted that the monsterlike form must be a photo of a seabird or a tree trunk, no one suspected that Mr. Wetherell had crafted it from a toy. In fact, faith in the claim and the photo led to fifty years of sightings and research to attempt to find and identify the beast. Expeditions, technology, and experts have dedicated time, money, and energy to seek out the rumored creature.

The deception behind the hoax remained a secret for over 60 years and was only conclusively revealed in 1993 when David Martin and Alastair Boyd investigated the myth and interviewed Mr. Wetherell's surviving stepson. From the son's perspective, The *Daily Mail* newspaper had humiliated and discredited Mr. Wetherell when he submitted the plaster footprints. To seek revenge, he created the photo of the monster to fool the publication. However, according to Mr. Wetherell's son, no one involved in the hoax had expected the publicity that the photo would generate. Their goal had been to fool the newspaper, not the whole world. However, even today, though his story has been conclusively discredited, many still travel to the Loch, and some claim to have caught a glimpse of an extraordinary creature in the water. This demonstrates how a hoax can perpetuate in public awareness even in light of contradictory evidence.

See also: Chadwick, Cassie; Fake News; Fraud; Hoax; Lightfoot, Lucy; Piltdown Man; Suspension of Disbelief.

Further Reading

Darnton, J. (1994). Loch Ness: Fiction is stranger than truth. *The New York Times*. Retrieved from https://www.nytimes.com/1994/03/20/weekinreview/loch-ness -fiction-is-stranger-than-truth.html

Kiernan, K. (2017). The Loch Ness Monster turns 83: The story of the Surgeon's Photograph. *Don't Take Pictures*. Retrieved from https://www.donttakepictures.com/ dtp-blog/2017/4/19/the-loch-ness-monster-turns-83-the-story-of-the -surgeons-photograph

Krystek, L. (2011). The surgeon's hoax. *The Museum of Unnatural Mystery*. Retrieved from http://www.unmuseum.org/mob/nesshoax.htm

Lyons, S. (2000). Birth of a legend. *Nova*. Retrieved from https://www.pbs.org/wgbh /nova/lochness/legend3.html

Locus of Control

Locus of control refers to the degree to which individuals feel as though they have control over the outcomes of events in their lives. Individuals with an internal locus of control feel empowered to impact and shape outcomes and events. These individuals feel as though they can influence others, achieve their goals, and effectively collaborate with the people around them. Individuals with an external locus of control feel as though the control over outcomes and events is external to themselves. In this sense, they feel limited control of the events that happen in their lives and do not feel as though they have the power to impact situations, make changes, or influence others. Locus of control is an aspect of personality that is shaped over childhood and stabilizes in adulthood. The degree to which individuals feel in control of their own lives is significantly correlated with how frequently they tend to engage in deception as a means of getting what they want.

People with an internal locus of control are more likely to take responsibility for their achievements as well as their failures and to take steps to modify their efforts to meet their goals. They tend to be honest, cooperative, and genuine because they believe they can resolve issues and effect change. They work hard and correlate increased effort with increased success. They tend to achieve more and be more motivated than those with an external locus of control because they feel effective and powerful in shaping their own lives. Due to this, they are less likely to engage in deception and instead seek honest means of influencing situations.

People with an external locus of control, alternatively, are likely to blame others for their failures and may even attribute their successes to luck. They are likely to be vulnerable to external influences, experience greater levels of stress, and engage in deception to try to conform to expectations or to get what they want. They put less effort into attempting to influence the outcome of events in their lives because they do not correlate effort with success. Because they feel limited control, they are likely to suffer from learned helplessness and resist the idea that they could take control of a situation and have the power to change the outcome. They are likely to be neurotic, depressed, and anxious. Teaching these individuals effective strategies to take control over the events, relationships, and situations in their lives can help alleviate these issues, though changing such personality traits requires rigorous effort and support.

Intelligence level tends to interact with locus of control to predict deceptive behavior. Individuals with lower scores on intelligence measures tend to score higher on measures of external locus of control. These individuals look to others for support, guidance, and expectations and are more likely to lie. Their lies serve as a means of self-protection because they believe there are no other solutions that could help them reach their goals. They may also lie to conform to the expectations of those who they feel have the control. This effect is particularly salient in children. Parents who have rigid or unrealistic expectations and pressure their children to achieve beyond their intellectual abilities tend to shape children to have an external locus of control. These children are then more likely to lie or cheat in an attempt to conform to expectations or as a means to reach their goals.

Dr. Peter Mudrack analyzed the connection between locus of control and Machiavellian tendencies. Through examination of a decade of research, he concluded that Machiavellianism is correlated with an external locus of control. Those who score high on traits of Machiavellianism likely view the world as unpredictable and uncontrollable through honest means such as hard work or genuine cooperation. Those who score high on Machiavellian traits are more likely to manipulate, deceive, and cultivate favor with those in power as a means to success. These individuals are also more likely to blame others for failure and take advantage of others whenever possible. Such behaviors seem quite rational when locus of control is taken into consideration. Thus, effort to change individuals' perceived level of control in situations could be an effective treatment of Machiavellian personality traits. If they feel their lives are controlled by external forces, it makes sense that they would try any means possible to achieve the outcomes they desire. They use their behaviors to manipulate people and events in situations where they perceive limited control.

See also: Academic Cheating; Intelligence; Machiavellianism; Motives for Lying; Personality.

Further Reading

Mudrack, P. E. (1990). Machiavellianism and locus of control: A meta-analytic review. *The Journal of Social Psychology, 130*(1), 125–126.

Schindler, W. J. (1975). *Locus of control and intelligence as predictors of overt lying behavior in nine through thirteen year old children not under and under expectancy pressure* (Unpublished doctoral dissertation). Kent State University, Kent, OH.

Low-Stakes Lies (See White Lies)

Lying

Though the term "lying" may frequently be used interchangeably with deception, lying is a specific form of deception that relies on deceptive verbal statements. Lying is an especially interesting form of deception because it relies on language skills and, thus, is uniquely human. This type of deception is thought to be a direct by-product of evolving within elaborate social groups. Though lying may not be beneficial when living in close-knit family groups, complete honesty can put one at a disadvantage as the size of the group expands. In order to compete successfully in these extended groups, lying is frequently an adaptive strategy to make and keep friends, to maintain an advantage, and to influence others. Telling the truth may undermine goals that could be easily achieved by masking, exaggerating, or telling outright lies. Thus, lying tends to emerge early in childhood and is honed over development in relation to the demands of the environment.

Initially, attempts at lying are relatively unsophisticated and ineffective. To be adept at lying, one must monitor and control cognitive abilities such as executive control of verbal and nonverbal expressions, emotional responses, and memory stores. Lying requires a sophisticated understanding of social expectations, social display rules, and social skills. Liars must coordinate their presentation of false verbal and nonverbal expressions and fabricate displays that are congruent with the lie. The liar must simultaneously inhibit true verbal and nonverbal expressions, control for leakage of genuine information, and fabricate information that aligns with the deceptive intent. To be successful at lying, one must also maintain consistency between the initial lie and follow-up information, behavior, and expressions.

Around age two, verbal lies are typically self-serving and emerge in circumstances where the child is attempting to avoid punishment or to gain rewards. These first attempts are almost always egocentric and ineffective since children are not monitoring their statements or nonverbal presentations due to a lack of understanding of their partners' perspective. These children also make no effort to maintain the lie in response to follow-up questions. By age three, children start to become aware of social display rules and offer verbal lies to conform to social expectations, to protect the feelings of others, and to smooth over social interactions. They may say they like a gift even if their nonverbal behaviors belie their verbal statements. Around four years of age, children begin to generate rudimentary intentional lies to influence the beliefs of others. These lies can be playful, defensive, aggressive, competitive, or protective, but still are marked by inconsistency between verbal and nonverbal behavior or between verbal statements and follow-up remarks. This is likely due to immature executive functioning and self-assessment skills.

Between the ages of six and eight, children begin to effectively use tactical strategies to escape detection and be more influential with their lies. Between these ages, children begin to coordinate their nonverbal expressions to support their verbal statements to create more effective deceptive displays. They are also likely to maintain the lie and answer follow-up questions in line with the reality they have fabricated. These more sophisticated skills are honed across childhood, and lying proficiency continues to advance into young adulthood, as executive control, theory of mind understanding, recursive awareness, and inhibitory control mature.

The capacity for language allowed for the emergence of lying behavior. Then as lying behavior emerged, the need to detect liars was then selected for, necessitating that liars develop even more discrete abilities. This evolutionary arms race likely drove the complexity of current language and deceptive abilities and likely influenced current language, cognitive abilities, emotions, and social abilities. Thus, though most people generally condemn lying behavior in children and in social partners, such abilities are uniquely human and are likely a stimulant and by-product of our massive cognitive evolution.

See also: Age Differences; Development of Deception; Evolution of Deception; Language; Recursive Awareness; Tactical Deception; Theory of Mind.

Further Reading

Debey, E., De Schryver, M., Logan, G. D., Suchotzki, K., & Verschuere, B. (2015). From junior to senior Pinocchio: A cross-sectional lifespan investigation of deception. *Acta Psychologica, 160*, 58–68.

LaFreniere, P. J. (1988). The ontogeny of tactical deception in humans. In R. Byrne & A. Whiten (Eds.), *Evolution of Social Intelligence* (pp. 238–252). Oxford University Press.

Smith, R. M., & LaFreniere, P. J. (2013). Development of tactical deception from 4 to 8 years of age. *British Journal of Developmental Psychology, 31*, 30–41.

Talwar, V., & Crossman, A. (2011). From little white lies to filthy liars: The evolution of honesty and deception in young children. *Advances in Child Development and Behavior, 40*, 139–179.

Talwar, V., Gordon, H. M., & Lee, K. (2007). Lying in the elementary school years: Verbal deception and its relation to second-order belief understanding. *Developmental Psychology, 43*(3), 804–810.

Lying at Work

Lying in the workplace is relatively ubiquitous and can occur at any level of an organization. Some employees lie to secure time off or other benefits, or to avoid consequences of uncompleted tasks; some managers lie to motivate employees, to secure support, or to mediate between employees and administrators; and some administrators lie in an attempt to encourage the perception of success of the organization. Employees may spontaneously engage in deceptive behavior, or it may be encouraged within the culture of the organization. In general, however, lying behavior tends to undermine the effectiveness and success of organizations. Employees who engage in deception at work tend to become less committed to the company over time and become less effective workers. Lying behavior tends to negatively influence the quality of work, trust between colleagues, and cooperative efforts, all of which are detrimental to the work environment.

Employees can lie about their qualifications when applying for a job, but even more commonly, they lie about things peripheral to their actual jobs once hired. They lie about why they are late, call out sick when they are not, and profess greater job satisfaction than they actually feel. They may claim to have missed emails or deflect blame to others for incomplete or poor performance, make excuses, exaggerate time or effort needed to complete a task, or commit to work that they do not intend to complete. Many lie in an attempt to impress their superiors or receive promotions or to avoid punishment for mistakes or late work. Some organizations even encourage lying behavior. For example, Drs. Sarah Jenkins and Rick Delbridge from Cardiff University analyzed an organization that encouraged receptionists to lie about their location. Off-site receptionists were asked to act as though they were on-site when responding to callers. Not only were they encouraged to lie, but they were also rewarded for their effectiveness of such deceptions.

Managers also may feel the need to alter the truth in order to motivate employees, to secure budgets, or to give the perception of success. Managers must balance the needs of the administration with the needs of the employees. This pressure may lead to managers exaggerating, omitting information, or lying to appease both extremes. Upper-level administrators also commonly engage in tactical deception strategies to compete more effectively with rival companies, to gain funding, or to mollify employees. Use of such deception may lead to it becoming an intrinsic value in the workplace that is embedded, maintained, and strengthened over time, likely to the detriment of the company as a whole. Such behaviors lead to the normalization of deception and lead to corruption within organizations.

Dr. Frank D. Belschak and his colleagues examined employees who scored high on traits of Machiavellianism to see the effects of deception in the workplace. Those who score high on traits of Machiavellianism are likely to have little trust in leaders, high stress, and engage in unethical behavior. Dr. Belschak and his colleagues found that these individuals tend to have manipulative, unethical, and counterproductive work behaviors. They tend to have a cynical worldview, do not tend to feel guilty about lies, and are more likely to make unethical decisions and exploit their employer. In addition, most report that they are dissatisfied with their jobs, are stressed at work, and feel low commitment to their company.

These more deceptive individuals are more likely to burn out, contribute poor performance, and have less effective interpersonal work interactions. Interestingly, since deceptive individuals can be goal-driven, they do illustrate cooperation and productivity when it is advantageous for themselves. Therefore, many rise to leadership positions. As leaders, they continue to engage in unethical behavior and are likely to create a negative feedback cycle within the workplace.

They engage in deception, distrust others, and are likely to create a stressful, distrustful work environment for their employees. These elements tend to create a work environment where the employees are not given autonomy or trust to do their jobs, and the employees are under greater stress. As a result, promotion of unethical individuals to leadership positions can reduce employee compliance, increase deception in the workplace, and create a less effective work environment. One deceptive team member decreases overall trust and performance and can damage collaboration and mutuality, or the sense of connection, coordination, and understanding, between team members.

In order to find ethical employees, many organizations use screening measures such as background checks, reference checks, and personality tests to learn about past and projected behaviors of potential employees. Some organizations use periodic screening measures such as drug or alcohol testing to discourage deception in the workplace and monitor productivity and effectiveness in annual evaluations. In extreme circumstances, polygraph testing may be used as a means to investigate thefts or corruption within the workplace.

See also: Competition; Costs of Lying; Machiavellianism; Motives for Lying; Paternalistic Lies; Polygraph Tests.

Further Reading

Belschak, F. D., Muhammad, R. S., & Den Hartog, D. N. (2018). Birds of a feather can butt heads: When Machiavellian employees works with Machiavellian leaders. *Journal of Business Ethics, 151*(3), 613–626.

Fuller, C. M., Marett, K., & Twitchell, D. P. (2012). An examination of deception in virtual teams: Effects of deception on task performance, mutuality, and trust. *Transactions on Professional Communication, 55*(1), 20–35.

Jenkins, S., & Delbridge, R. (2016). Trusted to deceive: A case study of strategic deception and lying at work. *Organizational Studies, 38*(1), 53–76.

Sackett, P. R., & Decker, P. J. (1979). Detection of deception in the employment context: A review and critical analysis. *Personnel Psychology, 32*, 487–506.

Lying to Children

Children's tendency to lie to their parents has been a topic of much research over the last two decades, but parents' tendency to lie to their children has also recently emerged as a topic of research. Though parents may discourage or actively punish lying behavior, many parents lie to their children to influence their emotional states as well as their behavior. Parents may make idle threats or exaggerate consequences in an effort to keep their children safe. Parents may also lie to their children to protect feelings and keep things private, or they may lie to others in the presence of their children. Dr. Penelope Brown wrote one of the first research papers to explore parental lying in fieldwork she conducted with Mayan farmers. Mayan parents primarily lied to their children to influence their behavior. For example, farmers would lie about wild animals to make sure their children stayed close to them and did not wander off.

Similar research has since been applied to American and Asian populations. Researcher Rachel Santos and her colleagues in Dr. Kang Lee's lab at the University of Toronto found that parents frequently lie about a range of things. Some common parental lies revolved around encouraging children to eat healthy food, saving money, consequences of bad behavior, and threats about abandoning the children if they do not cooperate.

Parents may lie in the context of play, teasing, or magical thinking such as telling stories about Santa Claus or the Tooth Fairy. Parents may also lie to promote positive feelings, such as to increase a child's self-esteem, or to promote appropriate behavior, such as to increase obedience or respect. Interestingly, parents who lie to their children also endorse that it is very important to teach their children to tell the truth. In a research study by Dr. Gail Heyman and her colleagues, adults were asked to rate an assortment of lies that parents may tell. In the study, all participants reported that their own parents had taught them that lying was unacceptable, yet their parents had lied to them during childhood.

A majority of parents (84% of U.S. parents and 98% of Chinese parents) reported having used instrumental lying (lying to influence others for selfish reasons) to encourage good behavior in their children. Most used false threats such as leaving the child behind, the police coming to get the child, or kidnappers coming if the child does not comply with behavioral expectations. The most common lie to influence behavior was to threaten to leave the child behind if they refuse to cooperate. Another common lie was that a parent would buy a requested toy later, even though the parent had no intention of doing so. Chinese parents told instrumental lies at higher rates than American parents in 15 out of the 16 examples. Chinese parents also reported higher acceptance of parental lying as a method of controlling behavior. The only exception was lying about the availability of junk food. American parents were more likely to lie about not having candy in the house. Interestingly, though Chinese parents were more likely to endorse and to use lying to control behavior; they were also more likely to punish children for lying behavior. Parents in both cultures were also likely to use lying to increase self-esteem and positive feelings, such as through play, encouragement, or care.

American parents admitted to using lies as a last resort when their children were not cooperating. Parents reported that lying may save time and decrease anxiety or protect the child from harsh realities. Due to widespread lying behavior in parenting, researchers were interested in whether lying to children increases the likelihood that the children will experience maladjustment and increased dishonest behavior later in life. Their findings suggest that adults who were lied to by their parents in childhood subsequently lied more to their parents in adolescence and adulthood and reported more maladjustment than participants who did not recall parental lying during their childhood. These results may partially stem from observational learning, socialization, and modeling. Less well-adjusted adults may also recall or infer more lying behavior during their childhoods than more well-adjusted, honest adults.

Some of the studied effects of being lied to during childhood include being more likely to lie in reciprocation and less confidence in parents' reliability.

Children who lie tend to exhibit increased externalizing and antisocial behaviors, increased delinquency and fighting behaviors, increased aggression, and decreased self-control. Children who lie to their parents are also at higher risk of depression, feelings of alienation, and increased anxiety. As stated, one study looking at the relationship of parenting by lying and later outcomes found consistent correlations. Specifically, researchers found that knowledge of parental lying during childhood correlated with increased lying behavior toward the parent in adulthood. Furthermore, this increased lying behavior is accompanied by greater rates of internalizing, externalizing, and antisocial personality traits in adulthood.

Overall, using lies to shape children's behavior is correlated with less positive outcomes in emotional adjustment later in life and poorer relationship quality. Regardless, this research shows that lying is quite common in parenting. However, in most circumstances, adults believe their parents told predominantly white lies and that their lies had benevolent and prosocial intentions.

See also: Age Differences; Cultural Differences; Development of Deception; Hypocrisy; Lying to Parents; Motives for Lying; Paternalistic Lies; Sex Differences in Lying Behavior.

Further Reading

Brown, P. (2002). Everyone has to lie in Tzeltal. In S. Blum-Kulka & C. Snow (Eds.), *Talking to Adults* (pp. 241–275). Lawrence Erlbaum Associates.

Cargill, J. R., & Curtis, D. A. (2017). Parental deception: Perceived effects on parent-child relationships. *Journal of Relationships Research, 8*, 1–8.

Heyman, G. D., Hsu, A. S., Fu, G., & Lee, K. (2013). Instrumental lying by parents in the US and China. *International Journal of Psychology, 48*(6), 1176–1184.

Heyman, G. D., Luu, D. H., & Lee, K. (2009). Parenting by lying. *Journal of Moral Education, 38*(3), 353–369.

Santos, R. M., Zanette, S., Kwok, S. M., Heyman, G. D., & Lee, K. (2017). Exposure to parenting by lying in childhood: Associations with negative outcomes in adulthood. *Frontiers in Psychology, 8*(1240), 1–9.

Lying to Parents

The ability to consider, construct, and maintain a plausible lie is a by-product of maturation as well as environmental influence. Children must develop cognitively before they can lie effectively, but lying behavior is also influenced by their familial relationships. Parental expectations, parenting style, and modeled behavior can encourage or discourage lying behavior. Early lies are almost always within the parent-child dyad and can be unwittingly supported by parents through their expectations, communications, and behaviors.

Children initially lie to parents as a way to meet expectations and avoid punishment. Most children are eager to please and are likely to lie when they do not measure up to parental expectations. Asking children who made the mess, who ate the cookie, or who broke the plate traps them into deceptive responses to avoid

How to Raise Honest Children

Social interactions are a complicated mix of honest communications and socially appropriate tact. Parents rate honesty as one of the top qualities they want to foster in their children. However, children must also be able to engage in socially appropriate interactions, which do not always call for the blunt truth. Thus, parents may be sending mixed messages by encouraging honesty and then admonishing blunt speech. In general, authoritative parents tend to be more successful in raising honest children. Those parents establish clear expectations and enforce consequences, yet calmly discuss the reasons behind the rules. Authoritative parents talk about why dishonesty is a problem, apologize for their own mistakes, and allow their children to explain and discuss the reasons behind naughty behaviors.

Though parents spend time establishing and enforcing rules, children also learn from watching. Thus, to have honest children, parents must be good role models. If parents model dishonest behavior, children learn that telling lies is acceptable. Most adults may use white lies to smooth over social interactions, but children may not discriminate between lies that are socially appropriate and lies that are not. Parents can also model honesty by being direct with children, particularly when they ask questions. Vague answers may come across as dishonest. Sometimes parents say "maybe" to deflect a request when the answer is actually no. This may smooth over the interaction for the parent, but it models dishonesty for the child.

Parents should also avoid setting the child up for dishonest behavior. For example, if a parent knows a child has engaged in naughty behavior, they should avoid asking the child who did it. This requires the child to self-incriminate or to lie. Since most children want to please their parents, such questions encourage lying. Instead, parents should calmly acknowledge what the child did and present a solution or consequence. Even adults may lie when feeling trapped, and lying can become a habit. Parents should avoid giving their children the opportunity to practice.

Parents of honest children spend time talking about the importance of honesty. Parents can praise people or storybook characters who were honest, especially in difficult situations. Additionally, parents can praise their children when they are honest. If parents admonish children for lying, they should also praise them for telling the truth. A key to effective parenting is to reward desired behaviors. If parents wish to increase honesty, they should provide more attention for honesty than for lies. Additionally, children frequently lie to avoid disappointing or angering their parents. Thus, if a child does tell the truth, parents need to stay calm. Reacting with anger punishes honesty rather than reinforcing it.

Parents can help children internalize honesty by reinforcing that telling the truth makes people feel good and is linked to positive emotions. Parents can discuss other people's feelings and help children start to identify when the truth will be hurtful to another person. Once children can recognize such situations, parents can help them figure out socially appropriate ways to be honest. As children develop, they may also need more autonomy. Adolescents may lie to maintain privacy or establish boundaries. When parents allow teens to decline discussing an issue or to keep some information private until they are ready to share, they lessen the need to lie.

parental disappointment. Parents who simply acknowledge the indiscretion, rather than forcing self-incrimination, and propose a solution are more likely to encourage future honest behavior. As children learn familial and societal expectations, they may begin to engage in prosocial and polite lies. They may also lie to garner respect from the parent or as part of fantasy play. These early lies are relatively naive and ineffective but may be used to lay the foundation for expectations of honesty.

Parenting style is directly correlated with how frequently children are likely to lie, particularly as children grow into adolescence and develop greater abilities to effectively deceive others. As proposed by pioneering research psychologist Dr. Diana Baumrind, authoritative and authoritarian parents have high expectations for their children and clear consequences for bad behavior. Authoritative parents, however, are warm toward their children, explain the reasons behind rules, and discuss how lying impacts others. Children of authoritative parents tend to develop greater empathy skills and are less likely to lie. When they do lie, they are more likely to feel guilty, to confess, and to work with their parents to resolve issues. Authoritarian parents, alternatively, are less likely to discuss reasons behind rules and more likely to enforce punishment without discussion. Children of authoritarian parents are more likely to hide their indiscretions and less likely to internalize moral values, leading to greater deceptive behavior over time.

Permissive parents have low or inconsistent expectations for their children. If they do have rules, there are no consistent consequences, and these parents spend less time talking about the ramifications of their children's behaviors. Children do not have clear boundaries and are likely to expect instant gratification. Their moral development lags behind that of children raised by authoritative or authoritarian parents, and they are more likely to lie to their parents, friends, teachers, and other authority figures to get what they want.

As children move into adolescence, parents may grow more concerned about lying behavior because their adolescents' choices may have more severe consequences. At this point, the quality of the parent-child relationship established over childhood becomes especially important. Parents who have established healthy relationships characterized by trust and open communication are less likely to have adolescents who engage in deception or concealment. Research by Dr. Matthew Gingo and his colleagues shows that as adolescents begin to establish their own sense of autonomy, it becomes important to them to make their own decisions, particularly about personal issues. If parents do not allow for such autonomy, adolescents are likely to engage in more deceptive behavior.

In Dr. Gingo's study, interviewed adolescents endorsed deception as an appropriate response to protect privacy, particularly when parents try to exert control over personal choices such as friends, dating, clothing, or hairstyles. These same adolescents did not endorse lying about activities such as personal safety, health, or homework, which they view as acceptable realms for parental influence. Parents who listen, give advice, and negotiate are likely to have adolescents who engage in less frequent deceptive behavior. In these relationships, adolescents endorsed not wanting to violate trust or damage the relationship. Adolescents who viewed their parents as demanding and inflexible, however, were significantly more likely to endorse lying. Adolescents who engage in delinquent behavior tend to show weaker attachment to their parents. Alternatively, facilitating strong, secure attachment tends to lead to less delinquent behavior.

Parental behavior is a major determinant of whether or not children and adolescents are likely to lie. Modeling lying behavior or encouraging it through entrapment or over control leads to more overall deceptive attempts within the relationship. Modeling honesty, discussing issues openly, and delineating between personal choices and core values can decrease lying behavior, though this may require concessions of power from the parent as they encourage healthy relationships and growth.

See also: Age Differences; DePaulo, Bella; Development of Deception; Lying to Children; Theory of Mind.

Further Reading

Baumrind, D. (2005). Patterns of parental authority and adolescent autonomy. *New Directions for Child and Adolescent Development, 108*, 61–69.

DePaulo, B. M., Kashy, D. A., Kirkendol, S. E., & Wyer, M. M. (1996). Lying in everyday life. *Journal of Personality and Social Psychology, 70*(5), 979–995.

Gingo, M., Roded, A. D., & Turiel, E. (2017). Authority, autonomy, and deception: Evaluating the legitimacy of parental authority and adolescent deceit. *Journal of Research on Adolescence, 27*(4), 862–877.

Tosone, C. (2006). Living everyday lies: The experience of self. *Clinical Social Work Journal, 34*(3), 335–348.

Warr, M. (2007). The tangled web: Delinquency, deception, and parental attachment. *Journal of Youth and Adolescence, 36*, 607–622.

Lying to Partners (See Romantic Relationships)

M

Machiavellian Intelligence (See Machiavellianism)

Machiavellianism

Machiavellian intelligence refers to a type of social intelligence in which one demonstrates the ability to interact in a sophisticated, and frequently deceptive, manner to influence the behavior of others to one's own advantage. This requires complex communication, social systems, and cognitive abilities. Machiavellian intelligence can be used for both competitive and cooperative initiatives, but the outcomes are usually for selfish gain. The term arises from Niccolo Machiavelli's book, *The Prince*, which extolled the idea that deceit, treachery, and force are warranted to be an expedient and effective leader.

In the 1970s, psychologists adopted the term "Machiavellianism" to describe a particular array of personality traits. Machiavellianism became correlated with the behavior of individuals who purposefully manipulate others for a self-serving goal. As a personality trait, Machiavellianism emerges as self-focus that is so ingrained that the individuals will manipulate, deceive, and exploit others to get what they want. In psychology, Machiavellian personality traits tend to correlate with narcissism and psychopathy.

Individuals who score high on levels of Machiavellianism tend to show distrust, a tendency toward manipulative behavior, and a greater likelihood of exploiting others. These individuals tend to engage in more short-term romantic relationships and use sex for dominance, power, or sexual satisfaction, rather than to increase intimacy or affiliation. They avoid relational commitment and are more likely to engage in cheating behaviors. Though men more frequently show these traits, women with high scores on Machiavellianism scales are more likely to pretend to orgasm when with a sexual partner. This pretense may serve to increase their partner's relationship satisfaction and to retain the partner. Sex is used to control the partner rather than for personal enjoyment, and in general, these women tend to be more possessive and controlling.

In psychology, there are tests for the level of Machiavellianism, and those who score high tend to endorse statements that encourage manipulating and using others to achieve goals. High scorers might say that the only bad thing about committing a crime is getting caught and that it is important to tell people what they want to hear to get them to do what you want. Those high on scales of Machiavellianism are more likely to lie, are confident in their ability to lie effectively, and endorse lying as acceptable for self-gain.

Individuals who score high on scales of Machiavellianism tend to take advantage of situations where boundaries are ambiguous, and they frequently manipulate situations to benefit themselves. They also tend to be cynical and detached and wait for opportunities to achieve an advantage over others. They tend to be relatively charismatic and convince others to cooperate until force is needed. They may mask their true intentions and maintain an exit strategy. They are often respected as effective in negotiations, but less desirable as colleagues, friends, or romantic partners.

Examples of modern-day Machiavellian personalities include characters such as Tony Soprano from the television show *The Sopranos*. Tony is willing to lie, manipulate, or kill to maintain his leadership position. Though Tony may want to be loved, he will settle for being feared. Lord Varys and Lord Baelish also embrace the Machiavellian archetype in their ongoing battle in *Game of Thrones*, the television series based on the fantasy novels of George R. R. Martin. Their ruthless, manipulative, and selfish ambition leaves no room for empathy or compassion.

Those who score high on levels of Machiavellianism tend to be focused on their own interests; prioritize their own needs over others; exploit, flatter, charm, or outright lie to get ahead; are cynical of morality and relationships; lack values or struggle with commitment or warmth; and only show empathy or emotions when it manipulates social interactions for their own benefit. Most individuals with these characteristics are resistant to treatment because they typically are not interested in changing. They are likely to manipulate relationships to maintain their position of power and endorse the sentiment that the ends justify the means.

Though those who score high on traits of Machiavellianism may be successful in business, most have difficulty developing psychological intimacy with others and sustaining personal relationships. Even at work, they are likely to have reduced trust in leaders, higher stress, and more unethical behavior, particularly if their employer has similar traits.

See also: Antisocial Personality Disorder; Coercion; Dark Triad; Gaslighting; Instrumental Lies; Intelligence; Lying at Work; Manipulation; Motives for Lying; Narcissism; Personality; Romantic Relationships; Social Intelligence.

Further Reading

Brewer, G., Abell, L., & Lyons, M. (2016). Machiavellianism, pretending orgasm, and sexual intimacy. *Personality and Individual Differences, 96*, 155–158.

Hartley, D. (2015, September 8). Meet the Machiavellians. *Psychology Today*. Retrieved from https://www.psychologytoday.com/us/blog/machiavellians-gulling-the-rubes/201509/meet-the-machiavellians

LaFreniere, P. J. (1988). The ontogeny of tactical deception in humans. In R. Byrne & A. Whiten (Eds.), *Evolution of Social Intelligence* (pp. 238–252). Oxford University Press.

Lucas, J. R., Gentry, K., Sieving, K., & Freeberg, T. M. (2018). Communication as a fundamental part of Machiavellian Intelligence. *Journal of Comparative Psychology, 132*(4), 442–454.

Machiavelli, N., & Wootton, D. (1995). *The Prince*. Hackett Publisher.

Malingering

Malingering is when an individual invents or exaggerates symptoms of a disorder in order to achieve external rewards. Malingering ranges from subtle changes in how one represents their symptoms to outright lies about physical or psychological experiences. For example, an individual may produce such symptoms as anxiety, depression, memory loss, or pain in order to avoid responsibilities, avoid military service, secure treatment or medication, or obtain financial compensation for injuries. In some cases, individuals repeat the lies so frequently they themselves may start to believe them.

Malingering differs from disorders such as Munchausen syndrome because the goal of malingering is an external incentive. Though both disorders involve voluntary presentation of fictitious symptoms, only malingering is tied to external gain. Malingering also differs from a diagnosis of hypochondriasis because in malingering individuals are intentionally producing the symptoms for the reward, not because they actually believe they are sick.

Malingering is relatively rare. Most people who engage in malingering have experience with the law, have a clear goal, and show behaviors inconsistent with the claimed illness or injury. They also usually have vague and transient symptoms, have poor impulse control, and have a history of dishonesty or exaggeration. Furthermore, since the symptoms are not genuine, treatment tends to be ineffective. Instead, treatment may lead to increased symptoms or reports of atypical changes in symptoms. Symptoms also tend to be grossly overexaggerated in comparison to results of medical diagnostic tests.

Because detecting malingering could be essential for treatment or for court cases around workers' compensation, psychological tests have been designed that detect malingering. Personality tests like the Minnesota Multiphasic Personality Inventory-2 have scales to detect an individual's tendency to exaggerate. Additionally, tests such as the Test of Memory Malingering and the Word Memory Test have been designed to detect level of effort. These tests seem difficult but are actually quite simple. Even those with traumatic brain injuries, diagnosed with depression, psychiatric inpatients, children, and elderly adults tend to do quite well, if they try. If patients fail these tests, it becomes clear that they are not putting forth genuine effort. Such disingenuous performance means that other symptoms may be exaggerated as well.

Though malingering may occur when an individual is attempting to avoid work or service, not all individuals who engage in malingering have such nefarious goals. Some individuals may exaggerate their own symptoms and intentionally perform poorly on neuropsychological tests in an effort to ensure their symptoms are detected. However, exaggerating the symptoms is counterproductive because accurate treatments cannot be prescribed based on inaccurate test results. Patients who feel heard and who are being taken seriously are less likely to exaggerate. Information that some of the tests are designed to show level of effort can also be explained to increase likelihood of good effort.

Individuals can engage in malingering one time, repeatedly, or by proxy. Events that involve a lawsuit, such as an accident or a workplace incident, may cause individuals to misrepresent their symptoms to gain external rewards. Malingerers may engage in symptom magnification and make a false report or exaggerate symptoms or injuries to obtain compensation, time off, or other medical benefits. In other cases, individuals prolong their reported symptoms, well beyond the time it should typically take injuries to heal. In some cases, the reports of symptoms become so extreme that they border on fantasy, or the patient may start to believe their own report.

In a review study completed in 2016, researchers found that in all 11 established cases of malingering studied, the motivation was financial. Malingerers were seeking disability funds, litigation settlements, or money collections. In two cases, the malingerer confessed, but in the others, neuropsychological measures were needed to diagnose the deceptive behavior.

Malingering by proxy has more recently been studied. In malingering by proxy, an individual reports symptoms in a child or other dependents to seek compensation. In some cases, parents coach their children or dependent adults to feign symptoms in order for the parent to gain external rewards such as medications, money, or other legal compensation. In many cases of malingering by proxy, child protective services eventually get involved because the enforced malingering borders on child abuse. Children are likely to suffer unnecessary medical procedures and may be given inappropriate medications and treatments, and they are also likely to have long-term psychological effects such as lower self-esteem, impaired self-image, and more difficulty with extrafamilial relationships. These children are more likely to learn to conform to the sick role and to be more dependent on others as they enter adulthood, perpetuating the problem.

See also: Benefits of Lying; Cognitive Dissonance; Exaggeration; Instrumental Lies; Munchausen Syndrome; Self-Deception.

Further Reading

Amlani, A., Grewal, G. S., & Feldman, M. D. (2016). Malingering by proxy: A literature review and current perspectives. *Journal of Forensic Science, 61*(S1), S171–S176.

Aronoff, G. M., Mandel, S., Genovese, E., Maitz, E. A., Dorto, A. J., Klimek, E. H., & Staats, T. E. (2007). Evaluating malingering in contested injury of illness. *Pain Practice, 7*(2), 178–204.

Gerson, A. R. (2002). Beyond the DSM-IV: A meta-review of the literature on malingering. *American Journal of Forensic Psychology, 20*(1), 56–69.

Iverson, G. L. (2007). Identifying exaggeration and malingering. *Pain Practice, 7*(2), 94–102.

Slovenko, R. (2006). Editorial: Patients who deceive. *International Journal of Offender Therapy and Comparative Criminology, 50*(3), 241–244.

Manipulation

Manipulation is the act of deceiving others in order to influence their behavior to one's own benefit. Manipulators can use several psychological principles to control their targets. They may use deception in the forms of false compliments, superficial charm, bribes, threats, coercion, or guilt to shape the behavior of others. There is such a wide range of manipulative techniques that skilled manipulators may go undetected. Individuals who are eager to please others or who have an external locus of control may fall victim to manipulation as they strive to please. Manipulators may lie, rationalize, evade, shame, seduce, flatter, or use excesses of emotion to get their way.

Individuals who are eager to please, too trusting, have low self-confidence, or are lonely may be especially vulnerable to being manipulated. They also are more likely to manipulate others in an attempt to get what they need. Manipulation generally has a negative connotation, but people who are good at manipulating others tend to be more successful. The ability to manipulate could help one gain resources, establish alliances, and attract others. However, manipulators tend to be selfish, have a need to feel superior to others, and are focused on personal goals. Since manipulation requires an ability to exploit others, those with a Machiavellian personality style tend to be expert manipulators. Those with antisocial or narcissistic personality traits also tend to use manipulation to achieve their goals. They tend to lack empathy, are impulsive, and do not readily consider the feelings of others.

Dr. David Buss and his colleagues from the University of Texas at Austin asked participants to think about how they use psychological manipulation to get others to do what they want, as well as how to get others to stop doing things. Based on their findings, five categories of manipulation emerged: reasoning, regression, silent treatment, coercion, and debasement. The reasoning category includes using reason to ask others to comply. This category relies less on manipulation and more on logical cooperation, unless the reasoning is excessively persistent. The other categories are more manipulative. The regression category relies on negative reinforcement. For example, participants would say things such as, "I complain until he does what I want." Other examples include pouting or sulking until one gets one's way.

The silent treatment includes withdrawing attention or other favors until the other person does what one wants. The coercive tactic includes exerting physical or psychological control over others or using compliments and flattery to get what one wants. Finally, the debasement tactic includes being self-deprecating in order to elicit sympathy to get the other to do what one wants. This is frequently a passive-aggressive strategy that is designed to undermine others' self-esteem or to make others feel guilty, or to portray oneself as a victim. Manipulators tend to place themselves in a physically dominant position, manipulate facts to blame the victim, display negative or hostile emotions, apply pressure, or are critical or sarcastic.

To better understand manipulation, researchers from the University of Michigan, Stanford University, and Harvard University examined tactics of manipulation. They found that manipulation can be used to elicit or to terminate behavior in others. When participants in their psychological study attempted to elicit a behavior in others, the use of reasoning and charm was most frequent. When they were attempting to terminate a behavior, however, coercion and the use of silent treatment were more common.

Preston Ni, a professor of communication studies, identified four characteristics of manipulative people. He stated that manipulative people are good at detecting weaknesses in others, will use such weaknesses to their own advantage, will plot to serve their own interests, and will continue to exploit others unless forcibly stopped. He also identified different categories of psychological manipulation including negative manipulation, positive manipulation, deception and intrigue, and strategic helplessness. Specifically, one may manipulate by acting superior and causing self-doubt in others; one may use compliments and insincere flattery to influence others; one may flat-out lie to confuse others; or one may pretend to be a victim to elicit sympathy and feelings of guilt from others.

Because manipulation can be subtle, it is frequently covert, indirect, and deceptive. Flattery or intimidation may shape behavior even without an individual's awareness. Most manipulators are not capable of asking for what they want directly. They may fear rejection, know that what they are asking for is unreasonable, or have external pressures that drive them. If individuals believe that they are being manipulated, the best strategy is to delay their response. Taking time to think about a situation may help individuals gain perspective to make a good choice for themselves independent of external manipulative pressures.

See also: Antisocial Personality Disorder; Bait and Switch; Borderline Personality Disorder; Coercion; Gaslighting; Locus of Control; Machiavellianism; Narcissism; Personality; Red Herring; Tactical Deception.

Further Reading

Buss, D. M., Gomes, M., Higgins, D. S., & Lauterbach, K. (1987). Tactics of manipulation. *Journal of Personality and Social Psychology, 52*(6), 1219–1229.

Lancer, D. (2014). Are you being manipulated? How to recognize the motives and tactics of manipulators. *Psychology Today*. Retrieved from https://www.psychologytoday.com/us/blog/toxic-relationships/201704/are-you-being-manipulated

Ni, P. C. (2015). *How to Successfully Handle Manipulative People*. Preston Ni Communication Coaching.

Shortsleeve, C. (2018). How to tell if someone is manipulating you—And what to do about it. *Time*. Retrieved from https://time.com/5411624/how-to-tell-if-being-manipulated/

Mate Selection (See Dating; Romantic Relationships)

Media

The widespread use of different kinds of media in modern day has created a multitude of platforms upon which to study deception. False information can be spread much more quickly than ever before and is much more difficult to contain. This false information can be spread knowingly or unknowingly, and once it is shared, the source is frequently obfuscated. Information, even false information, can be spread via news outlets, gossip sites, tweets, emails, social media platforms, or videos. Given the nature of electronic media, once information spreads, it is very difficult to isolate and erase. This puts much more responsibility on the consumer to fact-check, validate sources, and use critical thinking before blindly believing what they see or hear from media sources.

Though the purpose of journalism is to uncover the truth, many journalists commonly use casual deception. Journalists may use deception to get their story, to hide information that would be embarrassing to subjects, or to spin a story to benefit one side of an issue. Journalists frequently use lies of omission as a means of implying information to shape the beliefs of an audience. Deception may also emerge in the form of hidden cameras, staging, photo manipulation, or lying to protect a source. Stories may be skewed intentionally or unintentionally, and most stories contain bias. Even stories that are factually correct may have used deception as a means to that end.

False information is frequently much more salient and sensationalized than true information, and many readers do not evaluate what they read or view carefully. Beyond the spread of misinformation from news outlets or other news sources, social media is rife with deceptive attempts. When interviewed, most individuals willingly report engaging in deception on online sites and most expect that others are engaging in deception as well, making such sites perfect for deception research. Dr. Monica Whitty from the University of Warwick and Dr. Siobhan Carville from Queen's University, Belfast, were interested in how different types of deception are used in different types of media. They examined self-serving lies as well as other-oriented lies and examined their prevalence depending on the target of the lie as well as the type of media used. Self-serving lies are those that are told to protect the liar. These may serve to maintain a reputation, impress others, or avoid getting into trouble. Other-oriented lies are told to protect the person being lied to. For example, other-oriented lies may serve to protect the feelings of others.

Dr. Whitty and Dr. Carville found that participants within their research study told self-serving lies when they were communicating with people they did not know well. These individuals told self-serving lies more often in emails rather than over the phone or face-to-face. Almost 30 percent of males even admitted to lying about their gender in online chat rooms. Other common lies that emerged were lies about age, attractiveness, and interests. The individuals in their research study were more likely to tell other-oriented lies when talking with people who they knew well, and these lies did not vary by media type. When looking at telling the truth, participants told harsh truths more readily to those they did not know well by email. This aligns with the phenomenon of individuals being less inhibited and more aggressive online than in person.

Dr. Arun Vishwanath, from the University of Buffalo, examined Facebook users to determine the extent of deception within that social media platform as well as the predictors of who is likely to be deceived. Interviews revealed that young adults spend an average 40 hours a month using Facebook and check their feeds an average of 20 times a day. However, findings also revealed that 1 in 10 Facebook profiles are false accounts. These accounts are likely used for deceptive purposes, fraud, or scams. Because social media has become so pervasive, phishing attacks using social media platforms tend to have a success rate at around 40 percent. Given the amount of information that users willingly post on their Facebook page, accepting a false friend request may give the phisher everything they need to know to take advantage of the user. Facebook users also may provide credit card information to make purchases or donate to cleverly constructed phishing schemes.

Dr. Vishwanath also found that individuals' frequency of use of Facebook impacts their level of susceptibility to attacks. Behaviors become more automatic with increased usage, and thus, frequent users may be less sensitive to suspicious friend requests or social activity. Alternatively, those who have increased concern for privacy are less susceptible to attacks and are more suspicious of accepting friend requests or providing information. Habitual Facebook users have more friends, engage in more interactions, and are more susceptible to providing information to phishers. A basic level of suspicion and caution is important when communicating online to avoid deceptive attempts.

See also: Advertising; Alternative Facts; Catfishing; Doublespeak; Fact-Check; Fake News; Omission, Lies of; Online Dating; Phishing; Social Media; Sockpuppets.

Further Reading

Lee, S. T. (2004). Lying to tell the truth: Journalists and the social context of deception. *Mass Communication & Society, 7*(1), 97–120.

Vishwanath, A. (2015). Habitual Facebook use and its impact on getting deceived on social media. *Journal of Computer-Mediated Communication, 20*, 83–98.

Whitty, M. T. (2002). Liar, liar! An examination of how open, supportive and honest people are in Chat Rooms. *Computers in Human Behavior, 18*(4), 343–352.

Whitty, M. T., & Carville, S. E. (2007). Would I lie to you? Self-serving lies and other-oriented lies told across different media. *Computers and Human Behavior, 24*, 1021–1031.

Memory

The malleability of memory is an important consideration in the study of deception. Deceiving others by omitting information, fabricating false information, denying knowledge, or exaggerating or minimizing a situation can actually alter how one remembers an event. Memory can furthermore be shaped by implicit or explicit suggestions, predictions, and expectations. In most situations, subtle differences in the way individuals remember experiences are of no need for concern. However, in other situations, such as eyewitness testimony or police interrogations, accuracy is more important.

Dr. Miri Besken from Bilkent University examined the effect of lying on memory. Dr. Besken instructed some participants to lie about an event that occurred during the study. In a follow-up interview, when those individuals were asked to tell the truth, they remembered information they had lied about significantly better than true information. This research echoed findings from previous research paradigms where participants were asked to lie about a scene they witnessed and then were later asked to remember the actual event. In both studies, the participants recalled fabricated information at higher rates than true information. It is likely that memory is distorted by lies due to the fact that lies require more effort and are more demanding of cognitive resources than simply telling the truth. Generating lies also requires suppression of the truth, which may serve to reinforce the lie while suppressing the truth in cognitive processing.

Effortful processing is known as a key to enhancing memory. Successful students use this strategy to remember information when studying by self-quizzing or discussing concepts. Effortful engagement with information improves one's ability to remember it later. These same principles explain why the effort needed to construct and maintain a plausible lie enhances one's memory for the lie.

Because the creation of a convincing lie requires more cognitive effort than telling the truth, the lies are more easily remembered. Interestingly, most individuals are not aware of this impact of lying on memory performance. For example, participants in Dr. Besken's study predicted they would have more difficulty remembering the lies, contrary to how they actually performed.

The impact that lying has on memory is particularly important when considering the creation of false memories. Dr. Laura Paige and her colleagues from Brandeis University are extremely interested in how false memories are created during interrogation procedures. Since lying impacts the creation and recall of memories, it influences what one remembers about a situation. Lying about an event can shape the way an individual remembers the experience later. Additionally, the more times an individual repeats the fabricated memory, the greater their confidence in the experience. These impacts on memory likely stem from convolution of fabricated and real details, suppression of information, lack of rehearsal of actual information, and rehearsal of deceptive information. All of these impact an individual's ability to retrieve information and to identify or distinguish true from false information. Individuals who feign amnesia about a particular event remember less when trying to recall the information later, which demonstrates the strength and impact of purposeful suppression. It is also common for individuals who habitually lie to have difficulties in distinguishing truth from falsehoods. They start to believe their own lies and cease to recognize that they are exaggerating or overtly lying.

The malleability of memory is one of the reasons interrogators must be careful not to influence a witness's memory for an event with leading questions or assumptions. Sometimes merely suggesting information through word choice can shape a memory or interpretation of an event. For example, asking a witness to estimate how fast a car was going prior to *crashing* into another car may subtly shape the memory of the event as compared to asking how fast a car was going when it *bumped* another car. Word choice can shape how an event is remembered. Asking witnesses to speculate or repeatedly answer the same questions can also alter memory. Retrospectively, it becomes hard to discriminate between what one actually witnessed from what one speculated may have occurred, and repeating information solidifies it in memory, whether it is an accurate representation of reality or not.

See also: Exaggeration; False Memory; Reality Monitoring; Self-Deception.

Further Reading

Besken, M. (2018). Generating lies produces lower memory predictions and higher memory performance than telling the truth: Evidence for a metacognitive illusion. *Journal of Experimental Psychology: Learning, Memory, and Cognition, 44*(3), 465–484.

Otgaar, H., & Baker, A. (2018). When lying changes memory for the truth. *Memory, 26*(1), 2–14.

Paige, L. E., Rields, E. C., & Gutchess, A. (2019). Influence of age on the effects of lying on memory. *Brain and Cognition, 133*, 42–53.

Sun, X., Punjabi, P. V., Greenberg, L. T., & Seamon, J. G. (2009). Does feigning amnesia impair subsequent recall? *Memory & Cognition, 37*, 81–89.

Mental Effort

Mental effort, or cognitive load, refers to the amount of energy and attention that must be devoted to maintain a thought process. Most research shows that spontaneous lying takes more mental effort than telling the truth. When telling the truth, one must simply pull the information from memory. When lying, one must suppress the truth, fabricate a convincing lie, remember the lie, keep lies consistent, monitor the listener to ensure the lie is being believed, and adjust accordingly. Lying tends to promote greater activity in those brain areas responsible for complex tasks. This increased effort when constructing a lie is possibly noticeable to a trained observer and can provide a clue that the speaker is not being honest. Accordingly, researchers tend to use reaction time as a measure of honesty because those who are answering honestly need less time to respond than those who are fabricating information.

Though this difference in response time could be a good way to detect lying, there are a few difficulties. First, even statistically significant differences in the response times between honest and fabricated answers are very small and only readily detectable with computer analysis. Second, discrepancies in mental effort are only detectable if the individual is forced to respond as quickly as possible in the face of novel questions. Researcher Dr. Kristina Suchotzki from the University of Wurzburg and her colleagues found that if lies have been prepared ahead of time, there are no corresponding increases in mental effort. Thus, for the differences in the response latency associated with mental effort to be useful, questions must be unpredictable to require novel responses, and answers must be given immediately. When providing a rehearsed lie, the liar must suppress the truth, but having a lie prepared decreases the strain on the resources that a spontaneous lie demands. Thus, unexpected questions for which the individual does not have an answer prepared should show the biggest discrepancies between honest and fabricated response times. Such demands for precision make differences in mental effort and reaction time difficult to detect in typical face-to-face interrogations.

Because lying takes increased mental effort, some experts on lie detection believe that increasing overall cognitive load may make lying behavior easier to detect in real time because the individual would have fewer cognitive resources to devote to constructing and maintaining a plausible lie. This cognitive perspective of lie detection suggests an overload should more radically increase the amount of time it takes to construct a convincing lie, as compared to when an individual is telling the truth. To overload mental resources, interviewers may ask people to complete additional tasks while being interviewed or interrogated. They may also add time pressure by asking the person to answer the questions quickly, increase stress, or increase the intensity of physiological cues such as tiredness or hunger. All of these extra stressors increase demands on mental effort, which should increase the differences in response times between lying and honest responses.

During a literature review of cognitive load research, Dr. Bruno Verschuere and his colleagues from the University of Amsterdam identified problems with using cognitive load to detect deception. They found that increasing cognitive load by having the individual complete multiple tasks during the interview not only affected response times for fabricated answers but also increased the amount of time it took the respondent to tell the truth. The increased amount of time it took to tell the truth makes discriminating the truth from lies more difficult, and such response latencies may be misconstrued by an examiner as indicating a lie given that it would align with typical lie-telling response times.

Though research on the effectiveness of manipulating cognitive load on detecting lies is relatively mixed, all studies showed evidence of increased mental effort when lying. Across a wealth of studies throughout the last 20 years, telling the truth was never more demanding than telling a lie. This is because there are more demands on executive functioning when lying, including increased demands on working memory, response inhibition, and task switching. The reliance on these three areas when constructing and executing a lie increases the cognitive effort needed. In addition, lying tends to evoke more emotional arousal, which further prolongs reaction times.

See also: Cognitive Changes while Lying; Costs of Lying; Models of Lying; Neuroscience; Reaction Time; Theory of Mind.

Further Reading

Fernbach, P. M., Hagmayer, Y., & Sloman, S. A. (2014). Effort denial in self-deception. *Organizational Behavior and Human Decision Processes, 123*, 1–8.

Suchotski, K., Verschuere, B., Van Bockstaele, B., Ben-Shakhar, G., & Crombez, G. (2017). Lying takes time: A meta-analysis on reaction time measures of deception. *Psychological Bulletin, 143*(4), 428–453.

Verschuere, B., Kobis, N. C., Bereby-Meyer, Y., Rand, D., & Shalvi, S. (2018). Taxing the brain to uncover lying? Meta-analyzing the effect of imposing cognitive load on the reaction-time costs of lying. *Journal of Applied Research in Memory and Cognition, 7*, 462–469.

Vrij, A., Fisher, R., Mann, S., & Leal, S. (2006). Detecting deception by manipulating cognitive load. *Trends in Cognitive Sciences, 10*(4), 141–142.

Meyer, Pamela

Pamela Meyer is a professional lie detector and the author of *Liespotting: Proven Techniques to Detect Deception*. In 2013, she founded Calibrate, a company that trains business leaders and other professionals to spot or detect deception. Ms. Meyer is a certified fraud examiner and has an MBA from Harvard as well as an MA in Public Policy. She gained popularity through a 2011 TED talk entitled *How to Spot a Liar*, which has been listed as one of the 25 most popular TED talks of all time.

In her book, *Liespotting: Proven Techniques to Detect Deception*, she examines research on lying and lie detection and reveals that, on average, individuals are lied to 10–200 times a day. Strangers tend to lie to each other on average 3 times within the first 10 minutes of meeting, and married couples lie to each other once out of every 10 interactions. Furthermore, personality and gender differences are correlated with lying behavior. For example, extraverts lie significantly more than introverts, and men lie more to protect their reputation while women lie to protect others. She outlines why people lie and how to assess verbal and nonverbal cues to detect when others are lying.

In her book, Ms. Meyer presents the BASIC system, a conversation guide. Her BASIC guide outlines that interviewers should pay attention to baseline behavior, ask open-ended questions, study the deceptive clusters, intuit the gaps in answers, and confirm conclusions. She states that it is important to keep an open mind, not jump to conclusions, and to focus on the facts. She also identifies that individuals telling the truth tend to remember more salient details rather than simply details in a chronological order. Therefore, if an individual is going in strict chronological order when recounting an event, that may be an indicator that they are attempting to lie. She also notes there are telltale signs of lying such as emphatic denials, use of formal or distancing language, inclusion of irrelevant detail, attempts to stall, chattering fingertips, stiff bodies, sustained eye contact, fake smiles, and discrepancies between words and actions. For example, liars may say yes but shake their head no. However, all of these behaviors show individual differences, so to be good at detecting deception, it is important to know individuals' baseline behaviors and then to pay attention to changes during pertinent questions.

In addition to training individuals to detect lies, Ms. Meyer also examines why people lie. In line with other researchers, she identifies that most lies are cooperative. The liar and the willing believer work together to create a smooth social experience. In an interview with Dick Carozza of *Fraud Magazine*, Ms. Meyer explains that there are offensive and defensive motives for deception. Offensive reasons include securing a reward, gaining an advantage, creating positive impressions, or exercising power. Defensive reasons include avoiding punishment, protecting oneself or others, escaping awkward situations, or maintaining privacy. Additionally, lies can be told for more harmful purposes. For example, as of 2010, she presents that there were 997 billion dollars of corporate fraud in the United States alone.

To retaliate against such ubiquitous lying, Ms. Meyer proposes that facial recognition training, interrogation training, and a survey of field research can help business leaders to spot deceptive attempts. Her work is presented to a lay audience who want to improve their lie detection skills, and she claims that lie spotters can be trained to detect lies 90 percent of the time. She draws upon research such as that by Dr. Paul Ekman and Dr. Erika Rosenberg to make liespotting accessible to the masses. She challenges listeners to look and listen and presents that the basis of lie detection is a healthy sense of skepticism. She cautions that humans tend to have a truth bias and want to believe others to maintain relationships. Most people tend not to stop, listen, and evaluate and therefore are not likely to recognize lies. Additionally, lie detection is hard to practice. Even if one is suspicious that another may be lying, there is rarely feedback to know if one is correct. Ms. Meyer believes our inherent failure to detect deception is a by-product of an evolutionary arms race in which deceptive abilities are evolving as quickly as the detection abilities. Even today, as we strive to outwit phishers, these scammers continually alter their strategies. But, by using Ms. Meyer's techniques to detect deception, she believes that people can become much more savvy detectors.

See also: Deceiver Stereotype; Detecting Deception; Ekman, Paul; Evolution of Deception; Fraud; Language; Microexpressions; Motives for Lying; Nonverbal Behavior; Personality; Phishing; Reality Monitoring; Scams; Sex Differences in Lying Behavior; Truth-Default Theory.

Further Reading

Carozza, D. (2012). Spotting those elusive liars: An interview with Pamela Meyer, CFE, author of 'Liespotting' and keynoter at the 23rd annual ACFE Fraud Conference & Exhibition. *Fraud Magazine*. Retrieved from https://www.fraud-magazine.com/article.aspx?id=4294972760

Meyer, P. (2010). *Liespotting: Proven Techniques to Detect Deception.* St Martin's Press.

Meyer, P. (2011). *How to spot a liar* [Video file]. Retrieved from https://www.ted.com/talks/pamela_meyer_how_to_spot_a_liar/up-next

Microexpressions

Microexpressions are the unconscious, uncontrolled, and universal aspects of facial expressions. Facial muscles that are directly connected to the limbic system, where emotion signals originate, create microexpressions. When individuals experience emotions, the emotion signals are directly translated to the facial muscles at the same time they are being transmitted to the frontal cortex for conscious processing. Once the emotional signals are processed in the frontal lobe, individuals can decide whether to accentuate or conceal the emotional expression, but this process lags behind the initial display, causing a brief genuine microexpression that is unconscious and uncontrolled.

Since microexpressions are not consciously controlled, they reveal the emotions that individuals may attempt to conceal during deceptive attempts. Common emotions that occur when lying include fear, distress, guilt, contempt, disgust, and glee. An initial, reflexive display of one of these emotions that is immediately suppressed or masked provides observers a clue that the subsequent emotional display is not genuine, particularly if the microexpression does not match the verbal response being given. Microexpressions may only last less than half a second, so they are more easily observed in video footage that can be slowed down frame by frame.

Microexpressions differ from macroexpressions in length and cohesion. Macroexpressions are the conscious, displayed emotional expressions that are tailored to match the tone of the verbal content or situation, and they tend to last one to four seconds. These are the normal facial expressions that individuals see and display to communicate with those around them. Microexpressions are much briefer, are unconscious, and tend to match the actual internal state. Because they are so quick, observers are more likely to focus on the macroexpression that masks them and can easily miss the brief, genuine microexpression.

Examples of microexpressions are the lowered brows and narrowed eyes, flared nostrils, and clenched jaw that reveals a flash of anger. Similarly, pulling back with widened eyes, an opened mouth, and raised brows communicates surprise, even if these signs are immediately covered up and smoothed over into socially appropriate emotional displays. The disgust response from biting into a truly noxious or toxic substance can be read across language barriers, even if the individual is trying to cover up the response. When Dr. Paul Ekman asked research participants to cover up microexpressions, only about a quarter of them were able to do so about 2 percent of the time. However, because they are so fleeting, most observers do not recognize them without training.

Learning to watch for microexpressions allows observers a glimpse into the actual emotional state of a conversation partner. Microexpressions provide greater awareness of a partner's emotional state, conflicts between felt and expressed emotion, and potential efforts to deceive. However, since there are many reasons individuals may wish to conceal their emotional responses, a mismatch between initial and posed emotional expressions may not indicate guilt. Frequently, true emotional responses may not conform to cultural display rules. For example, laughing at a funeral or reacting angrily when working with a child is typically inappropriate, so adults may work to cover up these emotional displays.

Examination of microexpressions in a mock crime scenario revealed that microexpressions could be successfully used to differentiate liars from those telling the truth. Analysis of microexpressions from the first second after suspects made statements about their guilt was conclusive in discriminating liars from those who were telling the truth, particularly when analyzing individuals who were experiencing high-intensity emotions. Given this evidence that microexpressions can discriminate between lies and truths, computer technology or interrogation training may help security personnel more reliably discriminate between those who may be hiding information and those who are telling the truth.

Reading microexpressions has been the target of training programs across the United States to increase the effectiveness of detecting those who are engaging in deception. For example, the U.S. transportation agency has training programs to help officers more effectively and reliably identify suspicious passengers. Detecting microexpressions that are inconsistent with displayed expressions or verbal reports may reveal suspicious individuals. When Dr. Paul Ekman and Dr. Maureen O'Sullivan analyzed the ability to detect microexpressions, they found that U.S. Secret Service agents were significantly more successful than controls and that training programs such as the ones they complete can enhance the ability to detect microexpressions.

See also: Detecting Deception; Ekman, Paul; Emotional Effects; Facial Cues; Nonverbal Behavior; Wizard's Project.

Further Reading

Burgoon, J. K. (2018). Microexpressions are not the best way to catch a liar. *Frontiers in Psychology, 9*(1672), 1–5.

Ekman, P. (1991). Invited article: Face, voice, and body in detecting deceit. *Journal of Nonverbal Behavior, 15*(2), 125–135.

Frank, M. G., & Svetieva, E. (2015). Microexpressions and deception. In M. K. Mandal & A. Awasthi (Eds.), *Understanding Facial Expressions in Communication* (pp. 227–242). Springer.

Matsumoto, D., & Hwang, H. C. (2018). Microexpressions differentiate truths from lies about future malicious intent. *Frontiers in Psychology, 9*(2545), 1–11.

Microexpressions. (2018). *What are Microexpressions?* Retrieved from https://www .paulekman.com/resources/micro-expressions/

Porter, S., & ten Brinke, L. (2008). Reading between the lies: Identifying concealed and falsified emotions in universal facial expressions. *Psychological Science, 19*(5), 508–514.

Milgram's Obedience Experiments

Dr. Stanley Milgram's obedience experiments from the 1960s used deception to examine how social pressures, particularly from authority figures, can influence behavior. This series of experiments involved deceiving participants and encouraging them to deliver what they thought were painful and potentially deadly shocks to a fellow participant. Dr. Milgram discovered that a vast number of participants obeyed the directions of the experimenter to the extent of potentially killing their fellow participant. Such methodology raises ethical concerns and is potentially damaging for the psychological well-being of the participant.

In Dr. Milgram's study, in which he claimed to be studying how punishment affects learning, participants were assigned to the role of teacher or learner. In actuality, all participants were assigned to the role of teacher. Those who were assigned the role of the learner were actually confederates, or assistants, of the experimenter. The participant watched the confederate being hooked up to a machine with which the participant was asked to administer shocks following incorrect responses in the learning study. The experimenter instructed the participant to administer shocks at 15 volt (V) increments beginning at 15 V and continuing up to 450 V. A sample shock was given to the participant to convince them of the authenticity of the generator. The participant and the confederate were separated into different rooms but could communicate during the experiment via an intercom. Though the confederate was never actually shocked, he vocalized pain, desire to end the experiment, complaints of a heart condition, and eventual prolonged silence. If the participant expressed a desire to discontinue the shocks, the researcher simply responded that the experiment must continue.

In Dr. Milgram's first series of experiments, 65 percent of the participants continued until they had administered the 450 V deadly shock. All of the subjects administered at least 300 V. All participants were uncomfortable and displayed signs of tension and stress, though most quickly conformed when told that they must continue the experiment. Though such experiments raise ethics concerns, they did demonstrate how those in positions of power, even positions of perceived power, can radically influence the behavior of others.

There are several reasons that research participants conformed in Milgram's obedience study. Some of these include deference to authority, diffusion of responsibility, and the gradual increase in shock strength. Having an authority figure encourage them to continue lessened their feelings of responsibility though they still demonstrated signs of stress. Those who did discontinue the experiment tended to do so when the learner first requested to be released and expressed a wish not to continue. Participants who continued past that point tended to complete the experiment. Participants were likely to show signs of sweating, trembling, stuttering, and nervous laughter. However, since the increments of shocks slowly grew over the experiment, it was difficult for participants to know when to draw a line, especially if they continued past the point of the initial complaints, reflecting the foot-in-the-door phenomenon.

Such results can be applied to many different social situations. Individuals are likely to conform to those in positions of authority, regardless of the consequences.

Individuals are also likely to play their role as expected, which may have implications for treatment of prisoners, suspects, or prisoners of war. This highlights how important it is for those in positions of authority to behave ethically and why average individuals can commit heinous crimes under the guidance of unethical authority figures. Given the likelihood of the masses to conform to those in authority, the extreme need for checks and balances is highlighted as well as the widespread detrimental implications of deception.

Follow-up discussions with participants revealed that most participants were able to rationalize or justify their behavior. Most viewed the experimenter as a leader and felt justified in following his orders. Most trusted the experimenter to have good intentions and thought they were contributing to scientific research. Several felt that they were required to continue to fulfill their end of the contract by completing the research. In retrospect, however, most were horrified at their actions and at their willingness to harm another person simply because they were instructed to do so.

Dr. Milgram's initial and subsequent research illustrated that there are elements that increase obedience. In addition to the incremental increase in shock strength and prods from authority figures, participants were also likely feeling social pressures to be polite. They were also not given much time to think about the consequences. All of these elements contributed to the number of participants who continued the study to lethal proportions. The study highlights the effectiveness of coercive force and can caution against such measures when attempting to solicit the truth from a witness or suspect. The greater the perception of authority, the more likely an individual will conform.

See also: Coercion; Conscience; Corruption; Deception in Research; Ethics; Hypocrisy; Locus of Control; Minimization.

Further Reading

Hollander, M. M., & Turowetz, J. (2017). Normalizing trust: Participants' immediately post-hoc explanations of behaviour in Milgram's 'obedience' experiments. *British Journal of Social Psychology, 56*, 655–674.

Milgram, S. (1963). Behavioral study of obedience. *Journal of Abnormal and Social Psychology, 67*, 371–378.

Packer, D. J. (2008). Identifying systematic disobedience in Milgram's obedience experiments: A meta-analytic review. *Perspectives on Psychological Science, 3*(4), 301–304.

Russell, N. J. C. (2011). Milgram's obedience to authority experiments: Origins and early evolution. *British Journal of Social Psychology, 50*, 140–162.

Mimicry

Mimicry is an adaptation in which organisms mimic aspects of other organisms. The mimicked traits allow the individual to survive more readily than individuals who do not have those traits. In this way, mimicry functions at a basic evolutionary level to allow individuals within a species to survive. Mimicry is a form of deception where adapted traits mislead others, particularly predators. Though mimicry is not a conscious or purposeful mode of deceiving others, it is categorized as deception because it functions to mislead observers.

Mimicry traits evolved because those organisms who resemble other species have a selective advantage. The traits that emerge may falsely signal that the organism is poisonous, venomous, or otherwise dangerous. Presenting such signals discourages predators from pursuing or consuming them, allowing them to survive and reproduce more readily. Increased reproduction provides even more of the selected trait in the next generation. In this way, mimicry is supported by natural selection. The mimicry trait is a false signal, but predators may take it as an honest signal because the consequences of consuming a potentially poisonous meal is death. Those individuals who take the risk are more likely to also consume prey that are actually poisonous, which is detrimental to their survival and reproductive success. Over evolutionary time, cautious predators will be more likely to survive, making the mimicry traits even more effective, increasing their ratio in the population.

Mimicry is similar to camouflage, but rather than merging into a background to escape detection, species evolve physical traits or behaviors that mimic another species. There are several types of mimicry. Two examples of mimicry are Batesian mimicry and Mullerian mimicry. Batesian mimicry is when a species evolves distinctive markings that resemble a poisonous species to provide a false signal to predators. For example, the yellow and black markings on hoverflies strongly resemble those of wasps. Though hoverflies are harmless, predators tend to avoid them because of these features that make them resemble a stinging wasp.

In Mullerian mimicry, two species evolve to resemble one another, and both are toxic to predators. This double protection makes it even more likely that a foultasting, toxic experience will deter predators from both species. For example, both the Monarch butterfly and the viceroy butterfly have distinctive markings that have evolved to signal toxicity to predators. The markings make individual butterflies more likely to survive because predators learn that they do not make an appetizing meal. Thus, those individuals who have clear markings are less likely to be eaten and are more likely to pass on the markings to greater numbers of offspring.

Aside from physical markings, species can also evolve behavioral patterns that mimic other animals for personal gain. For example, one species of firefly, the Photuris, mimics the mating lights of other firefly species to draw in prey. Once an interested male approaches, drawn in by the signals of mating interest, the predatory beetle attacks and eats him. In this way, the mimicked behavior functions to make the Photuris more likely to survive and pass on this innate behavior to offspring, supporting and increasing its presence in the species.

Plants also have mimicry traits. For example, plants have evolved to have physical features or odors that attract insects for the purposes of pollination. Insects are attracted to the features or scents, attempt to reproduce, and thus cross-pollinate individual plants before moving on. Plants that have these odors are more likely to survive and be pollinated, increasing that trait in the species.

Mimicry works as long as the mimicked trait is typically an honest signal. If the species using mimicry start to outnumber those that are providing honest signals, the mimicry becomes less effective. Birds, for example, will quickly learn that markings do not belie danger if the poisonous species ceases to be present in the environment. To remain effective, the honest signals must outnumber the false signals or else they lose their communication value.

See also: Camouflage; Deception in Animals; Evolution of Deception; Signaling Theory.

Further Reading

Anderson, B., & Jager, M. L. (2019). Natural selection in mimicry. *Biological Reviews, 95*(2), 291–304.

Bond, C. F. (1988). The evolution of deception. *Journal of Nonverbal Behavior, 12*(4), 295–307.

Dalziell, A. H., & Welbergen, J. A. (2016). Mimicry for all modalities. *Ecology Letters, 19*(6), 609–619.

Minimization

Minimization is a type of deception that occurs when an individual has done something that creates anxiety and guilt. Rather than acknowledge the severity of the transgression, the individual instead minimizes the importance of the act. This may include rationalizing the behavior, coming up with excuses, or deciding that the behavior or consequences are not as severe as they really may be. Minimization is used to allay feelings of guilt associated with socially inappropriate behaviors. An individual may trivialize, make light of, or downplay their own role in a situation or the severity of the situation. It tends to occur during an experience of cognitive dissonance in which a thought and a behavior do not align. To alleviate the discomfort, the individual must either admit to the behavior or change their perception. Since changing a thought process is easier than changing a behavior, many will opt to minimize the severity of the act.

During minimization, individuals may phrase the description of a situation to make it seem less important. For example, they may say that it only happened once, it only happened a little bit, or it was not a big deal. They may also just claim that it was not intentional, and thus not their fault. They may blame the victim or come up with reasons why the behavior was acceptable. People minimize situations frequently as a self-protective measure or as a defense mechanism. They may feel guilty, stressed, or anxious about their own behavior, and minimizing it in their descriptions or thoughts can help alleviate some of that stress. Minimization may be a short-term solution for a problem. Understanding the severity of one's behavior and taking responsibility for changing the behavior, however, is needed for long-term psychological health.

Minimizations are often used during attempts to manipulate others. The goal is to convince oneself or others that a behavior is not as severe or detrimental as it is initially perceived. During minimization, an individual admits to a behavior but attempts to convince themselves or others it is not as bad as it seems. An individual may attempt to trivialize a behavior to explain why it was appropriate given the situation, and they may even be successful in convincing themselves or others. Typically, they externalize the blame, focus on what others did rather than their own behavior, and claim that the behavior was unintentional or not that bad.

This tendency to minimize the effects of a behavior is often seen in research on domestic violence. In order to maintain their own self-esteem and self-concept, abusers have a tendency to trivialize their own abusive actions so they can maintain their perception of themselves as a good person. They minimize their own role in the situation by blaming the partner, the situation, or trivializing the severity of the abuse. By minimizing the situation, the abuser does not respect the victim's concerns. They belittle their partner's perspective, undermine their confidence, or dismiss their concerns. Undervaluing the other person's worth makes confrontation of the minimization tactics less likely to occur.

The use of minimization can also be used as a tactic in interrogations. Interrogators may minimize the importance or severity of a crime in order to get a suspect to admit to committing it. Providing rationalization that makes the behavior seem logical or less severe may essentially trick the suspect into admitting that they did it, since they believe the interrogator is on their side.

See also: Cognitive Dissonance; Denial; Gaslighting; Locus of Control; Manipulation; Self-Deception.

Further Reading

Bear, A. L. (2015). Denying and minimizing is no way to cope. *Psychology Today*. Retrieved from https://www.psychologytoday.com/us/blog/charm-harm/201506 /denying-and-minimizing-is-no-way-to-cope

Kelly, C. E., Russano, M. B., Miller, J. C., & Redlich, A. D. (2019). On the road (to admission): Engaging suspects with minimization. *Psychology, Public Policy, and Law, 25*(3), 166–180.

Rogers, R., & Dickey, R. (1991). Denial and minimization among sex offenders. *Annals of Sex Research, 4*, 49–63.

Scott, K., & Straus, M. (2007). Denial, minimization, partner blaming, and intimate aggression in dating partners. *Journal of Interpersonal Violence, 22*(7), 851–871.

Models of Lying

Most models of lying assume there are measurable differences between behaviors, brain activity, and emotional experiences when someone is lying versus when they are telling the truth. Each model of lying attempts to provide effective and consistent means of distinguishing lies from truths. Models of lying make use of variations in behaviors, cognitive load, cognitive effort, complexity of speech, emotional reactions, and arousal levels to effectively detect lying. A few models of lying include the Cognitive Load Approach, Working Memory Model, Cognitive Strain Model, Strategic Model, Information Manipulation Theory 2, and Activation-Decision-Construction-Action Theory, among others.

The Cognitive Load Approach (CLA), described by Dr. Miron Zuckerman and Dr. Bella DePaulo and their colleagues, and the Working Memory Model (WMM), described by Dr. Siegfried Ludwig Sporer and Dr. Barbara Schwandt, both propose that increasing cognitive load, or the amount of information active in working memory, may allow interviewers to more easily discriminate between lies and the truth. These models suggest that lying puts more strain on working memory resources than telling the truth. When lying, one must create and remember a plausible lie; monitor and control nonverbal, paraverbal, and verbal cues; and monitor and adjust based on a partner's responses. Furthermore, activation of true information is an automatic process, so a liar must suppress true information while reporting deceptive information.

Based on the CLA or WMM, interrogators could increase the amount of information suspects are manipulating in working memory, such as by having them complete competing tasks during the interview, to stress these cognitive resources. Individuals who are telling the truth can still answer questions even when taxed. Individuals who are attempting to lie, however, will likely show delayed responses, longer pauses, less cohesive answers, and greater physiological changes. Those telling the truth can still respond quickly and effortlessly because they do not need to modify their answers or monitor their own plausibility or suspiciousness. Lying requires more effort because the liar must invent or modify information, stay plausible and noncontradictory, and monitor for suspiciousness; thus, increases in load may reduce their ability to lie effectively.

The Cognitive Strain Model similarly suggests that lying increases the demand of working memory and cognitive resources. This model suggests that lying taxes cognitive resources and that lies will reduce in complexity as a liar becomes fatigued. Furthermore, anything that adds to cognitive demand will reduce the complexity of language. Lying induces a level of complexity that truth-telling does not, demonstrated by participants in research studies who used more simplistic thinking and speech when asked to lie as compared to those who were asked to tell the truth. Thus, analysis of the complexity of a suspect's answers may help distinguish between true and fabricated responses. Some research shows, however, that increasing cognitive strain also slows reaction time for telling the truth. Thus, interrogators would need to take that into account when attempting to detect lies.

The Strategic Model, in opposition to the Cognitive Strain Model, suggests that a liar will adjust the complexity of lies depending on the perceived threats and benefits. In psychological research, participants did tend to manipulate the complexity of their lies to accomplish specific goals. Participants were likely to use ambiguous and simple lies, as predicted by the Cognitive Strain Model, unless they were lying to a suspicious partner. In those instances, liars were more likely to use assertive, elaborative, and complex lies.

Dr. Steven McCornack and his colleagues from Michigan State University propose that the Information Manipulation Theory 2 explains how people manipulate information when attempting to deceive, and what situations tend to evoke lying. In opposition to other theories, this theory proposes that lying does not necessarily place a greater load on cognitive resources than truth-telling. In fact, in some situations, low-stakes lies may be less effortful than telling the truth. This theory focuses on the quantity and quality of the information shared, the relevance of information, and the manner in which it is conveyed. Messages that diverge from the norm in any of these areas may signal lying.

A final example is the Activation-Decision-Construction-Action Theory (ADCAT) of lying proposed by Dr. Jeffrey Walczyk and his colleagues from Louisiana Tech University. This theory builds on the Information Manipulation

Theory 2 and the Working Memory Model. It also draws from other models of lying such as the Four-Factor Theory of deception that suggests lying involves arousal, guilt, cognitions, and control and from the Preoccupation Model of Secrecy that suggests attempted suppression of information can cause an individual to perseverate on the information until it becomes an obsession. In general, the ADCAT says that lying taxes cognitive resources due to automatic activation of the truth that must be suppressed, assessments of risk to decide whether or not to lie, construction of a plausible deception, and sincerity when delivering the lie. If lies have been rehearsed, they make fewer demands on cognitive resources than those that are unrehearsed. Unrehearsed lies will show higher rates of stereotypical behaviors associated with lying as well as more demand on cognitive resources, making them easier to detect.

For all theories of lying, practice and preparation facilitate believability of lies. Creating lies in the moment places greater demands on cognitive resources and makes them easier to detect. Some liars are effective because they have repeated the lie so many times that they can recite it from habit or start to believe it. Furthermore, practice lying improves those skills. Frequent liars lie more readily and with less effort than those who typically tell the truth.

See also: Language; Lying; Mental Effort; Microexpressions; Nonverbal Behavior; Reaction Time; Reality Monitoring; Self-Deception; Theory of Mind.

Further Reading

Burgoon, J. K. (2016). Deception detection accuracy. In C. R. Berger & M. E. Roloff (Eds.), *The International Encyclopedia of Interpersonal Communication* (1st ed., pp. 1–6). John Wiley & Sons.

Burgoon, J. K., Buller, D. B., Floyd, K., & Grandpre, J. (1996). Deceptive realities: Sender, receiver, and observer perspectives in deceptive conversations. *Communication Research, 23*(6), 724–748.

Gawrylowicz, J., Fairlamb, S., Tantot, E., Qureshi, Z., Redha, A., & Ridley, A. M. (2016). Does practice make the perfect liar? The effect of rehearsal and increased cognitive load on cues to deception. *Applied Cognitive Psychology, 30*, 250–259.

McCornack, S. A., Morrison, K., Palik, J. E., Wisner, A. M., & Zhu, X. (2014). Information Manipulation Theory 2: A propositional theory of deceptive discourse production. *Journal of Language and Social Psychology, 33*(4), 348–377.

Repke, M. A., Conway, L. G., III, & Houck, S. C. (2018). The strategic manipulation of linguistic complexity: A test of two models of lying. *Journal of Language and Social Psychology, 37*(1), 74–92.

Sporer, S. L., & Schwandt, B. (2006). Paraverbal indicators of deception: A meta-analytic synthesis. *Applied Cognitive Psychology, 20*(4), 421–446.

Vrij, A., Fisher, R., Mann, S., & Leal, S. (2006). Detecting deception by manipulating cognitive load. *Trends in Cognitive Sciences, 10*(4), 141–142.

Walczyk, J. J., Harris, L. L., Duck, T. K., & Mulay, D. (2014). A social-cognitive framework for understanding serious lies: Activation-decision-construction-action theory. *New Ideas in Psychology, 34*, 22–36.

Zuckerman, M., DePaulo, B. M., & Rosenthal, R. (1981). Verbal and nonverbal communication of deception. In L. Berkowitz (Ed.), *Advances in experimental social psychology, 14*, 1-57. Academic Press.

Motivational Impairment Effect

The motivational impairment effect describes how individuals who are highly motivated to deceive show more nonverbal signals of deception. Thus, those who try the hardest to deceive are also the most likely to be detected. Furthermore, individuals who are highly motivated to detect deception show a similar impairment in detection ability. Most psychological research shows that motivation increases performance for easy tasks but decreases performance for difficult tasks. Deceiving effectively and detecting deception are highly difficult tasks, which may explain why increased motivation may have a negative impact on performance.

The motivational impairment effect during deception may be due to the fact that those who are highly motivated to deceive tend to have greater physiological arousal, and such arousal is harder to conceal. The motivational impairment effect is the most noticeable when an observer knows the speaker well. However, in a research paradigm, Dr. Bella DePaulo and Dr. Bob Rosenthal found that participants were also able to detect the impairment in strangers, as long as the motivation to deceive was strong and the participants could both hear the liars and see their nonverbal behaviors. The motivational impairment effect was not demonstrated for white lies or for posed scenarios that did not elicit sufficient motivational arousal to impact performance. For example, the motivational impairment effect is typically not elicited by mock crime scenarios frequently used in research but is elicited when real crime scenarios or interviews are used. Only when a liar is sufficiently aroused and motivated to get away with the lie is their physiological arousal sufficient to impact their performance. Furthermore, those who are not aroused by lying, such as those with antisocial personality disorder, or those who feel justified in lying, do not show impaired performance.

Researchers also demonstrated that those who are highly motivated to detect deception show a similar decrease in performance. Dr. Stephen Porter and his colleagues from Grant MacEwan College found that participants who were highly motivated to detect deception in a research study actually performed less accurately, but with more confidence, than those in the low-motivation condition. Those who were highly motivated to detect deception had many false alarms where they rated true statements as false. When provided feedback about their judgments, however, performance did improve. Dr. Porter and his colleagues believe that the presence of feedback served as a reality check to the observer and mitigated the tunnel vision that highly motivated observers tend to show. This reality check allowed them to stop using only the stereotypical cues to make their judgments. Even with feedback, however, those who are highly motivated to detect deception did not perform better than those with low motivation.

The motivational impairment effect is a substantial issue in interrogation settings in which interrogators are highly motivated to detect deception. Interrogators who are overly enthusiastic about detecting deception or already believe the suspect is guilty are likely to detect deception even when it is not present. Those who are highly motivated to detect deception rely on the stereotypical cues of deception, such as averted gaze or fidgeting behaviors that do not, in fact, indicate deceptive attempts. In 1999, Dr. Saul Kassin and Dr. Christina Fong of Williams College found that participants provided with the Reid Technique training, which is typically provided to police to detect deception, actually performed worse than research participants who had not been trained. The trained individuals, however, were more confident in their incorrect judgments and provided more reasons for their judgments. This research highlights the importance of regular feedback and collaboration between interrogators to mitigate the tunnel vision that might ensue from being highly motivated and overconfident in detection skills.

Dr. James Forrest and Dr. Robert Feldman from University of Massachusetts at Amherst proposed that another explanation for this effect is that those who are highly motivated to detect deception tend to engage in central route processing. They found that motivated detectors engaged higher order cognitive processing and paid more attention to the verbal message and were likely to miss the nonverbal cues that may indicate deception. Those who were less motivated were more likely to use peripheral processing and noticed the subtleties and nonverbal cues of deception more readily.

See also: Antisocial Personality Disorder; DePaulo, Bella; Detecting Deception; Emotional Effects; Physiology; Polygraph Tests; Reid Technique.

Further Reading

DePaulo, B. M., & Kirkendol, S. E. (1989). The motivational impairment effect in the communication of deception. In J. C. Yuille (Ed.), *Credibility Assessment* (pp. 51–70). Springer.

DePaulo, B. M., Kirkendol, S. E., Tang, J., & O'Brien, T. P. (1988). The motivational impairment of fact in the communication of deception: Replications and extensions. *Journal of Nonverbal Behavior, 12*, 177–202.

DePaulo, B. M., & Rosenthal, R. (1979). Telling lies. *Journal of Personality and Social Psychology, 37*, 1713–1722.

Forrest, J. A., & Feldman, R. S. (2000). Detecting deception and judge's involvement: Lower task involvement leads to better lie detection. *Personality and Social Psychology Bulletin, 26*(1), 118–125.

Kassin, S. M., & Fong, C. T. (1999). I'm innocent!: Effects of training on judgments of truth and deception in the interrogation room. *Law and Human Behavior, 23*, 499–516.

Porter, S., McCabe, S., Woodworth, M., & Peace, K. A. (2007). 'Genius is 1% inspiration and 99% perspiration'... or is it? Investigation of the impact of motivation and feedback on deception detection. *Legal and Criminological Psychology, 12*, 297–309.

Motives for Lying

One's motives for lying depend on the situation, the history, and the individual. Individuals can lie to protect themselves or to protect others. They lie for instrumental reasons, such as to gain or maintain power over others, to acquire resources, or avoid punishment. They lie for relational reasons, such as to initiate or terminate relationships, avoid conflict, or protect oneself or others. Or they can lie for psychological reasons, such as to avoid embarrassment, project a favorable image,

Most Common Lies

Knowing what people tend to lie about may make it easier to spot lies as they occur. Though high-stakes lies are likely more salient, they are actually less common than white lies. On average, people tell a white lie on a daily or weekly basis, making everyone a victim and perpetrator of deception. These deceptions usually include tweaking the truth to conform to social norms, avoid hurting others, or bolster self-esteem. Some may get in the habit of making these small self-serving variations to the truth and actually influence their own perceptions of reality.

Many of the most common lies stem from conforming to societal expectations. Due to societal values, most people, women in particular, want to be perceived as younger and, men in particular, want to be viewed as more successful and financially stable than they may actually be. It is common, particularly in the United States, for individuals to lie about age or career. Furthermore, both men and women tend to lie about the number of sexual partners they have had. In the United States, men tend to exaggerate their number while women minimize their number to conform to societal expectations.

Lies are also commonly told to maintain or avoid relationships. Women are more likely to claim to be in a relationship, regardless of their actual relationship status. Telling a persistent suitor that they are in a relationship can be a safe way to tell a suitor they are not interested. Complimenting friends, particularly when asked, is also a common lie that maintains relationships. Telling the truth about one's perception of another person's weight, appearance, or abilities can cause needless conflict or hurt feelings about inconsequential things. It is important, however, to tell the truth when it does matter. If a friend is headed to a job interview, honest critique may help them be more prepared and successful.

Other common lies are those spun to avoid an interaction or confrontation, get out of a conversation, or off the phone or chat session. In these situations, butler lies are used to extract oneself from a conversation or commitment without hurting feelings. When engaged over social media, individuals commonly claim to be busy or tired, claim to have missed the message, say they will be right back, claim technical problems or loss of battery life, or tell any other white lie that allows them to exit the conversation without damaging the relationship. These lies are typically socially acceptable, even though the other individual is usually aware that they are being lied to.

Lies are also commonly told when initiating new relationships. Exaggerations to make one more attractive or interesting to the new partner or friend are common means of securing the attention of the other. Users of dating apps, for example, admitted to claiming to have interests that aligned with the partner's interests or exaggerating abilities to appear more interesting. In general, once relationships are established, less lying tends to occur. Not only does one tend to feel more comfortable being genuine once they have established intimacy, but being known also makes it more difficult to escape detection.

or to increase social desirability. Individuals can engage in low-stakes lies that have low reward yet low risk of punishment should they be discovered. They can also engage in high-stakes lies where the potential for reward is great but so is the potential for punishment if they are caught. People may lie out of a sense of entitlement, to alleviate discomfort, or simply to hurt others.

Dr. Paul Ekman, a foundational researcher in the field of deception, proposes that there are nine basic motives for lying. Dr. Ekman suggests that individuals lie to avoid punishment, obtain rewards, protect others, protect oneself, win admiration, exit awkward social situations, avoid embarrassment, maintain privacy, and exercise power over others. Additionally, when lying in an online context, different motives emerge. Those who lie online tend to do so to gain attention or acceptance or to appear more attractive or interesting to others; for privacy; as part of a fantasy or role-playing scenario; to maintain anonymity or to try out different parts of identity; for personal gain; and to avoid conflict.

Dr. Mark Miller further explains that the reasons people lie can be sorted along three theoretical psychological perspectives. These include the psychoanalytic perspective, the behavioral perspective, and the person-centered perspective. Psychoanalytic reasons for lying include avoiding uncomfortable thoughts, feelings, or experiences; decreasing anxiety or blame for something one has done; or gratifying one's desires. The behavioral perspective predicts that people lie simply to receive rewards or avoid punishment—that is, to gain or maintain power over others, acquire resources, or avoid negative consequences. The person-centered perspective predicts that people lie in order to receive positive regard from others, to be viewed as more competent, successful, or impressive, in order to increase a sense of self-worth. Likely a combination of these reasons is needed to fully explain motivations for lying.

Individuals tend to engage in low-stakes lies to maintain relationships, to smooth over or escape social interactions, or to pacify conversation partners. In these situations, lies are motivated by a desire to diffuse, end, or regulate social interactions. These lies do not tend to be malicious or even premeditated and are typically forgivable even if they are detected. Individuals who engage in high-stakes lies, or more serious deceptions, tend to be more intentional. These lies typically are motivated by a need to protect oneself. They may be told to save face, or to create a false impression about one's personal characteristics, qualities, or achievements to garner respect, pride, or security. They may be told to protect others or from a sense of resentment or indignation. They may be motivated by revenge or to vent anger. High-stakes lies tend to be more malicious. They may benefit the liar at the expense of the conversation partner. These lies are high stakes because they are less likely to be easily forgiven if detected and may result in reputation or relationship damage or legal action.

Though there are many motives for lying, research shows that lying behavior tends to be more common for individuals with poorer psychological health. Confident, competent, well-connected individuals are less likely to lie because they do not need to in order to achieve their goals. Thus, a primary motive for lying is a sense of discontent or uneasiness with oneself that is perpetuated by the lying behavior. Those interested in curbing lying behavior may start with building competence and self-esteem and surrounding oneself with honest social partners.

See also: Benefits of Lying; Butler Lies; Costs of Lying; Ekman, Paul; Instrumental Lies; Intelligence; Locus of Control; Models of Lying; Narcissism; Social Media.

Further Reading

Burgoon, J. K., Buller, D. B., Floyd, K., & Grandpre, J. (1996). Deceptive realities: Sender, receiver, and observer perspectives in deceptive conversations. *Communication Research, 23*(6), 724–748.

Drouin, M., Miller, D., Wehle, S. M. J., & Hernandez, E. (2016). Why do people lie online? "Because everyone lies on the internet." *Computers in Human Behavior, 64,* 134–142.

Ekman, P. (1997). Deception, lying, and demeanor. In D. F. Halpern & A. E. Voiskounsky (Eds.), *States of Mind: American and Post-Soviet Perspectives on Contemporary Issues in Psychology* (pp. 93–105). Oxford University Press.

Miller, M. J. (1992). The Pinocchio syndrome: Lying and its impact on the counseling process. *Counseling and Values, 37*(1), 25–31.

Rose, C., & Wilson, M. S. (2014). Perceptions of everyday deceptions: Individual differences in narcissism and psychopathy associated with black and white untruths. In A. Besser (Ed.), *Handbook of the Psychology of Narcissism* (pp. 229–248). Nova Science Publications.

Munchausen by Proxy (See Munchausen Syndrome)

Munchausen Syndrome

Munchausen Syndrome is a psychological disorder in which an individual acts as though he or she is ill and engages in behaviors to cause or promote the sickness. Individuals tend to engage in these behaviors to gain sympathy or maintain the attention they receive when they are unwell. Individuals who suffer from Munchausen Syndrome deliberately exaggerate or concoct stories and symptoms, deliberately hurt themselves, or alter diagnostic tests to gain attention. They tend to have dramatic and inconsistent medical histories; vague symptoms; high rates of relapse of treated disorders; extensive knowledge about illnesses, hospitals, and medical terminology; symptoms that are not observed by others; eagerness to engage in medical tests; a history of seeking medical treatment; and overall low self-esteem. In some cases, sufferers inject themselves with viruses or bacteria, cause physical injuries, or consume toxic substances to create a medical emergency to gain medical attention.

Though the cause of Munchausen Syndrome is unknown, researchers believe that there are both biological and psychological factors that influence its development. Many who develop Munchausen Syndrome suffered from abuse in childhood and have spent time in hospitals for legitimate illnesses. Some who suffer from Munchausen Syndrome later develop other psychological disorders such as schizophrenia or psychosis. Munchausen Syndrome is resistant to treatment due to the inherent reinforcement of attention from others. Treatment revolves around changing the self-harm behaviors and preventing the individual from seeking and receiving medical procedures that may be ordered by doctors who are unaware of the self-inflicted nature of the illnesses. Ultimately, the individuals need to address underlying psychological traumas that are driving their need to gain medical attention.

Munchausen Syndrome differs from hypochondriasis. Those with Munchausen Syndrome know they are not actually ill, or know they are the cause of their own illness, whereas those with hypochondriasis actually believe there is something wrong with them. Munchausen Syndrome also differs from malingering because those with Munchausen Syndrome are not faking symptoms to gain external incentives such as workers' compensation or settlements; they simply engage in the behaviors due to a need to maintain the sick role.

Munchausen by Proxy is a form of Munchausen Syndrome in which an individual causes sickness in another person. Though Munchausen Syndrome is more common in males, Munchausen by Proxy more often occurs in mothers who cause sicknesses in their children. This behavior allows them to serve as caregivers and to gain attention and sympathy from others. Mothers may cause sickness through feeding their child toxic chemicals, report symptoms that do not exist, or change test results to mislead medical personnel. Mothers then get to work with medical professionals and others to treat and protect their children. In this psychological disorder, moms are motivated by the attention and respect they receive from family, friends, and medical personnel. The mother takes on the role of the hero and publicly sacrifices her time and energy in caring for her child. If the child gets well, the mother may need to induce injury or illness to maintain the attention and the position of nurturer. In many cases, this cycle continues until the child's death. If the child does survive, he or she will likely be traumatized due to the medical interventions that were taken to treat the symptoms. These parents are not attempting to kill their children; they are just trying to keep them in the sick role to maintain the attention and ability to play the nurturing role.

Munchausen by Proxy can also emerge in individuals taking care of older adults or those with disabilities. The individual may cause a medical problem in the person under their care in order to get medical attention. Individuals who suffer from Munchausen by Proxy tend to have strong medical knowledge and go out of their way to create relationships with medical personnel. They also tend to act very devoted to the person under their care, share details about the amount of time and effort they devote to the person, and revel in the sympathy they get from others. Medical personnel may suspect Munchausen by Proxy when a patient has repeated and unusual illnesses, does not improve with treatment, has a caregiver who is delighted by abnormal test results, has frequent relapses, or has a sibling who also experiences frequent and unexpected illnesses.

Munchausen by Proxy is difficult to treat because most individuals who suffer from it do not see themselves as engaging in harmful behaviors. Their goal is to nurture, tend to, and help the person in their care. Individuals typically resist treatment and do not believe that their behavior is a problem. Since children, elderly, and disabled individuals are vulnerable populations, they typically need law enforcement interventions to protect their interests. Typically, children get better when they are away from the caregiver and long-term changes in custody are indicated.

See also: Compulsive Lying; Delusions; Exaggeration; Malingering; Motives for Lying; Neuroscience; Prevalence of Lying.

Further Reading
Huffman, J. C., & Stern, T. A. (2003). The diagnosis and treatment of Munchausen's syndrome. *General Hospital Psychiatry, 25*, 358–363.

Scheper-Hughes, N. (2002). Disease or deception: Munchausen by Proxy as a weapon of the weak. *Anthropology & Medicine, 9*(2), 153–173.

Slovenko, R. (2006). Editorial: Patients who deceive. *International Journal of Offender Therapy and Comparative Criminology, 50*(3), 241–244.

Wong, L., & Detweiler, M. B. (2016). Munchausen syndrome: A review of patient management. *Psychiatric Annals, 46*(1), 66–70.

Mutually Beneficial Lies (See Prosocial Lying)

Mythomania (See Compulsive Lying)

N

Narcissism

Narcissism is a personality trait that describes people who tend to be arrogant, grandiose, and exploitative. Those who score high on scales of narcissism tend to lack empathy for others and have a sense of entitlement and belief about their own worthiness. To achieve their goals of success and power, those with high levels of narcissism use deception to gain the advantage and get what they want. They may flatter others, con people into conforming to their desires, and outright lie. They feel the need for attention and admiration and seek out others who will help keep their ego inflated.

There are an array of components of narcissism, which are all correlated with self-assessed overestimations in lie detection and lie-telling ability. The Narcissism Personality Inventory examines seven of these components including authority, exhibitionism, superiority, vanity, exploitativeness, entitlement, and self-sufficiency. Those who rank high on the inventory express high confidence in their own abilities, regardless of their actual performance. They rate themselves as good at reading others, despite their documented lack of empathy. While some narcissists are good at identifying certain types of emotions such as anger, when it helps them to exploit others, they are predominantly bad at understanding others. For example, narcissists performed significantly worse than controls in a lie detection task but expressed significantly higher confidence in their ability to detect lies.

Research by Dr. Liza Zvi and Dr. Eitan Elaad from Ariel University in Israel demonstrated that typical people overestimate their abilities to detect lies and to convince people when they are actually telling the truth. However, most people do not overestimate their own ability to tell convincing lies. Lie telling is rated as more difficult than lie detection across a span of research studies. Dr. Zvi and Dr. Elaad found, however, that those who rate high on narcissism rate themselves high on lie-telling abilities. Since they are confident in their lie-telling abilities, they tend to tell more lies than the average person. They tend to tell lies to more people, more frequently, and engage in more counterproductive behaviors. At the opposite end of the spectrum, individuals who show little to no narcissistic qualities rate themselves as unconvincing liars and, thus, tend to tell the truth.

Interestingly, those with high levels of narcissism are also likely to engage in higher levels of self-deception. To maintain their inflated sense of self, they must twist reality to suit their own needs, to the extent of denying and exaggerating empirical facts. They tend to make self-beneficial claims, become hostile when challenged, and take credit only for good work. They view themselves as smarter and more attractive than others and do not seem to have a realistic sense of self.

Due to their use of flattery and charisma, narcissists tend to make good first impressions, but most have difficulty sustaining relationships beyond a first meeting because of their lack of empathy and understanding.

In general, narcissists tend to be controlling, blame others for errors, lack boundaries, make emotionally driven decisions, and are unable to work cohesively with a team. They spend more time assigning blame to others and taking credit for good work than they do focused on the goal or on the cohesiveness of the social group. Narcissism is negatively correlated with the personality trait of agreeableness.

Narcissism is traditionally very difficult to treat. Treatment for narcissism requires a willingness from the individual to face the truth to see through the self-deceptions that allow them to maintain the inflated sense of self. Since self-deception typically covers up feelings of unworthiness or low self-esteem, most narcissists are unwilling to engage in treatment. To get better, they would need to face their innermost fears and experience the feelings of doubt, failure, and inadequacy that the narcissistic traits allow them to avoid.

See also: Coercion; Dark Triad; Machiavellianism; Personality; Scams; Self-Deception.

Further Reading

John, O. P., & Robins, R. W. (1994). Accuracy and bias in self-perception: Individual differences in self-enhancement and the role of narcissism. *Journal of Personality and Social Psychology, 66*(1), 206–219.

Raskin, R., & Terry, H. (1988). A principle-components analysis of the narcissistic personality inventory and further evidence of its construct validity. *Journal of Personality and Social Psychology, 54*(5), 890–902.

Zvi, L., & Elaad, E. (2018). Correlates of narcissism, self-reported lies, and self-assessed abilities to tell and detect lies, tell truths, and believe others. *Journal of Investigative Psychology and Offender Profiling, 15*, 271–286.

Neuroscience

Advances in neuroscience may be key in determining the mechanisms that underlie lying behavior as well as the key to detecting deception. Research evidence has demonstrated that the prefrontal cortex, or the front part of the frontal lobe that controls executive functions such as planning, decision-making, and personality, is essential in successful deception. Additionally, brain regions in the limbic system, the emotion center of the brain, such as the amygdala, as well as the reward centers of the brain, such as the striatum, are also thought to be instrumental in successful deception. In an attempt to determine the exact mechanisms that allow individuals to lie, researchers such as Dr. Nobuhito Abe from Harvard University use neuroimaging techniques to examine brain activity in healthy individuals as well as those who lack the ability to lie. This comparison illustrates which regions are instrumental to successful deception.

Over the past decade, researchers have started using positron emission tomography (PET) and functional magnetic resonance imaging (fMRI) to get a more accurate picture of brain activity during lying attempts. Such studies have demonstrated that lying is associated with increased activation in the prefrontal cortex.

Researchers have also observed greater activation in the superior frontal gyrus and the anterior cingulate cortex during lying behavior. Differential activation has also been observed between spontaneous lies and well-rehearsed lies. Many different imaging techniques, populations, and procedures have been used over the past 10 years in an attempt to identify which brain structures are active during lying behavior. A common finding to these different studies is that the frontal executive system is active during deception. The dorsolateral, ventrolateral, and anterior prefrontal cortices have all been identified as particularly active during deception as well as the anterior cingulate cortex. These areas account for the increased demands on working memory, response selection, cognitive control, and emotion processing needed for successful deception.

Neuroimaging studies on pathological liars reveal an increase in white matter in the prefrontal cortex as compared to normal controls. It is unclear whether the increase in white matter contributes to lying behavior or if the practice of lying increases the amount of white matter, but it does indicate that the prefrontal cortex is involved with lying. This increase in neural matter likely allows practiced liars to process information more quickly, which would increase deceptive success. Individuals with more white matter in the prefrontal cortex tend to have higher verbal IQ scores, contributing to superior verbal abilities and potentially greater skill for creating false stories.

The striatum, a subcortical component of the motor and reward systems connected to the frontal cortex, also plays an instrumental role in deception. The striatum is sensitive to dopamine and regulates reward perception, decision-making, planning, and motivation. This is one part of the brain that is affected in Parkinson's disease, leading to difficulties with motor control and reward-seeking behaviors, likely accounting for why those with Parkinson's are not able to lie even when enticed with a reward. Additionally, the amygdala, a subcortical region of the brain involved with emotion signals, seems to play a role in deception. Likely the connection between the prefrontal areas and these subcortical regions (amygdala and striatum) shapes deceptive behavior.

In populations that struggle to deceive, such as individuals with Parkinson's disease, research has shown decreased metabolic activity (i.e., less activation) in the dorsolateral and anterior prefrontal cortices. Alternatively, stimulating the dorsolateral prefrontal cortex increases the speed and efficiency of deceptive responses. These findings provide further evidence that these regions are instrumental to deception. Methodologies such as transcranial magnetic stimulation (TMS) and transcranial direct current stimulation (tDCS) allow researchers to stimulate various brain regions to link activation and behavior. These methodologies are noninvasive and use magnetic fields and imperceptible electrical currents to alter or excite specific brain regions. Where fMRI and PET scans can measure brain activity that underlies behavior, TMS and tDCS change brain activity in precise locations, and then researchers observe resulting changes in behavior. While such stimulation does not produce outright lies, differences in reaction time, excitability of brain regions, and motor excitability were noted when participants received the stimulation immediately after lying, but the same excitability was not noted if the participant was telling the truth.

Though fMRI and PET technology has illustrated differential activity in areas of the prefrontal cortex and subcortical areas, this technology is still not able to detect lying behavior at an individual level. So far, such technology is not adequate to account for individual differences in brain activity despite its ability to detect average differences in activity between deceivers and truth-tellers.

See also: Concealed Information Test; Control Questions Test; Munchausen Syndrome; Parkinson's Disease; Physiology; Polygraph Tests.

Further Reading

Abe, N. (2011). How the brain shapes deception: An integrated review of the literature. *The Neuroscientist, 17*(5), 560–574.

Johnson, R., Jr. (2014). The neural basis of deception and credibility assessment: A cognitive neuroscience perspective. In D. C. Raskin, C. R. Honts, & J. C. Kircher (Eds.), *Credibility Assessment: Scientific Research and Applications* (pp. 217–300). Academic Press.

Luber, B., Fisher, C., Appelbaum, P. S., Ploesser, M., & Lisanby, S. H. (2009). Non-invasive brain stimulation in the detection of deception: Scientific challenges and ethical consequences. *Behavioral Sciences and the Law, 27*, 191–208.

Ofen, N., Whitefield-Gabrieli, S., Chai, X. J., Schwarzlose, R. F., & Gabrieli, J. D. E. (2017). Neural correlates of deception: Lying about past events and personal beliefs. *Social Cognitive and Affective Neuroscience, 12*(1), 116–127.

Noble Lies

Noble lies are those lies told by people in authority in an attempt to maintain safety, to establish order, or to garner cooperation. Noble lies are most commonly told by government or religious leaders. In these contexts, noble lies are similar to propaganda that is designed to enhance cooperation and further an agenda under the guise of promoting the public good. The intention of a genuine noble lie is to inspire purpose, give value, and provide vision to unify the masses. The goal of a noble lie is to create and inspire, rather than to merely deceive. Those who use noble lies do not believe the lies they tell, but craft them to motivate others to achieve societal goals. They justify the deception by focusing on the intended outcomes and benefits to society.

The term "noble lie" was originated by Socrates in Plato's *Republic* and is presented as a grand deception that persuades people to be satisfied with their class to maintain social stability and order and to convince people to work to be productive despite the discrepancy between the classes. Stories, myths, and noble lies were proposed as a means of providing a guide and an ideal for encouraging individuals to conform, help one another, and work for the collective good. These lies can help provide purpose and create a more stable society, according to Plato. Truths, alternatively, may drive a wedge between the classes, increase competition, and decrease harmony. In this sense, noble lies are framed as being more ethical than the truth, and the outcomes are judged rather than the means to the end.

Frequently, noble lies are told by religious leaders in order to produce cohesive motivations, goals, and social norms for large groups of people. Religious laws fall under the realm of noble lies because they are used to convince the masses to believe in laws of God to maintain order and good behavior. In this context, noble lies are used in an attempt to benefit society and to control and guide uneducated citizens. Such lies can unite people, garner cooperation, and prevent rebellion or conflict. The use of noble lies presupposes that those in authority have noble goals and unselfish motivations and that the common people are unable to make decisions for their own good. These lies are essentially paternalistic lies in which authority makes decisions for the public under the guise of working toward a common good. Such lies may be used to forward society, but they can also support corruption depending on the morality of those in power.

For Plato, noble lies were meant to be motivational and inspiring. He proposed that they should be formed in such a way to encapsulate philosophical truths about the world or about society that are presented in a way that less educated masses can understand. Through these lies, broader truths can be shared that benefit society and help individuals achieve meaning within their lives. Plato's noble lie was intended to inspire patriotism, promote care, and motivate individuals to have devotion to their own people. Noble lies are meant to be persuasive, fantastical, motivating, and pleasurable to entertain. Noble lies, according to Plato, are a medicine to soothe and stabilize the masses even in times of hardship or inequality.

Plato argued that a noble lie is a useful lie that is required to maintain unity and stability, and later philosophers agree that a well-told noble lie is effective due to the unity that it can create. Noble lies ensure solidarity within the classes and are used to protect the people from themselves and their own dissatisfactions. A well-told noble lie uses a falsehood or fictional story to communicate a noble truth. A well-constructed noble lie is told with noble intentions for the greater good, to illuminate peaceful solutions, and to shape views, in circumstances where the truth may have detrimental effects.

Modern society has radically changed since the time of Plato, and noble lies can spread much more quickly and have broader effects than ever before. A well-crafted noble lie may be difficult to discriminate from reasonable, honest arguments, and though the ideal noble lie has positive effects for all, the quality of the outcome depends on the intentions of the liar. Noble lies presume that those in power know what is best for the masses and always have positive intentions. In modern reality, noble lies used by ignoble leaders are more likely to splinter than unite.

See also: Alternative Facts; Categories of Deception; Corruption; Ethics; Fake News; Paternalistic Lies; Politics; Propaganda; Prosocial Lying; White Lies.

Further Reading
Partenie, C. (2018). Plato's myths. *The Stanford Encyclopedia of Philosophy*. Metaphysics Research Lab.
Plato. (2008). *The Republic* (B. Jowett, Trans.). Digital.com Publishing. (Original work published ca. 380 BCE)
Sun, Y.-J. (2017). Lies in Plato's Republic: Poems, myth, and noble lie. *FONS, II*, 87–108.

Nonverbal Behavior

Nonverbal behavior refers to the aspects of communication that go beyond the verbal message. Nonverbal behavior makes up a substantial part of human communications and can radically change the meaning of the words spoken. Controlled change of tone, pitch, facial expression, or body posture, can convey sarcasm, excitement, contempt, interest, concern, humor, or disapproval despite the words actually spoken. In research on detecting deception, attention to uncontrolled nonverbal cues may be key to deciphering the accuracy of the spoken words.

Researchers such as Dr. Paul Ekman believe that there are nonverbal behavioral cues to deceit that show in the face, body, voice, and speech. When all of these cues are taken into consideration, lying can be detected with quite high accuracy. Interestingly, however, most people tend to ignore the behavioral cues that would reveal lying and instead rely upon the words spoken. Thus, though there are nonverbal cues to deception, most people do not attend to them in a conversation, even when actively trying to determine the level of honesty.

Some nonverbal behaviors that have been studied in deception research are rate of speech, atypical pauses, gaze aversion, emotional expression, body movements, head movements, leg and foot movements, use of gestures, self-manipulations (e.g., scratching head or wrist), hand and finger movements, and other fidgeting behaviors. When interviewed, many people believe that liars will speak more slowly, pause more, avoid direct eye contact, and engage in more fidgeting, scratching, foot-jiggling, shifting, and body movements than truth-tellers. Unfortunately, truth-tellers may also sometimes engage in these behaviors, so they are not always reliable. Furthermore, experienced liars may actually endeavor to come across as more sincere and may specifically control these signs of deception. Novice liars, or experienced liars who have not had time to prepare, may reveal the most nonverbal cues to deception.

Dr. Ekman found that experienced liars actually tended to move less than those who were telling the truth. They did not fidget, but instead, held their bodies deliberately still. If the listener is paying attention, such rigid, controlled behavior may be noticeable and used to detect deceptive intent. When asked to predict what liars would do, raters predicted that liars would show an increase in nervous behaviors such as shifting and scratching, subtle movements such as foot-jiggling and hand and leg movements, and supportive behaviors such as nodding and hand gestures. However, liars did not show an increase in hand, leg, foot, or head movements and actually showed a decrease in these subtle movements, contrary to predictions.

Furthermore, when research participants attempted to control these subtle movements when asked to lie as part of the research paradigm, they were unable to do so successfully. Even when they were aware of the connection between lying and a decrease in subtle movements, they could not control their own decrease in subtle behaviors. Liars, instead, tended to increase supportive behaviors (e.g., head nodding and gestures) rather than subtle movements (e.g., hand, foot, and leg movements). Though most research involves low-stakes lies, examination of high-stakes lies (e.g., police interrogations) shows similar findings. Those who attempt to lie in high-stakes situations tend to make even fewer subtle movements and display even more behavioral rigidity.

Liars also may show signs of anxiety or guilt such as increased blinking, sweating, arousal, or vocal pitch. The more anxiety or guilt a person feels, the more likely they will be unable to control these signals. Lack of control may lead to feeling even more anxious and more aroused. Unfortunately, since individuals differ in their base level of blinking, sweating, and arousal, it may be hard to detect whether these behaviors increase unless the listener knows the speaker well or has a point of comparison. Of these signals, vocal pitch may be the most difficult to control, making it the most useful for detecting deception.

Though the average individual has been found to detect deception only at chance levels, attention to nonverbal cues can radically increase performance. Training to observe microexpressions, for example, can help listeners recognize when nonverbal and verbal messages do not align. Liars frequently show brief facial expressions of disgust, anger, or delight when engaging in deception. Though they may attempt to mask these expressions, microexpressions may still be observable, or the expressed emotion may not align with the verbal statements. Such inconsistencies may be key to detecting deception in real-time conversations.

Researchers found that individuals who had damage to the language centers in the brain were significantly better at detecting lies than healthy individuals, showing the importance of nonverbal behaviors in detecting deception. Individuals with aphasia, for example, dedicated more time attending to nonverbal cues and emotions than healthy controls and were significantly better at recognizing deceptive attempts. Thus, attention to nonverbal behaviors may be a key to learning to detect deception. Attending to things like vocal pitch, facial expressions, and body movements may allow for insight that is unachievable when listening to the verbal message alone. Comparison between the verbal and nonverbal cues may be similarly effective for detecting dishonesty.

See also: Deceiver Stereotype; Detecting Deception; Diversionary Tactics; Ekman, Paul; Eye Gaze; Facial Cues; Microexpressions; Physiology; Polygraph Tests; Vocal Changes when Lying; Wizard's Project.

Further Reading

Ekman, P. (1991). Invited article: face, voice, and body in detecting deceit. *Journal of Nonverbal Behavior, 15*(2), 125–135.

Etcoff, N. L., Ekman, P., Magee, J. J., & Frank, M. G. (2000). Lie detection and language comprehension. *Nature, 405*, 139.

Mann, S., Vrij, A., Leal, S., Granhag, P. A., Warmelink, L., & Forrester, D. (2012). Windows to the sound? Deliberate eye contact as a cue to deceit. *Journal of Nonverbal Behavior, 36*, 205–215.

Slessor, G., Phillips, L. H., Bull, R., Venturini, C., Bonny, E. J., & Rokaszewicz, A. (2012). Investigating the "deceiver stereotype": Do older adults associate averted gaze with deception? *The Journal of Gerontology, Series B: Psychological Sciences and Social Sciences, 67*(2), 178–183.

Vrij, A., Semin, G. R., & Bull, R. (1996). Insight into behavior displayed during deception. *Human Communication Research, 22*(4), 544–556.

O

Obstruction of Justice (*See* Fifth Amendment)

Occasional Liars (*See* White Lies)

Omission, Lies of

Lies of omission occur when an individual leaves out pertinent information when answering a question or telling a story. In this way, the person may deceive others without technically telling a lie. Lying by omission includes telling the parts of the truth that one knows a listener would respond well to and neglecting to mention any parts that may be controversial or upsetting. Lying by omission can result from a listener drawing an incorrect conclusion that the speaker does not correct. Lying by omission may also occur if one avoids a conversation or does not offer information that the other person does not know one has.

Paltering is an active form of lying by omission. Dr. Todd Rogers and his colleagues from Harvard University and the University of Pennsylvania describe paltering as more active than simple lies of omission because the speaker does not simply omit information but phrases honest statements in such a way to purposefully give a false impression. Such statements may be semantically accurate but are designed to provide the listener with a misleading impression. For example, an unfaithful partner may honestly assert that he or she is not having an affair, yet may omit that he or she had an affair in the past. Thus, the statement is semantically true, but if the affair ended prior to the assertion, even the previous day, the omission of that information is misleading.

Palterers may skew the truth by defining terms narrowly or playing with word tense. Most palterers justify their omissions by believing they are protecting others, maintaining relationships, and smoothing over social interactions. In this sense, paltering is easy to rationalize, which makes it less impactful on self-esteem than lies of commission and an easier choice for those in stressful situations than telling the truth. In a psychological research study, omissions and paltering were more common than outright lying or telling the whole truth. Omissions or paltering allowed the participants to maintain a sense of being an honest person while still reaping the benefits of avoiding the potential negative consequences of being honest.

Omission and paltering are very common strategies for negotiators and advertisers. Successful negotiators do not always give the entire truth, only those parts that they think will sway the listener. More information is provided only as needed. In marketing, advertisers or salespeople may engage in lies of omission by not revealing the negative aspects of a purchase. If the customer does not specifically ask, they do not divulge information, even though it would likely be pertinent to the decision to purchase. Not revealing the whole truth can give one an advantage over competitors without actually lying. Lying by omission will only be effective, however, if the listener is unaware that there is information that has been omitted and does not ask pertinent questions that would necessitate sharing more information or telling a more active lie such as a lie of commission.

Liars who engage in lying by omission or by paltering risk damage to their reputations if they are caught. Those who lie by omission may simply claim to have forgotten that information or that they did not think it was pertinent. Palterers have more accountability if caught framing or distorting the truth in a biased way to gain an advantage. Though those who palter are able to justify their behavior and maintain self-esteem to a greater extent than those who lie by commission, the damage to reputation is similar if caught. Lying by omission tends to have the least consequences to self-esteem or reputation damage if discovered.

Lies of omission tend to be difficult to detect because the information that is provided is accurate. Identifying what is not mentioned can be incredibly difficult because one might not even know to look for it. To spot such lies, one must be thorough when asking questions or know the speaker well enough to understand what is not being said.

See also: Bending the Truth; Categories of Deception; Cognitive Dissonance; Commission, Lies of; Fabrication; Minimization; Politics; White Lies.

Further Reading

Edwards, V. V. (2014). *How to tell if someone is lying: The ultimate guide.* Retrieved from https://www.scienceofpeople.com/how-to-tell-if-someone-is-lying/

Gino, F. (2016). There's a word for using truthful facts to deceive: Paltering. *Harvard Business Review.* Retrieved from https://hbr.org/2016/10/theres-a-word-for-using -truthful-facts-to-deceive-paltering

Rogers, T., Zeckhauser, R., Gino, F., Norton, M. I., & Schweitzer, M. E. (2017). Artful paltering: The risks and rewards of using truthful statements to mislead others. *Journal of Personality and Social Psychology, 112*(3), 456–473.

Online Dating

Online dating has become a common way for individuals to meet to form romantic, long-term relationships. By 2017, 66 percent of single individuals in the United States reported using an online dating site. Reasons for using dating sites ranged from seeking a long-term romantic relationship (84%); seeking friends, fun, or adventure (43%); and finding sexual partners (24%). Online dating sites are becoming more popular with expanding computer use, and individuals who use such dating sites report that the information provided in the dating profiles makes it easier to find compatible partners and avoid incompatible partners and facilitates conversation. By 2018, approximately 6 percent of individuals in committed long-term relationships met online. However, most individuals report that they are more likely to lie online than in person, making those who engage in online dating more likely to be victims (or perpetrators) of deceptive attempts.

Dr. Michelle Drouin and her colleagues from Purdue University Fort Wayne found that over half of online daters know that others present false information on their online profiles. Online platforms allow for disinhibition and a different perspective on honesty. Most report that everyone lies online and everyone knows everyone else is lying. For some individuals, the disinhibition of being online may make them more honest because it allows them to be genuine without interpersonal backlash. In general, however, online dating sites are rated as much less honest than other social media sites. However, since the goal of online dating is typically to meet someone offline, the lies cannot be too extreme. Slight embellishments to garner attention or come across as more attractive to others can enhance online attention, but claims that are too significant would be noticeable when meeting offline. Only in unusual circumstances, such as catfishing attempts, might someone tell more significant lies that would immediately be discredited should the individuals meet face-to-face.

Dr. Catalina Toma and her colleagues from Cornell University and the University of Wisconsin-Madison found that less attractive online daters were more likely to enhance their profile photographs and to lie about physical characteristics such as height and weight. Fewer people were likely to lie about things unrelated to physical traits. Attractive individuals on online dating sites also posted more photographs than less attractive individuals, and women tended to alter their photographs more frequently than men. This may be due to the finding that male participants were more critical of physical attractiveness than female participants.

Overall, the research shows that deception is rampant in online dating platforms but that most of the deceptions are quite small. Nine out of ten individuals examined by Dr. Toma lied about their height, weight, or age. However, the misrepresentations were quite minute, and likely not perceptible when meeting in person. There were a few exceptions where individuals made radical claims, and such examples are very salient, contributing to the expectation that most people are lying online. In general, men tended to overestimate their height, women tended to underestimate their weight, and both genders were equally likely to lie about age.

Those individuals who lied about their height or weight were also less likely to draw attention to those characteristics in their written profiles. Liars tended to emphasize and elaborate on characteristics that were truthful and tended to omit details and referred less frequently to things about which they were lying. Descriptions tended to successfully hide or distract readers from those characteristics.

Online lying can impact offline relationships. Thus, most online daters tend to exaggerate those qualities to which they think a romantic partner might be attracted. If lies are detectable when meeting in person, it serves as a deterrent for continuing the relationship. In Dr. Toma's study, perceiving that the other person lied online correlated with lower attraction and lower expectations of a future relationship. Thus, lying about attributes to make a partner more interested tends to backfire because once couples meet face-to-face, such lies deter interest. Those strategies that make someone successful at dating online may actually damage their ability to transition those relationships offline.

See also: Catfishing; Evolution of Deception; Language; Omission, Lies of; Prevalence of Lying; Romantic Relationships; Social Media; Sockpuppets.

Further Reading

Drouin, M., Miller, D., Wehle, S. M. J., & Hernandez, E. (2016). Why do people lie online? "Because everyone lies on the Internet." *Computers in Human Behavior, 64*, 134–142.

Hancock, J. T., Toma, C., & Ellison, N. (2007). The truth about lying in online dating profiles. *Online Representation of Self*, 449–452.

Sharabi, L. L., & Caughlin, J. P. (2019). Deception in online dating: Significance and implications for the first offline date. *New Media and Society, 21*(1), 229–247.

Toma, C. L., & Hancock, J. T. (2010). Looks and lies: The role of physical attractiveness in online dating self-presentation and deception. *Communication Research, 37*(3), 335–351.

Toma, C. L., & Hancock, J. T. (2012). What lies beneath: The linguistic traces of deception in online dating profiles. *Journal of Communication, 62*(1), 78–97.

Optimism Bias

An optimism bias is a cognitive bias that characterizes individuals who believe that good things will happen to them and negative outcomes are less likely to occur. Optimists are more likely to notice and embrace positive outcomes and less likely to pay attention to negative outcomes. Individuals who have an optimism bias believe that they are safe, healthy, not at risk of injury, and will be successful in their pursuits. They believe they are not likely to be the victim of disease, crime, injury, or failure. An optimism bias can lead to increased self-esteem and confidence, but having such a bias can also lead to increased risk-taking behavior and more self-deception. In general, those with an optimism bias tend to lie less frequently because they have the expectation that they can work things out honestly.

Having an optimism bias facilitates better mental health and increases likelihood of success. Attending primarily to positive stimuli and having positive expectations increase positive emotions, which averts symptoms of depression and anxiety and reduces feelings of stress. Positive expectations also increase self-esteem, which creates a feedback loop for increased future success. Positive expectations also heighten success rates due to increased effort, productivity, and persistence and contribute to better cardiovascular health and a stronger immune system. Optimists tend to cope more effectively with setbacks and are overall happier and healthier. Alternatively, pessimists are more likely to notice negative stimuli and negative events in their environment rather than the positive.

However, in situations where the consequences are not positive, having an optimism bias can lead to increased rates of self-deception. An optimism bias could come into play when individuals engage in risky behaviors, such as smoking or

drug use. Because an optimism bias skews one away from negative expectations, optimistic individuals may believe that they will not suffer the negative effects from such behaviors. The self-deception allows for the alleviation of cognitive dissonance and allows the individual to engage in risky behaviors without worrying about the consequences. An optimism bias might also lead individuals to only attend to data that support what they want to hear. That way, they can maintain their bias without experiencing the discomfort of being inconsistent.

People with an optimism bias frequently overestimate their own abilities and expectations for success. While such expectations may lead to greater success, they may also lead individuals to engage in more risky behavior or situations for which they are unprepared. These people tend to predict that their abilities are better than average and that they will succeed in a competitive situation. If they are unsuccessful, they may be more likely to blame others or to blame the situation rather than to take responsibility for the failure. This can both protect mental health and lead to an unrealistic assessment of the event, which may lead them to engage in similar situations again in the future. Such optimism can undermine accuracy when predicting performance. So, though a certain level of optimism is beneficial for health and happiness, excessive optimism may lead to failure, injury, or heightened risk.

Most optimists have an internal locus of control. They feel as though they have control in a situation and can control the outcome. They tend to initiate, evaluate, and make more positive predictions about the future than those who are less optimistic. They expect to live longer, have better luck, and do not expect to be the victim of accidents or crimes. They expect to stay healthy, physically and mentally. These positive expectations tend to reduce anxiety and depressive symptoms. The obvious problem is that many of these things are not actually under an individual's control. So those with an optimism bias may suffer from these things unexpectedly, and while they tend to be honest with others, they may be more likely to lie to themselves to maintain their positive attitude.

See also: Cognitive Dissonance; Cognitive Distortion; Consequences of Lying; Denial; Emotional Effects; Locus of Control; Self-Deception; Truth-Default Theory.

Further Reading

Kress, L., & Aue, T. (2019). Learning to look at the bright side of life: Attention bias modification training enhances optimism bias. *Frontiers in Human Neuroscience, 13*(222), 1–10.

Schweizer, K., Beck-Seyffert, A., & Schneider, R. (1999). Cognitive bias of optimism and its influence on psychological well-being. *Psychological Reports, 84*, 627–636.

Segerstrom, S. C. (2001). Optimism in attentional bias for negative and positive stimuli. *Society for Personality and Social Psychology, 27*(10), 1334–1343.

Van der Leer, L., & McKay, R. (2017). The optimist within? Selective sampling and self-deception. *Consciousness and Cognition, 50*, 23–29.

Windschitl, P. D., Rose, J. P., Stalkfleet, M. T., & Smith, A. R. (2008). Are people excessive or judicious in their egocentrism? A modeling approach to understanding bias and accuracy in people's optimism. *Journal of Personality and Social Psychology, 95*(2), 253–273.

Othello Error

The "Othello Error," a term first used by Paul Ekman in his book *Telling Lies*, refers to Othello, a Shakespearian character who incorrectly interpreted his wife's nervous behavior as deception. The Othello Error thus refers to the nervous behavior that truth-tellers may exhibit if they are concerned about whether or not their claims will be believed. Due to increases in stress and the resulting physiological reactions, nonverbal behaviors may mimic behavior typical of liars, even when individuals are telling the truth. The Othello Error tends to be most problematic in interrogations or during direct questioning when an innocent individual is anxious or intimidated and thus exhibits nervous behaviors typical of a liar.

Dr. Ekman cautioned that lie detectors must remain aware that arousal is not sufficient to conclude someone is lying. Those telling the truth can become emotional when worried about consequences or if they feel they are suspected of lying. Physiological arousal due to this stress can complicate established lie detection measures. Behavioral and physiological reactions of an anxious truth-teller can mimic those of someone who is lying. Dr. Ekman also articulates that having preconceptions about another person can bias the judgments of the interviewer. If interviewers believe that a suspect or witness is lying, they will be more likely to interpret ambiguous behaviors as evidence of deception.

In political or legal situations, the Othello Error can have serious consequences. In a political climate where preconceptions about race and ethnicity can trigger suspicion, the Othello Error is likely to create a negative feedback loop. Prejudices or biases can lead observers to be more suspicious of certain ethnic groups, and individuals belonging to such groups are more likely to be detained, arrested, or disbelieved. Those same individuals are more likely to experience increased physiological arousal, due to a history of being the target of prejudice and discrimination, which is then interpreted as deceptive intent.

Professor Lenese Herbert from Washington and Lee University challenged the use of Dr. Ekman's Facial Action Coding System following the 9/11 attacks. Dr. Herbert argued that use of this system creates a prejudice against minorities' faces and makes the U.S. Security Personnel more likely to make the Othello Error when attempting to identify potential terrorists. Minority groups become the target of increased suspicion and may react by exhibiting more anxious behaviors. Those who belong to target minority groups are more likely to be seen as criminals and to be arrested, interrogated, or accused of a crime. This leads to the situation where even innocent members of the minority group feel anxiety and nervousness when faced with law enforcement personnel. This anxiety and nervousness may come across as guilt or suspicious behavior, and the individuals are even more likely to be targeted or detained.

Sanctioning assumptions based on race decreases the accuracy of true deception detection and increases error. Until interviewers or researchers can discriminate between anxious behaviors resulting from guilt and anxious behaviors resulting from fear, such nonverbal cues must be treated with caution. Furthermore, different cultures have different cultural display rules. Cultural display rules are learned through socialization processes and guide which emotions or behaviors are appropriate to show in which situations. When an individual from one culture attempts to judge an individual from another culture based on their nonverbal cues, they must know what is typical for the other group. For example, different cultures have different norms for presence and duration of eye contact. If a suspect is avoiding eye contact, an interviewer may interpret that as suspicious behavior when it may merely be a cultural norm.

Established interrogation techniques can increase the likelihood of the Othello Error. The Behavior Analysis Interview, for example, examines the nonverbal and verbal behaviors of a suspect to assess likelihood of guilt. However, an innocent suspect who is unfamiliar with the interview process or who is worried about not being believed may show heightened physiological arousal to the questions, making interviewers vulnerable to making the Othello Error. Additionally, the Control Questions Test attempts to assess guilt by the varying level of emotional arousal to different questions. Unfortunately, assuming arousal indicates guilt leads to the Othello Error. Innocent suspects may show arousal, and guilty suspects may be able to control their emotions to fool the experimenter. The Concealed Information Test attempts to avoid this error by presenting questions in a way to minimize physiological arousal in innocent suspects, but findings still need to be interpreted with caution, and interviewers need to be aware of the bias inherent in believing a suspect is guilty.

See also: Behavior Analysis Interview; Brokaw Hazard; Concealed Information Test; Control Questions Test; Cultural Differences; Ekman, Paul; Motivational Impairment Effect; Polygraph Tests; Reid Technique.

Further Reading

Ekman, P. (1985). *Telling Lies: Clues to Deceit in the Marketplace, Politics, and Marriage*. Norton.

Herbert, L. (2007). Othello error: Facial profiling, privacy, and the suppression of dissent. *Ohio State Journal of Criminal Law, 5*(79), 79–129.

P

Paltering (See Omission, Lies of)

Paraverbal Communication (See Vocal Changes when Lying)

Parkinson's Disease

Parkinson's disease is a progressive disorder that primarily affects the nervous system. Individuals with Parkinson's disease suffer from a gradual loss of neurons in the brain. Symptoms include resting tremors in one or both hands, stiffness, slowing of movement, slurred speech, muted facial expressions, rigidity of muscles, difficulty in maintaining posture and balance, and difficulty in writing. Parkinson's disease also causes cognitive dysfunction and executive functioning deficits, and individuals may experience difficulty thinking, dementia-like symptoms, and heightened difficulty in deceiving others. Many of these symptoms are caused by a diminished amount of the neurotransmitter dopamine in the brain.

Neuropsychological research has demonstrated that patients with Parkinson's disease display cognitive inflexibility and an uncommon tendency toward honesty. Some researchers have noted that individuals who develop Parkinson's disease later in life tend to be more honest even prior to its emergence. These individuals tend to be hardworking, serious, relatively inflexible, and unusually honest, even prior to the development of the disease. Researchers have identified two mechanisms that likely explain why those with Parkinson's struggle with deception. First, the prefrontal cortex, the area of the brain associated with executive functioning and motor control (and deceptive behavior), is specifically affected in patients with Parkinson's. Second, decreased dopamine production decreases the level of motivation and reward that is associated with deceptive success.

Given the executive functioning deficits associated with Parkinson's disease, it is unsurprising that those suffering from this disorder demonstrate deficits in effective lying behavior. In a neuropsychological research study, Dr. Nobuhito Abe and his colleagues found that individuals with Parkinson's disease demonstrated less brain activity in the prefrontal cortex as compared to healthy controls. Additionally, these patients had poorer performance on other executive functioning tasks as well. Thus, the ubiquitous honesty characteristically displayed by patients with Parkinson's is likely a result of brain dysfunction caused by the degeneration in the prefrontal cortex.

The decreased levels of dopamine in patients with Parkinson's also cause a dysfunction in the dopamine reward system. Not only are individuals with Parkinson's disease unable to lie effectively when asked to, but they also struggle to deceive when lying would lead to high levels of reward. In a research study, participants were rewarded for accuracy in a prediction task. Participants provided a self-report of how well they predicted information in a task, and they were rewarded for reporting high accuracy. For example, individuals were asked to privately predict whether a star would appear on the right or left of the screen and then to report whether or not their prediction was accurate. Individuals with Parkinson's disease tended not to retroactively lie about their predictions and thus performed at chance levels. Healthy controls, alternatively, reported high levels of accuracy, indicating deceptive behavior to increase rewards.

Decreased ability to deceive is also found in other patient populations that display tremors, like those found in patients with Parkinson's. In a psychological study comparing healthy individuals, individuals with Parkinson's disease, and individuals with essential tremors (a common movement disorder characterized by tremors but without the cognitive dysfunction common in Parkinson's disease), Dr. Francesca Mameli and her colleagues, found that all three groups showed similar brain activation and success when providing truthful responses in a research paradigm. On trials when the participants were asked to lie, however, the individuals with the essential tremor and the individuals with Parkinson's disease were significantly less successful in providing deceptive responses than the group of healthy controls. Furthermore, all groups had significantly longer reaction times when lying, and those with essential tremors were significantly slower than both those with Parkinson's disease and healthy controls.

Thus, research demonstrates that individuals with Parkinson's disease struggle to produce successful attempts at deception when prompted and also tend not to choose to lie when left to their own devices. Neuropsychological research indicates that typical neural degeneration in patients with Parkinson's causes a deficit in prefrontal executive control when instructed to lie. Decreased levels of dopamine throughout the brain also causes a deficit in the dopamine reward system, and thus, patients with Parkinson's do not opt to lie when given the opportunity to win rewards for even white lies.

See also: Neuroscience; Physiology; Reaction Time; White Lies.

Further Reading

Abe, N., Fujii, T., Hirayama, K., Takeda, A., Hosokai, Y., Ishioka, T., Nishio, Y., Suzuki, K., Itoyama, Y., Takahashi, S., Fukuda, H., & Mori, E. (2009). Do parkinsonian patients have trouble telling lies? The neurobiological basis of deceptive behaviour. *Brain, 132*(5), 1386–1395.

Abe, N., Kawasaki, I., Hosokawa, H., Baba, T., & Takeda, A. (2018). Do patients with Parkinson's Disease exhibit reduced cheating behavior? A neuropsychological study. *Frontiers in Neurology, 9*, 378.

Mameli, F., Tomasini, E., Scelzo, E., Fumagalli, M., Ferrucci, R., Bertolasi, L., & Priori, A. (2013). Lies tell the truth about cognitive dysfunctions in essential tremor: An experimental deception study with the guilty knowledge task. *Journal of Neurology, Neurosurgery & Psychiatry, 84*(9), 1008–1013.

Mayo Clinic. (2018, June 30). *Parkinson's disease.* Retrieved from https://www.mayo clinic.org/diseases-conditions/parkinsons-disease/symptoms-causes/syc -20376055

Paternalistic Lies

Paternalistic lies are generally altruistic lies that are told with the intention of help-ing or protecting others. They are frequently told by those in positions of power who have the authority to make decisions and choices for subordinates and who use paternalistic lies to maintain harmony. Parents often use paternalistic lies when they tell white lies to children to shape their behavior. Paternalistic lies can also be used in relationships to influence a partner, or they can be used on a broader soci-etal scale. Sometimes doctors lie to patients to increase hope and maintain positive attitudes, police lie to victims to keep them calm or make them more comfortable, teachers lie to students to support and encourage, spouses lie to partners to main-tain the relationship, and governments lie to the populace to maintain order. The goal of telling a paternalistic lie typically revolves around decreasing stress, increasing mental health, and maintaining relationships.

Though paternalistic lies are told specifically to benefit others, they are still a type of manipulation and deception and can have unforeseen consequences. Pater-nalistic lies tend to undermine autonomy and can interfere with another person's goals and beliefs. When telling such lies, one has to infer what is actually best for the other person. Matthew Lupoli and his colleagues found the most individuals do not like being the targets of paternalistic lies. Even if the lie has benefits com-pared to being told the truth, those who are lied to are less satisfied than those who were told the truth. They found that those who were lied to question the intentions of the liar, feel as though their autonomy has been violated, and do not appreciate the other trying to predict what is best for them.

The detriment of telling paternalistic lies revolves around the inability to fore-see what is best for others. For example, one may choose to lie to protect another's feelings or to boost another's confidence, but sometimes getting honest feedback is better for growth, intimacy, and changes in future behavior. Honest feedback can help others learn and be more successful, avoid embarrassment, and enhance trust. Governments may make laws and frame legislation with the best intentions for society, but history has shown that even those in positions of power are not always right. Legitimizing slavery or preventing equality is a measure of paternal-ism that undermines the autonomy of others. Though those making such rules may believe they are doing what is best for society, even noble intentions can result in immoral decisions and behaviors.

Paternalistic lies are generally considered more acceptable if the target is a minor or otherwise impaired. Making decisions for a child or for someone who is suffering from dementia may be more ethical than allowing them to make damag-ing decisions for themselves. Parents may know what is best for the child and may not be completely honest as a way of reaching a goal. Telling paternalistic lies to those who are mentally incapacitated or irrational may help keep them safe and encourage healthy behaviors.

Though paternalistic lies are not usually told for malicious purposes, they do take control away from the person being lied to. Those who tell paternalistic lies tend to assume that they know what is best for the other person and they do not allow other people to judge for themselves. If other individuals are not in a position to make such a judgment, then paternalistic lies may be ethically justified. However, if others are in a position to make decisions for themselves, then paternalistic lies may undermine autonomy and ultimately damage trust. Only if the person is incapacitated, irrational, or in immediate danger, would paternalistic lies be justified. Lying to keep someone safe in the short term may be more ethical than telling the truth and allowing them to be injured. Beyond those specific situations, paternalistic lies tend to benefit the liar more than the target, even if the liar had altruistic intentions.

See also: Coercion; Dementia; Ethics; Lying to Children; Noble Lies; Politics; Prosocial Lying; White Lies.

Further Reading

Korsgaard, C. M. (2020). Is there a moral justification for paternalistic lies? *ABC Religion & Ethics*. Retrieved from https://www.abc.net.au/religion/christine-korsgaard-is-there-moral-justification-for-paternalis/11950108

Lupoli, M. J., Levine, E. E., & Greenberg, A. E. (2018). Paternalistic lies. *Organizational Behavior and Human Decision Processes, 16*, 31–50.

Stokke, A. (2018). Paternalistic lying and deception. In K. Grill & J. Hanna (Eds.), *The Routledge Handbook of the Philosophy of Paternalism (Chapter 20)*. Taylor and Francis.

Pathological Liars (See Antisocial Personality Disorder; Compulsive Lying)

Pennebaker, James W. (See Linguistic Inquiry and Word Count Analysis Program)

Perjury

Perjury is deception by witnesses or defendants in the courtroom during a trial. Perjury specifically refers to the situation when witnesses or defendants have taken an oath to tell the truth but then present information that they know to be false. Defendants or witnesses predominantly commit perjury to avoid punishment for themselves or for a partner or friend. Because perjury has such widespread implications for the outcome of criminal cases, it is considered to be a felony and is punishable by fines or jail time.

Perjury can be difficult to detect or to prove, even for those with experience. Though judges, lawyers, interrogators, and others within the legal system may face and have more experience with attempts at deception, Dr. Paul Ekman and Dr. Maureen O'Sullivan found that most judges, police officers, and interrogators can only detect lies at about chance levels, similar to the average person. This widespread inability to conclusively discriminate between honest and dishonest behavior means that perjury may frequently go undetected. Furthermore, the presence of perjury could have a significant impact on the outcome of a case.

Dr. Ekman and Dr. O'Sullivan did find that those who work in the legal system are more likely to rate true statements as lies than the average individual, who is more likely to rate lies as the truth. Since part of their job is to detect lies, they are likely more skeptical of what others say, may already believe the defendant is guilty, or may have more experience with lying behavior. All of these elements change the way these individuals perceive statements. Whereas most individuals have a truth bias, when working with known criminals, most are more likely to assume that the defendant is lying. Because interrogators and lawyers are aware of the likelihood of perjury, they tend to purposefully monitor nonverbal cues that may signal dishonesty. However, most cues endorsed by police officers and interrogators as signaling dishonest behavior are unsubstantiated, and research has shown that such cues are unreliable.

Perjury is not a new concern. As early as 1934, researchers were already interested in investigating the presence of lying in the courtroom. Because lying was found to be quite common, those in the legal system instituted a process of witnesses and defendants swearing an oath to tell the truth before testifying. This oath was designed to encourage ethical behavior and even invokes the name of God in an attempt to elicit honesty. Being convicted of perjury, furthermore, results in severe penalties if an individual is found to be lying. Unfortunately, unless the defendant or witness confesses, it is not always possible to conclusively determine whether they committed perjury. Therefore, even lawyers and judges are aware that swearing an oath does not guarantee an honest statement. Given that, cross examination emerges as more important than the oath to tell the truth.

To be guilty of perjury, defendants or witnesses may tell bald-faced lies or they may palter. Paltering essentially involves making true statements that are purposefully misleading, by omitting key information, denying knowledge about an event, or making statements out of context. In any of these instances, the witness, suspect, or defendant is purposefully trying to mislead the court after swearing an oath of honesty. In an effort to reduce perjury, the Fifth Amendment of the Constitution was put in place stating that an individual cannot be required to self-incriminate. Thus, an individual on trial can plead the Fifth, meaning that they are opting not to answer a question and are exercising their right to remain silent rather than being self-incriminating or committing perjury.

Because it is difficult to prove that someone purposely lied, many individuals accused of perjury go unpunished. Through a psychological study, Drs. Stephanie Crank and Drew Curtis from Angelo State University examined how often individuals are likely to engage in perjury and how external incentives impact perjury behavior. They found that the number of people who engage in perjury exceeds the number that is reported to the Bureau of Justice Statistics. This is likely because many of the individuals who engage in perjury are never charged. Interestingly, most individuals are more likely to engage in perjury to help a partner than to help themselves.

See also: Bald-Faced Lies; Benefits of Lying; Costs of Lying; Fifth Amendment; Instrumental Lies; Motivational Impairment Effect; Nonverbal Behavior; Omission, Lies of; Polygraph Test; Truth-Default Theory.

Further Reading

Crank, S. D., & Curtis, D. A. (2020). And nothing but the truth: An exploration of perjury. *Journal of Police and Criminal Psychology.* https://doi.org/10.1007/s11896-020 -09383-1

Ekman, P., & O'Sullivan, M. (1991). Who can catch a liar? *American Psychologist, 48,* 913–920.

Hibschman, H. (1934). You do solemnly swear or that perjury problem. *Journal of Criminal Law and Criminology, 24*(5), 901–913.

Personality

The tendency to deceive others varies predictably with different personality traits. Research demonstrates significant correlations between deceptive behavior and each of the Big Five personality traits: extraversion, neuroticism, agreeableness, openness to new experience, and conscientiousness. Specifically, extraversion, neuroticism, and openness positively correlate with deceptive behavior, while agreeableness and conscientiousness are negatively correlated with the tendency to deceive. Additionally, other factors of personality such as narcissism and psychopathy, self-esteem, psychological health, and intelligence level also correlate with deceptive behavioral tendencies.

Extraverts, or those individuals who are driven by outside stimuli and social engagement, are more likely than introverts to engage in deceptive behavior. However, this tendency is mediated by intelligence levels. Extraverts who are highly intelligent are the most likely to lie, whereas extraverts who score low on measures of intelligence are less likely to lie. Introverts, or those who do not require outside stimuli to remain motivated, are less likely to engage in deceptive behavior, regardless of intelligence level. This difference may be due to the differences in sensitivity to social rewards. Extraverts are highly tuned in to the social world, while introverts place less emphasis on social interactions. Thus, extraverts are more likely to lie to gain social approval or social standing than introverts. Furthermore, less intelligent individuals, regardless of personality, are less successful at deceiving others and thus less likely to attempt such behaviors.

Above-average scores on measures of neuroticism and openness to new experience are also correlated with tendency to engage in deceptive behavior. Neurotic individuals tend to be more self-conscious, more anxious, and more worried about how they are perceived by others, and are thus more likely to lie to attempt to create a favorable impression. They are also more likely to deceive themselves and more likely to use lies to promote or smooth over social interactions. Individuals who are open to new experiences are also more likely to attempt deceptive strategies. Overall, open individuals are likely to have more experience in social situations, which may lead to more opportunities to deceive than those who do not frequently engage in new experiences.

Higher scores on the personality dimensions of agreeableness and conscientiousness are negatively correlated with lying behavior. More agreeable individuals are less likely to choose a deceptive strategy and more likely to interact honestly with others. Highly conscientious individuals are also less likely to attempt to deceive. These individuals tend to engage in more honest behaviors and tend to feel and express more guilt about past indiscretions.

Beyond the Big Five personality traits, other dimensions of personality also correlate with deceptive behavior. For example, those individuals who demonstrate antisocial personality traits, such as narcissism or psychopathy, tend to lie more frequently than their peers. Narcissists tend to lie to promote and bolster themselves, while psychopaths may lie for sheer pleasure or for self-gain. Those who score high on traits of psychoticism also tend to lie more frequently to themselves and to others. Manipulative individuals are more likely to lie to protect their own reputations or to get what they want, and those with moral disengagement are likely to lie without much thought to the feelings or perceptions of others.

Low self-esteem also correlates with increased lying behavior. Individuals with low self-esteem may try to make themselves look and feel better by exaggerating their own qualities and achievements to others. Lying behavior is directly correlated to low self-esteem, high anxiety, and poorer psychological health.

In addition to the relationship of personality to lying behavior, the ability to detect deception is also tied to personality. Those who score high on measures of extraversion, openness to experience, and agreeableness tend to more accurately detect deception from others. These enhanced abilities may result from increased social experience, social interest, and social status that arises from extraverted, open, and agreeable behavior. High scores on measures of trust, however, regardless of level of sociability, have been found to correlate with lower accuracy at discriminating between lies and the truth.

Overall, researchers such as Dr. Bella DePaulo have found that liars tend to be more manipulative than those who lie less frequently; they are more irresponsible, and they care more about how other people perceive them. Most lies are not meant for nefarious goals. Instead, liars are frequently socially driven, want to make a good impression, and want other people to like them. Many people use lies to try to create an image of themselves that will please others. Since liars also tend to be extraverted and open to new experiences, they may be more focused on others, and their lies may serve to maintain social cohesion rather than simply to deceive.

See also: Antisocial Personality Disorder; Conscience; DePaulo, Bella; Detecting Deception; Intelligence; Locus of Control; Machiavellianism; Manipulation; Narcissism; Prosocial Lying; Self-Deception; White Lies.

Further Reading

Chiu, S., Hong, F., & Chiu, S. (2016). Undergraduates' day-to-day lying behaviors: Implications, targets, and psychological characteristics. *Social Behavior and Personality, 44*(8), 1329–1338.

DePaulo, B. M. (2004). The many faces of lies. In A. G. Miller (Ed.), *The Social Psychology of Good and Evil* (pp. 303–326). Guildford.

Sarzynska, J., Falkiewicz, M., Riegel, M., Babula, J., Margulies, D. S., Necka, E., Grabowska, A., & Szatkowska, I. (2017). More intelligent extraverts are more likely to deceive. *PLoS ONE, 12*(4), 1–17.

Spencer, S. D. (2017). Examining personality factors in deception detection ability. *Psi Chi Journal of Psychological Research, 22*(2), 106–113.

Philosophy (See Ethics)

Phishing

Phishing refers to strategies used online to manipulate others. Phishers may present misleading information to hook a target or may act on a target's weakness to prompt a response. Typically, phishing aims to elicit credit card information, passwords, or other online information that can be used to make a profit. Phishers make their emails appear legitimate to gain personal or financial information. Companies now frequently hire technicians to help educate employees about phishing attempts in order to keep sensitive corporate information private.

The term "phishing" was coined in 1993 when an individual used a hacking program to steal details from America Online profiles. The phenomenon has only increased in the interim decades, with phishers targeting banks, political campaigns, companies, personal emails, and social networking sites. A vast majority of organizations fall victim to phishing attempts, with over a billion phishing attempts in 2018 alone. Though many organizations provide training, phishing attempts have become more and more difficult to detect, siphoning millions of dollars from organizations and individuals each year.

Phishing attempts may include attaching malicious software to emails, soliciting information, cloning a genuine website to confuse users, pop-up windows at the top of legitimate sites asking for login information, fake news links, cloning of supervisor emails, and URL redirection. Other examples include emails warning that an account will be deactivated unless the target follows a link and provides information and fake threats from the governments unless the target pays a specified fee. Phishers may also use blatant requests from a prince in Nigeria who is offering a large payout for a small upfront sum, and fictitious emails from "tech support," which request remote access to the target's computer to fix a problem. Phishers may also pose as friends who need money or information. In these situations, many people may send money for emergency needs without confirming with their friend.

There are several types of phishing including spear phishing, whaling, and clone phishing. Spear phishing involves sending personalized emails to targets within organizations asking for payments or personal information. Whaling involves targeting those who are in positions of power within the organizations. In both cases, the emails appear genuine and look as though they originated from a supervisor or business partner. Clone phishing attempts to direct targeted employees to external websites. Once the users are on the site, they are asked to log in using personal information, including passwords or other information. Hundreds of corporate brands have been mimicked through such attempts, leading to billions of dollars of fraud each year. Training programs aimed at helping users identify phishing attempts are used nationally to combat this growing problem. Anti-phishing software has also been developed, with varying levels of success.

To date, the best way to combat phishing attempts is by educating users. Employees need to be trained to not click on links or download attachments from unexpected emails, to log into websites independently rather than using links provided in emails, to assess the sender's email address, to confirm in person regarding emailed requests, and to not send sensitive information over email. Employees must cultivate a sense of concern for privacy and security, question instructions given via email, understand institutional policies and procedures to be able to detect inconsistencies, have technical knowledge to detect problems, and take responsibility to investigate requests. To deter phishing, companies must use technology to detect phishing attempts, and they must train their employees to be sophisticated users.

One research group at the University of Buffalo studied the intended victims of phishing schemes. Their results showed that most people do not fully process phishing emails, and information embedded in the emails significantly influences users. Urgency cues in the email increased stress and decreased attention to other cues of deception. For example, when the email conveyed urgency, users were more likely to overlook poor grammar or spelling and less likely to assess the sender's email address. Those with habitual patterns online and high email loads were also more likely to fall victim to phishing attempts. Those who were overwhelmed by email tended to respond or comply without analyzing the request. Many phishing attempts use statements to create fear, threat, excitement, or urgency to encourage immediate responses. Thus, the most vulnerable users are those who inadequately process the requests within an email due to high email load, urgency cues, and poor processing of email content. The most successful way to combat phishing is through careful processing and cultivating suspicion of emails that convey urgency or make requests electronically.

See also: Dark Triad; Fake News; Instrumental Lies; Machiavellianism; Manipulation; Narcissism; Social Media; Sockpuppets.

Further Reading

Akerlof, G. A., & Schiller, R. J. (2015). *Phishing for Phools: The Economics of Manipulation and Deception*. Princeton University Press.

Curtis, S. R., Rajivan, P., Jones, D. N., & Gonzalez, C. (2018). Phishing attempts among the dark triad: Patterns of attack and vulnerability. *Computers in Human Behavior, 87*, 174–182.

Vishwanath, A., Herath, T., Chen, R., Wang, J., & Rao, H. R. (2011). Why do people get phished? Testing individual differences in phishing vulnerability within an integrated, information processing model. *Decision Support Systems, 51*, 576–586.

Wright, R., Chakraborty, S., Basoglu, A., & Marett, K. (2010). Where did they go right? Understanding the deception in phishing communications. *Group Decision and Negotiation, 19*(4), 391–416.

Physiology

Whenever an individual experiences a stress response, there is a typical cascade of physiological effects. This automatic response is initiated by hormones such as cortisol and adrenaline that activate the autonomic nervous system, producing a fight or flight response. This response increases blood flow to the limbs and increases breathing rates to increase oxygen, promote alertness, and activate the nervous system. In deceptive situations, particularly when an individual is highly motivated to conceal information, this cascade of physiological effects is triggered. These changes are the basis of polygraph tests that measure autonomic arousal, and attentive observers may be able to detect such reactions to detect lying in everyday situations.

During attempts at deception, most individuals show this stress response that increases breathing rates, reactivity, facial expressions, pupil dilation, and fidgeting behaviors driven by increases in adrenaline. Though subtle, all of these changes can be noticeable to a skilled observer. Increased alertness also places increased demands on cognitive systems, which may make it more difficult for individuals to think quickly or respond normally, further adding to discrepancies in their behaviors.

There are individuals who lack the typical physiological stress responses that accompany lying behavior. Some individuals who rate high on levels of psychopathy do not show the typical stress response, nor do they exhibit the corresponding changes in physiology. About 4 percent of the general population can pass a polygraph test because they do not experience these physiological changes that the polygraph relies on to detect lying. Furthermore, individuals who feel justified in lying may not show a physiological stress response when lying. For example, white lies often create very little arousal because individuals do not feel guilty or concerned about being discovered. This means that more significant lies show greater physiological changes, which creates a motivational impairment effect.

Dr. Leanne ten Brinke from the University of Denver and her colleagues from the University of Michigan and the University of California, Berkeley, found that participants in a research study even had increases in their own physiological arousal levels when observing liars in real scenarios. This physiological reaction was largely unconscious and went unnoticed by most of the participants. The researchers' follow-up work revealed the usefulness of teaching participants to attend to their own physiological signals when attempting to detect lying behavior, because recognizing changes in one's own physiology can be a key to detecting the increases in arousal that tend to accompany lying behavior in others.

This instinctual response of detecting liars reveals itself in studies where participants are asked to select a partner for a cooperative task. Participants are more likely to choose people who regularly tell the truth rather than people who regularly lie, when asked to select a partner from a group of strangers. Participants rated people who tell the truth as more likable and more attractive than those who lie more frequently, even though the participants did not have information about the individual's lying behaviors. When asked to make social judgments, participants were more likely to rate liars more negatively and were more likely to avoid them, as compared to those who typically tell the truth.

Since it can be socially damaging to accuse another person of lying, many individuals are likely to ignore their instincts and generally opt to trust others, leading to a trust bias. This trust bias tends to be common in all but highly threatening situations, at which point observers are more likely to trust their instincts to make judgments. Thus, higher threat likely leads to both increased physiological arousal in the liar and greater ability to detect lies in the observer. In most psychological research on lie detection, there is very little threat, and thus, lie detection abilities may be difficult to elicit within the laboratory. Posed scenarios may not evoke sufficient physiological arousal to allow an individual to detect lying behavior. In Dr. ten Brinke's study, people could detect lies in real crime scenarios but not those told in mock crime scenarios, likely because the mock crime scenarios did not elicit sufficient physiological reactions in the liar or the observer.

Though such research sheds light on potential deception detection ability, other research shows that such measures are subject to individual differences. For example, Dr. Geoffrey Duran and his colleagues from the University of Lyon found that individuals who have lower resting heart rates were better at detecting lies than individuals with higher resting heart rates. If changes in one's own physiological arousal can be used as a means to detect others' lying behaviors, then changes in one's own heart rate may be easier to detect if one has a lower resting heart rate. This means that physiological features of the detector may also influence lie detection ability.

See also: Antisocial Personality Disorder; Detecting Deception; Models of Lying; Motivational Impairment Effect; Neuroscience; Nonverbal Behavior; Polygraph Tests; Truth-Default Theory.

Further Reading

Duran, G., Tapiero, I., & Michael, G. A. (2018). Resting heart rate: A physiological predictor of lie detection ability. *Physiology and Behavior, 186*, 10–15.

Pozzato, L. R. (2010). Interpreting nonverbal communication for use in detecting deception. *The Forensic Examiner, 19*, 86–97.

ten Brinke, L., Lee, J. J., & Carney, D. R. (2019). Different physiological reactions when observing lies versus truths: Initial evidence and an intervention to enhance accuracy. *Journal of Personality and Social Psychology: Interpersonal Relation and Group Processes, 117*(3), 560–578.

Piltdown Man

The Piltdown Man was a revolutionary archeological find by amateur archaeologist Charles Dawson near Piltdown, Sussex, in 1908. He provided evidence of bones of a previously unknown human ancestor, which provided an evolutionary link between apes and modern humans, subsequently named the Piltdown Man. Though there was some controversy surrounding the find, Charles Dawson found a second skull a few years later at another site. For those who were unconvinced about the veracity of his first discovery, the emergence of a second skull seemed to confirm the findings. However, Dawson never revealed exactly where the skulls were found and was the only one on the team to make any discoveries. Further findings also ceased upon Dawson's death in 1916. Both finds were exposed as forgeries over 41 years later, and thus, the Piltdown Man became known as a long-standing archeological hoax.

Post hoc examination of the bone fragments revealed that they included altered bones from orangutans, chimpanzees, and modern humans. By 1953, examination of the evidence demonstrated that the bones had been purposely stained and shaped to give the appearance of a genuine ancient human fossil. Since most of the scientific community believed that the Piltdown man was the missing link between humans and earlier ancestors, the research on human evolution was misdirected for several decades. Other findings were ignored in favor of studying the Piltdown Man, and theories of evolution were based on the Piltdown Man's brain size, tooth structure, and jaw shape, radically confounding the field.

Uncovering the hoax took decades because it was not until 1953 that scientific techniques had progressed enough to sufficiently analyze the specimens. The application of a fluorine dating test demonstrated that the fossils were not old enough to fit the era from which they were thought to originate. They were in fact bones from modern species. The abrasions on the bones were also found to be too even to be produced by natural wear, the shape was atypical, and dental putty had been used to create an amalgamation of species. In addition, further inspection under modern microscopes showed evidence of scratches that appeared to be made by an abrasive. The bones had also been artificially stained to give them the appearance of age. Thus in the 1950s, researchers were able to draw more accurate conclusions about the bones' likely origins even if they could not conclusively say from what species the bones actually originated.

More recent technology has allowed researchers to test the DNA of the specimens. During an eight-year study that continued until 2016, researchers concluded that the bones came from several humans and a single orangutan. Since all of the specimens were consistent in stain, gravel, and dental putty used, researchers believed that they were forged by the same individual. The bones from both archaeological sites came from the same orangutan, and the teeth were ground down to appear more human. Though there have been several suspects over the years, researchers still believe Charles Dawson is the most likely perpetrator. He was the one who found the bones at both sites and had the scientific knowledge to prepare such forgeries. Furthermore, as he continued to make discoveries over his career, each new finding seemed tailor-made to fit scientific projections. It is likely that he observed the reactions and projections made based on earlier findings, and created subsequent findings to fit those expectations. His ability to create evidence that fit expectations likely contributed to his success in deceiving the scientific community.

See also: Commission, Lies of; Hoax; Hwang Woo-Suk; Instrumental Lies; Lightfoot, Lucy; Loch Ness Monster; Manipulation.

Further Reading

Hancock, P. (2015). *Hoax Springs Eternal: The Psychology of Cognitive Deception.* Cambridge University Press.

Pavid, K. (2016, August 10). Piltdown man hoax findings: Charles Dawson the likely fraudster. *Natural History Museum*. Retrieved from https://www.nhm.ac.uk /discover/news/2016/august/piltdown-man-charles-dawson-likely-fraudster.html

Webb, J. (2016, August 16). Piltdown review points decisive finger at forger Dawson. *BBC News*. Retrieved from https://www.bbc.com/news/science-environment-37021144

Weiner, J. S., Oakley, K. P., & Le Gros Clark, W. E. (1953). The solution of the Piltdown problem. *The Bulletin of the British Museum (Natural History), 2*(3), 141–149.

Placebo Effect

A placebo is an innocuous treatment that has benefits due to its psychological rather than biological effects. When given placebos, patients frequently feel better because they believe the placebo will help. From a psychological perspective, the mere act of taking a medication or receiving a treatment may be sufficient to stimulate actual improvement. Typically, the goal of giving a placebo is to create this placebo effect. Placebos are likely the most common drugs throughout history, but today, placebos are more commonly used in medical research to determine whether a new treatment has an effect on a disorder or a disease beyond the effects of a placebo. Medical research compares groups who receive the experimental treatment with groups who receive a placebo to see if the treatment actually has a therapeutic effect beyond what is achieved by the placebo.

In addition to their use in research, there is a debate of whether placebos can ethically be prescribed to treat medical disorders. In research, most participants endorse the use of placebos due to their documented beneficial effects. Research participants, additionally, endorsed the use of placebo prescriptions in tandem with other medications to achieve the most benefit or as acceptable when there is no other treatment available. In 2014, Dr. Nkaku Kisaalita and his colleagues from the University of Florida demonstrated in a medical trial that even patients who took a medicine labeled "placebo" perceived beneficial effects and reduction in pain compared to individuals who did not take anything. The mere act of taking a pill convinced their brains of impending relief, causing it to curb pain signals. Eating healthy food, exercising regularly, and engaging in self-care can also stimulate the placebo effect. Individuals feel better even before enough time or repetition has elapsed to see actual benefits.

Though participants in research may endorse the use of placebos, some doctors assert that the use of placebos violates their oath of honesty because they are essentially lying to their patients. Some doctors avoid outright deception by simply telling their patients that they are prescribing a medication that has been shown to have beneficial effects. Doctors may not disclose that it is a placebo, and they do not claim any specific effects beyond that it has made patients with similar symptoms feel better. A proactive patient may push further to gather information about the medication, which then may necessitate the reveal of the placebo.

General suggestions to physicians for placebo use include that the doctor should only prescribe them if he or she actually believes that the placebo will be beneficial for the patient. Placebos should also never be given in the place of other medications that would be more effective, unless the side effects of other medications are too great for the patient to endure. If the placebo does not cause improvement, it should be discontinued, and doctors are encouraged to tell the truth if the patient asks. Given that research participants who knew they were receiving a placebo still showed improvement, doctors could admit that they were prescribing a placebo that had demonstrated beneficial effects for other patients.

One example of placebo use is the use of iron pills in sub-Saharan Africa with terminally ill patients. Patients are routinely prescribed these pills and told that the pills will make them feel better. Though the iron pills are not a cure for the illness, patients commonly demonstrate overall improvements in health due to their belief in the medication. There is still healthy debate about the morality of such practice, but in these situations, there are no other available medications, and the treatment does provide significant benefits for most patients.

Thus far, neurologists cannot specifically pinpoint how placebos work. Prescription drugs target specific receptor sites in the brain and cause changes in the way pain signals are transmitted. Different medications target different receptor sites, and medical research specifically documents how they interact to relieve symptoms. Placebos, alternatively, seem to function at a broader level. They do not target a specific receptor site but instead impact the patient's perceptions and expectations. Ingesting a placebo tends to lower anxiety, cultivate an expectation of relief, and cause a cascade of neurological activity that results from these positive expectations. Though there are no specific effects at the receptor level, there are measurable changes in symptoms due to these psychological changes.

See also: Benefits of Lying; Deception in Research; Dementia; Ethics; Instrumental Lies; Malingering; Prosocial Lying; Self-Deception.

Further Reading

Ambrose, E. G. (2007). Placebos: The nurse and the iron pills. *Journal of Medical Ethics, 33*(6), 325–328.

Gold, A., & Lichtenberg, P. (2014). The moral case for the clinical placebo. *Journal of Medical Ethics, 40*(4), 219–224.

Kisaalita, N., Staud, R., Hurley, R., & Robinson, M. (2014). Placebo use in pain management: The role of medical context, treatment efficacy, and deception in determining placebo acceptability. *Pain, 155*(12), 2638–2645.

Plagiarism

Plagiarism is the act of claiming credit for someone else's work. Plagiarism is primarily a concern in academia and research, but can also be a problem in journalism, art, or any other field that relies on individual creations and contributions. Plagiarism is considered a type of fraud, copyright infringement, and academic dishonesty. Though plagiarism is typically not prosecuted in the legal system, in academia, it can result in academic failure, expulsion, suspensions, revocation of degrees, or loss of reputation. Plagiarism can consist of copying another's work word for word, paraphrasing without proper citations, or purchasing academic papers written by someone else and submitting them as one's own.

Many students claim a sense of ignorance when confronted with plagiarism. A major problem in academia is ensuring that students understand plagiarism so that they can take responsibility for completing their own work. Some institutions have used contracts or educational resources or even provided entire courses directed at educating about plagiarism. Even then, many students show confidence in understanding plagiarism, yet still cite insufficiently or incorrectly in practice. Furthermore, students may directly copy from online sources and then endorse a statement that they are completing good research. Plagiarism is such a concern in academia that most institutions of higher learning purchase software designed to detect it.

Dr. Chris Park from Lancaster University concludes that there are a host of factors that are correlated with plagiarism and cheating in general. Students plagiarize out of ignorance, because they are desperate to achieve a grade, because they have too many other responsibilities, because they do not feel capable, because it is easier, or because they have not been punished for in the past. Students are more likely to plagiarize if English is not their first language and they are struggling to express their thoughts. Students who are young, male, struggling academically, active socially, have low confidence, are under high pressure from parents or instructors, do not feel like they will be caught, or who are not interested in the subject are more likely to plagiarize. Furthermore, the increased reliance and availability of information on the internet make it easier to plagiarize than ever before.

There are personality and individual characteristics that are correlated with plagiarism. Younger male students who are struggling academically are more likely to engage in plagiarism. The pressure to succeed may drive students to engage in such behaviors to increase their grades. Aggressive individuals who have an external locus of control are less likely to take responsibility for their actions and more likely to plagiarize. A culture of plagiarism can also increase its frequency. Students who witness other students cheating are more likely to cheat themselves. Furthermore, professors who do not take plagiarism seriously or who do not express their views about plagiarism tend to have students who are more likely to plagiarize. Instructors who lecture against plagiarism, yet do not punish it when it is discovered, tend to have students who continue to plagiarize. However, instructors who are open about academic integrity, emphasize honest behaviors, and punish cheating tend to have students who plagiarize less frequently.

Most research on plagiarism has been conducted at the university level. However, some researchers have also looked at plagiarism at the professional level. Dr. Benson Honig from McMaster University and Dr. Akanksha Bedi from Bishop's University examined journal articles and found that 25 percent of the papers contained plagiarism. One key element to explain this high rate is the amount of pressure that is on researchers and professors to publish in addition to their academic and service work. There is high competition for publications as well as time and institutional pressure for work to be of high quality and high impact. Researchers who were not held accountable in their undergraduate and graduate work were more likely to have poorer research habits, have decreased attention to detail, and neglected to properly cite their research. Dr. Honig noted that the levels of plagiarism increased over 7 percent over the course of 10 years.

Many journals do not yet have a plagiarism policy in place, nor do they use plagiarism software prior to publication. Similar to classrooms, the best way to prevent professional plagiarism is by having a clear system with consequences in place. Regular use of detection software can also decrease plagiarism because students and professionals know that their work will be checked. With modern technology, plagiarism can be easier to detect, but also more difficult to police. Furthermore, as education moves online, particularly at higher levels, methods to detect and decrease plagiarism become more and more necessary.

See also: Academic Cheating; Fraud; Locus of Control; Motives for Lying; Personality.

Further Reading

Honig, B., & Bedi, A. (2012). The fox in the hen house: A critical examination of plagiarism and members of the Academy of Management. *Academy of Management Learning & Education, 11*(1), 101–123.

Park, C. (2003). In other (people's) words: Plagiarism by university students—Literature and lessons. *Assessment & Evaluation in Higher Education, 28*(5), 471–488.

Poole, C. H. (2004). Plagiarism and the online student: What is happening and what can be done? *Journal of Instruction Delivery Systems, 18*, 11–14.

Polite Lies

Cross-culturally, lying is considered to be an immoral behavior. Lying serves to decrease the clarity and quality of communication, undermines trust, and is detrimental to mental and physical health. Polite lies, however, are those lies used to protect feelings and to conform to social norms. Use of these lies develops over childhood, and adults engage in polite lies frequently to smooth social interactions and maintain relationships. When studied, the use of polite lies was endorsed as more socially acceptable than telling the truth, even by participants who sanctioned honesty.

Polite lies tend to emerge around age three. Though selfish lies are the most common through early childhood, children start to be able to consider and engage in polite lies in specific situations. By age seven, children also start to evaluate polite lies differently from other types of lies. Children consider the difference in motivation behind prosocial, polite, and selfish lies and adjust recommended punishments accordingly. Even children recommend lying to protect others and consider the intention behind the lie when evaluating the morality of the lie. Researchers Dr. Him Cheung and his colleagues from the Chinese University of Hong Kong found that by age seven, children rate polite lies as acceptable and rate selfish lies as well as the blunt truth as unacceptable. These children recognized the importance of the intention behind the lie as being important for its acceptability.

Dr. Jennifer Lavoie and her colleagues from McGill University and John Jay College of Criminal Justice found that the ability to engage in polite lies developed with age and with theory of mind development. Children who engaged in polite lies tended to be older, had a well-developed theory of mind ability and had better social skills than those children who engaged in instrumental lies. Dr. Lavoie suggests that children use their lies selectively to achieve goals and that such behavior seems to shift from self-motivated lies to other-motivated lies over development. Children start to use lies to protect relationships and enhance interpersonal connections as they age rather than to simply gain a reward or avoid punishment.

The use of polite lies increases through adolescence with a more thorough understanding of culture rules, socialization, and desire for social acceptance. With age, individuals use polite lies to maintain relationships, sustain friends, and gain respect. Adolescents who continue to use selfish lies or engage in blatant honesty, alternatively, had more difficulties with interpersonal skills and relationships. Those individuals with greater understanding of theory of mind were also better at understanding and using prosocial and polite lies. They lied more effectively, controlled leakage more readily, and showed more empathy. Children with the lowest theory of mind development were most likely to tell instrumental, self-serving lies.

Dr. Felix Warneken and Dr. Emily Orlins from Harvard University found that by age seven, children are more likely to use polite lies when another individual is displaying sadness or when an adult models such lies. Thus, children do not ubiquitously lie just to be polite, but they decide when to use it to purposefully influence others. They are more likely than adults to tell the truth about another person's performance if the other individual is not displaying sadness. In this manner, children use lies as a way of engaging in prosocial behavior. By age 11, children reference the desire to be polite when asked about why they would lie in a situation.

Though lying is frequently studied throughout early development and tends to decrease with age, polite lies are required to conform to social expectations throughout the life span. The desire to be honest and the need to be socially appropriate places competing demands on adult behavior. Dr. Matt Blanchard and Dr. Barry Farber from Columbia University examined the tendency for adults to engage in polite lies even in situations where the truth would be more beneficial. They found that in therapy sessions, 93 percent of respondents admitted to lying to maintain social cohesion with their therapists. The most common reasons that respondents gave were to be polite, to avoid upsetting the therapist, and to ease social discomfort. Clients were likely to pretend to like their therapists' comments or to continue to engage in therapy even when they wanted to end the sessions.

Honesty is a prerequisite for progress in therapy, so dishonesty, even for the sake of politeness or social cohesion, is detrimental to therapeutic outcomes. To decrease such lying behavior, therapists need to address issues of safety, trust, and confidentiality throughout their sessions and endeavor to maintain empathy and positive regard even when a client is honest rather than polite.

See also: Butler Lies; Categories of Lying; Consequences of Lying; Instrumental Lies; Motives for Lying; Prosocial Lying; Recursive Awareness; Theory of Mind; White Lies.

Further Reading

Blanchard, M., & Farber, B. A. (2016). Lying in psychotherapy: Why and what clients don't tell their therapist about therapy and their relationship. *Counselling Psychology Quarterly, 29*(1), 90–112.

Cheung, H., Chan, Y., & Tsui, W. C. G. (2016). Effect of lie labelling on children's evaluation of selfish, polite, and altruistic lies. *British Journal of Developmental Psychology, 34*, 325–339.

Lavoie, J., Yachison, S., Crossman, A., & Talwar, V. (2017). Polite, instrumental, and dual liars: Relation to children's developing social skills and cognitive ability. *International Journal of Behavioral Development, 41*(2), 257–264.

Warneken, F., & Orlins, E. (2015). Children tell white lies to make others feel better. *British Journal of Developmental Psychology, 33*, 259–270.

Politics

Deception in politics is so common that psychological and political researchers have developed theories to explain its use and practice. Though many politicians may outright lie, discrete forms of deception commonly used by politicians include paltering, partially answering questions, answering a different question than what was asked, or avoiding questions all together. Though individuals who use these tactics may avoid outright lying, they do engage in evasion, omission, or impression management, all of which are housed under deceptive techniques. Two such theories that explain how the public views politicians who dodge or avoid questions include the Information Manipulation Theory 2 and the Truth-Default Theory.

Information Manipulation Theory 2 (IMT2) suggests that most politicians, with some obvious exceptions, do not outright lie. Instead, they manipulate information. That is, they tell parts of the truth, omit important information, and skew details to align with their own goals in order to pacify their audiences and garner support. For particularly sensitive topics, they may decline from responding, or more commonly, they provide a distraction answer that is off-topic.

In the Truth-Default Theory (TDT), the basic assumption is that most people tend to believe what they are told, particularly if the information comes from members of a close group. This assumption of truth makes them more easily deceived. In political parties, group affiliation can make individuals much more susceptible to deception, depending on the strength of their ideology. In general, strong affiliation with a political group strongly decreases the ability to detect deception from politicians within that party. When examined more closely, researchers found that there were differences along party lines. Specifically, Democrats were more likely to detect an attempt at avoiding a question than Republicans and were likely to reduce ratings of trustworthiness as a result, regardless of the candidate's political affiliation.

In his research examining the impact of political deception, Dr. David Clementson from California State University reported on how these two theories impact voters. First, Dr. Clementson noted that, as predicted in the Truth-Default Theory, observers frequently do not notice when a question has been avoided or redirected. If politicians provide an answer on a similar topic as the question asked, most listeners are distracted and, when asked, demonstrate that they are entirely oblivious to the dodge. When probed, the listeners misreport what question must have been asked to elicit such a response. In some cases, the answers provided grossly diverged from the question asked, yet most listeners remained oblivious to the dodge. However, Dr. Clementson noted that when voters do become aware that politicians are avoiding or dodging important questions or issues, there can be long-standing consequences, particularly for voters who do not have strong ties to the party or candidate. When individuals detect that candidates have avoided a question or are manipulating information, it increases the levels of suspicion and distrust of the politician. Individuals become disinterested, impatient, and are less likely to engage in the democratic processes. Since manipulation of information has become quite common in political debates, many voters have become disillusioned and frustrated with the political process as a whole.

Deception in politics is not a new problem. Even the story of George Washington admitting to chopping down a cherry tree as a child because he could not tell a lie is a confabulation that was made up to make him appear more virtuous. Politicians, as a whole, have garnered reputations of being manipulative and deceptive in order to gain and maintain power. Campaign promises and political stances are carefully crafted to secure votes and many struggle to follow through once elected. Though American political history is rife with scandals and deceptions such as Watergate, the Teapot Dome, and the Iran-Contra Affair, this is not a problem unique to the United States. One recent example of dishonesty in the political arena is Luiz Inácio Lula da Silva, the former president of Brazil, who was sentenced to nearly 10 years in prison for corruption and money laundering. Another example is Ehud Olmert, the former Israeli prime minister who was indicted on charges of bribery, fraud, obstruction of justice, and breach of trust. A final example is Nicolas Sarkozy, the former French president who faced charges including corruption and illegal campaign financing.

See also: *Art of War, The*; Astroturfing; Blue Lies; Consequences of Lying; Conspiracy Theories; Corruption; Fake News; Gaslighting; Hypocrisy; Instrumental Lies; Models of Lying; Noble Lies; Omission, Lies of.

Further Reading

Clementson, D. E. (2018). Effects of dodging questions: How politicians escape deception detection and how they get caught. *Journal of Language and Social Psychology, 37*(1), 93–113.

Gerlach, P., Teodorescu, K., & Hartwig, R. (2019). The truth about lies: A meta-analysis on dishonest behavior. *Psychological Bulletin, 145*(1), 1–44.

Michener, G., & Pereira, C. (2016). A great leap forward for democracy and the rule of law? Brazil's Mensalao Trial. *Journal of Latin American Students, 48*, 477–507.

Willsher, K. (2018, March 29). *Nicolas Sarkozy to face trial for corruption and influence peddling*. Retrieved from https://www.theguardian.com/world/2018/mar/29/nicolas-sarkozy-to-face-trial-for-corruption-and-influence-peddling

Polygraph Tests

Polygraph tests are probably the most well-known lie detection methodologies. These tests use changes in physiological reactions to detect deception. In the early 1900s, polygraph testing started with a simple measure of changes in blood pressure. In the 1930s, measures of heart rate, respiratory rate, and sweat production were added as additional physiological measures of the anxiety response that might signal deceptive attempts. There are many questioning techniques used with the polygraph measures such as the Control Questions Test and the Concealed Information Test. One major critique of the polygraph test is that though a physiological response is correlated with lying behavior, there are many confounding variables that must be taken into consideration. For example, excitement, fear, and anger also induce similar physiological responses. And some liars may feel no anxiety when lying, making the results invalid. Thus, the polygraph test can measure arousal, but such reactions do not conclusively mean that the individual is lying.

Modern polygraph tests depend on analysis of psychophysiological reactions that tend to accompany lying behavior. The polygraph device monitors changes in breathing patterns, changes in blood pressures, and changes in electrodermal activity to assess whether someone is having an emotional reaction or experiencing increased arousal when asked a question or during a verbal response. Different theoretical frameworks are used when assessing suspected deception. One is based on emotions and uses changes in heart rate and electrodermal responses to determine guilt. The emotional-based measures run the risk of false positives because even innocent people may be anxious, feel guilty, or fear consequences if they are not believed. A second framework is based on cognitive responses and uses changes in brain activity to determine guilt. Cognitive-based approaches measure event-related potentials, or the changes in electrical activity in the brain, that tend to occur when a stimulus is meaningful. This event-related potential is used to reveal whether crime-specific information is meaningful to suspects who claim no knowledge of an event.

Several different methodologies can be used when administering a polygraph test. The most common test used during a polygraph session is the Control Questions Test (CQT). In this technique, interviewers ask questions of varying relevancy to the situation and compare the individual's physiological reactions when responding to the questions. The underlying idea is that the questions that hold the most immediate threat to the individual will elicit the strongest emotional (and physiological) response. For an individual who committed the crime, the questions relevant to the crime (e.g., did you commit this specific crime?) should elicit the greatest physiological change. For those uninvolved with the crime, the comparison or control question (e.g., have you ever stolen anything?) would elicit a greater physiological response than questions about the current crime with which they were uninvolved.

A less common paradigm used during a polygraph test is the Concealed Information Test. In this version of a polygraph interview, suspects are asked multiple-choice questions about the crime in question. One of the responses is accurate and the others are plausible alternatives. Physiological arousal and event-related potentials in response to the multiple-choice answers are measured. Reacting specifically to the correct answers during the interview demonstrates that the individual may be concealing information about the crime.

When polygraph tests were first designed, interrogators believed that the physiology of lying was specific and detectable. With continued research, however, it appears that similar physiological responses can occur in many situations. Additionally, some populations, such as individuals with psychopathy, conduct disorder, and antisocial personality disorder, fail to show typical physiological responses. Therefore, in situations such as a polygraph test, which are constructed to elicit an arousal response, some individuals, particularly those who are the most likely to commit crimes, may not have the expected anxiety spike when attempting to deceive. Delinquent boys, for example, were found to have a lower sweat response in arousing situations when compared to non-delinquent boys. Such individuals have a lower level of natural arousal and may seek out stimulation, such as dangerous and impulsive activities, to maintain arousal. Thus, polygraph tests can fail to detect lying depending on the individual being interviewed, and they should be used to gather information rather than as a definitive measure of guilt.

See also: Antisocial Personality Disorder; Behavior Analysis Interview; Concealed Information Test; Control Questions Test; Detecting Deception; Motivational Impairment Effect; Reid Technique.

Further Reading

Ben-Shakhar, G., & Elaad, E. (2003). The validity of psychophysiological detection of information with the guilty knowledge test: A meta-analytic review. *Journal of Applied Psychology, 88*(1), 131–151.

Ford, E. B. (2006). Lie detection: Historical, neuropsychiatric, and legal dimensions. *International Journal of Law and Psychiatry, 29*, 159–177.

Hahm, J., Ji, H. K., Jeong, J. Y., Oh, D, H., Kim, S. H., Sim, K., & Lee, J. (2009). Detection of concealed information: Combining a virtual mock crime with a P200-based guilty knowledge test. *CyberPsychology & Behavior, 12*(3), 269–275.

Verscheure, B., Crombez, G., Koster, E. H. W., & De Clercq, A. (2007). Antisociality, underarousal and the validity of the Concealed Information Polygraph Test. *Biological Psychology, 74*, 309–318.

Prevalence of Lying

A plethora of research on the prevalence of lying has reported that the average American adult tells about one lie a day. Adults report a tendency to lie about their feelings, their income, their accomplishments, their sex lives, and their ages. In another study, 93 percent of adults reported lying at work or in business, and 96 percent reported lying to friends or family. Ninety percent of undergraduate job candidates reported lying during a job interview. Additionally, research shows that 82 percent of adolescents lie to their parents about money, alcohol, friends, dating, parties, or sex. In an anonymous survey, 92 percent of university students reported lying to a sexual partner.

However, in a national survey conducted by Dr. Kim Serota and her colleagues from Michigan State University, 60 percent of respondents actually reported telling no lies. While Dr. Serota's data did show that the average adult lies one to two times a day, as commonly reported in previous studies, there was high variation in lying behavior among participants, and 5 percent of the respondents actually accounted for half of the lies. Prevalence of lying seems to vary widely, and it may

Types of Liars

People lie for many different reasons. Many liars tell lies as a way to avoid shame, guilt, persecution, conflict, or loss of relationships, or to achieve praise or acceptance. Others tell lies for more selfish reasons, such as to manipulate others into helping them to achieve goals. Still others seem to lie with no apparent goal or forethought. Additionally, individuals vary in the frequency of lying, with some lying very rarely and others almost constantly.

The most common type of liar is the white liar. White liars use small, low-stakes lies to help others, to avoid confrontations, or to smooth over social situations. Lies are usually socially appropriate in nature and conform to cultural norms. In many instances, white liars may simply omit information as a means of altering another's perception, and most do not even count them when asked if they ever lie. Furthermore, many justify their white lies by believing they are harmless or actually beneficial, though negative health effects result even from telling white lies.

Occasional liars are also very common. Whereas white liars may omit, alter, exaggerate, or imply information that is not true, occasional liars are those who tell outright lies. As implied by the name, these individuals only lie occasionally, and most feel immediate remorse and guilt about their lies. Occasional liars may lie to avoid a social engagement, in an attempt to impress someone, or due to feeling trapped in a situation. Frequently, occasional liars feel bad enough about their behavior that they admit to the lie and ask forgiveness.

Not all liars are as innocuous. Some liars use lies to manipulate others. Pathetic liars, for example, use lies to solicit sympathy or support from others. Typically, these liars use lies to attain material resources or emotional support. These liars tend to be manipulative and escalate as they progress. Pathetic liars tend to have low self-esteem, a low sense of self-efficacy, and an external locus of control. Most pathetic liars do not feel remorse for their lies, and feel they do not get as much support and sympathy that they deserve.

Other types include compulsive, habitual, and pathological liars. Compulsive liars tell lies even when they have no reason to lie. They are addicted to lying and struggle to control the behavior. They may or may not intend their lies to be malicious, and they may fool new acquaintances, but their lies are so persistent that they struggle to form long-term, trusting relationships. Habitual liars use lies to make themselves appear more impressive, important, or exceptional than they really are. These individuals may have learned to lie in childhood as a self-protective measure and lie so frequently that they cease to be aware that they are lying. Additionally, their lies tend to grow in magnitude until their lies are far-fetched and unbelievable. Pathological liars also compulsively tell lies, but their lies tend to be of a self-protective nature. Pathological liars tell lies to avoid things that are uncomfortable, to feel safe, or to prevent others from detecting their weaknesses. Pathological liars may get so good at lying that it may be difficult to distinguish their truths from their falsehoods.

Finally, sociopathic liars lie without regard to other people's feelings or well-being. They are not empathetic, nor do they feel shame for their lies. They are manipulative and resistant to changing their behavior. They lie to get their own way or to achieve a goal, without regard for others. They tend to be charming and charismatic, and use their lies to manipulate others. Unlike compulsive, habitual, and pathological liars, they have a clear self-serving goal.

be the case that most individuals are relatively honest, and that only a few prolific liars skew the data. When the survey was expanded, Dr. Serota found that more than 90 percent of the respondents reported at least one lie over the course of a week, but most lied significantly less than once a day.

In such an experiment, one must take into account that the data are self-reported and that different individuals may have different definitions of deception. Some may only count antisocial lies and discount white lies while others may count any attempt to deceive. Also, individuals may misperceive their own lying behavior and muddy it with impression management, exaggeration, omissions, or prosocial lies. To add validity to the self-report measures, Dr. Serota and colleagues created a game paradigm that gave the participants the opportunity to cheat to be more successful at the game. Individuals who self-reported as liars were more likely to cheat at the dice game when given the opportunity, demonstrating that those who report lying do seem to engage in more deceptive behavior than those who report they rarely lie.

An additional research study carried out by Dr. Kim Serota and Dr. Timothy Levine in the United Kingdom confirmed that most people seem to be honest most of the time. This may be one of the reasons it is so difficult to detect when someone does lie. If the behavior is infrequent, then one would not expect the lie and would not be suspicious. Based on their data, lying seems to be less frequent than what deception research has suggested, and the frequency of lying is not evenly distributed across the population. For those who do lie, about 80 percent of the lies would be categorized as white lies. Only 20 percent of lies told are big lies or high-stakes lies that create risk if caught.

Dr. Madeline Smith and her colleagues from Northwestern University and Cornell University found similar data when studying lies via text messaging. Analyzing participants' text messages allowed Dr. Smith to eliminate the bias of memory. Since most people may not remember lies told in the moment, looking at the history of their messages allowed for analysis over several days. Just as Dr. Serota found, deception via text message was not normally distributed. Seventy-five percent of individuals told one lie in 30 messages. However, Dr. Smith identified five prolific liars who lied at a rate substantially higher than average. These results are consistent with those that found that the top 5 percent of liars tell a quarter to a half of all lies told. This supports the idea that everyone lies occasionally but only a few lie consistently.

Prolific liars may need their own research study and may constitute their own population that is distinct from occasional liars. Occasional liars may tell up to one big lie a week, whereas prolific liars tell up to three high-stakes lies and six white lies a day. Occasional liars decrease in lying frequency as they develop into adulthood, but prolific liars continue to lie, perhaps having learned in childhood that too much honesty has negative consequences. Prolific liars are four times more likely to get caught lying, nine times more likely to be fired from a job due to dishonesty, and four times more likely to lose a partner due to dishonesty. Interestingly, prolific liars do not express more guilt than occasional liars.

See also: Butler Lies; Categories of Deception; Machiavellianism; Motives for Lying; Narcissism; Omission, Lies of; Personality.

Further Reading

Serota, K. B., & Levine, T. R. (2015). A few prolific liars: Variation in the prevalence of lying. *Journal of Language and Social Psychology, 34*(2), 138–157.

Serota, K. B., Levine, T. R., & Boster, F. J. (2010). The prevalence of lying in America: Three studies of self-reported lies. *Human Communication Research, 36*, 2–25.

Smith, M. E., Hancock, J. T., Reynolds, L., & Burnholtz, J. (2014). Everyday deception or a few prolific liars? The prevalence of lies in text messaging. *Computers in Human Behavior, 41,* 220–227.

Primates

Though forms of deception have been documented in many species, nonhuman primates demonstrate forms of deception that are closest to the higher-order deception seen in humans. Dr. David Premack and Dr. Guy Woodruff completed a battery of studies in the 1970s on deception in chimpanzees. In their research, they found evidence that primates were able to use deception to successfully deceive their handlers. At least one chimpanzee in their studies was able to conceal and fabricate information. In one paradigm, they allowed chimpanzees to witness the concealment of a banana. Thus, the chimpanzees knew the location of the banana, but they were unable to reach it on their own. Then trainers would enter and would either retrieve the banana for the chimpanzee when the chimpanzee indicated where it was or would eat the banana when the chimpanzee indicated where it was. One chimpanzee, Sarah, learned to engage in deception when faced with the trainer who had a history of eating the banana. After several trials in which the trainer ate the banana after she helped him locate it, she started to feign ignorance, refused to assist him, or indicated incorrect information.

Though Sarah's behavior was not the norm for chimpanzees, it does provide interesting anecdotal evidence of the mental abilities with respect to primates for deceptive ability. Another primate who demonstrated simple skills in tactical deception was Koko, a gorilla who was taught sign language. During her PhD work at Stanford University, Dr. Francine Patterson taught Koko sign language starting in infancy. Koko understood and used 22 signs by age 18 months and more than 600 over her lifetime. She also was able to understand some spoken English words and to respond to her trainers via sign language. In one instance, Koko was noted to use sign language to deflect blame to her trainer, Kate, for breaking a sink. She also blamed Kate for breaking a toy. In both cases, her use of deception was ineffective because of a seeming lack of recursive awareness. She did not demonstrate the awareness that such accusations were not believable because Kate was not strong enough to break the sink and was not present when the toy was broken. Michael, another gorilla raised with Koko, also engaged in simple deception when he blamed Koko for ripping a jacket. When pressed, he admitted he ripped it himself.

Primates have also demonstrated deception outside of laboratory experiments. In 1987, Dr. Roger Lewin researched and reviewed evidence for deception in primates. One example he outlines revolves around a natural observation of baboons. In his example, a young baboon watched another baboon find food. Then the young baboon cried, drawing his mother's attention. She came and chased off the other baboon. At that point, the young baboon immediately stopped crying and approached and ate the food. In another example, a young chimpanzee watched while researchers hid some food. The chimpanzee ignored the food until no other members of the troop were around, at which point, he uncovered and ate the hidden food. Primates have also demonstrated the ability to use bluffs. For example, confronted chimpanzees will avert their faces to hide their facial expressions, such as expressions of fear. Once they have controlled the expression, they will turn back to their adversaries.

Many other observations exist, and the only remaining controversy is whether or not these observations are representative of higher-order, intentional deceptions. It is unclear whether or not these behaviors indicate willful, developed understanding of intentionality or if they are learned through previous experience and conditioning. For example, a chimpanzee may learn the connection between moving toward food and having it taken away by a stronger, more dominant peer. Therefore, the avoidance behavior while in the presence of others may be a learned behavior based on previous consequences rather than indicating an understanding of others' states of mind and willful intentions to shape the perceptions of others.

See also: Bluffs; Deception in Animals; Evolution of Deception; Recursive Awareness; Tactical Deception.

Further Reading

Bond, C. F. (1988). The evolution of deception. *Journal of Nonverbal Behavior, 12*(4), 295–307.

Hall, K., & Brosnan, S. F. (2017). Cooperation and deception in primates. *Infant Behavior & Development, 48*(Part A), 38–44.

Lewin, R. (1987). Do animals read minds, tell lies? *Science, 238*, 1350–1351.

Patterson, F., & Linden, R. (1981). *The Education of Koko*. Hold, Rinehart, and Winston.

Premack, D., & Woodruff, G. (1978). Does the chimpanzee have a theory of mind? *Behavioral and Brain Sciences, 1*(4), 515–526.

Prisoner's Dilemma

The Prisoner's Dilemma is a game paradigm originally proposed by Dr. Merrill Flood and Dr. Melvin Dresher in the 1950s. The Prisoner's Dilemma explores the likelihood of cooperation or deceit in a variety of situations. Initially, the Prisoner's Dilemma asked participants to decide whether they would cooperate with a partner in a competitive environment. The paradigm is framed as though the participants are two accomplices who are being interrogated for a crime. They are not allowed to see or speak to one another before or during the interrogation. Since there is not enough evidence for a conviction, if both accomplices refuse to indict the other, they will both serve a small sentence. However, if one person chooses to betray their accomplice, then the betrayer will go free and the accomplice will receive the full punishment for the crime. If they both indict one another, they split the full punishment.

From a logical perspective, the safest and most rational decision in this dilemma is to betray one's partner. That is the only way to ensure shorter jail time. However, when played over multiple trials, betraying one's partner tends to lead to one's partner retaliating, so over the long term, it is actually more beneficial to cooperate. This strategy is risky unless the partner is trustworthy because a betrayal can cause an individual to suffer the most.

In the game paradigm, the participant has no contact with the accomplice, similar to separating suspects into two interrogation rooms. However, varying the description of the accomplice can influence the strategy chosen. Participants tend to be the most cooperative if the accomplice is a friend or family member or if they were told that they will play with the same partner repeatedly. A sense of cooperation tends to emerge in these situations, and each individual is less likely to betray the other. However, describing accomplices as varying in attitude, values, or experiences may decrease the tendency toward cooperation.

In an interesting version of the game, Dr. Matthew Mulford and colleagues from the London School of Economics and Political Science manipulated the reported attractiveness of the accomplice. In his version of the dilemma, he allowed the participants to view photographs of their accomplices. After viewing the photographs, the participants were asked to choose whether to participate in the game with that accomplice. Rather than jail time, Dr. Mulford used money as the tangible reward. For example, if neither competitor betrayed the other, they each received a small reward. If they both betrayed one another, they received no reward. If only one of them betrayed, that person received the highest reward and the other lost money.

Two interesting things emerged from this study that demonstrated enhanced opportunities and enhanced cooperation for attractive individuals. First, individuals were more likely to choose to participate in the game after viewing a photograph of an attractive accomplice. Second, the level of attractiveness was predictive of the likelihood of cooperation. Attractive men were more likely to cooperate with their accomplice, and they were most likely to cooperate when paired with an attractive female partner. Attractive women were less likely to cooperate and only chose to play with highly attractive partners. Thus, attractive women tended to win almost double that of women who rated themselves as unattractive. The implications of this research can be easily applied to the labor market. Attractive individuals are more likely to be approached and engaged and more likely to find cooperative partners when employed than less attractive individuals.

In the 1980s, Dr. Robert Axelrod held a computer tournament that challenged individuals to determine the best strategy to use during the Prisoner's Dilemma to maximize benefits. Dr. Anatol Rapoport won the tournament with a relatively simple strategy known as the tit-for-tat strategy. The tit-for-tat strategy encourages cooperation and punishes defection. Specifically, during the Prisoner's Dilemma, the tit-for-tat strategy directs an individual to begin by cooperating with a partner. This teaches the partner that one is trustworthy and cooperative. If the partner defects, then the individual must defect on the very next trial. This teaches the partner that defections will be punished. However if the partner cooperates, then the individual must cooperate on the very next trial, demonstrating forgiveness.

The tit-for-tat strategy tends to establish an equilibrium of cooperation, especially for long-term partnerships. This strategy is applicable to everyday life. When engaging in relationships with others, a tit-for-tat strategy can encourage altruism and cooperative behavior. If a partner cheats or engages in deception, they need to be held accountable immediately. However, if they genuinely apologize, forgiveness strengthens the relationship. In current society, most individuals are quite adept at keeping accounts of the behavior of others. If another person engages in dishonest behavior, it stands out and tends to be remembered. Individuals also tend to advertise signs of cooperative behavior in order to encourage collaboration from others. Additionally, many people will value their own reputations as a means of signaling that they are trustworthy and worthy of cooperation. In this way, cooperation is encouraged within everyday relationships in order to reach collaborative goals, and deception is discouraged and becomes less beneficial.

See also: Evolution of Deception; Politics; Tactical Deception.

Further Reading

Axelrod, R., & Hamilton, W. D. (1981, March 27). The evolution of cooperation. *Science, 211*(4489), 1390–1396.

McNally, L., & Jackson, A. L. (2013, July 7). Cooperation creates selection for tactical deception. *Proceedings of the Royal Society B: Biological Sciences, 280*(1762). https://doi.org/10.1098/rspb.2013.0699

Mulford, M., Orbell, J., Shatto, C., & Stockard, J. (1998). Physical attractiveness, opportunity, and success in everyday exchange. *American Journal of Sociology, 103*, 1565–1592.

Stewart, A. J., & Plotkin, J. B. (2013). From extortion to generosity, evolution in the iterated prisoner's dilemma. *Proceedings of the National Academy of Sciences.* https://doi.org/10.1073/pnas.1306246110

Propaganda

Propaganda refers to information that is presented as fact to influence the attitudes of large groups of people about an organization, such as a government, a branch of religion, or a cultural group. Propaganda is typically designed to elicit an emotional reaction to sway attitudes or create stereotypes for or against the group in question. Because propaganda can be pervasive and widely disseminated in a population, people may not even realize they are being influenced. In the United States, for example, from childhood, individuals are inundated with pro-American viewpoints, news stories, websites, products, songs, and television shows that largely disregard alternative perspectives.

Typically, propaganda is associated with governments and is used to control or shape the beliefs of a nation. Such propaganda demonizes and dehumanizes political enemies to spread fear and hate and garner support for government causes. For example, propaganda was used extensively in the United States through World War II and the Vietnam War, buffering the military efforts, solidifying the support of the American people, and dehumanizing the enemy.

Different categories of propaganda include white propaganda, black propaganda, and gray propaganda. As articulated by Dr. Howard Becker of the University of Wisconsin, white propaganda is the blatant spread of information presented as fact to influence groups of people and to align them with the position of those in power. It targets other cultural groups or nationalities and only presents one side of issues, and its influence is typically undetectable by the people it persuades.

Black propaganda is misinformation that appears to come from within the group being targeted. In general, it is presented as though it was created by the very people it is serving to influence. This is a savvy form of propaganda that relies on the loyalty within a group. Individuals who identify with the source are more likely to buy into the message. Sockpuppets or meat puppets, for example, may be used to spread misinformation to undermine or discredit a person, group, or product without revealing the true source of the information.

Gray propaganda includes messages in which the source of information is anonymous. This type of propaganda is more common in the internet age where anyone can spread information relatively anonymously online.

Most groups, political or religious, do not admit the use of propaganda. Instead, euphemisms such as public diplomacy or information management attempt to provide a softer term of the acts of changing public perception. For example, U.S. Information Agency employee Nancy Snow reported that in the early 1990s their mission was to alter, revise, and improve the United States' image to the world in an attempt to counter the perception of the United States as aggressive and a threat to world peace.

Obviously in today's political climate, propaganda is still at the forefront of political campaigns. Recently, Johan Farkas from Malmo University and Dr. Marco Bastos from the University of London examined thousands of tweets from the Internet Research Agency (IRA) in St. Petersburg. The tweets originated from a list of accounts that were given to the U.S. Congress by Twitter as part of an investigation regarding Russia's meddling in the 2016 U.S. presidential election. These researchers analyzed and coded tweets from the IRA and demonstrated the spread of extensive propaganda targeting U.S. citizens.

Johan Farkas and Dr. Bastos found numerous disguised accounts that employed different techniques targeting different countries and political agendas. Most activity mimicked news outlets and worked to amplify discontent as well as concerns about public safety. Among the tweets were those promoting rumors, conspiracy theories, and emotional statements and those that encouraged online or offline violence. They also contained accounts impersonating American, British, German, and Italian reporters.

The accounts examined demonstrated a variety of specific campaigns tailored to propaganda efforts. These included accounts impersonating conservative patriots who promoted Donald Trump and conservative values; accounts impersonating Black Lives Matter activists who twisted the issues and discouraged African Americans from voting; and accounts impersonating news outlets to undermine trust in the media. In all cases, the propaganda served to promote rumors, undermine accurate information, elicit emotional reactions, and push political agendas, frequently without the consumer being aware of the influence. Thus, though the Internet age provides access to more information, many consumers do not take the time to critically assess the veracity of the information being provided or the validity of the source, making even modern consumers subject to influence.

See also: Alternative Facts; Blue Lies; Doublespeak; Fake News; Gaslighting; Noble Lies; Politics; Red Herring.

Further Reading

Bastos, M. T., & Farkas, J. (2019). "Donald Trump is my president!" The internet research agency and propaganda machine. *Social Media and Society, 5*(3), 1–13.

Becker, H. (1949). The nature and consequences of black propaganda. *American Socio-logical Review, 14*(2), 221–235.

Farkas, J., & Bastos, M. (2018). IRA propaganda on twitter: Stoking Antagonism and tweeting local news. *Proceedings of the 9th International Conference on Social Media & Society* (pp. 281–285). https://doi.org/10.1145/3217804.3217929.

Hutchinson, W. (2006). Information warfare and deception. *Informing Science, 9*, 213–223.

Schechter, D. (2004). Selling the Iraq war: The media management strategies we never saw. In Y. R. Kamalipour & N. Snow (Eds.), *War, Media, and Propaganda: A Global Perspective* (pp. 25–32). Rowman & Littlefield Publishers.

Snow, N. (2004). From bombs and bullets to hearts and minds: U.S. Public diplomacy in an age of propaganda. In Y. R. Kamalipour & N. Snow (Eds.), *War, Media, and Propaganda: A Global Perspective* (pp. 17–24). Rowman & Littlefield Publishers.

Prosocial Lying

Prosocial lying refers to when lies are told to help facilitate social interactions or to protect others. Though most research on deception focuses on antisocial or instrumental lies, most everyday lies are prosocial. As defined by Dr. Maurice Schweitzer and Emma Levine from the University of Pennsylvania, prosocial lies are false statements that are meant to deceive and to benefit the target. There are different types of prosocial lies, including altruistic lies and mutually beneficial lies. Altruistic lies are prosocial lies that are costly for the liar yet benefit the target. Mutually beneficial lies are prosocial lies that benefit the liar as well as the target. Prosocial lies are always told to benefit another, unlike white lies, which may be prosocial or self-serving. Additionally, prosocial lies may be low-stakes lies similar to white lies or they may be high-stakes lies, such as black lies.

Though prosocial lies are recognized as lies, even children do not rate them as negatively as other types of lies. Prosocial lying is considered a social skill, and it is used to conform to cultural display rules. Prosocial lies protect feelings and serve to maintain social relationships. In addition, humans are relatively poor at detecting prosocial lies. This may illustrate the lack of need to detect such deception. If others are lying for our benefit, it likely does not benefit us to detect such mistruths. Taking prosocial lies at face value can help preserve relationships, maintain self-esteem, and decrease anxiety and stress.

Researchers Dr. Michelle Eskritt from Mount Saint Vincent University and Dr. Kang Lee from the University of Toronto found that by age 10, children engaged in effective prosocial lying and were able to pass off prosocial lies without detection at rates similar to that of adults. This is likely a result of socialization pressures to be nice rather than honest. In the United States, there is inherent social pressure to tell prosocial lies. Children practice them more regularly and without corresponding levels of guilt that emerge when telling instrumental or black lies. Prosocial lies may be more accepted and less challenged by adults than antisocial lies, making prosocial lies more difficult to detect, likely due to their socially appropriate nature.

Prosocial lies are very common in everyday communication. Individuals lie more readily when their lies benefit someone else than when they benefit themselves. Furthermore, when lying to benefit someone else, brain activity differs from lying for self-serving reasons. Lying to benefit another individual does not produce the same negative emotional reactions that tend to accompany antisocial lies. Lying for prosocial means is more socially and morally acceptable and reduces negative feelings toward lying, stimulating a different pattern of activation in the brain than other types of lying behavior.

The acceptability of prosocial lies varies by culture. Dr. Piotr Szarota from the Polish Academy of Sciences and Dr. Katarzyna Cantarero from SWPS University in Poland found that, in the United States, prosocial liars are rated as more likable but less respectable than those who tell the truth. In Poland, however, prosocial liars were rated as less likable, less respectable, and as worse friends than those who told the truth. In both cultures, individuals who tell the truth are generally respected more than even prosocial liars. However, the reasons for the lie also matters. In countries that have individualistic cultures, such as the United States, lying to protect a friend is rated more highly than other types of prosocial lies. In countries with collectivistic cultures, such as Japan, lies that protect the group are rated more highly. In countries such as Poland, where frankness is the cultural norm, those who told the truth, regardless of whether it was hurtful, were rated more highly.

The amount of time a parent spends talking about the feelings, thoughts, and beliefs of others correlates to a child's understanding and use of prosocial lies. Parents with multiple children are more likely to refer to mental states than parents with only one child. Thus, children with siblings are more likely to learn about empathy and about how they can influence others at earlier ages than only children. As a result, children with siblings typically engage in prosocial deception earlier than those who are an only child.

See also: Black Lies; Blue Lies; Consequences of Lying; Cultural Differences; Development of Deception; Ekman, Paul; Emotional Effects; Motives for Lying; Neuroscience; Noble Lies; Paternalistic Lies; Theory of Mind; White Lies.

Further Reading

Eskritt, M., & Lee, K. (2017). Detection of prosocial lying by children. *Infant and Child Development, 26*(1), 1–17.

Levine, E. E., & Schweitzer, M. E. (2015). Prosocial lies: When deception breeds trust. *Organizational Behavior and Human Decision Processes, 126*, 88–106.

Szarota, P., & Cantarero, K. (2019). Do we really like helpful liars? Apparently not everywhere. *Current Psychology, 38*, 764–768.

Williams, S., Moore, K., Crossman, A. M., & Talwar, V. (2015). The role of executive functions and theory of mind in children's prosocial lie-telling. *Journal of Experimental Child Psychology, 141*, 256–266.

Pseudologia Fantastica (See Compulsive Lying)

Puffery

Puffery is an exaggeration that expresses a distorted view of a situation or person. It may include false praise, false advertising, or a distorted view of an individual or product. Puffery tends to downplay opposing views and exaggerates qualities to influence the public's perception. Puffery may include marketing claims such as the "best burger in the world" or personal claims as having "the best mom in the world."

Puffery frequently emerges at the beginning of relationships when one individual wants to impress another. The person may extremely exaggerate their own qualities and abilities or compliment the other person excessively. This emergence of puffery may be engaging, or it may simply come off as insincere and impede the development of intimacy. Politicians also tend to engage in puffery in an attempt to impress constituents. During campaigns, excessive or extreme promises may be made without regard to reality. This can create disappointment and frustration once the individual is elected and is unable to live up to their claims.

Though puffery may be used in personal and political relationships, it is even more common in advertising. Advertisements that use puffery are often entertaining and contain hyperbole. They liberally use superlatives that claim that an item or person is the best, newest, or fastest. The claims are frequently a matter of opinion, making them difficult to regulate, and are used to draw attention to an item and suggest that it is worthwhile, even if the literal message is obviously an exaggeration. Puffery can be persuasive because it sways an audience to have positive expectations about a person or item; thus, it may create an implicit bias.

Researchers Dr. Archishman Chakraborty and Dr. Rick Harbaugh describe puffery as cheap talk that attempts to persuade buyers with humor and exaggeration rather than verifiable data. Advertisers may claim that a product is cheaper, better, faster, or more effective without actually providing a counter-product as a comparison point. Some researchers argue that puffery is harmful because it misleads susceptible buyers and has implicit influences even on those who are skeptical. Rather than addressing actual qualities of the product, it serves to hype the product through mega exaggerations.

Dr. Defeng Yang and Dr. Ninghui Xie from Jinan University and Dr. Sarena Su from the University of California, Berkeley, examined the effect of advertisements that used puffery on consumers. In general, puffery increased customers' expectations about the products and did increase product sales. However, when expectations were not met, puffery resulted in loss of trust. In fact, products advertised using high puffery tended to get lower product evaluations from consumers regardless of their overall quality.

Other differences they found in consumers' reactions to puffery revolved around their thinking styles. In general, holistic thinkers tended to be influenced more strongly when moderate levels of puffery were used to describe a product, as compared to high levels of puffery or no puffery. For example, holistic thinkers, or "big-picture" thinkers who see things as a whole, tended to be more impressed if a product was claimed to be better than others, rather than the best. In contrast, analytical thinkers did not tend to be influenced by varying levels of puffery. Thus, for advertisers, moderating use of puffery may be more effective than claiming to be the best.

Dr. Yang and colleagues recognized that consumers who had less knowledge about the product were more susceptible to puffery, and that advertisement placement matters. For example, puffery in professional magazines primarily read by experts tended to be taken as more truthful and thus was more effective than puffery in popular magazines. However, if the readers of the popular magazines did not know much about the product, puffery was more effective. Those who know a lot about the product were negatively influenced by puffery. Advertisers must know their audience and format to judge whether puffery would be effective in that context.

Though puffery may be used as a method to increase sales or impress others, it can backfire if others realize they are being misled or if puffery comes out as deceptive. Use of puffery by individuals, politicians, or advertisers may also make people more suspicious about any claims made. Using puffery can cause reputation damage, lower consumer ratings, and interfere with the development of healthy relationships.

See also: Advertising; Doublespeak; Politics; Propaganda; Social Media.

Further Reading

Chakraborty, A., & Harbaugh, R. (2014). Persuasive puffery. *Marketing Science, 33*(3), 382–400.

Xu, A. J., & Wyer, R. S., Jr. (2010). Puffery in advertisements: The effects of media context, communication norms, and consumer knowledge. *Journal of Consumer Research, 37*(2), 329–343.

Yang, D., Xie, N., & Su, S. J. (2019). Claiming best or better? The effect of target brand's and competitor's puffery on holistic and analytic thinkers. *Journal of Consumer Behavior, 18*, 151–165.

Pyramid Schemes (See Scams)

R

Reaction Time

Reaction time, or how quickly individuals can respond after being presented with stimuli, is widely used throughout psychological research. Measuring how quickly an individual can process and respond to a question and comparing that time to the amount of time it takes him or her to respond to other questions can reveal which areas the individual must spend greater time thinking about before providing a response. For deception research, lying is hypothesized to take greater cognitive effort, and thus, when lying, individuals would need more time to process the situation, inhibit information they do not wish to share, fabricate a plausible lie, and provide an answer.

Reaction time is particularly useful in detecting deception when respondents have not had time to prepare a cover story because it takes time to construct plausible information. Thus, during interviews, questions should not be provided beforehand, and respondents should be asked to answer as quickly as possible. Even a four-second delay between the presentation of the question and the response provides most individuals ample time to construct a plausible story. To alleviate the effects of such delays, asking the individual to tell their story in the reverse order or asking them unanticipated questions about their story tends to strain liars more than truth-tellers and their follow-up responses take longer, which signals potential deception to those who are paying attention to such cues.

Dr. Kristina Suchotzki and Dr. Bruno Verschuere and their colleagues demonstrated that even when individuals had time to prepare a cover story, their reaction time remained longer when lying than when telling the truth. This indicates a stability of delay in deception, even in practiced and prepared individuals. Since there are individual differences in processing and response times, control questions are needed to delineate between an individual's response times when telling the truth and when lying, and there must be a sufficient number of questions to find average differences between lies and the truth.

Cognitive models of deception explain that lying takes more time because greater cognitive resources are needed to inhibit, construct, and remember information. Liars must create a plausible lie, remember their lies so they do not contradict themselves, monitor their own nonverbal behaviors, assess their audience to make sure they are believed, and inhibit true information. Brain imaging studies show greater brain activation during lying behavior as compared to when telling the truth as individuals monitor, assess, fabricate, and speak. Additionally, increased emotional arousal contributes to longer reaction times, so the more anxious individuals are about lying or about being caught, the greater the reaction time differences will be between their lies and true statements.

Early research using reaction time to detect lying behavior was inconsistent, likely due to insufficient measurement technology. With modern technology, there has been a resurgence in reaction-time research. A meta-analysis of reaction-time research reveals that with appropriate measures, there is evidence that lying takes more time than telling the truth, even when the individual is prepared with a lie. From a cognitive perspective, when presented with a question, the truth is automatically activated, and successful lying depends on suppressing and overcoming that automatic first response.

Reaction time, therefore, has the potential to be an effective method of distinguishing between lies and the truth. More research is needed to outline the basic requirements for its effective use. Methodologies such as the exact instructions, stimuli presentation pace, number of trials, and proportion of lie-versus-truth trials need to be tested and standardized to find peak efficiency of such measures. Additionally, for reaction time to be used as an accurate discrimination between lying behavior versus truth-telling behavior, respondents would need to provide an immediate response to questions, baseline comparison data for each individual would need to be measured, and use of computer software to detect subtle differences in reaction time would be required.

Deceptive ability relies on both behavioral and cognitive control. Successful deception requires use of attention, memory, inhibition, and executive monitoring systems in the brain. Successful deception also requires ample motivation and a sense of reward for deceptive success. Neuroimaging studies demonstrate that lying behavior activates the frontal and parietal cortex, the cerebellum, the striatum, the insula, and the thalamus. Such widespread activation increases the amount of time spent processing, which leads to slower reaction times for lying versus honest responses.

See also: Control Questions Test; Detecting Deception; Emotional Effects; Mental Effort; Models of Lying; Motivational Impairment Effect; Neuroscience; Physiology; Polygraph Tests; Recursive Awareness.

Further Reading

Suchotzki, K., Verschuere, B., Van Bockstaele, B., Ben-Shakhar, G., & Crombez, G. (2017). Lying takes time: A meta-analysis on reaction time measure of deception. *Psychological Bulletin, 143*(4), 428–453.

Verschuere, B., Suchotzki, K., & Debey, E. (2015). Detecting deception through reaction times. In P. A. Granhag, A. Vrij, & B. Verschuere (Eds.), *Detecting Deception: Current Challenges and Cognitive Approaches* (pp. 269–291). Wiley-Blackwell.

Reality Monitoring

Reality monitoring is the process of recognizing the difference between memories about things that actually happened and things one simply imagined or fabricated. According to the reality monitoring theory, when one actually experiences an event, the memories about that event are formed through perceptual processes and contain sensory, spatiotemporal, and emotional details. The individual may remember the taste, touch, smell, sight, or auditory information wrapped up in the experience. When one constructs or fabricates an event however, the memories are internally constructed, and sensory details are missing or must be imagined. Thus, fabricated events are more likely to contain higher-order cognitive processing and reasoning rather than sensory information, and such memories are likely stored differently in the brain. Due to these differences in the formation and storage of memories, reality monitoring may be an effective way for observers to detect deception.

When using the reality monitoring theory to detect deception in a research paradigm, Dr. Michael Logue and his colleagues from Brock University found that, when lying, participants used fewer visual, auditory, spatial, and temporal details. Instead they used significantly more higher-order cognitive operations such as inferences, descriptions of thoughts, and opinions. Therefore, though reality monitoring is not necessarily related to deception, it may be an effective way to detect deception since it may help observers distinguish between real versus fabricated reports.

To study how the reality monitoring theory may reveal deception, Dr. Aleksandras Izotovas, from the University of Portsmouth in the United Kingdom, and his colleagues engaged in a study where participants were shown a video of a mock incident and were then asked to describe what happened. Some participants were instructed to lie and others were asked to tell the truth. When analyzing the descriptions of the incident, researchers blind to the condition were able to distinguish between the liars and the truth-tellers based on the quality of the information provided. Those who were telling the truth described the incident in more detail and with more sensory information than those who fabricated descriptions. Furthermore, during a follow-up interview two weeks later, additional differences emerged. Those who had told the truth showed evidence of memory decay, and they remembered fewer details than during the initial interview. However, those who were in the lying condition demonstrated a stability bias and remembered their original lies in detail. Though the truth-tellers remembered less, even after a two-week delay, they still reported more sensory information such as visual and temporal details, such as when the event occurred or the sequence of events, than those who lied. Likely, the liars engaged higher-order processes when constructing convincing lies, and due to that mental effort, they remembered their lies about the event better than those who had simply told the truth.

In a study at Bar-Ilan University in Israel, researcher Galit Nahari drew similar conclusions using a different methodology. In Dr. Nahari's study, participants were asked to leave the laboratory for 30 minutes and then return. Half of them were asked to go about their normal business and engage in at least three tasks before returning. The other half were asked to complete a mock crime, which included accessing a key to a professor's office, logging onto his computer, copying down a chemical formula, and then passing it to a confederate. They were cautioned not to let anyone see them committing the mock crime and to report back in 30 minutes. Individuals in each group were then interviewed about the events.

During the interview, those who engaged in the crime were instructed to try to convince the naive interviewer that they had not been involved with the mock crime. If they were successful, they would win money. Thus, they needed to lie about their whereabouts for 30 minutes. Those who were asked to go about their normal business were simply asked to tell the examiner what they had done during that time. As would be predicted by the reality monitoring theory, those who were telling the truth provided more perceptual details than those who were lying. Though all of the liars fabricated details, they did not reach the same level of specificity as those who were telling the truth. This may be because some details are difficult for liars to fabricate. In a follow-up interview two weeks after the event, those who told the truth remembered fewer details about the event than those who lied. In this study, as well as in the previous study, participants did not seem to accurately assess and account for typical declines in memory when trying to deceive others.

An understanding of reality monitoring may be particularly important within eyewitness testimony and in understanding the creation of false memories. If interviewers provide enough sensory details when describing an event, individuals may start to struggle to distinguish between real and imagined memories. Additionally, individuals who engage in frequent deceptions can struggle with reality monitoring and tend to develop a blurred line between actual and fabricated reality. Reality monitoring also can fail when trying to remember things that happened a long time ago. As memories naturally fade, individuals tend to fill in information, and it becomes part of their memory even if it is inaccurate.

See also: Cognitive Distortion; Detecting Deception; Emotional Effects; False Confessions; False Memory; Language; Malingering; Memory; Neuroscience; Self-Deception.

Further Reading

Brandt, V. C., Bergstrom, Z. M., Buda, M., Henson, R. N. A., & Simons, J. S. (2014). Did I turn off the gas? Reality monitoring of every day actions. *Cognitive Affective Behavioral Neuroscience, 14*(1), 209–219.

Izotovas, A., Vrij, A., Hope, L., Mann, S., Granhag, P. A., & Stromwall, L. A. (2018). Facilitating memory-based lie detection in immediate and delayed interviewing: The role of mnemonics. *Applied Cognitive Psychology, 32*, 561–574.

Johnson, M. K., & Raye, C. L. (1981). Reality monitoring. *Psychological Review, 88*, 67–85.

Logue, M., Book, A. S., Frosina, P., Huizinga, T., & Amos, S. (2015). Using reality monitoring to improve deception detection in the context of the cognitive interview for suspects. *Law and Human Behavior, 39*(4), 360–367.

Nahari, G. (2018). Reality monitoring in the forensic context: Digging deeper into the speech of liars. *Journal of Applied Research and Memory and Cognition, 7*, 432–440.

Recursive Awareness

Recursive awareness is an ability that builds on cursory theory of mind to facilitate higher-order social intelligence and effective deceptive ability. Theory of mind is the understanding that others have thoughts, memories, desires, intentions, and beliefs. To successfully deceive, deceivers must have a mature theory of mind to understand what the receiver believes to be able to manipulate their understanding to create a false belief. Recursive awareness takes this ability one step further and suggests that to be truly effective in deceiving others, the individual must not only be aware that they can influence others' thoughts, memories, desires, intentions, and beliefs but must also have the recursive awareness that the social partner may also be attempting to influence, manipulate, or deceive the individual as well. A mature theory of mind is a necessary first step for effective deception, but the ability to monitor and assess whether one's lies are believed and adjust accordingly and awareness of whether the other is also attempting to manipulate is a higher-order ability that must be developed to ensure successful deceptive ability.

Dr. Rachelle Smith and Dr. Peter LaFreniere examined the development of recursive awareness and found that this ability does not mature as early as initial developments in theory of mind. By age five, children start to be able to conceal the truth as needed in a competitive game paradigm. This demonstrates an awareness of theory of mind and an understanding that one can conceal information to effectively mislead others. Four-year-olds had difficulty in this task and were just as likely to reveal the information as to conceal it. In this competitive card game, children were asked to look at a card in a standard deck of playing cards and then to give the experimenter a clue about the color of the card by either pointing to a red card or a black card. If the experimenter successfully guessed the color of the card, she won the card. If the experimenter guessed incorrectly, the child won the card. The winner of the game was the one who won the most cards. Thus, the children were motivated to mislead the adult, and the adult was motivated to watch the child carefully to try to detect deceptive attempts.

Four-year-olds frequently showed the card as they were looking at it themselves, verbalized the color, and used a predictable strategy when trying to mislead the adult, such as pointing at the incorrect color every time throughout the game. A savvy adult quickly learned how to read the child's clue to guess the correct answer. By age six, children demonstrated more awareness of the need to hide the card carefully and provided more false information. They were not able to inhibit subtle cues such as looking or orienting their body toward the right answer even as they pointed to the wrong answer.

By age eight, the children had a much better grasp of recursive awareness. They provided misinformation to the adult and manipulated cues effectively. For example, they fabricated leaking information by glancing toward the wrong color as they pointed to the correct color. Following the trial, they articulated that they knew if they glanced at the wrong color the experimenter would believe that it was an accident and would believe that wrong color was the correct answer. Furthermore, on the subsequent trial, the eight-year-olds would glance to the correct color instead of the incorrect color and then articulate that they knew that the experimenter would believe that they were trying the same strategy again and would choose the opposite card. In this way, eight-year-olds demonstrated an ability to understand not only that the experimenter had their own thoughts and intentions but also that the experimenter would be attempting to read the child's behaviors to get insight into the child's intentions. Being able to manipulate the belief of the other required manipulating those signals effectively to create a false belief.

In real-life situations, individuals must understand the motivations and intentions of others in order to effectively interact and be aware that the other is also attempting to gain insight into one's own intentions. Such insight is needed to be successful in negotiations, as well as in both cooperative and competitive situations. One may need to bluff and provide masked or fabricated intentions in order to ultimately be successful. Until one understands what cues others may read, however, this is a difficult task. Though deception can have ethical implications, it is necessary for effective social intelligence. Knowing when and how to lie effectively enhances all realms of social life. To be effective in business, negotiations, and competitive situations, and to be able to cooperate effectively, one must understand the desires of others and be able to communicate one's own intentions and desires as needed.

See also: Bluffs; Competition; Ekman, Paul; Eye Gaze; Facial Cues; Social Intelligence; Tactical Deception; Theory of Mind.

Further Reading

Shultz, T. R., & Cloghesy, K. (1981). Development of recursive awareness of intention. *Developmental Psychology, 17*(4), 465–471.

Smith, R. M., & LaFreniere, P. J. (2009). Development of children's ability to infer intentions from nonverbal cues. *Journal of Social, Evolutionary, and Cultural Psychology, 3*(4), 315–327.

Smith, R. M., & LaFreniere, P. J. (2011). Development of tactical deception from 4 to 8 years of age. *British Journal of Developmental Psychology, 31*, 30–41.

Wimmer, H., & Perner, J. (1983). Beliefs about beliefs: Representation and constraining function of wrong beliefs in young children's understanding of deception. *Cognition, 13*(1), 103–128.

Red Herring

The term "red herring" refers to a deceptive attempt in which one uses flawed reasoning or distraction to mislead an audience about a pertinent topic. The distraction may or may not be an intentional attempt to deceive, but serves to undermine progress toward a goal and to add noise to an argument. The term "red herring" stems from a nineteenth-century story in which a smoked herring was used to divert hunting dogs from their prey. The smell of the smoked herring misled the pack and was a way to end or confuse the hunt. This story has developed into an idiom that includes any attempt to mislead or divert an audience from their original goal or intention. A red herring can be used as a literary device, to intentionally mislead or redirect others, to gain an advantage when one does not have a strong position, or to distract others from a controversial issue.

In literature, a red herring can be used to increase suspense and allow for surprise reveals later in the story. Planting a suspicious character in a story, for example, may distract or divert a reader from the true criminal to allow for a more satisfying twist at the end. Red herrings are also commonly used in parenting, business meetings, or negotiation. Purposefully inserting irrelevant yet connected information can successfully turn the conversation to a more agreeable topic or to manipulate the outcome of the conversation.

Red herrings are frequently used in politics to divert attention from relevant issues. Raising unrelated concerns or topics in response to difficult questions can distract an audience, and if they are used skillfully, the audience may not even realize that their questions were not addressed. Politicians may successfully use red herrings to divert the conversation to topics about which they have more to share or that reveal greater success. Presenting an irrelevant piece of information may distract listeners or adversaries from the topic at hand or shift the topic altogether. Red herrings may also be used in academia, such as through distractors in exam questions to more fully test students' abilities and understanding of the material.

When using a red herring, a person is essentially shifting the focus of the conversation to manipulate the outcome. In some cases, the new issue is similar enough that others are genuinely distracted. Furthermore, red herring statements frequently are successful because most are designed to introduce a topic that is agreeable to the listener. The agreement between opponents distracts from the original issue, which will frequently remain unaddressed now that both sides have found common ground, even if that ground does not address the original issue. In this case, it is easy to overlook that the argument has shifted, making red herrings a strong deceptive strategy in many cases.

An example of a red herring that distracts or diverts attention from the real issue has emerged in the Black Lives Matter movement. The "All Lives Matter" response to the "Black Lives Matter" movement is an excellent example of the red herring logical fallacy. Rather than addressing the issue, the "All Lives Matter" response simply distracts from the real issue being discussed. This red herring may be used due to ignorance or blatant racism, but it serves to derail the movement by shifting attention away from the issue and by attempting to invalidate and shut down the conversation by redirecting the conversation.

To address red herrings, one must be aware when a discussion has shifted to a different issue or a different aspect of an issue. One must also notice when the shift, even if the new topic is a worthy issue, introduces a topic that is irrelevant to the first topic being discussed. One can acknowledge that the new issue is important, but irrelevant or even counterproductive, and redirect the focus of the conversation back to the initial point. Red herrings may be unintentional or purposefully used to manipulate. They may be used to end a conversation or to help one rationalize their point of view to reduce anxiety or discomfort. In either case, their use is unproductive to resolve issues, and most merely serve to distract, manipulate, confuse, and avoid confronting or resolving issues.

See also: Cognitive Dissonance; Diversionary Tactics; Gaslighting; Manipulation; Politics; Smoke and Mirrors.

Further Reading

Currall, J. E. P., Moss, M. S., & Stuart, S. A. J. (2008). Authenticity: A red herring? *Journal of Applied Logic, 6*(4), 534–544.

Tindale, C. W. (2007). *Fallacies of Diversion: Fallacies and argument appraisal.* Cambridge University Press.

Reid Technique

The Reid Technique is an interrogation procedure developed by John Reid that is particularly successful at eliciting confessions from uncooperative suspects. His company, John E. Reid and Associates, is known for training interrogators in the Reid Technique of interrogation, which is commonly used by law enforcement personnel. The Reid Technique starts by analyzing the facts and engaging in a Behavior Analysis Interview to identify situations in which Reid's interrogation techniques are appropriate. Because the Reid Technique is accusatory and likely to elicit a confession, even from innocent suspects, interrogators need to be convinced of the suspect's guilt before applying the practice. A major criticism of the technique is the heightened rate of false confessions, and there has been some debate about whether law enforcement personnel should continue to use the practice. In theory, the Behavior Analysis Interview weeds out innocent suspects, and then the Reid Technique is used to get guilty suspects to admit to their part in the crime.

Methods used in the Reid Technique include asserting that the interrogator knows that the suspect is guilty and indicating the wealth of evidence against the suspect, whether real or fictional. During the interrogation, interrogators maintain physical closeness and eye contact, and attempt to create a calm environment where the suspect feels safe to tell the truth. The interrogator also does most of the talking and constructs not only what happened but also provides plausible excuses for why the behavior may have been reasonable. Reid's technique suggests asking "alternative questions" in which the interrogator provides two choices of why the suspect committed the crime, with innocence not being an option. One of the provided choices is less threatening and more socially appropriate than the other. However, when the suspect takes either option, even the more socially appropriate option, they admit guilt. Once guilt is admitted, the interrogator records the statements and has the suspect sign it.

Though the goal of the Reid Technique is to identify guilty suspects without eliciting false confessions, there has been a question of how well it makes that distinction. It is nonviolent, but does not have the same level of theoretical and empirical validation as the Concealed Information Test. Due to this, law professor Brian Gallini proposed that confessions based on the Reid Technique should be inadmissible in court. In his research, he demonstrated that about two-thirds of state police departments train their officers with the Reid Technique. He noted that during the interrogation, the interrogator displays unwavering confidence that the suspect is guilty. Such confidence is one prerequisite of eliciting false confessions or even planting false memories. Innocent individuals may grow anxious, confused, or scared under such presumptions and start to show nonverbal behaviors of arousal, which may also be taken as signs of guilt. The interrogation procedures are designed to increase arousal, incentivize confessions, and provide rationalizations or justifications for the suspect to accept. Through the use of physical proximity, eye contact, and alternative questioning, the interrogator arguably engages in coercion. Because of this high risk, many countries prohibit the technique; however, it is still commonly used in the United States.

Research on lie detection has demonstrated that police officers perform no better than the general public at detecting lies. Most individuals detect lies at about chance levels, and those who are motivated to detect lies tend to perform worse, yet tend to be more confident in their accuracy. Thus, motivated police officers who assume a suspect is guilty may be prone to errors and not realize their mistakes. Though the Reid Technique does seem to be effective at eliciting confessions, it does not address the human error of being able to distinguish between true confessions and false confessions. Dr. Saul Kassin and Dr. Christina Fong of Williams College found that research participants who were trained in the Reid Technique actually performed worse at judging guilt than participants who did not receive training, yet were more confident in their abilities. Confessions based on the Reid Technique are also commonly accepted in court and influence the verdict regardless of how they were obtained.

In 2017, Douglas Wicklander and David Zulawski, two former employees of John E. Reid & Associates, announced that their company, Wicklander-Zulawski & Associates, would no longer use the Reid Technique when training law-enforcement personnel throughout the United States due to the high rates of false confession. They note the Reid Technique relies too heavily on deception, coercion, and aggression, and are moving toward training based on research of less risky methods. In response, John E. Reid & Associates announced that they stand behind their method and continue to adapt it for increased efficacy.

See also: Behavior Analysis Interview; Coercion; Concealed Information Test; Detecting Deception; False Confessions; Motivational Impairment Effect; Polygraph Tests.

Further Reading

Gallini, B. R. (2010). Police "science" in the interrogation room: Seventy years of pseudo-psychological interrogation methods to obtain inadmissible confessions. *Hastings Law Journal, 61*, 529–577.

Kassin, S. M., & Fong, C. T. (1999). I'm innocent!: Effects of training on judgments of truth and deception in the interrogation room. *Law and Human Behavior, 23*, 499–516.

Zulawski, D. E., Wicklander, D. E., Sturman, S. G., & Hoover, L. W. (2001). *Practical Aspects of Interview and Interrogation* (2nd ed.). CRC Press.

Reverse Psychology

There are several empirically validated strategies that individuals use when trying to influence others. Examples include the door-in-the-face tactic, the foot-in-the-door phenomenon, and reverse psychology. The door-in-the-face tactic is when individuals ask for a large favor, which is usually denied, and then immediately ask for a smaller favor. This smaller favor is more likely to be granted, because it seems more reasonable in comparison to the larger favor. The foot-in-the-door phenomenon occurs when individuals ask for small favors and then slowly ramp up what they ask for over time. Since the other individual has complied in the past, it becomes more difficult for them to say no in the future. Reverse psychology relies on the phenomenon in which individuals who feel threatened seek to relieve the distress by engaging in the behavior that is the opposite of what is asked. Thus, at times, asking for the opposite of what one wants may drive another to engage in the behavior one was actually seeking. Such forms of deception use an understanding of social psychology to manipulate others.

One example of reverse psychology is when an individual expresses doubt or scorn at the actions of another in order to drive the other to become more committed to prove the individual wrong. This indirect influence can be risky because if the other tends to be agreeable and easily swayed, then reverse psychology is not likely to work. Instead, the other individual may do what was asked, which is the opposite of what was actually wanted. If the other individual is known to be disagreeable, however, presenting the opposite point of view may cause them to take a counterpoint, and they can be manipulated to comply. Knowing and understanding an opponent can greatly increase the chance of success when using reverse psychology.

When using reverse psychology, individuals present the opposite of their true intentions. They strategically misrepresent their own beliefs in order to influence others. When engaging in a debate, they may present an opinion opposite to what they actually believe in order to increase the chances of getting what they want. They may express doubt about their own competence to solicit support and opportunities from a partner or supervisor. Overuse of such strategy, especially with the same conversation partners, can backfire if others become aware that such a strategy is being used. At that point, the other individual may simply agree, and the reverse psychology does not work.

Reverse psychology can be used in parenting, in relationships, in politics, in competitions, and in marketing. Researcher Dr. Geoff MacDonald, from the University of Toronto, and his colleagues examined the pervasiveness of reverse psychology and examined how frequently it is used as a strategy to influence others. Two-thirds of the participants in their research study provided valid examples of times they used reverse psychology to influence others. Based on participants' self-report, such strategies were successful about two-thirds of the time. They found that reverse psychology was frequently used to seek reassurance from others. Individuals reported minimizing their own abilities or expressing self-doubt to elicit reassurance or compliments from others. Such a strategy can be risky because there is a chance that the other will agree with one's negative self-assessment, which can lead to increased self-doubt. Such tactics may also lead to increased reliance on reassurance seeking due to the reward of receiving positive feedback.

Dr. Emily Hofstetter from Linkoping University and Dr. Jessica Robles from Loughborough University examined the use of reverse psychology in competitive games. In competitive situations, deception tends to be socially acceptable and expected. To gain a competitive advantage, players use strategies to maximize success and to undermine opponents. Strategies may include threat, deception, persuasion, or manipulations such as reverse psychology. For example, by advertising the intentions to make a weak move, a player may receive advice for stronger moves and thus can engage in such stronger moves with the social sanction of the group rather than experience censure from initiating a tough play. Players may also help or encourage others to make plays that will actually benefit themselves on their next turn, under the presence of helping the opponent. Particularly in games such as role-playing games where the play is a combination of cooperative and competitive action, reverse psychology can increase personal success under the pretense of helping the group.

Reverse psychology can also play a strong role in marketing strategy. One example is to provoke the impression of scarcity to manipulate consumers into buying the product. Retailers may limit how many items an individual may buy to create the impression of a scarcity. Furthermore, marketers can increase customer satisfaction by decreasing customer expectations. By decreasing expectations and then meeting those low expectations, they can increase overall satisfaction. Using reverse psychology in marketing can also mean less advertising, which means less advertising costs. By creating an under-the-radar brand and not attempting to convince people to buy it, some savvy marketers have created niches of high-demand items. Providing less information, less service, less choice, and less availability can create an increased demand for the product. Like other types of reverse psychology, this can backfire, but it is an increasing strategy in marketing and advertising. Traditional marketing makes extensive promises of satisfaction, whereas reverse psychology marketing does not. Thus, the under marketed product frequently exceeds expectations rather than products in traditional markets, which may not be able to live up to the advertised qualities and standards and features.

See also: Advertising; Cognitive Dissonance; Manipulation; Politics; Puffery; Smoke and Mirrors; Tactical Deception; Transparent Lies and the Illusion of Transparency.

Further Reading

Hofstetter, E., & Robles, J. (2018). Manipulation in board game interactions: Being a sporting player. *Symbolic Interaction, 42*(2), 301–320.

MacDonald, G., Nail, P. R., & Harper, J. R. (2011). Do people use reverse psychology? An exploration of strategic self-anticonformity. *Social Influence, 6*(1), 1–14.

Sinha, I., & Foscht, T. (2007). *Reverse Psychology Marketing: The Death of Traditional Marketing and the Rise of the New "Pull" Game*. Palgrave Macmillan.

Romantic Relationships

Deception is common in romantic relationships, particularly in situations where partners feel they need to edit information to avoid arguments or to fulfill relationship expectations. Dr. Bella DePaulo and her colleagues found that over 90 percent of individuals in a research study admitted that they have lied to a romantic partner. Most admit to withholding information or avoiding issues in order to maintain cohesiveness. These researchers even noted that individuals tend to tell the most serious lies to romantic partners, while less substantial lies are told to friends and acquaintances.

Though lying tends to be common in romantic relationships, most partners demonstrate a truth bias, which means that they do not expect their partner to lie to them, nor are they likely to detect lies when they occur. This creates an interesting mismatch, because lies are more common between committed romantic partners than in any other type of relationship, yet these lies are the least likely to be detected.

Deception in romantic relationships often develops when one partner does not respond well to honesty. Honesty has been shown to increase intimacy, but in partnerships where it increases hostility, individuals may choose to lie to avoid a conflict. Successful deception in this case may have short-term positive benefits and deter negative reactions. Lies may also be used to keep a partner at a distance. Individuals with high anxiety use more deception to avoid feeling vulnerable or to avoid disappointing their partners. Unfortunately, lies for any reason tend to serve as a barrier to true intimacy and decrease overall relationship satisfaction. And although individuals show more difficulty in detecting deception when it is enacted by romantic partners, when it is revealed, the ramifications are greater than in other relationships.

The types of lies told in romantic relationships vary significantly by sex. Women tend to lie more to protect the feelings of the romantic partner or in attempts to secure or strengthen relationships. Men are more likely to lie about their level of wealth, physical ability, or emotions in order to secure a sex partner. Both sexes, however, use deception to avoid conflict. Individuals commonly avoid tense topics that may start a fight. They also will lie to buffer their partner's self-esteem. Additionally, in about 30–50 percent of marriages, lies are used to cover up infidelity. Dr. Gayle Brewer and her colleagues from the University of Liverpool found that women with mistrusting, manipulative, and exploitative personality traits were also more likely to fake an orgasm during sex with their committed partner. Those women were also more likely to use sex to control or dominate their partner and use of such deception did facilitate affiliation or intimacy following sexual intercourse.

Deception is common in committed relationships and perhaps even more common in casual sexual relationships. Relationships in which friends engage in sexual intercourse tend to have fewer explicit rules surrounding the boundaries of the relationship. Though the lack of boundaries can be an advantage to individuals who are not interested in commitment, they can also lead to more deceptive situations. Frequently, one partner may hope that the relationship turns into something more, but omit telling their partner so as to not add pressure, lose the sexual relationship, or violate the boundaries of the friendship. Both partners may end up feeling deceived if they are not at similar levels of interest and commitment. Typically, these relationships are characterized by less communication, and thus each partner must infer their partner's intentions.

Detecting or suspecting dishonesty in committed relationships is correlated with negative outcomes for the relationship. Suspecting or detecting dishonesty contributes to lower levels of relationship satisfaction, lower levels of commitment, and more attempts at retaliation. Lying to a romantic partner leads to decreased intimacy and increased feelings of isolation. Being deceived by a romantic partner can lead to feelings of betrayal and depression, increased anxiety about future abandonment, and a heightened need for approval. Alternatively, partners who can find ways to maintain or increase honesty in their relationships tend to have the highest satisfaction ratings and greatest feelings or intimacy and commitment.

See also: Betrayal; Catfishing; Dating; DePaulo, Bella; Evolution of Deception; Infidelity; Machiavellianism; Online Dating; Sex Differences in Lying Behavior; Social Media; Truth-Default Theory.

Further Reading

Brewer, G., Abell, L., & Lyons, M. (2016). Machiavellianism, pretending orgasm, and sexual intimacy. *Personality and Individual Differences, 96*, 155–158.

Cole, T. (2001). Lying to the one you love: The use of deception in romantic relationships. *Journal of Social and Personal Relationships, 18*(1), 107–129.

Hollander, D. (1995). *101 Lies Men Tell Women and Why Women Believe Them*. Harper Collins.

Quirk, K., Owen, J., & Fincham, F. (2014). Perceptions of partner's deception in friends with benefits relationships. *Journal of Sex & Marital Therapy, 40*(1), 43–57.

Roggensack, K. E., & Sillars, A. (2014). Agreement and understanding about honesty and deception rules in romantic relationships. *Journal of Social and Personal Relationships, 31*(2), 178–199.

Tosone, C. (2006). Living everyday lies: The experience of self. *Clinical Social Work Journal, 34*(3), 335–348.

S

Saarni, Carolyn

Carolyn Saarni was an educational and developmental psychologist who primarily researched emotional development and the impact of social competence over childhood. Most deception researchers note that having good emotional control is a prerequisite for effective deception. Dr. Saarni contributed to deception research by empirically demonstrating how individuals tend to use deception in everyday life. She demonstrated how children develop an understanding of deception and learn to separate appearance from reality as they start to realize that an individual may feel one way but act in another way.

Dr. Saarni earned her PhD in educational psychology at the University of California, Berkeley, in 1971. She launched her research career at New York University in 1971, and during her tenure there, she primarily examined children's emotional development. In 1980, Dr. Saarni returned to California and took a position at Sonoma State University where she taught counseling, developmental theory, and research, topics that were unconventional for the time. Dr. Saarni not only highlighted what children understand about emotions but also examined how they learn to control their facial expressions and verbal responses in social settings to conform to social expectations. She laid the groundwork for the understanding of emotion regulation or the ability to regulate and control emotion signals and emotional expressions. She was interested in how children learn to mask what they feel and how they behave in actual social situations in response to socialization pressures.

One of Dr. Saarni's research paradigms, the disappointing gift task, has become foundational in the field of developmental psychology. In this task, children from first, third, and fifth grades were asked to engage in a research study. The children were told that they could earn a gift if they worked hard and completed the work provided. During the first session, each child earned a desirable gift. During the second session, however, they were given a disappointing gift. Dr. Saarni was interested in how children would reveal or control their emotions when confronted with such a disappointment. She found that younger children were more likely to show genuine negative emotions and behaviors in response to the disappointing gift. Older children, particularly those with a mature theory of mind, were more likely to cover up their negative response and demonstrate polite, deceptive emotions and behavior. Dr. Saarni found that boys were more likely to show a genuine, disappointed response, where girls were more likely to engage in socially appropriate deception and respond positively when interacting with the experimenter.

Dr. Saarni's research highlighted how deception is commonly used to conform to social norms and cultural display rules. For example, children are often taught to act pleased and say thank you when given a gift, whether they want it or not. In this way, adults send children mixed messages by encouraging them to be honest, yet admonishing them if they tell the truth. Dr. Saarni's research also demonstrated the typical socialization differences between boys and girls that result in differences in emotional control by the elementary school level. These age and sex differences have become targets of study in subsequent psychological research.

Dr. Saarni revealed how deceptive behavior is socially sanctioned in everyday culture. To be socially appropriate, one must practice controlling and regulating one's own emotional display. Such practice lays the groundwork for successful deception in a variety of contexts. She also showed that emotion regulation skills rely on socialization pressures, theory of mind development, and social interaction. Despite universal emphasis on the importance of honesty, she demonstrated how deception is widely encouraged to protect the feelings of others, avoid punishment, and receive rewards.

See also: Age Differences; Cultural Differences; Detecting Deception; Development of Deception; Facial Cues; Polite Lies; Prosocial Lying; Recursive Awareness; Sex Differences in Lying Behavior; Theory of Mind; White Lies.

Further Reading
Cole, P. M. (2018). A festschrift for Carolyn Ingrid Saarni. *European Journal of Developmental Psychology, 15*(6), 623–630.

Feldman, R., Jenkins, L., & Popoola, O. (1979). Detection of deception in adults and children. *Child Development, 50*, 350–355.

Gross, D., & Harris, P. L. (1988). False beliefs about emotion: Children's understanding of misleading emotional displays. *International Journal of Behavioral Development, 11*(4), 475–488.

Lewis, M., & Saarni, C. (1993). *Lying and Deception in Everyday Life.* Guilford.

Saarni, C. (1979). Children's understanding of display rules for expressive behavior. *Developmental Psychology, 15*, 424–429.

Saarni, C. (1984). An observational study of children's attempts to monitor their expressive behavior. *Child Development, 55*, 1504–1513.

Saarni, C. (1988). Children's understanding of the interpersonal consequences of dissemblance of nonverbal emotional-expressive behavior. *Journal of Nonverbal Behavior, 12*, 275–294.

Saarni, C. (1999). *The Development of Emotional Competence.* Guilford.

Saxe, Leonard

Dr. Leonard Saxe is a psychologist and researcher from Brandeis University who demonstrated that there are no concrete physiological signals that can conclusively determine that someone is lying. Because of this, he raised awareness about the lack of validation of commonly-used polygraph tests. Research and consultations such as those from Dr. Saxe led to decreased use of polygraph testing, particularly in the workplace. Despite such research, test results are still frequently accepted as evidence in criminal or employee court cases.

In a revealing 1985 study, Dr. Saxe worked with staff of the television show *60 Minutes* to demonstrate the ineffectiveness of polygraph testing. In the expose,

CBS hired four polygraph examiners and asked them to interrogate employees accused of stealing camera equipment. For each polygraph examiner, a different employee was identified as the suspect. Following the test, each polygraph examiner identified the predetermined suspect as the guilty party. In actuality, no equipment was stolen, and all of the suspects were innocent. The study demonstrated that the use of polygraph testing was ineffective because the interviewers' preconceived expectations influenced the results in all four cases. One may argue that the use of polygraph testing may successfully induce a guilty person to confess, but according to Dr. Saxe, the risk of false confessions and false findings is unacceptably high.

The underlying idea of a polygraph test is the premise that arousal increases when individuals attempt to deceive others. In that sense, polygraph tests do not measure deception; they measure arousal level. However, Dr. Saxe cautioned that arousal due to attempts at deception is indistinguishable from arousal stemming from other sources. Arousal may stem from the fear of being caught in a lie, but it can also result from general anxiety, worry that one will not be believed, discomfort with the situation, or worry that others will be upset. Furthermore, Dr. Saxe demonstrated in later research that guilty individuals who believed the polygraph would detect their attempts at deception did demonstrate more arousal during interview proceedings. Guilty individuals who did not believe that the test would be able to detect their deception did not show increases in arousal levels during polygraph procedures. This also suggests that the test is ineffective at identifying deception.

Given the lack of validity provided for polygraph tests, Dr. Saxe argues that it may be more effective for researchers to focus on how and when lying is used rather than on its detection and punishment. Understanding which situations provoke lying could provide more information about increasing honesty than merely being able to detect deception. In a series of research studies, Dr. Saxe and his colleagues identified predictable situational effects that make people more likely to lie. For example, more than 85 percent of individuals in a research study admitted to lying to a romantic partner about a previous relationship. Almost all of the liars rationalized their lies by saying they were protecting their partner. Another situation that tends to elicit lying behavior is the student-teacher relationship. In a role-playing experiment, students were much more likely to lie about their reasons for missing an assignment when asking for an extension if the assignment was worth a lot (75% of their grade) and if their reason for missing it was not good (such as a hangover). In such situations, it was much easier for students to justify telling a lie to avoid the consequences of telling the truth.

Based on this research, Dr. Saxe encourages creating social environments that encourage honesty. One such environment would be to stop punishing people for honesty. Allowing people to admit to mistakes and remedy them may be more effective than the threat of punishment that encourages individuals to lie. Rather than merely identifying liars, understanding the conditions that elicit lies and shaping such environments to promote honesty may be a more effective way to increase honesty. Research on deception demonstrates that most deception is not premeditated but is simply a result of social pressures. Deception is most commonly used to smooth social interactions, be socially appropriate, and maintain relationships. Thus, situational variables may be important in determining whether it is likely someone will engage in deception, and controlling such variables can decrease deception attempts.

Dr. Saxe identifies that the ability to detect deception is important at all levels. Deception in the workplace, criminal trials, and even in matters of national security is ubiquitous and frequently difficult to detect. However, he cautions that physiological tests such as polygraph tests, as well as paper and pencil honesty scales for integrity, have not been validated. A reliance on arousal puts interrogators at risk for detecting arousal that does not stem from guilt and punishing innocent parties. Furthermore, an understanding of an individual's level of integrity may not be effective if situational variables align to encourage lying.

See also: Behavior Analysis Interview; Control Questions Test; Deceiver Stereotype; Detecting Deception; False Confessions; Lying to Parents; Motivational Impairment Effect; Polygraph Tests; Prosocial Lying.

Further Reading

Adelson, R. (2004). The polygraph in doubt. *Monitor on Psychology, 35*(7), 71.

Saxe, L. (1991). Lying: Thoughts of an applied social psychologist. *American Psychologist, 46*(4), 409–415.

Saxe, L. (1994). Detection of deception: Polygraph and integrity tests. *Current Directions in Psychological Science, 3*(3), 69–73.

Saxe, L., Dougherty, D., & Cross, T. P. (1985). The validity of polygraph tests: Scientific analysis and public policy. *American Psychologist, 40*, 355–366.

Scams

A scam is a scenario in which a con artist exploits the trust of victims in order to make a profit. Scams and scammers, historically known as confidence men, or con men, use trickery, charm, and suave deception to take advantage of others. Scams can include get-rich-quick schemes, extortion, impersonation, fraud, identity theft, phishing attempts, rigged gambling events, fake charities, pyramid schemes, and workers' compensation schemes, among many others. Some scams target individuals and others target corporations.

Edward Smith, a former con man, described his methods and provided insight into psychological principles used to select and fool victims in his 1922 book *Confessions of a Confidence Man: A Handbook for Suckers*. He stated that those who feel the most secure are actually in the greatest danger of being scammed. He outlined stages of an investment scam and described the need for small benefits to the victim followed by sudden time pressure for the victim to invest for bigger payouts. Incremental benefits to victims throughout an investment scam create the image of legitimacy and makes victims believe that there will be higher payouts if they fully invest. Time pressure also decreases critical thinking and provides the illusion that they must act fast or lose a big opportunity.

The psychological pressures used in scams mirror those that make advertising strategies such as bait and switch so successful. Victims (or consumers) are lured in by the promise of big payoffs (or good deals) under false pretenses, and only after they are committed (either contractually or psychologically) is the true situation revealed. In many instances, for both strategies, the consumer or victim may not know a swindle has taken place. Consumers may believe that they missed the opportunity by being late or are convinced by a savvy salesperson to spend more once they are committed to purchasing. Victims may believe that it was simply bad luck or unforeseen circumstances that made them lose money.

In a meta-analysis of research on internet scams, researcher Gareth Norris from Aberystwyth University and his colleagues found specific psychological traits that make some individuals more susceptible to being victims of scams. They found that the bulk of scams, particularly internet scams, do not target specific people but are sent out in mass quantities. However, personality traits of the receivers may influence which individuals become a victim. Individuals with an external locus of control are more susceptible to time-limited messages. Those with neurotic tendencies tend to have higher susceptibility, while those who are conscientious seem to be less susceptible. Mood, socioeconomic status, and how genuine the scam appears to be also impact the susceptibility of the user.

To protect oneself against scams, individuals need to recognize the signs of danger. If an opportunity seems too good to be true, an individual should take time to do some research. If others have encountered a similar scam, there will likely be information online. One should always double-check when friends, family, or charities are requesting money via text or email. One should never pay money to receive an unsolicited prize and should be careful of paying upfront for offers. Particularly when being pressured, it is important to take time to consult an expert or do some research. One must also be aware of the fine print when accepting free trial offers. The fine print may contain cancellation fees or other monetary commitments following the trial. Savvy internet users know never to open attachments in unsolicited emails and only enter login credentials on home pages searched independently, not through unsolicited email links. Older adults tend to be particularly vulnerable to scams because they become less sensitive to detecting deception. They also tend to have declines in processing speed, which increases the time they need to fully think through consequences.

In 2019, billions of dollars were lost to scams. With the rise of internet usage, scammers have access to more people more quickly, and money can be lost well before scams are detected. Almost 30 billion spam emails are sent every day, and if only a small percentage of those reach a naive victim, the success rate of scams can still be costly to individuals and organizations.

See also: Advertising; Bait and Switch; Fine Print; Fraud; Hoax; Impersonator; Locus of Control; Personality; Phishing; Sockpuppets.

Further Reading

Burnes, D., Henderson, C. R., Sheppard, C., Zhao, R., Pillemer, K., & Lachs, M. S. (2017) Prevalence of financial fraud and scams among older adults in the United States: a systematic review and meta-analysis. *American Journal of Public Health 107*(8), 13–21.

Federal Trade Commission. (2020). *10 things you can do to avoid fraud.* Retrieved from https://www.consumer.ftc.gov/articles/how-avoid-scam

Henderson, L. (2000). *Crimes of Persuasion: Schemes, Scams, Frauds.* Coyote Ridge.

Norris, G., Brookes, A., & Dowell, D. (2019). The psychology of Internet fraud victimisation: A systematic review. *Journal of Police and Criminal Psychology, 34,* 231–245.

Skiba, K. (2020). Consumer fraud complaints hits record high. *AARP.* Retrieved from https://www.aarp.org/money/scams-fraud/info-2020/ftc-fraud-complaints-rise.html

Smith, E. H. (2010). *Confessions of a Confidence Man: A Handbook for Suckers.* Sunwise Books.

Secret Societies (See Espionage)

Self-Deception

Self-deception refers to the ways in which individuals' thoughts, desires, and expectations shape the way they perceive reality. Self-deception is universal, is largely unconscious, and is difficult to identify or control. Self-deception involves rationalizing contradictory information to maintain one's own worldview. When people attempt to deceive others, they frequently engage in self-deception first, which makes them more effective deceivers. Alternatively, evidence shows that when one attempts to deceive others, it often results in self-deception, making it a cyclical process.

Self-deceptions can occur at the individual or group level. At the individual level, individuals may convince themselves that they are more attractive, intelligent, or ethical than they really are; that significant others will appreciate their efforts; and that they would be able to detect if another person is lying. Examples of group-level self-deceptions include assertions by politicians that American interference will be welcomed in other societies, that scientific breakthroughs will be wholly beneficial, and that climate change is not occurring.

Occasional self-deceptions may help maintain psychological health because skewing reality can decrease stress and anxiety for situations beyond one's control. For example, researchers Dr. Josip Hrgovic and Dr. Ivana Hromatko from the University of Zagreb found some adaptive benefits of self-deception. Specifically, women from households of low socioeconomic status were less depressed when they engaged in self-deception. The self-deceivers were more likely to rate their living conditions as significantly better than did non-self-deceivers. Women who had more accurate appraisals of their living conditions also had the highest depression scores. Thus, at least in some situations, self-deception involves suppressing those things that threaten self-esteem or mental stability, to maintain psychological health.

Occasionally, self-deception allows individuals to appear more confident and more competent than they may be in reality. Since confidence tends to be interpreted as competence and people tend to defer to competent individuals, self-deception may be an effective strategy to convince oneself and others of one's abilities. Excessive self-deception, however, is correlated with psychological disorders.

Signs that You Are Lying to Yourself

Though most people put effort into trying to determine whether others are lying, it may be a better use of one's time to determine whether one is lying to oneself. People tend to lie to themselves because it is comforting and convenient. Admitting to deficits or problems can be damaging to self-esteem or it may require effort to rectify the situation. It is much easier to blame others, rationalize behaviors, or otherwise self-deceive than to make substantive changes.

Self-deception may not be easy to detect, but there are several predictable signs of which one may become aware. One sign of self-deception is the consistent pattern of blaming others for situations. Another is the need to justify one's own behaviors to oneself or others in order to feel settled. Those who engage in self-deception routinely avoid taking responsibility for decisions and outcomes, provide a plethora of excuses for any problems, and refuse to listen to feedback. They frequently feel like frauds and are anxious, and their emotions tend not to match their words. They may say, or even believe, they are fine but find they have to fight to hold back anger or tears when confronted about decisions or actions.

Self-deceivers tend to make many goals and plans, yet rarely follow through. They commit to too much and are unable to complete everything successfully or on time. They may also express values that are contrary to their behaviors and assert extreme, yet inconsistent, viewpoints, depending on what they think others want to hear. Self-deceivers tend to be uncomfortable in their own skin and do not have a clear sense of who they are or what they want.

Recognizing and admitting to self-deception is difficult because it necessitates that one takes steps to confront insecurities and change one's behaviors. To decrease self-deception, individuals may need to take responsibility for mistakes, end relationships, or change jobs. However, most of those individuals who do the work to decrease self-deception find that they have decreases in anxiety, increases in self-esteem, and heightened feelings of self-efficacy and self-worth. Those who are more honest with themselves also tend to have more genuine relationships with others, fewer psychological health problems, and fewer stress-related physical complaints. They learn to value and trust their own opinions and demonstrate more self-confidence.

To begin the process of decreasing self-deception, individuals can spend time identifying situations that make them feel uncomfortable, genuinely acknowledge their own strengths and weaknesses, ask questions, and listen objectively to others. Self-deceivers tend to avoid taking responsibility for errors because they are too harsh on themselves and cannot withstand the self-inflicted pressure of being wrong. Thus, they may benefit from clearly articulating and working toward achievable goals; consciously forgiving themselves for weaknesses, flaws, and quirky characteristics; and celebrating small accomplishments.

The tendency to engage in self-deception, deception of others, or honest behavior becomes a habit. Self-deceivers may need to be constantly mindful of their self-deceptions and consciously correct their lies until they break the habit. Recognizing the behavior pattern may be the most difficult step in the process, and correcting the behavior takes sustained effort. Once the pattern is altered, however, it becomes easier to be honest with oneself and with others.

Narcissists, for example, engage in self-deception to maintain their elevated sense of self, and depressed individuals may maintain their depression through self-deceptive beliefs. Interestingly, high levels of self-deception are found among not only very successful individuals, such as politicians, religious leaders, and terrorists, but also among those diagnosed with psychological disorders. North Americans tend to score higher on self-deception than individuals from Asia.

Self-deception likely involves psychoanalytic processes such as repression, denial, and rationalization. Repression is the suppression of uncomfortable or unacceptable thoughts or emotions. Denial is the refusal to believe or think about information that is anxiety provoking. Rationalization is using excuses to justify undesirable behavior, such as the rational argument that smoking is relaxing, leading to the self-deception that it is therefore beneficial. Use of these defense mechanisms can lead to cognitive distortions and a skewed perception of the implications of one's behaviors.

Self-deception also includes strategies such as misinterpretation, selective attention, or selective evidence gathering. Self-deception is perpetuated through social interactions. Individuals may seek out others who reinforce their self-deceptions, avoid those who may challenge them, and selectively share information that shapes how others view them, which impact how they view themselves. Deceiving others may spur self-deception, and self-deception also serves to more effectively deceive others. Stronger convictions cultivated through self-deception allow one to be more persuasive because individuals are more effective communicators when they believe in what they are saying. Self-deception goes hand in hand with self-persuasion. When we attempt to persuade others, we also persuade ourselves.

Engagement in self-deception emerges in childhood when children engage in pretend play. Though they logically know that their fantasy play is not real, they are able to suspend their disbelief and eliminate the distinction between reality and fantasy for the length of play. Such pretend play may lay the groundwork for later self-deception. Self-deception frequently involves avoiding information that does not align with what one wants to believe. However, self-deception differs from poor information gathering because true self-deception involves an awareness of contradictory information that one rationalizes or chooses to ignore. Self-deception involves a bias that causes one to reach preferred conclusions regardless of contradictory evidence, and one's memories are distorted to align with what one wants to believe.

See also: Alternative Facts; Cognitive Dissonance; Cognitive Distortion; Delusions; Denial; False Memory; Memory; Narcissism; Suspension of Disbelief; Truth-Default Theory.

Further Reading

Dings, R. (2017). Social strategies in self-deception. *New Ideas in Psychology, 47*, 16–23.

Hrgovic, J., & Hromatko, I. (2018). Self-deception as a function of social status. *Evolutionary Behavioral Sciences*. http://dx.doi.org/10.1037/ebs0000143

Shean, G. D. (1993). Delusions, self-deception, and intentionality. *Journal of Humanistic Psychology, 33*(1), 45–66.

Smith, M. K., Trivers, R., & von Hippel, W. (2017). Self-deception facilitates interpersonal persuasion. *Journal of Economic Psychology, 63*, 93–101.

Triandis, H. C. (2011). Culture and self-deception: A theoretical perspective. *Social Behavior and Personality, 39*(1), 3–14.

Self-Serving Lies (See Black Lies; Instrumental Lies)

Sex Differences in Lying Behavior

Examination of sex differences in deception is a highly researched area, yet the findings, to date, have been mixed. Individual research studies have been inconsistent in demonstrating whether one sex lies more frequently than the other. The majority of studies find that men tend to be more dishonest than women, though some studies show no difference, and one revealed that women lie more than men. One explanation for this inconsistency is that men and women differ in the content, motivations, and intentions behind their lies. Thus, the type of lie being assessed in an experiment may alter the behavior of the participants and impact the results.

Dr. Philipp Gerlach and Dr. Ralph Hertwig from the Max Planck Institute for Human Development, and Dr. Kinneret Teodorescu from the Israel Institute of Technology completed a meta-analysis of 565 psychological experiments on deception and found that, across studies, men lied significantly more than women. When all results were averaged, 42 percent of men and 38 percent of women lied. However, these differences were influenced by the type of lies, the risk involved with lying, the individuals involved, and the size of the potential reward.

When analyzing the body of research, overall results show that in childhood, boys are more likely to lie to parents and other adults than girls. Young men tell lies for their own benefit rather than to protect the feelings of others. Men are more likely to tell high-stakes lies that involve higher risk and have less fear of punishments if caught in the lie. Men lie about their socioeconomic status and their consumption of alcohol and drugs. Men also tell lies about their physical or cognitive abilities, their past achievements, and their past sexual partners. Men are more likely to lie during anonymous conversations, particularly when a monetary benefit can be secured, than when engaging with someone with whom they have a relationship. Overall, men are more likely than women to tell self-serving lies for personal gain, but men are also more likely to tell lies that benefit others.

Results for women revealed that, from childhood, girls and women tell lies to foster intimacy and protect others' feelings more than do boys and men. Women rate being supportive and protecting other people's feelings as more important than telling the truth. This is especially strong in younger women. Women lie to increase intimacy and to promote increase in self-esteem. On average, women are concerned about the welfare of others and moderate their lying behavior to avoid hurting those around them. Women are also more likely to lie when engaging with an individual with whom they will interact again in the future than when engaging in an anonymous conversation. Women engage in less high-risk lying behavior and are more concerned about being caught than are men.

Though men report higher confidence in telling lies than women, cognitive research shows that, when lying, men took significantly longer to construct the lie. Furthermore, male brains had enhanced activation as compared to women when lying, conceivably indicating increased effort to control and monitor behavior and information. Women frequently score higher on verbal working memory tasks, show less impulsivity, and engage in more multitasking than men, which might provide women with the deceptive advantage should they seek to exercise it.

However, Dr. Taku Sato and Dr. Yoshiaki Nihei from Tohoku University in Japan showed that, though lying may be more effortful for men, men tend to lie with more confidence, increasing the likelihood they will be believed. Since women tend to feel more anxious or guilty about lying, they come across as less confident and, consequently, less believable. Interestingly, however, women expressed more confidence in detecting lies than did men, which correlated with women earning higher scores in detecting deception.

See also: Age Differences; Benefits of Lying; Black Lies; Categories of Deception; DePaulo, Bella; Detecting Deception; Instrumental Lies; Mental Effort; Motives for Lying; Polite Lies; Prevalence of Lying; Prosocial Lying; Reaction Time; Romantic Relationships.

Further Reading

Chiu, S., Hong, F., & Chiu, S. (2016). Undergraduates' day-to-day lying behaviors: Implications, targets, and psychological characteristics. *Social Behavior and Personality, 44*(8), 1329–1338.

DePaulo, B. M., Kashy, D. A., Kirkendol, S. E., & Wyer, M. M. (1996). Lying in everyday life. *Journal of Personality and Social Psychology, 70*(5), 979–995.

Gerlach, P., Teodorescu, K., & Hartwig, R. (2019). The truth about lies: A meta-analysis on dishonest behavior. *Psychological Bulletin, 145*(1), 1–44.

Marchewka, A., Jednorog, K., Falkiewicz, M., Szeszkowski, W., Grabowska, A., & Szatkowska, I. (2012). Sex, lies and fMRI—Gender differences in neural basis of deception. *PLoS ONE, 7*(8), e43076.

Sato, T., & Nihei, Y. (2009). Gender differences in confidence about lying and lie detection. *Tohoku Psychologica Folia, 67*, 71–73.

Sherlock Holmes Effect

The Sherlock Holmes effect describes the natural tendency for innocent bystanders to be curious about the details of a crime. The theory is that an individual who witnesses a crime will have a natural curiosity to understand what happened, who did it, and how it was carried out. Those who committed the crime, on the other hand, will show less curiosity because they already know what happened and who did it. Thus, suspects who are guilty should show less interest during a discussion about an event as compared to one who is innocent.

The concept of the Sherlock Holmes effect is named for the fictional police consultant created by Sir Arthur Conan Doyle. Sherlock Holmes' forte was observation and deduction. He demonstrated a supernatural logical reasoning ability that allowed him to draw conclusions from minute details that tended to evade the notice of the police. The Sherlock Holmes effect reflects this inherent interest to analyze crime scenes, spot evidence, create theories to test, and draw conclusions. According to the Sherlock Holmes effect, innocent individuals will ask more questions, be interested in sharing ideas and thoughts, and want to discuss possible scenarios of what may have happened. Guilty people, however, are more distracted by concealing their own guilt and are more likely to focus on controlling their own behaviors than interacting with the interviewers.

The Sherlock Holmes effect is most likely to be observed when the individual has a personal connection to the crime. For example, if a crime occurs in one's workplace, apartment building, or neighborhood, individuals tend to be the most interested in figuring out and discussing what might have happened. For the effect to be observed, the individual must have time to think about the crime in order to develop theories about what might have happened or who might be responsible. The person must also be interested in solving the mystery and willing to work with the police. Individuals who do not meet these criteria are not likely to show the behaviors, making the effect less useful; however, it does provide a simple screening tool that may prevent innocent individuals from being interrogated.

The Behavior Analysis Interview (BAI) procedure commonly used by police in the United States uses the Sherlock Holmes effect to screen out innocent subjects before more in-depth interrogations. The BAI makes this assumption that innocent people will speculate more than deceivers. The idea is that innocent individuals are more likely to try to logically reason about the details of a crime. Thus, when asked questions such as "Who could have committed the crime?" or "How could this crime have been committed?" innocent individuals will likely provide wide-ranging, logical, and speculative solutions to these questions. They are more likely to discuss their thoughts about an incident, and many are willing to make guesses or discuss suspicions, whereas guilty parties will exert more energy into controlling their own behaviors and concealing their connections. This tends to make guilty individuals come across as less forthcoming and more guarded. Guilty individuals are less likely to share information and are less interested in the crime because they already know who committed it. They are more interested in misrepresenting information than trying to solve the case. Thus, guilty people tend to share less information and have shorter verbal responses, and their responses do not reveal thought about what might have happened. This theoretical difference in how individuals will approach the questions provides an initial guide for screening out those who are likely innocent.

The Sherlock Holmes effect has some limitations because it relies on behaviors that are comparative in nature, and different individuals may not react in a consistent manner when being interviewed. If the crime does not feel personal, if innocent suspects are not interested in helping the police, or if they are anxious about proving their own innocence, they will likely show less interest, more anxiety, and may follow a behavior pattern more similar to a guilty suspect. Furthermore, experienced criminals may understand this effect and may provide detailed and speculative answers as would be expected for an innocent suspect. Thus, the Sherlock Holmes effect can serve as a generally reliable guide but cannot conclusively prove that someone is or is not attempting to deceive.

See also: Behavior Analysis Interview; Detecting Deception; False Confessions; Language; Social Intelligence.

Further Reading

Blair, J. P. (2008). The Behavioural Analysis Interview: Clarifying the practice, theory and understanding of its use and effectiveness. *International Journal of Police Science and Management, 10*(1), 101–118.

Kholodny, Y. (2008). Interrogations using a polygraph in Russia: 15 years of legal application. *European Polygraph, 2*(4), 73–82.

Moffitt, K. (2009). Deception detection theory as a basis for an automated investigation of the Behavior Analysis Interview. *Americas Conference on Information Systems, AMCIS 2009 Doctoral Consortium, 21.*

Signaling Theory

Signaling theory is a biological concept that explains how signals have evolved within and between species to provide information. Signals may include physical features or behaviors that allow for communication between individuals. Initially, researchers believed that signals evolved to provide clearer communication about things like sexual interest, reproductive potential, and potential for survival. However, once such honest and clear signals evolved, the potential for deceptive false signals emerged. Honest signals may include things such as warning calls in birds to signal that predators are near, mating dances in birds to signal fertility, or body markings that warn of toxins or reproductive potential. For example, insects, amphibians, reptiles, and fish tend to have variations in brightness of body markings. In general, brighter markings correlate with higher levels of toxicity if eaten, a phenomenon known as aposematism. The bright body markings function as a warning signal to predators, and they are effective because there are predictable ramifications if predators attack. Thus predators have evolved to avoid such prey.

Once these honest signals have been established, they then may be manipulated in order to deceive. Genetically weak birds, frogs, or butterflies may evolve similar color patterns as toxic species to successfully deceive a predator. Since predators have learned to avoid the bright color patterns, brighter variants of a nonpoisonous species also survive more readily because they deceive predators with their bright displays. If these false signals are too common, the signaling system collapses. A predator that eats a bright frog and does not experience toxic effects will learn that such signals are false. However, if most brightly colored animals are toxic, cheaters can take advantage of them to secure benefits.

Evolutionary biologists explain how animals, with or without conscious awareness, constantly send false signals to confuse, scare, or ward off predators. Some butterflies have evolved patterned wings that mimic toxic plants or poisonous prey, and these signals protect them from attack. Male cuttlefish can morph their coloring to mimic a female to infiltrate a harem and then mate with the females from the harem of a dominant male. Birds can produce false warning calls to clear a foraging area so they can have free rein to feed. Antelope have been shown to spring up and down in front of a lion to demonstrate their spryness to deter pursuit. Since such spryness typically means that the antelope would escape, the lion may choose not to engage. Injured antelope who can fake the spryness can deceive the lion with this false signal. Male deer will roar at each other to determine a victor without actual physical confrontation. In this way, a weaker deer who can fake a strong roar may actually win a battle without ever physically engaging. This only works as long as the roars are usually an honest signal and actually indicative of strength and likelihood of physical domination.

Given the link between signals and ability or future behavior, researchers now believe that, though signals do facilitate communication, their function may be to benefit the sender rather than to simply facilitate honest communication. Signals may have evolved to be more and more convincing to influence others rather than to be merely more accurate. Humans also may take advantage of signaling theory. Humans provide signals in their clothing, self-presentation, and behavior to attract mates, secure competitive advantages, or signal cooperation. For example, males may wear expensive clothing or watches or drive expensive cars to signal success to attract females. They may take more risks to communicate increased testosterone and fertility. Females may accentuate their waist-to-hip ratio with clothing choices or communicate signs of youth through use of cosmetics and lotions. Such dishonest signaling helps secure a reproductive partner, even for individuals with less beneficial genetic potential.

Signaling theory proposes that most signals do help facilitate communication between or among species. However, once honest signals have been established, dishonest signals are likely to emerge. These dishonest signals must remain infrequent enough for them to remain convincing. If a signal is frequently dishonest, it will no longer be believed, and the communication value will be altered.

See also: Competition; Deception in Animals; Instrumental Lies; Mimicry; Tactical Deception.

Further Reading

Blount, J. D., Speed, M. P., Ruxton, G. D., & Stephens, P. A. (2009). Warning displays may function as honest signals of toxicity. *Proceedings of the Royal Society B, 276*, 871–877.

Clark, R., & Kimbrough, S. O. (2017). Social structure, opportunistic punishment and the evolution of honest signaling. *PLoS ONE, 12*(12), 1–28.

Dawkins, R., & Krebs, J. (1978). Animal signals: information or manipulation? In J. Krebs & N. B. Davies (Eds.), *Behavioural Ecology: an Evolutionary Approach* (pp. 282–309). Blackwell Scientific Publications.

Hawkes, K., & Bird, R. B. (2002). Showing off, handicap signaling, and the evolution of men's work. *Evolutionary Anthropology, 11*, 58–67.

Slander (See Defamation)

Smoke and Mirrors

Smoke and mirrors is a deceptive strategy that stems from an act put on by stage magicians during the vaudeville era of the late 1800s in which literal smoke and mirrors were used to create illusions. For these magicians, smoke and mirrors could create the illusion of an apparition or conceal a sleight of hand to entertain audiences. The term "smoke and mirrors" also came to refer to the practice of diverting an audience's attention away from the deception being performed. The saying now refers to any act of obscuring or embellishing the truth with misinformation or distraction. The proverbial practice of smoke and mirrors is still used by illusionists, manipulators, advertisers, companies, criminals, politicians, and individuals as they hide actions or practices from audiences, consumers, police, or other observers.

In the modern day, figurative smoke and mirrors are used by organizations and companies in order to maintain a favorable public image, by individuals to justify behaviors, and by politicians to conceal unpopular policies. Dr. Patricia Bromley and Dr. Walter Powell demonstrated the use of smoke and mirrors to conceal the gap between policy and practice in organizations. They showed that organizations may create policies to persuade observers that issues are being addressed even if those policies are never actually put into practice. This creates a smoke and mirror effect because the policies create the illusion of the practice. Emphasis on accountability and transparency can reduce this discrepancy and policies may need to change to reflect practices, or practices must change to conform to established policies.

Companies may also use smoke and mirrors in their advertising campaigns. For example, the tobacco industry uses selective advertising that downplays or omits the negative effects of smoking to create an illusion of popularity, sophistication, and relaxation associated with cigarette use. In this sense, they obscure the truth and embellish with information that increases the likelihood that individuals will use the product. Those who buy into these perceptions of smoking are more likely to purchase and use the products.

Drs. Hugh Klein, Claire Sterk, and Kirk Elifson from Emory University demonstrated how smokers also use the smoke and mirror strategy to justify their cigarette use. They found that smokers consistently report that smoking helps them reduce depressive feelings as well as feelings of anxiety, and it feels pleasurable and helps them focus. Additionally, the more benefits they perceive, the more likely they will smoke more frequently. Thus, shaping perceptions, even through the deceptive use of smoke and mirrors, can shape behavior, and those who smoke are more likely to accept the positive advertisements about smoking. After interviewing almost 500 adult smokers, these researchers found that smokers downplay the negative effects and embellish the positive effects. These individuals were likely to accentuate the benefits of smoking and emphasize relaxation, the calming effect, and the enjoyment of the practice. Those who embellished the truth were likely to smoke more cigarettes, engage in chain-smoking, and had a negative attitude toward quitting.

Those who engage in illegal activities may also use smoke and mirrors to create the illusion of innocence. By creating alibis, planting or hiding evidence, and stoutly claiming innocence, criminals may convince friends, family, and police that they were not involved with a crime. Savvy criminals may redirect attention to other suspects or otherwise try to shape the views of interviewers or interrogators.

Finally, political candidates may use a tactical smoke and mirrors strategy to obscure unpopular policies. By ignoring, obfuscating, or redirecting attention from unpopular policies and emphasizing topics that people agree on, even if they are of less importance, the general populace can be deceived and redirected. In this sense, smoke and mirrors can be a diversionary tactic or a bait and switch strategy that leaves the population unaware that they have been deceived or misled.

The use of smoke and mirrors tends to confuse issues, from the effect of climate change to public policies, to building relationships. Use of smoke and mirrors occurs when individuals bring up conflicting, distracting, and tangential topics to divert attention away from the issue at hand. Its use can be effective for tactical deception and manipulating the perceptions of others by directing attention away from salient issues to prevent the deceived from even knowing that deception took place.

See also: Advertising; Bait and Switch; Catfishing; Cognitive Dissonance; Diversionary Tactics; Fraud; Impersonator; Manipulation; Phishing; Politics; Puffery; Red Herring; Reverse Psychology; Self-Deception; Sherlock Holmes Effect; Tactical Deception.

Further Reading

Bromley, P., & Powell, W. W. (2012). From smoke and mirrors to walking the talk: Decoupling in the contemporary world. *The Academy of Management Annals, 6*(1), 483–530.

Klein, H., Sterk, C. E., & Elifson, K. W. (2014). Smoke and mirrors: The perceived benefits of continued tobacco use among current smokers. *Health Psychology Research, 2*(2), 1519. https://doi.org/10.4081/hpr.2014.1519

Social Intelligence

Social intelligence revolves around how well individuals understand themselves and others. Those with high social intelligence tend to demonstrate self-awareness and the ability to interact effectively with others. They tend to be excellent at communication and navigating social interactions. They have a heightened theory of mind, are good at judging intentions in social situations, and have a good memory about others' desires and goals. They are likely to effectively gain and maintain power and popularity among their peers. Though those with high social intelligence do not necessarily use it for nefarious means, their effectiveness at reading others can make them skilled deceivers. They are good at gauging how others will interpret information and act in different social situations.

Those who score high on measures of social intelligence also tend to show high emotional intelligence and strong language abilities. They are effective at reading facial expressions and understanding how others think and feel. They are able to draw inferences and are good at directing and shaping interactions. They tend to be empathetic, have good social skills, and are good at presenting themselves in socially acceptable ways. They can carry on conversations with different people, are emotionally and verbally expressive, and are comfortable engaging in social interactions. They have a solid understanding of how to change their behavior to match the social situation and tend to be viewed as leaders. They are good listeners, are able to grasp what is not being said, and are able to present a positive impression. Though social intelligence can be improved with practice and attention, some people are naturally better and more interested in observing and understanding others.

Social intelligence is a key to effective deception as well as deception detection. Individuals with high social intelligence tend to be better at noticing nonverbal cues in a conversation than those with low or average social intelligence. They also tend to be better at reading others to tell if their own lies are being believed. Because they are paying attention and are sensitive to social cues, they are more likely to notice discrepancies, emotional leaks, or changes in arousal levels. Those with high social intelligence tend to use deception to facilitate cooperation between groups, to increase diplomacy in sensitive situations, or to be successful in competitive events. High social intelligence correlates with effective social competition, understanding social dynamics, and coping with complex social exchanges.

Those with high social intelligence are good at using their own experiences to make sense of the experiences of others. They tend to be introspective and have strategies for competing and cooperating effectively with others. They are able to attribute mental states to others based on what they themselves would likely think or feel in a similar situation. They use gratitude, sympathy, and deception to gain an advantage. They tend to have good self-control and self-regulation skills including emotion regulation. Social intelligence is likely the most influential factor in both telling and decoding lies. Those with high social intelligence tend to be able to read facial expressions, understand how others may be feeling, and understand how to effectively manipulate or bargain with others.

Social intelligence can be used to create solid cooperative alliances, effective marketing campaigns, or solid political alliances at a global level. Low social intelligence can lead to acting in offensive or socially inappropriate ways. Those with low social intelligence do not conform well to new cultural norms, have difficulty reading strangers, and are more likely to offend than to engage. Social intelligence, therefore, is important for political leaders, marketing researchers, and others in positions of power. There is a fine line between cooperation and competition, and only those with high social intelligence can negotiate a cooperative alliance that also confers a competitive advantage.

Social intelligence is likely a by-product of a long evolutionary history. Interactions in social groups have selected social skills that allow individuals to interact more effectively to survive and reproduce. Being able to read others allows one to gain an advantage, find mutually beneficial solutions, and be a savvy social partner. An understanding of social intelligence is required for effective advertising and marketing and cooperative alliances and to gain a competitive advantage.

See also: Benefits of Lying; Detecting Deception; Evolution of Deception; Intelligence; Language; Machiavellianism; Nonverbal Behavior; Recursive Awareness; Tactical Deception; Theory of Mind; Wizard's Project.

Further Reading

Gallup, G. G. (1998). Self-awareness and the evolution of social intelligence. *Behavioural Processes, 42*, 239–247.

Ganaie, M. Y., & Mudasir, H. (2015). A study of social intelligence & academic achievement of college students of district Srinagar, J&K, India. *Journal of American Science, 11*(3), 23–27.

O'Sullivan, M. (2005). Emotional intelligence and deception detection: Why most people can't "read" others but a few can. In R. E. Riggio & R. S. Feldman (Eds.), *Applications of Nonverbal Communication* (pp. 215–253). Lawrence Erlbaum Associates.

Riggio, R. E. (2014). What is social intelligence? Why does it matter? *Psychology Today*. Retrieved from https://www.psychologytoday.com/us/blog/cutting-edge-leadership /201407/what-is-social-intelligence-why-does-it-matter

Smith, R. M., & LaFreniere, P. J. (2009). Development of children's ability to and for intentions from nonverbal cues. *Journal of Social, Evolutionary, and Cultural Psychology, 3*(4), 315–327.

Smith, R. M., & LaFreniere, P. J. (2011). Development of tactical deception from 4 to 8 years of age. *British Journal of Developmental Psychology, 31*, 30–41.

Social Media

Increased use of social media platforms such as Facebook, Twitter, Instagram, Snapchat, and MySpace is correlated with increased attempts to deceive. About two-thirds of people who use social media report that they have lied online. Ninety-eight percent of users also believe that others are likely to exaggerate, alter, or outright lie when interacting on a social media site. The most common suspected lie is about physical appearance, but users also expect that others may lie about things like gender, occupation, and personal characteristics. Reasons for lying include attempting to appear more attractive, protecting privacy, and conforming to social norms or expectations.

Types of online deception include trolling, impersonation, concealment, and lies about one's own characteristics such as gender, appearance, income, career, or age. In fact, when analyzed, about half of online daters reported that they have lied about their age, appearance, relationship status, weight, or interests. People are more likely to lie on sites where they will remain anonymous than on sites where they may eventually meet the people with whom they are communicating.

Dr. Elizabeth Wright and her colleagues from Queensland University of Technology examined social media sites such as Instagram and Facebook and found that individuals use these platforms to express themselves, to communicate, and to be creative, but they are also likely to engage in behaviors to gain attention and elicit social approval. Strategies include using filters and hashtags to get attention as well as using software to radically alter photos. Since Instagram is primarily focused on posting pictures to promote oneself rather than on building relationships, most people use it to increase popularity, to document and showcase their own lives, and to seek validation. Furthermore, Dr. Tara Dumas and her colleagues from Western University in Ontario found that those individuals who spent more time editing photos, taking selfies, updating their accounts, and presenting an ideal version of themselves scored higher on scales of narcissism. Those individuals were also likely to spend more time scrolling through social media sites to keep tabs on others. Additionally, more time spent on Instagram, Facebook, and MySpace was correlated with a weak sense of belonging, less stable personal relationships, loneliness, and isolation.

Such research demonstrates that a large part of deceptive behavior on social media sites revolves around attempts to seek validation, attention, and approval from others. Those with lower self-esteem, higher levels of narcissism, and fewer offline relationships are the most likely to engage in dishonest behavior to gain attention and validation through online platforms. Those who feel secure, integral to their peer group and who have strong same-sex friendships are less likely to exaggerate or outright lie online. They feel accepted, validated, and worthy, and do not need to alter others' perceptions to win approval.

As of 2016, 87 percent of young adults were found to be connected to social media sites. Given this huge proponent of usage, social media is influencing the way young people communicate. Since most deception detection is revealed through nonverbal communication, communicating online makes the detection of deception much more difficult. Most people understand and expect to be deceived given the nature of the platform, and most recognize that it is easier to get away with lies online as compared to in-person conversations. Use of social media has also given young adults a sense of anonymity in their opinions and conversations, leading to expression of opinions that they may not be comfortable expressing in face-to-face conversations.

Online use allows anyone to create an alternate identity. Furthermore, individuals can create and maintain false identities without much risk of being detected. Under such identities, individuals can live out fantasies, express extreme opinions, and feel less inhibited by social morals than they may when operating under their true identities. This may be freeing for some individuals who do not fit the social norms, but it also allows scammers to manipulate and deceive others more readily. As Dr. Wright and her colleagues note, the tendency to deceive others online is related to problems with self-worth, relationships, depression, and anxiety. Individuals who suffer from these problems may be more likely to use the anonymity of the internet to seek assurance and validation, or the increasing reliance on social approval and validation may contribute to the development of these disorders.

Social media can be empowering or inhibiting. Individuals can use it to socialize, learn, grow, and institute change on global levels. Individuals can use it to explore aspects of their own personalities, to connect with others with similar beliefs, lifestyles, or values. Or, individuals can use it to create superficial, impersonal, unhealthy personas; to seek validation; or to take advantage of others. Social media makes deception easier because the users can be anonymous, fake, and undetectable, and as a result, most users are or should be reasonably suspicious of those with whom they connect via the internet.

See also: Catfishing; Exaggeration; Impersonator; Online Dating; Prevalence of Lying; Scams; Sockpuppets; Trolling.

Further Reading

Drouin, M., Miller, D., Wehle, S. M. J., & Hernandez, E. (2016). Why do people lie online? "Because everyone lies on the internet." *Computers in Human Behavior, 64*, 134–142.

Dumas, T. M., Maxwell-Smith, M., Davis, J. P., & Giulietti, P. A. (2017). Lying or longing for likes? Narcissism, peer belonging, loneliness, and normative versus deceptive like-seeking on Instagram in emerging adulthood. *Computers in Human Behavior, 71*, 1–10.

Wright, E. J., White, K. M., & Obst, P. L. (2018). Facebook false self-presentation behaviors and negative mental health. *Cyberpsychology, Behavior, and Social Networking, 21*(1), 40–49.

Sociopathic Liars (*See* Antisocial Personality Disorder; Compulsive Lying)

Sockpuppets

The term "sockpuppet" refers to an online identity that is created for deceptive purposes. An individual may create multiple sockpuppets in order to praise, denounce, advocate for, or support an idea, website, individual, product, or organization. A sockpuppet may be used to create the impression of a larger body of support for an issue or to spread misinformation, fear, uncertainty, or doubt throughout a group. For example, authors may create sockpuppet accounts to post favorable reviews about their own work, to increase the perception of interest or sales. Typically, a user creates several fake sockpuppet accounts to manipulate a target audience or to create the impression of a strongly united public opinion.

The phenomenon of online sockpuppets is a relatively new concept, yet there are already multiple types. A strawman sockpuppet is used when an individual wants to undermine one side of a debate. One may create a strawman sockpuppet and use it to post ridiculous claims that appear to come from the side of the issue that one wants to discredit. The claims of a strawman sockpuppet are presented as uneducated and ignorant, which makes them easy for the opposition to refute. The claims of a strawman sockpuppet serve to discredit an idea and overshadow more rational arguments on that side of the issue. Such actions may make proponents of the opposing viewpoint more avid or undermine the commitment of those who are aligned with the strawman's purported side. This strategy has been used in political campaigns, marketing programs, and public relation initiatives, and serves to spread fear, uncertainty, and doubt.

A meatpuppet, alternatively, is an individual who is recruited to publicly advocate for a point of view. Meatpuppets are recruited to comment on products, issues, or on public websites to draw attention to issues or to create the perception of widespread interest in an issue or product. Their commentary may give the issue or product more credibility and a higher rating. Individuals who serve as meatpuppets may be hired to sell a product or push forward an idea, including government propaganda. Frequently, strawman sockpuppets and meatpuppets are used in tandem to undermine one side of an issue (or candidate) and support the other.

Sockpuppets have emerged in several fields including business, politics, and journalism. For example, John Mackey, the chief executive of Whole Foods, used a sockpuppet for over seven years to promote Whole Foods, to argue with critics, and to criticize the competition. Tad Furtado, policy director for a New Hampshire Republican representative, posed as a sockpuppet on Democratic blogs to undermine the opposing party. Michael A. Hiltzik, winner of a Pulitzer Prize for Best Reporting, used a sockpuppet to comment and feud with readers. Donald Trump even posed as his own official spokesperson, John Barron, and commented on news stories about the Trump family for years.

One extreme example of sockpuppetry is the 50 Cent Party in China. Starting in 2004, the Chinese government began hiring individuals to post comments on the internet. At its peak, this online army was represented by upward of two million fake accounts, used to post almost 500 million comments to promote the Chinese government and to sway public opinion on hot issues. These individuals were paid to comment on message boards and social media sites. Individuals could even earn a professional license as an *internet opinion analyst* that helped them hone their skills in propaganda.

Given the growing body of offenders and the strength sockpuppets have to manipulate public opinion, researchers have invested in creating programs to detect sockpuppets in online forums. One way that sockpuppets may be identified is through analysis of IP addresses of suspected sockpuppets, since multiple sockpuppets are likely one person posting from a single computer. Programs have also been created to analyze writing style, such as alphabet count, pattern of use of emoticons and common keywords, word usage, or writing style, and to analyze nonverbal behaviors, such as the number of revisions and timing of interactions. Since sockpuppets controlled by the same user tend to interact at the same time, the timing of their interactions do not tend to show the typical delay that characterizes the interactions of normal users. Software to detect sockpuppets has success rates from 70 to 99 percent depending on the social platform under analysis.

With the anonymity of the digital age, sockpuppetry is likely to become more rather than less common. The ease of creating email addresses and online personas allows for individuals to easily create multiple online identities to stage conversations, commentaries, or critiques to sway public opinion. Use of such strategies for political campaigns or policy work can have far-reaching implications. The easiest way to combat sockpuppetry is to unplug and gather information in person from offline, genuine, sources.

See also: Alternative Facts; Catfishing; Corruption; Fake News; Phishing; Politics; Propaganda; Social Media.

Further Reading
Boehler, P. (2013, October 3). Two million 'internet opinion analysts' employed to monitor China's vast online population: Government employees trawl through blogs and social media to dissect public opinion. *South China Morning Post: China Insider.* Retrieved from https://www.scmp.com/news/china-insider/article/1323529/two-million-employed-monitor-chinese-public-opinion

Elsner, K. (2013, November 27). China uses an army of sockpuppets to control public opinion—And the US will too. *Liberty Voice.* Retrieved from https://guardianlv.com/2013/11/china-uses-an-army-of-sockpuppets-to-control-public-opinion-and-the-us-will-too/

Stone, B., & Richtel, M. (2007, July 16). The hand that controls the sock puppet could get slapped. *The New York Times.* Retrieved from https://www.nytimes.com/2007/07/16/technology/16blog.html

Yamak, Z., Saunier, J., & Vercouter, L. (2018). SocksCatch: Automatic detection and grouping of sockpuppets in social media. *Knowledge-Based Systems, 149*, 124–142.

Suspension of Disbelief

Suspension of disbelief is a cognitive phenomenon during which individuals deny or set aside critical thinking and reasoning and willingly believe the unbelievable.

Suspension of disbelief predominantly comes into play when enjoying a movie, book, or other work of fiction where the reader immerses oneself in the fantasy world and willingly believes unrealistic storylines. While such dismissal of reality may aid enjoyment of a fictional work, it can also serve to color beliefs about real-life events as well. It may be easier to believe a partner's lie, even if it is quite ridiculous, than to face a harsh truth. Thus, individuals may willingly suspend their reason to maintain their perceptions of reality, even if the chosen beliefs are not very realistic. In this way, people may distort their perceptions in order to maintain their beliefs.

The term "suspension of disbelief" originated in 1817 by poet Samuel Taylor Coleridge, who asked readers to suspend their disbelief for a moment while reading his fantastical work. Since that time, it has been applied to a phenomenon that one experiences when faced with all kinds of poetry, theater, books, movies, and other fictional experiences. A willing suspension of disbelief does not necessarily mean that the viewer or reader honestly believes what is happening, but that they believe it for the moment. Subcortical parts of the brain, such as the limbic system, are activated, causing viewers to feel genuine emotions for and about the fictional characters and allowing them to invest in the story. Willing suspension of one's disbelief causes individuals to reject their own critical awareness of the constraints of reality and immerse themselves in the story. If a work of fiction is well done, it may only be in retrospect that the audience pauses to critically evaluate the story line, find plot holes, or recognize the fantastical elements. A suspension of disbelief allows viewers to experience the rush of terror when characters are facing vampires, feel exhilaration when superheroes defy the laws of physics, or experience the satisfaction of perfect poetic justice for the end of any drama.

People primarily refer to the idea of a willing suspension of disbelief when discussing works of fiction. In real life, however, a willing suspension of disbelief may allow individuals to see the best in others, take people at their word, or discount evidence for things one does not want to believe. Understanding one's own tendency to engage in suspension of disbelief may be important to learn to detect deception or gain logical knowledge, particularly when it conflicts with previous beliefs. The human mind is very good at willingly ignoring contradictory evidence in favor of finding evidence that fits what one wants to believe and may make people more susceptible to being deceived. One must consider evidence, context, and opposing viewpoints to overcome one's tendency to blindly believe others.

The general tendency of suspending one's disbelief can also lead to inaccuracies of knowledge. One way that this emerges is through historical fiction. Books and movies based in history may be based on true events that are elaborated to make a more interesting story. Those who suspend their disbelief and accept the events as true are likely to have an inaccurate comprehension of history or facts. Additionally, simply believing what one sees, hears, or reads accounts for the startling influence of fake news, propaganda, and social media. Shutting off logical reasoning and critical thinking allows people to be influenced by information that is not always couched in reality. There is a time and place to engage a willing suspension of disbelief. Such suspension can accentuate a theatrical experience but can be a detriment if not overcome for issues in reality. Political decisions, scientific decisions, and environmental policies need to be based on critically evaluated reasoning.

See also: Alternative Facts; Blue Lies; Cognitive Dissonance; Cognitive Distortion; Emotional Effects; Fake News; Half-Truths; Memory; Propaganda; Reality Monitoring; Red Herring; Social Media.

Further Reading

Holland, N. N. (2008). Spiderman? Sure! The neuroscience of disbelief. *Interdisciplinary Science Reviews, 33*(4), 312–320.

Holland, N. N. (2014). What brain activity can explain suspension of disbelief? *Scientific American Mind, 25*(1), 74.

Walton, K. L. (1978). Fearing fictions. *The Journal of Philosophy, 75*(1), 5–27.

T

Tactical Deception

Tactical deception occurs when an individual uses specific, purposeful tactics or strategies to deceive others to intentionally achieve a goal. Tactical deception involves consciously misrepresenting one's intentions to misdirect a social partner's attention or understanding of a situation. Tactical deception requires monitoring one's own behavior, monitoring the reactions of a social partner, and adjusting one's strategy accordingly to successfully manipulate the interaction. The development of tactical deception abilities correlate with developments of theory of mind.

Dr. Rachelle Smith from Husson University and Dr. Peter LaFreniere from the University of Maine examined the emergence of tactical deception ability over childhood. A competitive game paradigm required children to monitor their own behavior as well as the behavior of a competitive partner to gain strategic advantage in a game. Developmental increases in success rates were found across childhood. Children between ages four and six were likely to leak information through facial expressions and behaviors. They would grin when attempting to deceive, look toward the correct answer in a guessing game, and blurt out answers when asked, explicitly revealing information. Between ages six and eight, children were more effective at stifling cues, hiding facial expressions, and controlling their eye gaze to engage in more successful tactical strategies. A competitive partner had to rely on leaked or accidental cues to gain insight. By age eight, children moved beyond simply attempting to stifle cues and started to fabricate false information to mislead or confuse a social partner. These children would look at the wrong answer, use an irregular playing strategy, and provide false facial expressions to actively influence the expectations, beliefs, and behavior of a competitive social partner.

This research demonstrated that inhibiting information is relatively naive and simplistic because stifling behavior signals to a social partner that something is missing or it may allow information to leak through. A more savvy strategy, as demonstrated by older children and adults, is to fabricate misleading information that covers for missing or suppressed information. Such fabricated information smooths over gaps and, if done well, may keep a social partner from being aware that deception has occurred.

Through adolescence and adulthood, tactical strategies become more honed, and facial expressions, verbal statements, and false signals can be used to gain a competitive or cooperative advantage in business negotiations, athletic contests, political debates, relationships, or during wartime. The use of tactics to deceive, misinform, or mislead the enemy dates back to ancient times, as documented in Sun Tzu's military guide, *The Art of War*. Leaking misinformation to an enemy can influence their tactical decisions, cause confusion, intimidate, and secure the advantage. Ancient Greek stories talk of the Trojan horse used to mislead and defeat Troy, Mongolian armies feigned retreat, George Washington used deceptive strategies to win the American Revolutionary War against the larger British forces, and examples of tactical strategies underlined both World War I and World War II.

Tactical deception is common in humans, but forms of it can also be seen in other animal species. Dr. David Premack and Dr. Guy Woodruff demonstrated that chimpanzees can engage in quite clever deceptions to influence the behavior of trainers. In their research, chimpanzees witnessed a banana being hidden out of their reach. Over a number of trials, two trainers interacted with the chimpanzees. The kind trainer would give the banana to the chimpanzee when the chimpanzee indicated where it was hidden, but the villainous trainer would eat the banana himself when shown where it was hidden. One chimpanzee, Sarah, began to use a form of tactical deception when faced with the villainous trainer. She would feign ignorance and refuse to indicate where the banana was hidden or would indicate an incorrect location. Whether such deceptions are based on a tactical understanding of intentions or simply due to conditioning is still under debate.

Another primate who demonstrated simple skills in tactical deception was Koko, a gorilla who was taught sign language. Koko was noted to use sign language to deflect blame for naughty behavior. Since tactical deception requires self-awareness and modification of one's own behaviors to influence the beliefs and actions of others, there is debate about whether other animals, such as birds and insects, engage in true tactical deception. Birds may make fake warning calls to distract members of their group from a food source, and insects may mimic the color patterns of other species, but these examples may indicate behavior modification and evolutionary adaptation rather than true tactical strategies.

See also: Art of War, The; Deception in Animals; Development of Deception; Espionage; Instrumental Lies; Mimicry; Primates; Recursive Awareness; Signaling Theory; Theory of Mind.

Further Reading

LaFreniere, P. J. (1988). The ontogeny of tactical deception in humans. In R. Byrne & A. Whiten (Eds.), *Evolution of Social Intelligence* (pp. 238–252). Oxford University Press.

Premack, D., & Woodruff, G. (1978). Does the chimpanzee have a theory of mind? *Behavioral and Brain Sciences, 1*(4), 515–526.

Smith, R. M., & LaFreniere, P. J. (2013). Development of tactical deception from 4 to 8 years of age. *British Journal of Developmental Psychology, 31*, 30–41.

Theory of Mind

Theory of mind is likely the most imperative development that underlies successful deception abilities. Theory of mind is the understanding that others have thoughts, intentions, and beliefs. Theory of mind ability, introduced by Dr. David Premack and Dr. Guy Woodruff almost 50 years ago, allows humans to engage in perspective-taking, empathy, persuasion, and diplomacy, as well as deception and manipulation. To effectively deceive another person, deceivers must have an understanding of what the receiver believes in order to manipulate that belief.

Theory of mind develops predictably over childhood and is correlated with emerging deceptive abilities. Children under the age of five usually do not lie convincingly because they do not have the awareness necessary to be plausible in their deceit. They may be unaware of the cues that others will use to detect deceptive attempts, such as a smear of chocolate on the cheek of a child who is denying stealing the cookies, or unaware of what the other already knows or thinks. Young children struggle to manipulate their own behaviors to make their story more convincing because, without theory of mind, they are unable to take the other's perspective.

Story paradigms, known as false-belief tasks, are used to assess the development of theory of mind abilities. In false-belief tasks, children are provided with information that a social partner does not have. Then the children are asked to make a prediction about the belief or behavior of the partner. If the child has a mature theory of mind, the lack of information is factored into the prediction of the other's response. Children without a mature theory of mind attribute their own knowledge to the social partner and make predictions about the behavior of the other accordingly. Usually by the age of five, children can start making more accurate predictions about what a social partner may think or do due to this emerging ability to consider what the partner does or does not know.

Those with mature theory of mind ability can take the perspective of their conversational partners. Such perspective-taking allows individuals to interact successfully in competitive and cooperative interactions. Consideration of what the other believes is needed to prevent misunderstandings, to negotiate effectively, or to deceive others. Successful deception requires monitoring one's partner; assessing what they know, suspect, or believe; and monitoring one's own behavior to further influence their perception. By manipulating the beliefs of others, one can plant false expectations and beliefs to achieve one's own ends. Theory of mind also allows individuals to effectively use white lies to protect the feelings of others or smooth social interactions. Understanding what information may hurt another is a prerequisite for altering the information to assure one is not causing harm and can allow individuals to conceal true feelings in order to respect social norms. To maximize theory of mind abilities, one must be aware not only of the beliefs and expectations of others but also of the others' awareness of one's own thoughts and expectations.

Theory of mind ability is predominantly believed to be unique to humans. Our ability to understand the mental representations of others allows for deceptive abilities relatively absent in even our closest primate relatives. Evolution of theory of mind abilities were likely driven by social competition and an evolutionary arms race of increasingly subtle attempts at deception coupled with more savvy detection abilities.

The strategic management of verbal and nonverbal expressive behavior to achieve goals necessitates a mature theory of mind. In turn, a mature theory of mind contributes to effective tactical deception. The ability to take another's perspective allows for effective strategies when attempting to convey false or misleading information or to conceal true information. Though rudimentary theory of mind develops around age five, these abilities continue to emerge with maturation and experience over childhood and over adult development.

See also: Age Differences; Deception in Animals; Development of Deception; Evolution of Deception; Machiavellianism; Primates; Recursive Awareness; Tactical Deception.

Further Reading

Baron-Cohen, S., Leslie, A. M., & Frith, U. (1985). Does the autistic child have a "theory of mind"? *Cognition, 21*, 37–46.

Carrington, S. J., & Bailey, A. J. (2009). Are there theory of mind regions in the brain? A review of the neuroimaging literature. *Human Brain Mapping, 30*, 2313–2335.

El Haj, M., Antoine, P., & Nandrino, J. L. (2017). When deception influences memory: The implication of theory of mind. *The Quarterly Journal of Experimental Psychology, 70*(7), 1166–1173.

Premack, D., & Woodruff, G. (1978). Does the chimpanzee have a theory of mind? *Behavioral and Brain Sciences, 1*(4), 515–526.

Smith, R. M., & LaFreniere, P. J. (2009). Development of children's ability to infer intentions from nonverbal cues. *Journal of Social, Evolutionary, and Cultural Psychology, 3*(4), 315–327.

Smith, R. M., & LaFreniere, P. J. (2011). Development of tactical deception from 4 to 8 years of age. *British Journal of Developmental Psychology, 31*, 30–41.

Wellman, H. M. (1990). *The Child's Theory of Mind.* MIT Press.

Transparent Lies and the Illusion of Transparency

Transparency plays a dual role in the realm of deception. First, transparent lies, or obvious lies, can be used when liars are not actually intending to deceive others. Second, the illusion of transparency is the widely held erroneous belief that observers will be able to tell the difference between truths and lies. Not only do most individuals believe they will be able to distinguish between the lies and truths of others, but they also believe that others will know when they are being honest or deceptive as well.

Transparent lies are those lies that the sender, or liar, does not try to hide and may even wish to be uncovered. These lies may be common when the sender feels the need to lie because telling the truth would be socially unacceptable. They may use body language, facial expressions, tone of voice, intonations of sarcasm, and other such nonverbal behaviors intentionally in concordance with the lie to convey the actual meaning. This form of lie-telling differs from other forms of deception because the sender is not intentionally trying to deceive others. Such lies may confuse non-native speakers but otherwise are easily parsed by listeners.

Transparent liars are not believed when they are lying. Their statements may be taken as jokes or sarcasm or may otherwise influence an interaction. Transparent liars may use lies to turn the conversation away from uncomfortable topics, to inject humor into stressful situations, or to share their beliefs in a less direct, less hurtful way. Alternatively, some liars may intend to deceive but are ineffective and thus may also be called transparent liars. Ted Ruffman and his colleagues found that individuals tend to become more transparent with age. Older adults in their study were more transparent when lying, and young adults were able to detect the lies of older adults more easily than the lies of other young adults. Additionally, older adults also showed less effectiveness at detecting lies.

The illusion of transparency refers to the tendency for individuals to overestimate others' abilities to accurately assess whether they are telling the truth or lying. Most people hold a strong belief that others will know when they are telling the truth and that their lies will be detected. In a research study by Dr. Thomas Gilovich and his colleagues, participants significantly overestimated the extent to which observers would be able to detect their lies. The participants predicted that observers would be able to detect their lies almost 50 percent of the time. However, their results showed that observers accurately detected lies only about 25 percent of the time. Furthermore, participants believed that others would believe them when they were telling the truth, and though observers' abilities to detect honesty had greater accuracy than detecting lies, their accuracy rates still revolved around chance levels.

The illusion of transparency becomes particularly relevant during criminal investigations. Because most people believe that others will know when they are telling the truth, innocent individuals are more likely to waive their Miranda rights than guilty individuals. Innocent individuals believe that, since they have nothing to hide, police officers or interrogators will recognize that they are telling the truth. However, this belief may increase the number of false confessions because innocent suspects who waive such rights may then be at the mercy of interrogation tactics that have been shown to elicit false confessions. These errors are particularly common with young suspects, such as adolescents or individuals with lower cognitive functioning. Young suspects and individuals with lower cognitive functioning are also more likely to waive their rights to please authority figures or to gain the immediate satisfaction of being able to go home, and they assert that their innocence will be evident.

See also: Age Differences; Detecting Deception; False Confessions; Fifth Amendment; Nonverbal Behavior; Truth-Default Theory.

Further Reading

Gilovich, T., Savitsky, K., & Medvec, V. H. (1998). The illusion of transparency: Biased assessments of others' ability to read one's emotional states. *Journal of Personality and Social Psychology, 75*, 332–346.

Levine, T. R. (2016). Examining sender and judge variability in honesty assessments and deception detection accuracy: Evidence for a transparent liar but no evidence of deception-general ability. *Communication Research Reports, 33*(3), 188–194.

Mandelbaum, J. (2014). *Exploring the Illusion of Transparency When Lying and Truth-Telling: The Impact of Age, Self-Consciousness, and Framing.* CUNY Academic Works.

Ruffman, T., Murray, J., Halberstadt, J., & Vater, T. (2012). Age-related differences in deception. *Psychology and Aging, 27*(3), 543–549.

Treason (See Espionage)

Trolling

Trolling is a term for posting deceptive information online with the purpose of misleading or redirecting a conversation for personal amusement. Trolling behavior can include any practices that deceive or disrupt social interactions, particularly online, when there is no apparent purpose for the behavior. Trolling can be a form of harassment, used for entertainment, or may be used to achieve a goal. Trolls, or those who engage in trolling behavior, may use controversial, deceptive, or negative comments to divert a conversation or interrupt dialogue. Those who engage in such behavior commonly have personality traits that align with the Dark Triad. The Dark Triad traits include narcissism, Machiavellianism, and psychopathy. Trolls are frequently intelligent and typically do not believe the information they post.

Internet trolls may use this behavior for entertainment, for strategic means, or for domination. Their goal may be to create upset in an online forum and to disrupt the flow of conversation. Trolls may spread misinformation or cause group members to turn against each other. Organizations may use trolls to manipulate public opinion in order to gain support for a product, and governments may use trolls to further a political agenda. Trolls can be strategically used to plant seeds of doubt within a group. Because trolls are frequently anonymous, they tend to be less inhibited and are hard to regulate.

Dr. Evita March and Dr. Jessica Marrington report that over one-third of millennials admit to engaging in trolling behavior online, particularly in conversations about politics and religion. One form of trolling, flame trolling, is aggressive, deceptive, and disruptive, and success is achieved when the troll lures others off-topic. Another type of trolling is kudos trolling, which is used for personal entertainment. Trolling behaviors are purposefully provoking, and though most people endorse the intention of ignoring trolls, such behaviors tend to elicit frustration, annoyance, and anger. In their research study, only those participants who engaged in past trolling behaviors thought that it was entertaining. Those same individuals also had higher scores on measures of sadism and psychopathy.

Researchers Dr. Barbara Lopes and Dr. Hui Yu investigated the connection between trolling behaviors and Dark Triad personality types. They found that those who scored higher on the psychopathy score were more likely to troll Facebook profiles, and tended to believe it is acceptable to hurt others for personal gain or for personal pleasure. Thus, it is not surprising that those individuals are more likely to bully, manipulate, or troll others online. Interestingly, those individuals were more likely to show this personality trait online than in face-to-face interactions. This may be one reason that trolling is so prevalent in online forums.

Dr. Keita Masui completed similar work looking at the connection between loneliness and trolling. In a research study with 513 participants, he found that loneliness was a positive predictor of internet trolling, especially for individuals high on the traits of Machiavellianism and psychopathy. He also found that victims of internet trolling had higher rates of depression and anxiety as a response. Both groups of individuals showed increased negative emotions and more difficulty in creating interpersonal relationships online.

Dr. Kevin M. Kniffin and Dr. Dylan Palacio from Cornell University looked at the incidents of trolling during sports competitions. These researchers found that trolling behavior most commonly not only focused on undermining and critiquing competitors' playing abilities but also included unfounded comments on physical appearance, athleticism, personal relationships, sexual behavior, families, and affiliates. This commentary and trolling behaviors serve to undermine confidence, leading to decrease in performance. Such behaviors were most common within esports but were found among males playing in-person contact sports as well.

Trolling is similar to cyberbullying, but frequently trolls do not know their victims. Many trolls will escalate the behavior until they get a response. In this way, trolling can be malicious and harmful to the target. Dr. Krista Howard and colleagues from Texas State University found that trolls tend to demonstrate higher need for engagement in social media, engage in a lot of self-comparison to others, and are more likely to be male.

See also: Astroturfing; Catfishing; Dark Triad; Machiavellianism; Narcissism; Politics; Red Herring; Sex Differences in Lying Behavior; Social Media; Sockpuppets.

Further Reading

Howard, K., Zolnierek, K. H., Critz, K., Dailey, S., & Ceballos, N. (2019). An examination of psychosocial factors associated with malicious online trolling behaviors. *Personality and Individual Differences, 149*, 309–314.

Kniffin, K. M., & Palacio, D. (2018). Trash-talking and trolling. *Human Nature, 29*, 353–369.

Lopes, B., & Yu, H. (2017). Who do you troll and why: An investigation into the relationship between the Dark Triad Personalities and online trolling behaviours toward popular and less popular Facebook profiles. *Computers in Human Behavior, 77*, 69–76.

March, E., & Marrington, J. (2019). A qualitative analysis of internet trolling. *Cyberpsychology, Behavior, and Social Networking, 22*(3), 192–197.

Masui, K. (2019). Loneliness moderates the relationship between Dark Tetrad traits and internet trolling. *Personality and Individual Differences, 150*, 1–5.

Truth-Bias (See Truth-Default Theory)

Truth-Default Theory

The Truth-Default Theory is the idea that most people have a truth bias. This means that most individuals assume that others are telling the truth, even when there is evidence to the contrary. The Truth-Default Theory explains why most people are so poor at detecting deception. Even in suspicious situations, most people still assume that others are telling the truth. This is likely due to the fact that most people are generally honest or rationalize lies, so they assume others are honest as well. If an individual believes that telling the truth will lead to negative outcomes such as hurting the feelings of others, being punished, being embarrassed, or damaging relationships, they may rationalize telling a lie, but they see these

How to Confront Someone Who Is Lying

People lie for many different reasons, and psychological research indicates that most people are not good at detecting lies. Most of the time lies save face and smooth awkwardness, so they benefit social interactions. The liar may be attempting to impress or may feel threatened, and the lies will cease once trust has been established. If the lies continue after a relationship has been established, however, there tends to be negative impacts on relationship satisfaction. Being able to identify when confrontation is needed and how to effectively confront a liar can be instrumental in improving relationship quality in personal and professional realms.

Some general tips to follow when confronting a liar is to analyze the type of lie being told, stay calm, and plan the confrontation. First, document the lies and think about why the person may be lying. Decide if the lies are worth addressing. White lies smooth social interactions. Story embellishments make people feel good about their experiences. Small lies are likely not worth correcting. If everyone knows the lies are occurring, just enjoy the story. If lies are being used to manipulate others or if someone is lying about responsibilities or relationships, however, they may need to be addressed to salvage relationships and trust.

If a confrontation is needed, talk to the person in private and come prepared with specific evidence. Most liars will be savvy at deflecting blame and rationalizing behaviors, so calmly providing hard evidence can be more effective than being drawn into an emotional appeal or defense. Experienced liars will have excuses and conflicting information to confuse and divert accusations. It is easy to be swayed by charismatic liars, and practiced liars may be able to twist accusations and come off as the victims. In such situations, having evidence is key. Provide specific examples and give the liar an opportunity to explain. They may admit to the lie and apologize or give reasoning that makes sense. If they do get defensive, a confronter needs to be firm in what behaviors will be tolerated. If the goal is to maintain the relationship, boundaries may need to be articulated and consequences set in place.

In situations where it is important to maintain relationships, such as long-term romantic relationships, friendships, or work partnerships, a good practice is to document the conversation and the decisions reached and share it with the other person to ensure agreement and understanding. If the liar has reasonable motivations, work together to find a solution. For people who lie frequently, confrontation and articulation may not be immediately successful. Lying becomes a habit, and it may take a while for them to become aware of and curb their own behavior. If the relationship is important to maintain, the evidence-gathering and confrontation cycle may need to happen several times to support long-term behavioral changes.

Ultimately, individuals are responsible for their own behaviors. Those who confront can control their own behaviors by withdrawing from the relationship or establishing and upholding clear consequences for behavior, but the liar will need to make the choice to work on being honest. An effective confronter will approach the conversation with good intentions and attempt to sort out the issues rather than arguing or accusing. A confronter must also be willing to follow through with the consequences set in order to see effective change. Many people regret lies as soon as they are told, and a chance to correct themselves in a nonthreatening way may provide a successful solution to the situation.

instances as exceptions rather than typical, so they do not tend to be prevalent in memory. Additionally, it can be beneficial to believe others when they choose to lie in order to avoid social embarrassment or promote cohesion.

Evidence collected in support of the Truth-Default Theory demonstrates that most people assume that others are honest, which is why most individuals are so vulnerable to being deceived. Though research on detecting deception tends to show that most people can distinguish between truth and deception about 50 percent of the time, this is likely a distorted view of reality. In fact, most individuals are likely to detect truths at a much greater rate than 50 percent of the time due to the truth bias. However, they likely detect lies at a much lower rate; thus, the ability to distinguish between the two balances out to about chance levels.

Dr. Timothy Levine from the University of Alabama at Birmingham proposed the veracity effect. The veracity effect describes the tendency for individuals to have high accuracy when judging true statements, likely because most individuals judge almost every statement to be true. Therefore, when an individual tells the truth, most others believe them. Individuals only tend to struggle when being told lies. When being lied to, most individuals still think the other is telling the truth. Though a truth bias does contribute to a marked inability to detect deception, Dr. Levine proposes that this bias is an adaptive response that facilitates communication and the stability of relationships. Though it makes individuals vulnerable to deception, most people are honest most of the time, so analyzing every statement for signals of honesty would be a waste of energy and would make communication less productive and efficient and relationships less stable.

Most research supports Dr. Levine's proposal. Most people are honest most of the time. Most lies are told by a few prolific liars. Thus, typically, it makes sense to believe others most of the time. In line with this, most lies are believed, and detection typically only occurs after the fact if the individual confesses or if future evidence contradicts earlier beliefs. The tendency for an individual to believe others lays a foundation for deceptive success. Those who choose to manipulate others and to actively deceive are likely to be believed, at least in the short term.

Because individuals are likely to assume that others are telling the truth, relying on instinctual detection abilities may be very ineffective. Dr. Levine suggests effort and critical evaluation of the statements of others is a more accurate avenue to detect lies than intuition. Accurate assessment is difficult because there is no one conclusive clue that someone is lying. Furthermore, most lies, even suspected lies, are never confirmed, so there is limited feedback from which to learn. To detect lies, one must actively analyze changes in personal mannerisms, inconsistencies between statements, or discrepancies between verbal and nonverbal presentations. Contrary to other researchers such as Dr. Bella DePaulo and Dr. Albert Vrij, Dr. Levine suggests that intuition will lead us to believe others due to our truth-default, and only through critical analysis is one likely to detect lies. Unfortunately, conscious methods of deception detection also show limited success. The motivational impairment effect has illustrated that those who are most motivated to detect lies can overcome the truth-default bias. However, in these circumstances, they actually exhibit poorer lie detection skills, yet increased confidence, so they make even more errors than the average individual.

See also: DePaulo, Bella; Detecting Deception; Motivational Impairment Effect; Optimism Bias; Reality Monitoring; Social Intelligence; Vrij, Aldert.

Further Reading
Bond, C. F., Jr., & DePaulo, B. M. (2006). Accuracy of deception judgments. *Personality and Social Psychology Review, 10,* 214–234.

Levine, T. R. (2014). Truth-default theory (TDT): A theory of human deception and deception detection. *Journal of Language and Social Psychology, 33*, 378–392.

Levine, T. R. (2019). Five reasons why I am skeptical that indirect or unconscious lie detection is superior to direct deception detection. *Frontiers in Psychology, 10,* 1354.

Serota, K. B., & Levine, T. R. (2014). A few prolific liars: Variation in the prevalence of lying. *Journal of Language and Social Psychology, 34*(2), 138–157.

Tuskegee Syphilis Study

The Tuskegee Syphilis Study was a research study by the U.S. Public Health Service in collaboration with the Tuskegee Institute that was conducted from 1932 to 1972. This study has come to be an exemplar for the damage that deception in research can cause. The goal of the study was to examine the long-term health effects of syphilis in 400 African American males. At the time of the study, around 35 percent of men in Tuskegee, Alabama, who were of reproductive age had syphilis, commonly known as bad blood, and treatments were relatively ineffective and toxic. To study the effects of the disease, these men were recruited and were told that they would receive medical treatment. Rather than treatment, they were given placebos. Even when an effective treatment was discovered in the 1940s, the men were not treated because clinicians wanted to continue to study the effects of the disease. By the time the study was discontinued, a majority of the men suffered from syphilis-induced heart disease, CNS effects, bone degeneration, sores, rashes, fever, hair loss, headaches, body aches, fatigue, organ failure, sensory failure, or death.

The study was initially planned to last between six months and one year with follow-up treatment for those infected with the disease. When funding for the treatment phase was lost, however, researchers decided to continue the study without informing the participants in order to study the long-term effects of the disease. Participants were told that the invasive tests needed for the study, such as spinal taps and blood tests, were special free treatments designed to improve their health.

By 1934, researchers started publishing results from the study, outlining the detrimental health effects of untreated syphilis. In 1936, researchers received the first pushback for purposefully withholding treatment. In response, local doctors were recruited to pacify critics but were instructed not to actually treat the disease. By 1945, penicillin was introduced, which effectively treated the disorder without toxic effects. However, researchers actively prevented the participants from seeking or receiving treatment. Stanley Schuman, MD, and his fellow researchers summarized the study in the *Journal of Chronic Diseases* in 1955, reporting that 39 percent of their participants died, 70 percent remained untreated, 23 percent had inadequate treatment, and 7 percent had managed to get treatment despite barriers put in place. Results show that the life expectancy of an individual with untreated syphilis is 17 percent shorter than a healthy individual.

Throughout the 1960s, concerns were raised about ethical violations of the study, but they were ignored by both the experimenters and the Public Health

Service. The Center for Disease Control deemed that the study should continue until all subjects had died, and their bodies could be studied. Only when the details were released to the press in the 1970s did the experimenters receive enough pressure to terminate the study and treat the participants. The U.S. Government then paid a modern-day equivalent of 52 million dollars to participants and their families, agreed to provide free medical treatment, and established institutional review board (IRB) regulations and bioethical centers to prevent future unethical research.

In retroactive analysis of the study, the researchers attempted to justify the research by asserting that these underprivileged African American males would never have acquired treatment anyway and that the study results are beneficial for the future of medicine. They also pointed out that participants received meals when at the clinic, were provided with rides to the clinic, were given free treatment for other ailments throughout the duration of the study, and were provided with funeral benefits. Despite these justifications,128 of the participants died from syphilis-related complications during the study, many spread the disease to intimate partners, and many offspring were born infected.

Such experiments radically violate today's ethical standards for research and serve to create mistrust in the research process. Due to such history of exploitation and mistreatment, many African Americans continue to show decreased participation in research and decreased utilization of medical services. Dr. Vicki Freimuth and her colleagues from the Centers for Disease Control and Prevention in Atlanta, Georgia, examined the barriers such events have created for participation in research. They found lingering effects in their research sample, including limited knowledge about research, distrust of researchers, and inaccurate understanding about the informed consent process, all of which create a barrier to recruitment. Their participants voiced a lingering suspicion and distrust in research procedures that need to be overcome to further medical research and treatment. African Americans lead the nation with regard to health concerns and are at higher risk for a range of chronic conditions. More participation in research is needed to design and implement adequate medical care, but many individuals understandably choose not to participate due to this history of unethical and harmful behavior.

See also: Costs of Lying; Deception in Research; Ethics; Milgram's Obedience Experiments; Placebo Effect.

Further Reading

Alsan, M., & Wanamaker, M. (2018). Tuskegee and the health of black men. *The Quarterly Journal of Economics, 133*(1), 407–455.

Center for Disease Control and Prevention. (2020). *U.S. Public Health Service Syphilis Study at Tuskegee*. Retrieved from https://www.cdc.gov/tuskegee/index.html

Freimuth, V. S., Quinn, S. C., Thomas, S. B., Cole, G., Zook, E., & Duncan, T. (2001). African American's views on research and the Tuskegee Syphilis Study. *Social Science and Medicine, 52*, 797–808.

Schuman, S., Olansky, S., Rivers, E., Smith, C. A., & Rambo, D. S. (1955). Untreated syphilis in the male Negro: Background and current status of patients in the Tuskegee study. *Journal of Chronic Diseases, 2*(5), 543–558.

V

Veracity Effect (*See* Truth-Default Theory)

Vocal Changes when Lying

Research on nonverbal behaviors associated with lying has revealed a range of vocal behaviors that tend to accompany lying. These include paraverbal communication behaviors such as speech rate, response latency (increased time needed to initiate a response), use of fillers, repetition, and vocal pitch, which all tend to vary predictably with lying behavior. People who are lying, particularly if they are inexperienced or anxious, tend to speak more slowly; take longer to start to answer questions; use more fillers, such as ahs, ums, and uhs during their responses; repeat themselves more while responding; and have detectable increases in their vocal pitch.

Both slowed speech rate and increased time needed to initiate a response reveal the increased cognitive demands needed to construct a lie, particularly if the individual is trying to make the lie sound plausible. In such situations, the person who is lying needs time to think of a convincing response, contrary to those who are telling the truth who do not have to exercise caution or worry about sounding believable. If the person who is lying has rehearsed the response, the speech rate and response latency may more closely mimic someone who is telling the truth. However, in these situations, the liar will likely use more repetition and fillers to prevent the listener from asking probing questions or otherwise interrupting. Keeping control of the conversation and filling the time prevents the other from asking questions that might arouse suspicion or reveal holes in the fabricated story.

In addition to changes in the speed and quality of conversation, changes in vocal pitch, or how high or low a person's voice typically sounds, also correlate with lying behavior. When an individual is lying, his or her vocal pitch tends to increase. Since vocal pitch arises from the amount of tension in the vocal tract, it can be directly influenced by the emotions typically associated with lying. When a speaker is happy, angry, or anxious, their typical pitch can increase by as much as 100Hz due to increased tension in the vocal tract. Thus, lying is not the only reason that one's pitch would increase, but it does give the listener a clue that the speaker is particularly aroused.

To examine vocal changes during lying behavior, Dr. Gina Villar, Dr. Joanne Arciuli, and Dr. Helen Paterson, from the University of Sydney, asked participants to provide honest and deceptive opinions about controversial social issues. These opinions were then analyzed for vocal quality and veracity. When lying, participants used fewer words, gave fewer details, spoke more slowly, and had a noticeably higher vocal pitch than when telling the truth. Interestingly, their research also suggests that vocal pitch may be a more useful marker for detecting deception than other nonverbal behaviors because vocal pitch is less susceptible to conscious control than behaviors such as eye gaze or fidgeting.

Behaviors that align with the deceiver stereotype, such as averted eye gaze and fidgeting movements, tend to be understood and manipulated by experienced liars. For example, research shows that practiced liars tend to actually make more eye contact than is typical in order to convince the audience and appear more truthful. Vocal pitch, however, tends to show the opposite trend. Dr. Villar and colleagues demonstrated that participants who were aware of the connection between higher pitch and lying had even more severe increases in vocal pitch when lying. Since increased pitch is associated with increased tension and anxiety, being aware of the increase in pitch likely only increases anxiety, producing an even higher pitch. Thus, to successfully manipulate vocal pitch, a liar would have to alter his or her overall physiological arousal, which is arguably more difficult than simply maintaining eye contact.

Though paraverbal communication behaviors have been found to shift predictably when lying, normal speech rate, response latency, and vocal pitch vary from individual to individual. For example, typical vocal pitch varies among individuals and between genders, (e.g., male voices tend to have a lower pitch (100–150Hz) than female voices (200–250Hz)), so there is not one vocal pitch that reveals that another individual is lying. Instead, these qualities of speech must be assessed in the context of the individual's typical behavior. The ability to pick up on changes in vocal behaviors would require a basis for comparison. One would need to know the individual's typical speech rate, response latency, and vocal pitch in order to identify changes that would reveal dishonesty (or, at least, emotionality). Familiarity with the individual's typical behaviors or at least a comparison conversation is required to reliably discriminate among paraverbal variations.

See also: Deceiver Stereotype; Detecting Deception; Emotional Effects; Nonverbal Behavior; Physiology.

Further Reading

DePaulo, B. M., Lindsay, J. J., Malone, B. E., Muhlenbruck, L., Charlton, K., & Cooper, H. (2003). Cues to deception. *Psychological Bulletin, 129*(1), 74–118.

Juslin, P. N., & Laukka, P. (2001). Impact of intended emotion intensity on cue utilization and decoding accuracy in vocal expression of emotion. *Emotion, 1*(4), 381–412.

Sporer, S. L., & Schwandt, B. (2006). Paraverbal indicators of deception: A meta-analytic synthesis. *Applied Cognitive Psychology, 20*(4), 421–446.

Villar, G., Arciuli, J., & Paterson, H. (2013). Vocal pitch production during lying: Beliefs about deception matter. *Psychiatry, Psychology and Law, 20*(1), 123–132.

Vrij, A., & Semin, G. (1996). Lie experts' beliefs about nonverbal indicators of deception. *Journal of Nonverbal Behavior, 20*(1), 65–80.

Vrij, Aldert

Aldert Vrij is a social psychologist at the University in Portsmouth in the United Kingdom who has written over 400 articles and book chapters on lie detection. He is the author of *Detecting Lies and Deceit: Pitfalls and Opportunities*. He is a preliminary researcher in the area of deception, and he presents a wealth of research on nonverbal and verbal cues to deception as well as lie detection. Over the past 30 years, his research has spanned examining the use of children's testimony in the courtroom; detecting deceit using verbal, nonverbal, and physiological behaviors; and examining police officers' abilities to detect lies. He has also examined the use of cognitive load to facilitate lie detection, given suggestions on how experts can improve detection abilities, and explored cultural differences in lie detection. Through empirical tests of interview techniques, reality monitoring, and the creation of false memories, he has provided suggestions and critiques of traditional interrogation procedures.

Given his extensive research, Dr. Vrij is an expert in many aspects of lie detection. Though he demonstrates that analysis of nonverbal behavior and speech content can help reveal lying behavior, he proposes that proactive tactical strategies are more effective in detecting lying than merely observing behaviors. Increasing cognitive load, asking unexpected questions, asking interviewees to tell their story in the reverse order or carry out a secondary task, and maintaining eye contact are all strategies that tend to increase lie detection accuracy as compared to simply observing verbal or nonverbal cues during speech.

In *Detecting Lies and Deceit: Pitfalls and Opportunities*, Dr. Vrij explains why people lie, the gender and personality differences in lying behavior, and how to detect lies. He analyzes common lie detector tools, such as the Behavior Analysis Interview; explores the impact of reality monitoring; and demonstrates the consistency of vocal changes when lying. He presents nonverbal, verbal, and written analysis techniques for lie detection and outlines physiological responses that tend to emerge during deceptive behavior. Finally, he explores common errors in lie detection and provides guidelines for more effective lie detection skills.

Dr. Vrij suggests that most individuals have an illusion of transparency, which means they believe others will know when they are lying. Individuals also endorse the belief that they would be able to tell if someone else was lying to them. This is not the case. Most individuals demonstrate a truth bias and assume that others are generally honest, and thus, most tend not to suspect lying except in exceptional circumstances. Most also never get feedback about their suspicions of lying and thus do not know if their suspicions were accurate, which means it is hard to hone the skill. Furthermore, many people are motivated to believe lies because most lies are told to maintain relationships, prevent embarrassment, and maintain social appropriateness.

Dr. Vrij notes that most people, even interrogators, rely on erroneous cues when attempting to detect deception, and his research shows that there are no clear verbal or nonverbal behaviors that conclusively depict deception. Even when using lie detector tests that have been specifically designed to detect deception, experienced liars may be able to use countermeasures to create the impression of honesty. Anxious individuals may demonstrate physiological responses that indicate lying, even when they are being honest. Dr. Vrij's empirical tests of the Behavior Analysis Interview demonstrate that the underlying assumptions of the interview procedure are not supported. For example, in his research design, truthtellers also behaved in an evasive and anxious manner, which is directly contrary to the assumptions made by the BAI. Through this work, Dr. Vrij demonstrates the flaws with current deception detection procedures and offers cautions as well as suggestions for more effective techniques.

See also: Behavior Analysis Interview; Deceiver Stereotype; False Confessions; Language; Motivational Impairment Effect; Nonverbal Behavior; Personality; Physiology; Reality Monitoring; Sex Differences in Lying Behavior; Transparent Lies and the Illusion of Transparency; Truth-Default Theory; Vocal Changes when Lying.

Further Reading

Vrij, A. (2008). *Detecting Lies and Deceit: Pitfalls and Opportunities* (2nd ed.). Wiley.

Vrij, A. (2010). Why professionals fail to catch liars and how they can improve. *Legal and Criminological Psychology, 9*(2), 159–181.

Vrij, A., Edward, K., Roberts, K. P., & Bull, R. (2000). Detecting deceit via analysis of verbal and nonverbal behavior. *Journal of Nonverbal Behavior, 24*, 239–263.

Vrij, A., Mann, S., & Fisher, R. P. (2006). An empirical test of the behaviour analysis interview. *Law and Human Behavior, 30*, 329–345.

Vrij, A., Mann, S. A., Fisher, R. P., Leal, S., Milne, R., & Bull, R. (2008). Increasing cognitive load to facilitate lie detection: The benefit of recalling an event in reverse order. *Law and Human Behavior, 32*, 253–265.

Vrij, A., Mann, S. A., Kristen, S., & Fisher, R. P. (2007). Cues to deception and ability to detect lies as a function of police interview styles. *Law and Human Behavior, 31*, 499–518.

W

Wetherell, Marmaduke (See Loch Ness Monster)

White Lies

White lies are low-stakes deceptive statements that are used to smooth over social interactions or conform to cultural norms. Types of white lies include butler lies, exaggerations, minimizations, agreements, fibs, and bluffs. White lies may be prosocial and told out of kindness or compassion, but they may also be self-serving. For example, one may tell a white lie to protect someone's feelings, to buffer someone else's self-esteem, to avoid embarrassment, or in an attempt to impress others. White lies frequently stem from an effort to act in a socially appropriate fashion within a group. For example, during their development, children must learn to control their facial expressions, learn to keep some opinions to themselves, and recognize when it is socially appropriate to lie.

Common white lies include denying responsibility for small antisocial acts, underestimating how long something will take to encourage cooperation, or acting as if one knows more about a topic than one actually does. They also include expressing pleasure for unwanted gifts, complimenting friends to increase their self-esteem, lying about one's age or number of sexual partners, acting more confident than one actually feels, exaggerating details to make a story or past achievements more impressive to others, or lying about personal details on dating profiles. Most white lies are relatively acceptable and are told to preserve or improve social relationships or self-esteem. Most are told out of a sense of empathy or kindness, rather than for nefarious purposes. Even children recognize these mistruths as lies, but they do not rate them as negatively as antisocial lies that are told to purposefully manipulate another person.

Most white lies are told for prosocial reasons, and many times everyone knows that the truth is being stretched. White liars also tend to lie only occasionally. However, as illustrated by Dr. Neil Garrett and colleagues from University College London, telling white lies actually desensitizes the amygdala to dishonest behavior. Thus, telling even white lies tends to lead to an escalation in dishonesty in the future. One, in a sense, adjusts to telling lies, and the process starts to feel more comfortable. Getting caught in a lie, even a white lie, can also tarnish one's reputation. Though a white lie may seem innocuous in the moment, it can make others less willing to believe future communications. Though others may not appreciate brutal honesty in the moment, it does give one a sense of credibility in future conversations.

Just as telling white lies comes easier with practice, avoiding the necessity to lie also improves with practice. A good alternative to lying is to skirt around the unacceptable truth. Finding an element of truth to offer and avoiding lies can be just as acceptable in a social situation. Even if individuals do not love a friend's new haircut, they can probably honestly say that they like how confident it seems to make the friend feel. In this sense, brutal honesty is not necessarily the antithesis of white lies. Respectful honesty can maintain relationships, business reputations, and personal identity better than white lies when dealing with sensitive issues.

Telling a white lie can also change how one views a situation and alter future behavior. Dr. Jennifer Argo from the University of Alberta, and Dr. Baba Shiv from Stanford University, demonstrated that when participants were induced to lie to protect the feelings of the experimenter, they subsequently gave significantly higher ratings of the experimenter and were much more likely to donate money, tip, or give a good review of the service provided in the experiment. Likely, by lying, the individuals felt a sense of cognitive dissonance that they then sought to alleviate by aligning their behavior with their lie. Thus, when telling a white lie, individuals may actually facilitate self-deception and adjust their memories, beliefs, and behaviors to align with the lie to alleviate guilt.

See also: Black Lies; Blue Lies; Bluffs; Butler Lies; Categories of Deception; Cognitive Dissonance; Exaggeration; Fibs; Minimization; Motives for Lying; Online Dating; Polite Lies; Prosocial Lying; Self-Deception; Social Intelligence.

Further Reading

Argo, J. J., & Shiv, B. (2012). Are white lies as innocuous as we think? *Journal of Consumer Research, 38*(6), 1093–1102.

Broomfield, K. A., Robinson, E. J., & Robinson, W. P. (2002). Children's understanding about white lies. *British Journal of Developmental Psychology, 20*, 47–65.

Garrett, N., Lazzaro, S. C., Ariely, D., & Sharot, T. (2016). The brain adapts to dishonesty. *Nature Neuroscience, 19*, 1727–1732.

Oesch, N. (2016). Deception as a derived function of language. *Frontiers in Psychology, 7*, 1–7.

Talwar, V., & Lee, K. (2002). Emergence of white-lie telling in children between 3 and 7 years of age. *Merrill-Palmer Quarterly, 48*(2), 160–181.

Weinstein, B. (2019). *Three reasons why white lies are the worst solutions to your problems.* Retrieved from https://www.forbes.com/sites/bruceweinstein/2018/02/28/three-reasons-why-white-lies-are-the-worst-solutions-to-your-problems/?sh=75817824650e

Wizard's Project

The Wizard's Project was a research study started in the 1980s that examined individual differences in the ability to detect lies. Dr. Paul Ekman and Dr. Maureen O'Sullivan, from the University of San Francisco, tested over 20,000 individuals and found a select group (around 50 individuals out of the 20,000 tested) who could detect lies with 80 percent accuracy across different situations and types of deception. They termed these individuals Truth Wizards, as they seemed to have an extraordinary skill at a task in which most people score around chance levels.

Participants in Dr. Ekman and Dr. O'Sullivan's study consisted of untrained individuals as well as professionals who specialize in detecting deception. Participants included government officials, police officers, lawyers, psychologists, investigators, interrogators, and college students, among others. Most (99.75%) of those individuals fell short of Truth Wizard status. In fact, even police officers and psychiatrists tended to score similarly to first-year college students. Only secret service agents were apt to meet the criteria of being a Truth Wizard, and those identified were typically superior interviewers, federal judges, or forensic psychologists.

Participation in the study consisted of completing three lie deception tasks. These tasks included attempting to detect deception related to emotions, opinions, and crimes. To gain Truth Wizard status, participants had to accurately detect lies across all three scenarios. Psychologists tended to be more successful in detecting lies about emotions and opinions, while law professionals tended to be better at detecting lies about crimes. This is likely a result of a natural talent coupled with training in those areas. So, if performance were to be separated by type of lie, more participants would have gained Truth Wizard status for their specialty area. It was highly uncommon to perform well in all three scenarios, however.

The emotion deception task involved watching videos of female student nurses who were watching either a graphic surgical procedure or a peaceful nature film. All the student nurses were asked to act like they were watching a nature film. Since the participants could not see the screen the student nurses were watching, they had to determine whether the student nurses were lying about which film they were watching based on their emotional reactions. The opinion deception task involved watching videos of men who were asked for their opinions on topics they felt strongly about. Some men were asked to describe their opinion truthfully and others were asked to pretend they held the opposite opinion. Participants then were asked whether or not they thought each man was telling the truth or lying. The crime deception task involved watching videos of men who were asked to deny that they stole $50. Some of the participants had stolen the money and some had not. Participants watched one-minute video clips of the men's denials and had to judge whether or not they were telling the truth.

The emotion deception task was found to be the most difficult to judge accurately. Also, as noted earlier, the experience of the participant (law enforcement or psychological training) correlated with performance on the different tasks. Computer analyses revealed that facial movements did differ between truth-tellers and liars for all of the tasks, with more disgust and anger being displayed by the liars. Most individuals, however, did not detect this difference during rating.

Once Truth Wizards were identified, Dr. Ekman and Dr. O'Sullivan observed them as they completed lie detection tasks to deduce what factors the Truth Wizards used to make accurate assessments of lying behavior. Dr. Ekman and Dr. O'Sullivan also interviewed the Truth Wizards about their lives and history and gave them a series of psychological tests such as personality inventories and IQ tests. The Wizards had no significant sex difference, were mostly middle aged (40–60), and tended to refer to nonverbal cues and inconsistencies between verbal statements and nonverbal behavior when analyzing the videos in all three tasks. Wizards tended to pay attention to emotional and cognitive cues when making their assessments. They noted microexpressions of emotions, such as delight, anger, or disgust, which did not fit with the verbal message. These microexpressions are the uncontrolled, fleeting, facial expressions that reveal genuine emotion despite a deceiver's attempt to mask such emotions.

Truth Wizards also tended to notice subtle inconsistencies in rate of speech, hesitations, odd phrases, and effortful or interrupted speech. They were keen observers and noticed changes and abnormalities in the verbal and nonverbal reports. Most Truth Wizards tended to have natural ability as well as professional training to hone their skill. Only four of the fifty identified Truth Wizards were not in a law enforcement profession and almost all fifty had a special interest in lie detection.

One of the four individuals who was not in law enforcement was Renee Ellory, who publishes the *Eyes for Lies* blog. Ms. Ellory has a natural ability to detect deception without any formal training. She has featured many high-profile criminal cases on her blog and provides her opinion about which defendants and witnesses are lying and which are telling the truth. Based on retroactive assessment of her posts, she demonstrates a 95 percent accuracy rate for cases that were later solved and a 100 percent accuracy rate for cases over the last five years. She is especially good at picking up on microexpressions, particularly those at odds with what should be called for given the situation.

Understanding how Truth Wizards detect deception may be key to creating effective training programs for professionals who rely on such skill. Dr. O'Sullivan reports that training in detecting microexpressions can significantly improve an individual's ability to recognize potential liars. Renee Ellory, since being identified as a Truth Wizard, now offers training programs and engages in consulting work for investigators. Training investigators to pay attention to the signals that Truth Wizards use to detect deception may increase their ability to detect lies.

See also: Detecting Deception; Ekman, Paul; Emotional Effects; Intelligence; Microexpressions; Nonverbal Behavior; Social Intelligence; Vocal Changes when Lying.

Further Reading

Camillieri, J. (2009, January 21). Truth Wizard knows when you've been lying. *Chicago Sun Times*, 20.

Ekman, P. (1991). Invited article: Face, voice, and body in detecting deceit. *Journal of Nonverbal Behavior, 15*(2), 125–135.

McDonald, G. (2004, October 14). *Lying and deceit—The Wizard's Project: Can you spot a liar? Experts studying deception learn from the 'wizards' of lie detection*. Retrieved from https://www.eurekalert.org/pub_releases/2004-10/ama-lad100804.php

O'Sullivan, M., & Ekman, P. (2004). The wizards of deception detection. In P. A. Granhag & L. A. Strömwall (Eds.), *The Detection of Deception in Forensic Contexts* (pp. 269–286). Cambridge University Press.

Y

Yellow Journalism (See Fake News)

Index

Page numbers in **bold** indicate the location of main entries.

Abe, Nobuhito, 124, 206, 221
Academic cheating, **1–2,** 56, 156, 235
  common reasons, 1
  in online education, 2
  plagiarism, 1, 2, 45, 147, 234–236
Activation-Decision-Construction-Action
  Theory (ADCAT), 196, 197
Adelson, Rachel, 97
Advertising, **2–5,** 19, 21, 51, 90, 128, 137,
  138, 214, 247, 251, 252, 262, 263, 270,
  280, 282
  Ad Standards (formerly Advertising
    Standards Canada), 4
  embedded, 4
  false advertising, 2, 14, 19, 90, 250
  Federal Trade Commission, 2, 4, 14, 19,
    137, 138
  incomplete comparison claims, 3
  semantic confusion, 2, 3
  See also Bait and switch; Bluffs;
    Clickbait; Competition; Fine print;
    Puffery; Reverse psychology; Smoke
    and mirrors
Age differences, **5–7**
  See also Nonverbal cues; Theory of
    mind
Agreeableness, 82, 206, 226, 227, 258,
  259, 262
Alternative facts, **7–8**
Altruistic lies, 27, 31, 223, 249
  See also Prosocial lies; Prosocial lying
Alzheimer's, 135
Alzheimer's Association, 135
Amazeen, Michelle, 127
Amnesia, 5, 94, 95, 185
  feigning, 94, 95, 185
Amygdala, 124, 206, 305

Anderson, Anna, **9–10,** 151
  Romanov, Anastasia, 9–10, 151
  Schanskowska, Franziska, 9
Anger, 11, 26, 29, 51, 98, 102, 109, 110,
  120, 125, 160, 173, 189, 201, 205, 211,
  240, 273, 294, 307, 308
Animals, 11, 33, 41, 42, 86–87, 164, 170,
  193, 278, 290
  abuse of, 11
  camouflage in, 41, 42
  deception in, 86–87, 290
  mimicry in, 42, 86, 192–194, 290
  See also Organisms
Anterior cingulate cortex, 207
Antisocial lies, 27, 45, 154, 243, 249,
  250, 305
  See also Black lies; Instrumental lies
Antisocial personality disorder (ASPD),
  10–12, 43, 170, 198, 227, 241
  sociopathy, 10
Anxiety, 16, 23, 24, 26, 29, 36, 63, 71, 73,
  76, 77, 85, 91, 92, 95, 97, 98, 110, 111,
  120, 131, 135, 153, 155, 171, 172, 179,
  194, 201, 210, 216, 217, 218, 227, 234,
  240, 241, 249, 259, 264, 269, 272, 273,
  274, 277, 280, 284, 294, 302
Aphasia, 211
Area 51, 71, 115, 144, 145
Arciuli, Joanne, 301
Argo, Jennifer, 306
Arnold, Benedict. *See* Espionage
Arousal, 10, 11, 23, 28, 36, 37, 54, 55, 57,
  65, 73, 79, 96, 97, 108, 109, 118, 124,
  125, 131, 187, 195, 197, 198, 210, 211,
  218, 219, 230, 231, 240, 241, 253, 260,
  269, 270, 282, 301, 302
  autonomic, 230

Arousal (*cont.*)
  brain and nervous system, 109
  cognitive, 55
  of deception, 124
  emotional, 10, 11, 23, 36, 73, 108, 118,
    187, 219, 253
  hyper-arousal, 28
  motivational, 198
  physiological, 73, 97, 198, 218, 219, 230,
    231, 240, 302
  signals of, 36, 211
  See also Control Questions Test;
    Polygraph tests; Physiology; Saxe,
    Leonard
Art of War, The, **12–13,** 290
Astroturfing, **14–15**
  front groups, 14
Atypical pause, 98, 210
Autism, 7, 15–17, 71, 127
Autism spectrum disorder (ASD), **15–17**
Autonomy, 45, 93, 144, 170, 173, 174, 223,
  224, 230
Aydogan, Gokham, 61–62
Axelrod, Robert, 246
Azizli, Nicole, 82

Bait and switch, **19–20,** 270, 280
  See also Diversionary tactics; False
    advertising; Federal Trade
    Commission; Half-truths; Scams
Baker, Alysha, 156
Bakos, Yannis, 138
Bald-faced lies, **20–22,** 32
Barefaced lie. *See* Bald-faced lies
Baron-Cohen, Simon, 125
BASIC system, 188
Bastos, Marco, 248
Baumrind, Diana, 174
Bavelas, Janet, 112
Beauducel, Andre, 54
Becker, Howard, 247
Bedi, Akanksha, 235
Behavior Analysis Interview (BAI),
  22–24, 99, 219, 277, 304
Behavioral perspective, 201
Belschak, Frank D., 169
Bending the truth, **24–25,** 144
Benefits of lying, **25–28,** 68, 69,
  70, 76, 108, 110, 117, 118, 154,
  156, 168, 196, 208, 214, 223, 264,
  272, 278
Besken, Miri, 184–185

Betrayal, **28–30,** 77, 115, 245–246, 264
Big Five personality traits, 226–227
  agreeableness, 82, 206, 226, 227, 262
  conscientiousness, 68, 81, 226, 227, 271
  extraversion, 187, 226, 227
  neuroticism, 166, 226, 271
  openness to new experience, 226, 227
Bigley, Elizabeth. *See* Chadwick, Cassie
Birnbaum, Gurit, 83
Bishara, Norman, 75
Black lies, **30–31,** 249
Black Lives Matter (BLM), 248, 259
Blanchard, Matt, 237
Blinking, 125, 210, 211
Blood pressure, 29, 64, 73, 97, 109, 110,
  239, 240
Bloom, Charlie, 76
Bloom, Linda, 76
Blue lies, **31–32,** 100
Bluff, 26, **33–34,** 45, 155, 245, 258, 305
Body movements, 60, 98, 124, 125,
  210, 211
Bold-faced lies. *See* Bald-faced lies
Borderline personality disorder (BPD),
  34–36, 63
Boynton, Marcella, 88
Bradley, Michael, 73
Brewer, Gayle, 264
Brokaw Hazard, **36–37**
Bromley, Patricia, 280
Brown, Penelope, 170
Bullshit. *See* Careless liars
Bushway, Ann, 2
Buss, David, 153, 181
Bussey, Kay, 45
Butler lies, **37–39,** 45, 76, 200, 305

Calibrate. *See* Meyer, Pamela
Camouflage, 26, **41–42,** 86, 193
  in animals, 41, 86, 193
  in the military, 42
  See also Deception in animals
Careless liars, **42–44,** 45
Carnegie, Andrew, 47, 48, 151
Categories of deception, 41, **44–45,** 107,
  120, 154, 192, 243
Catfishing, **46–47,** 215
  Catfish: The TV Show, 46
  Joseph, Max, 46
  Schulman, Nev, 46
  See also Phishing
Chadwick, Cassie, **47–49,** 151

Chakraborty, Archishman, 251

Charm, 11, 48, 49, 63, 34, 178, 180, 181, 242, 270

Charlatans, **49–50**

Cheating. *See* Academic cheating; Infidelity

Cheung, Him, 236

Cho, Charles, 14

Clandestine operations. *See* Diversionary tactics; Espionage

Clickbait, **50–52,** 129

Coercion, 11, **52–54,** 94, 131, 136, 141, 180, 181, 192, 260, 261

Cognitions, 197

Cognitive
   ability, 5, 8, 27, 54–55, 99, 101, 118, 128, 129, 155, 160, 167, 168, 177, 275
   arousal, 55
   bias, 216
   complexity, 159, 160, 163
   control, 125, 167, 207, 254
   cues, 308
   decline, 5, 92
   demands, 85, 196, 301
   depleting, 70
   development, 63, 100, 172
   differences, 54, 55
   dissonance. *See* Cognitive dissonance
   dysfunction, 221, 222
   effort, 55, 124, 164, 185, 187, 195, 253
   factors, 131, 255
   function, 54, 293
   growth, 27
   inflexibility, 221
   intelligence, 156
   interpretations, 29
   lies, 44, 275
   load, 55, 99, 159, 186, 187, 195
   maturation, 99, 101, 144
   model, 253
   perspective, 186, 254
   potential, 160
   process, 54, 79, 92, 124, 133, 160, 163, 184, 199, 255
   resources, 54, 133, 159, 184, 186, 196, 197, 253
   responses, 70, 240
   strain, 159, 196
   systems, 230
   See also Cognitive Strain Model; Mental effort

Cognitive-based approach, 240

Cognitive-behavioral therapy, 91

Cognitive changes while lying, **54–55**

Cognitive dissonance, 51, **55–57,** 58, 66, 75, 141, 148, 194, 217, 286, 306
   See also Suspension of disbelief

Cognitive distortion, 34, **57–59,** 102, 103, 124, 133, 141, 184, 250, 274, 287, 297
   in sexual offenders, 58
   unethical amnesia, 58
   See also Alternative facts; Borderline personality disorder; Diversionary tactics; Fabrication; False memory; Gaslighting; Memory; Minimization; Puffery; Suspension of Disbelief

Cognitive Load Approach (CLA), 195, 196

Cognitive Strain Model, 159, 195, 196

Collectivist cultures, 32, 78, 148

Collusion. *See* Conspiracy theories

Commission, lies of, 44, **59–61,** 98, 124, 213, 214

Comparison Question Test. *See* Control Questions Test

Competition, 1, 8, 13, 14, 15, 24, 26, 33, 60, **61–62,** 68, 75, 81, 86, 90, 102, 110, 114, 115, 118, 119, 125, 177, 196, 208, 214, 217, 235, 237, 245–246, 257, 258, 262–263, 279, 282, 285, 289, 291, 295
   athletic, 13, 26, 33, 61, 102, 103, 289, 295
   between classes, 208
   in business or marketing, 3, 14, 61, 62, 68, 90, 196, 214, 258, 282, 285, 289
   in dating or romance, 62, 83, 289
   in games, 15, 33, 60, 125, 257, 262–263, 289
   in nature, 86, 279
   oxytocin, 62
   in political campaigns, 14, 62, 90, 102, 103, 285, 289
   in research, 235
   social, 237, 282, 289, 291
   in war, 13, 289
   See also Academic cheating; *Art of War, The*; Astroturfing; Bluffs; Diversionary tactics; Prisoner's dilemma; Sockpuppets; Strategies of successful bluffers; Tactical deception

Compliments, 27, 108, 117, 152, 180, 181, 182, 200, 251, 262, 305

Compulsive lying, 43, **62–64,** 242

Con, 47, 48, 49, 151, 205, 270
　See also Chadwick, Cassie; Charlatans;
　　Impersonator; Scams
Concealed Information Test (CIT), **64–66,**
　72, 73, 99, 132, 219, 240, 260
Conditioned behavior, 86
Conduct disorder, 241
Confabulation. See False memory
Confronting, 13, 21, 43, 45, 54, 58, 64, 77,
　83, 91, 95, 109, 113, 148–149, 153,
　195, 200, 235, 242, 245, 259, 267, 273,
　278, 296
Conscience, 11, **66–68**
Conscientiousness, 68, 81, 226, 227, 271
Consequences, 2, 11, 23, 24, 27, 30, 31, 33,
　34, 53, 54, 55, 68–70, 74, 76, 89, 96,
　100, 110, 115, 116, 117, 131, 135, 154,
　155, 168, 170, 171, 173, 174, 191, 192,
　193, 194, 201, 213, 214, 216, 217, 218,
　223, 236, 239–240, 245
　See also Consequences of lying
Consequences of lying, 24, 27, 30, 34,
　54–55, **68–70,** 76, 89, 96, 100, 117,
　135, 154, 172, 201, 213, 214, 218, 223,
　243, 269, 271, 296
　See also Benefits of lying; Costs of
　　lying; Defamation; Lying at work;
　　Lying to parents; Othello Error;
　　Polygraph tests
Conspiracies. See Conspiracy theories
Conspiracy theories, 48, **71–72,** 115, 144,
　164, 248
Continued influence effect of
　misinformation (CIEM), 7, 8
Contempt, 89, 189, 210
　of court, 64
Conway, Kellyanne, 7
Control questions, 253
Control Questions Test (CQT), **72–74,** 99,
　219, 240
Cooperation, 11, 27, 32, 52, 62, 66, 68, 75,
　93, 111, 112, 135, 136, 143, 155, 165,
　166, 169, 171, 177, 178, 181, 188, 208,
　209, 230, 245, 246, 247, 258, 260,
　263, 279, 282, 289, 291, 305
　advantages of, 289
　by abusive parents in therapy, 136
　effects of oxytocin on, 62
　in business, 68, 155, 289
　in children, 135, 155, 171
　by dementia patients, 93
　in corruption, 75

in games or sports, 246, 263, 289
in suspects, 246, 260
at work, 169
　See also Prisoner's dilemma
Corruption, **74–76,** 169, 170, 209, 239
Corruption Perception Index, 74
Costs of lying, 27, 68, **76–77**
　See also Benefits of lying;
　　Consequences of lying
Couwenberg, Judge Patrick, 63
Covert operations. See Diversionary
　tactics; Espionage
Cover-ups. See Espionage
Crime scenarios, 54, 65–66, 190, 198, 231
Criminal behavior, 11, 54, 71, 82, 95, 136,
　151, 224
Criminal investigations, 72, 132, 134, 268,
　270, 293, 308
Critical thinking, 7, 8, 126, 129, 182, 270,
　286, 287
Crop circles, 144
Cultural differences, **78–79,** 303
　in corruption, 75
Cultural display rules, 84, 100, 190, 218,
　249, 267
Curtis, Drew, 225
Curtis, Shelby R., 82

Dahlen, Eric R., 120
Dark Triad, 30, **81–82,** 294
　psychopathy, 30, 31, 81–82, 115, 177,
　　226–227, 230, 241, 294
　See also Machiavellianism; Narcissism;
　　Personality
Dating, 53, **82–84,** 174, 241
　See also Online dating
Dawson, Charles. See Piltdown Man
Debasement, 181
Debey, Evelyne, 5–6
Deceiver stereotype, **84–86,** 121, 122, 302
Deception
　in animals. See Deception in animals;
　　Primates
　detecting. See Detecting deception
　development of. See Development of
　　deception
　direct, 88
　evolution of. See Evolution of deception
　Four-Factor Theory of, 197
　higher-order, 86–87, 244–245, 255,
　　256–257
　indirect, 88

by journalists, 182
nonverbal indicators, 84
reactive, 61
in research. *See* Deception in research
in social groups, 55
Deception flowchart, 93
Deception in animals, **86–87,** 278, 290
See also Primates
Deception in research, **87–89,** 147, 298
false feedback, 88–89
level of professionalism, 88–89
task deception, 88–89
See also Milgram's obedience
experiments; Tuskegee Syphilis
Study
Defamation, **89–91**
in the Internet age, 90
political tool, 90
See also Slander
Defense mechanism, 94, 95, 194, 274
Delusions, **91–92,** 113–114
See also Erotomania
Dementia, **92–94,** 135, 221, 223
Denial, 44, **94–95,** 124, 160, 188, 274, 307
DePaulo, Bella, 21, 44, **95–97,** 195, 198,
227, 263, 297
See also Categories of deception
Depression, 24, 27, 29, 46, 63, 107, 110,
120, 152, 166, 172, 179, 216, 217, 264,
272, 273, 280, 284, 294
Detecting deception, 2, 6, 10–11, 13, 15–16,
20, 30, 33, 36, 37, 55, 59, 65, 73, 74,
78–79, 82, 85, 95–96, **97–99,** 107,
109, 118, 120, 121, 122, 124, 125, 130,
139, 143, 153, 155, 156, 157, 160, 163,
179, 186, 187–188, 190, 195, 196, 197,
198–199, 200, 201, 205, 206, 207, 208,
210, 211, 214, 215, 218, 224–225, 227,
228–229, 230–231, 238, 239–241, 243,
249, 253–254, 255, 257, 261, 263, 269–
270, 271, 272, 273, 276, 281, 284, 287,
291, 293, 295, 302, 303–304, 306–308
age differences, 6, 96, 121–122, 174,
293–297
difficulty in, 10–11, 15–16, 125, 143,
156, 160, 186, 198–199, 224–225, 228,
231, 238, 241, 243, 249, 264, 270, 271,
273, 284
feeling cues, 107
functional magnetic resonance imaging,
206–208
gender differences, 96, 276
thinking cues, 107
See also Behavior Analysis Interview;
Brokaw Hazard; Concealed
Information Test; Control Questions
Test; Cultural differences; DePaulo,
Bella; Ekman, Paul; Evolution of
deception; Fraud; Linguistic Inquiry
and Word Count analysis program;
Meyer, Pamela; Polygraph tests;
Reality monitoring; Reid Technique;
Sherlock Holmes Effect; Truth-
Default Theory; Vrij, Aldert;
Wizard's Project
Development of deception, **99–101,** 107
primary lies, 100
secondary lies, 100
tertiary lies, 100
See also Ekman, Paul
Disappointing gift, 16, 100, 267
paradigm, 100
Disappointing gift task. *See* Saarni,
Carolyn
Disengagement, 67, 227
Disgust, 26, 98, 107, 109, 125, 189, 211,
307, 308
Distress, 28, 29, 58, 91, 94, 131, 135, 153,
189, 262
Diversionary responses, 143
Diversionary tactics, **102–103,** 280
covert operations, 103, 114–115
in politics, 102
in sports, 103
See also Espionage
DNA test, 10
Domestic violence, 152, 195
Door-in-the-face tactic. *See* Reverse
psychology
Dopamine, 207, 221, 222
reward system, 222
Double agent. *See* Espionage
Doublespeak, **103–105**
enhanced interrogation, 104
ethnic cleansing, 104
Dresher, Melvin, 245
Drouin, Michelle, 215
Dumas, Tara, 283
Duping delight, 109
Dyad, 172
Dyadic, 143

Ebner, Natalie, 140
Effortful process, 8, 184

Ekman, Paul, **107–109,** 124, 125, 188, 189, 190, 200, 210, 218, 224, 225, 306, 307
  feeling cues, 107
  Lie to Me, 107
  thinking cues, 107
  See also Microexpressions; Othello Error; Wizard's Project
Elaad, Eitan, 205
Electrodermal activity, 64, 73, 240
Elifson, Kirk, 280
Ellory, Renee, 308
Elvish, Ruth, 93
Embellishment, 25, 215, 296
  See also Exaggeration
Emotional effects, **109–111**
  duping delight, 109
Emotional health, 109, 156
Emotional intelligence, 156, 281
  See also Intelligence; Social intelligence
Emotions, 11, 29, 34, 35, 51, 52, 53, 58, 73, 86, 94, 102, 107, 108, 109–111, 120, 126, 151, 156, 160, 163, 164, 168, 173, 178, 181, 189, 190, 205, 211, 216, 218, 240, 264, 267, 273, 274, 287, 294, 301, 307, 308
  anger, 11, 26, 29, 51, 98, 102, 109, 110, 120, 125, 160, 173, 189, 201, 205, 211, 240, 273, 294, 307, 308
  anxiety, 16, 23, 24, 26, 29, 36, 63, 71, 73, 76, 77, 85, 91, 92, 95, 97, 98, 110, 111, 120, 131, 135, 153, 155, 171, 172, 179, 194, 201, 210, 216, 217, 218, 227, 234, 240, 241, 249, 259, 264, 269, 272, 273, 274, 277, 280, 284, 294, 302
  contempt, 89, 189, 210
  depression, 24, 27, 29, 46, 63, 107, 110, 120, 152, 166, 172, 179, 216, 217, 264, 272, 273, 280, 284, 294
  disgust, 26, 98, 107, 109, 125, 153, 189, 211, 307, 308
  distress, 28, 29, 58, 91, 94, 131, 135, 189, 262
  fake, 156
  fear, 102, 107, 131, 145, 152, 189, 206, 218, 229, 240, 245, 247, 285
  genuine or true, 107, 109, 110, 125, 126, 189, 190, 267, 287, 308
  glee, 98, 107, 125, 189
  guilt (as emotion), 5, 10, 11, 21, 31, 34, 35, 36, 53, 56, 57, 58, 67, 68, 76, 94, 95, 96, 110, 152, 169, 174, 180, 181,

182, 189, 190, 194, 197, 210, 218, 219, 227, 230, 240, 242, 243, 249, 276, 306
  hate, 163, 247
  hidden, 107, 125
  jealousy, 29, 114
  masked, 11, 91, 109, 178, 189, 211, 267, 308
  negative, 29, 35, 58, 94, 109, 156, 160, 163, 181, 250, 267, 294
  positive, 11, 29, 107, 163, 169, 170, 172, 216
  regulating, 34, 91, 156, 207, 267–268
  simulated, 96, 109
  suppression of, 26, 54, 58, 96, 100, 118, 189, 254, 272, 274
  surprise, 15, 73, 99, 189
  See also Saarni, Carolyn
Empathy, 10, 27, 30, 43, 53, 67, 81, 153, 174, 178, 181, 205, 206, 237, 242, 250, 281, 291, 305
Equivocation, 103, **111–113**
Erotomania, **113–114**
Eskritt, Michelle, 6, 249
Espionage, 103, **114–116**
  Arnold, Benedict, 115
  clandestine operations, 102, 103, 114–115
  covert operations, 52, 72, 102, 103, 114–115
  cover-ups, 114–115
  Defense Personnel Security Research Center, 115
  double agents, 114–115
  See also Coercion; Diversionary tactics
Ethics, 30, 33, 57, 58, 60, 61, 62, 67, 68, 75, 88, 92, 93, **116–117,** 130, 139, 146, 147, 148, 170, 178, 191, 192, 208, 223, 224, 225, 233, 258, 272, 298, 299
  American Dental Association, 117
  American Medical Association, 117
  American Psychological Association, 116, 117
  codes of ethics, 116–117
  Institutional Review Board, 88, 104, 117, 299
  social contract theory, 116
  See also Cognitive distortion; Tuskegee Syphilis Study
Euphemisms, 103, 104, 248
  See also Doublespeak

Evasion, 13, 23, 83, 102, 112, 180, 238, 276, 304
  See also Diversionary tactics; Equivocation
Event-related potential, 240
Evolution of deception, 41, 86, **118–119,** 153, 160, 168, 188, 192, 193, 278, 290, 291
  See also Deception in animals; Recursive awareness; Tactical deception; Theory of mind
Evolutionary arms race, 119, 160, 168, 188, 291
Exaggeration, 4, 6, 14, 15, 24, 25, 30, 44, 45, 47, 51, 52, 56, 60, 63, 64, 69, 77, 84, 110, **119–121,** 127, 143, 144, 147, 155, 167, 169, 170, 179, 184, 185, 200, 202, 205, 215, 227, 242, 243, 250–251, 283, 284, 305
  See also Bending the truth; Malingering; Puffery
Exclusionary words, 160
Executive functioning, 5, 6, 100, 124, 155, 168, 187, 206, 207, 221, 222, 254
Extraversion, 187, 226, 227
Eye gaze, 16, 23, 79, 84, 98, **121–122,** 125, 289, 302
Eye contact, 23, 37, 79, 85, 97, 98, 121, 122, 125, 188, 210, 219, 260, 302, 303

Fabrication, 5, 16, 24, 30, 44, 45, 47, 48, 52, 60, 77, 90, 94, 95, 98, 101, **123–124,** 126, 128, 133, 134, 144, 146, 147, 160, 167, 168, 184, 185, 186, 187, 196, 244, 253, 254, 255, 256, 257, 258, 289, 301
Facial action coding system (FACS), 107, 218
  See also Ekman, Paul
Facial cues, **124–126**
  See also Eye gaze; Microexpressions
Fact-check, 7, 21, **126–128,** 141, 145, 182
  FactCheck.org, 127
  Snopes.com, 127, 145
Factitious disorder, 63
  See also Munchausen syndrome
Fake news, 7, 51, 90, 126, **128–130,** 145, 228, 287
Fallon, Laura, 52
False advertising, 2, 14, 19, 90, 250
  See also Astroturfing
False-belief task, 291

False confessions, 22, 33, 52, 53, 65, 73, **130–132,** 136, 260–261, 269, 293
  coerced-compliant, 131
  coerced-internalized, 131
  voluntary, 131
  See also Reid Technique
False future behavior, 102
False information, 5, 51, 52, 54, 57, 59, 89, 90, 94, 100, 123, 124, 127, 130, 182, 183, 184, 185, 215, 257, 289
False memory, 95, **132–134,** 185, 256, 260, 303
  See also Memory
False signals, 119, 193, 278, 289
  See also Signaling theory
Farber, Barry, 237
Farkas, Johan, 248
Fear, 102, 107, 131, 145, 152, 189, 206, 218, 229, 240, 245, 247, 285
Federal Trade Commission (FTC), 2, 4, 14, 19, 137, 138
Feedback loop, 37, 43, 56, 77, 160, 216, 218
Feeling cues, 107, 108
Feldman, Robert, 26–27, 199
Feltovich, Nick, 61
Fibs, 45, **134–135,** 305
Fidgeting, 23, 26, 84, 85, 98, 121, 198, 210, 230, 302
Fifth Amendment, **135–137,** 225
Fillers, 97, 163, 164, 301
Fine print, 19, **137–138,** 271
Flattery, 178, 180, 181, 182, 205, 206
Flood, Merrill, 245
Fong, Christina, 199, 261
Foot-in-the-door phenomenon, 191, 261
  See also Milgram's obedience experiment; Reverse psychology
Foot-jiggling, 210
Forrest, James, 199
Four-Factor Theory of deception, 197
Fraud, 2, 4, 46, 48, 49, 51, 121, **139–140,** 144, 146, 147, 151, 152, 183, 187, 188, 229, 234, 239, 270, 273
  insurance claims, 139
  susceptibility to, 139–140, 271, 287
  See also Charlatans; Hwang Woo-Suk; Identity theft; Phishing; Plagiarism; Scams
Fraud Magazine, 188
Freud, Sigmund, 133
Frontal lobe, 92, 189, 206

Functional magnetic resonance imaging
    (fMRI), 92, 206, 207, 208
Fundamental attribution error, 148
    See also Hypocrisy

Gallini, Brian, 260
Garrett, Neil, 305
Gaslighting, 52, 102, 103, **141–142**
    See also Diversionary tactics
Gaze aversion, 84, 85, 97, 121, 122, 198,
    210, 245, 302
    See also Eye gaze
Gbadamosi, Gbolahan, 50
Gender differences, 96, 187, 302, 303
    See also Sex differences in lying
    behavior
Gerlach, Philipp, 275
Gestures, 16, 84, 85, 97, 210
Gilovich, Thomas, 293
Gingo, Matthew, 174
Gino, Francesca, 57–58
God, 208, 225
Gordon, Andrew, 7–8
Government, 14, 71, 72, 75, 103, 104,
    114, 115, 208, 223, 228, 247, 285,
    286, 294, 299, 307
Guadagno, Rosanna, 84
Guilty Knowledge Test. *See* Concealed
    Information Test
Guitar, Amanda, 153

Half-truths, **143–144**
    diversionary responses, 143
    See also Bending the truth
Hand movements, 85, 210, 221
Harbaugh, Rick, 251
Heart rate, 97, 110, 231, 239, 240
Hendrick, Clyde, 137
Hertwig, Ralph, 275
Heyman, Gail, 171
High-stakes lies, 30, 31, 55, 76, 82, 109,
    155, 200, 201, 210, 243, 249, 275
    See also Black lies
Hira, Shinji, 65
Hoax, 47, 49, **144–146,** 162, 164, 165, 232
    crop circles, 144
    War of the Worlds, The, radio broadcast,
    145
    Wilson, Dr. Robert Kenneth, 145, 164
    See also Conspiracy theories; Loch
    Ness Monster; Lightfoot, Lucy;
    Piltdown Man
Hochhauser, Mark, 104

Hofstetter, Emily, 262
Hollander, Dory, 83
Honig, Benson, 235
Hormones, 110, 230
Howard, Krista, 295
Hrgovic, Josip, 272
Hromatko, Ivana, 272
Hwang Woo-Suk, **146–147**
Hypochondriasis, 179, 202
Hypocrisy, **148–149**

Identity lies, 155
Identity theft, 46, 151, 270
    See also Impersonator; Scams
Illusion of transparency, 292, 293, 303
    See also Transparent lies and the
    illusion of transparency
Impersonator, **151–152**
    imposter syndrome, 152
Impression management, 50, 144, 148,
    238, 243
Impulsivity, 11, 20, 34, 81, 82, 179, 181,
    241, 275
Incomplete comparison claims, 3
Individualistic cultures, 78, 148, 250
Infidelity, 28, 29, 141, 142, 148, **152–154,**
    213, 264
Information Manipulation Theory 2
    (IMT2), 195, 196, 238
Informed consent, 104, 117, 299
Inhibitory control, 5, 27, 58, 100, 163,
    168, 183, 215, 253, 254, 257, 284,
    289, 294
Institutional Review Board (IRB), 88, 104,
    117, 299
    See also Ethics
Instrumental lies, **154–155,** 169, 236, 249
Intelligence, 2, 11, 12, 13, 63, 83, 114, 115,
    152, **155–157,** 166, 226, 272, 294
    cognitive intelligence, 156
    emotional intelligence, 156, 281
    level, 11, 166, 226
    See also Machiavellianism; Social
    intelligence
Internet Research Agency (IRA), 248
Interrogation, 22, 33, 36, 52, 55. 99, 104,
    123, 130, 131, 132, 133, 134, 136,
    141, 163, 184, 185, 186, 188, 190, 195,
    198, 210, 218, 219, 245, 246, 260, 277,
    293, 303
    methods, tactics, or techniques, 36, 131,
    132, 195, 219, 260, 293
    See also Reid Technique

Intimacy, 11, 25, 45, 53, 68, 76, 83, 84, 110, 133, 144, 153, 177, 178, 200, 223, 251, 264, 275, 299
Introvert, 187, 226
Investigator bias, 131
Izotovas, Aleksandras, 255

Kassin, Saul, 199, 261
Katz, Amy, 53
Kaylor-Hughes, Catherine, 92
Kelly, Anita, 77, 111
Kisaalita, Nkaku, 233
Klein, Hugh, 280
Kniffin, Kevin M., 295
Knopp, Kayla, 153
Kocur, Dagna, 34
Koko the gorilla, 87, 244, 290
    See also Primates
Korean cloning scandal. *See* Hwang Woo-Suk
Kouchaki, Maryam, 57–58

LaFreniere, Peter, 60, 101, 118, 125, 257, 289
Lamarche, Veronica, 53
Lancer, Darlene, 76
Language, 26, 79, 97, 98, 100, 107, **159–161**, 162, 163, 167, 168, 188, 189, 196, 211, 235, 244, 281, 290, 292
    barriers, 189
    body, 26, 97, 98, 107, 292
    sign, 87, 244, 290
Lavoie, Jennifer, 154, 236
Leal, Sharon, 139
Lee, Kang, 6, 32, 171, 249
Leg movements, 23, 85, 210
Leue, Anja, 54
Levine, Emma, 27, 249
Levine, Timothy, 243, 297
Lewin, Roger, 244
Liars, types of, 242
    careless liars, 42–44
    compulsive liars, 63–64, 242
    habitual liars, 69, 242
    occasional liars, 242, 243
    pathetic liars, 242
    pathological liars, 43, 207, 242
    prolific liars, 76, 242–243, 297
    prosocial liars, 30, 69, 250
    sociopathic liars, 11, 242
    white liars, 30, 242, 305
Libel. *See* Defamation
Lie detector tests, 109, 303

See also Polygraph tests
Lies, types of, 30, 44, 45, 69, 101, 108, 236, 249, 264
    altruistic lies, 27, 31, 223, 249
    bald-faced lies, 20–22, 32
    black lies, 30–31, 249
    blue lies, 31–33, 100
    bluff, 26, 33–34, 45, 155, 245, 258, 305
    butler lies, 37–39, 45, 76, 200, 305
    catfishing, 46–47, 215
    commission, 44, 59–61, 98, 124, 213, 214
    cover-ups. *See* Espionage
    fibs, 45, 134–135, 305
    half-truths, 143–144
    high-stakes lies, 30, 31, 55, 76, 82, 109, 155, 200, 201, 210, 243, 249, 275
    hoax, 47, 49, 144–146, 162, 164, 165, 232
    identity lies, 155
    instrumental lies, 154–155, 171, 236, 249
    low-stakes lies, 76, 108, 196, 200, 201, 210, 242, 249, 305
    malingering, 56, 63, 120, 178–180, 202
    noble lies, 208–209
    occasional lies, 154
    omission, 21, 44, 59, 60, 98, 124, 182, 213–214, 238, 243
    other-oriented lies, 183
    paternalistic lies, 209, 223–224
    perjury, 136, 137, 224–226
    polite lies, 5, 16, 37, 38, 45, 69, 100, 101, 173, 236–238
    primary lies, 100
    prosocial lies, 27, 30, 31, 45, 68, 96, 99, 100, 243
    puffery, 250–252
    relational lies, 154, 155, 199
    secondary lies, 100
    self-deception, 20, 24, 27, 56, 58, 76, 91, 94, 95, 110, 114, 123, 148, 205, 206, 216, 217, 272–274, 306
    self-serving lies, 183, 275
    tertiary lies, 100
    transparent lies, 16, 292
    white lies, 27, 30, 31, 45, 69, 76, 93, 110, 172, 173, 198, 200, 222, 223, 230, 242, 243, 249, 291, 296, 305–306
Liespotting: Proven Techniques to Detect Deception. See Meyer, Pamela
Lightfoot, Lucy, 144, **161–162**

Limbic system, 109, 189, 206, 287
Linguistic Inquiry and Word Count
  (LIWC) analysis program, 159,
  162–164
  Pennebaker, Dr. James W., 159, 162–163
Lloyd, E. Paige, 79
Loch Ness Monster, 144, 145, **164–165**
  Boyd, Alastair, 165
  Martin, David, 165
  Wetherell, Marmaduke, 145, 164, 165
Locus of control, 67, 71, 156, **165–167,**
  180, 217, 235, 242, 271
  Mudrack, Peter, 166
Logue, Michael, 255
Lopes, Barbara, 294
Low-stakes lies, 76, 108, 196, 200, 201,
  210, 242, 249, 305
  See also White lies
Lying, **167–168**
Lying, models of. *See* Models of lying
Lying, motives for. *See* Motives for lying
Lying, prevalence of. *See* Prevalence of
  lying.
Lying at work, 77, **168–170,** 241
Lying to children, 5, 25, 135, 155,
  170–172, 223
  See also Fibs
Lying to parents, 5, 25, 45, 100, 144, 154,
  166, **172–175,** 241, 275
Lying to partners. *See* Romantic
  relationships

MacDonald, Geoff, 262
Machiavellian intelligence. *See*
  Machiavellianism
Machiavellianism, 30, 31, 73, 74, 81, 82,
  153, 166, 169, **177–178,** 181, 294
  Game of Thrones, 178
  Lord Baelish and Lord Varys, 178
  Machiavelli, Niccolo, 177
  Machiavellian intelligence, 177
  Martin, George R. R., 178
  Prince, The, 177
  Tony Soprano, 178
  See also Dark Triad
Macroexpressions, 189
Malingering, 56, 63, 120, **179–180,** 202
  by proxy, 180
  Test of Memory Malingering, 179
  Word Memory Test, 179
Mameli, Francesca, 222
Mandal, Eugenia, 34–35

Manipulation, 4, 35, 52, 74, 81, 102, 119,
  141, 143, **180–182,** 183, 195, 196, 210,
  223, 238, 239, 262, 291
  silent treatment, 181
  See also Information Manipulation
  Theory 2
Mann, Samantha, 122
March, Evita, 294
Marchand, Marie, 20
Marrington, Jessica, 294
Martin, Ryan C., 120
Masui, Keita, 294
Mate selection. *See* Dating; Romantic
  relationships
McCornack, Steven, 196
Meatpuppet, 285
Media, 7, 8, 15, 51, 90, 104, 114, 126, 127,
  128, 129, 136, **182–184,** 248
  in the European Union, 15
  in the United States, 15
  See also Clickbait; Fact-check; Fake
  news; Social media
Memory, 5, 7, 8, 9, 124, 133–134,
  184–185, 254
  See also False memory
Mental effort, 54, 55, **186–187,** 255, 303
Mental health, 10, 26, 46, 53, 68, 69, 70,
  76, 77, 110, 111, 121, 162, 216, 217,
  223, 236
Merckelbach, Harald, 94
Meyer, Pamela, **187–189**
Microexpressions, 107, 108, 124, 125,
  189–190, 211, 308
  See also Ekman, Paul; Facial cues;
  Nonverbal behavior; Wizard's Project
Milgram's obedience experiments, 88,
  191–192
Military, 12, 13, 42, 103, 104, 114, 115,
  179, 247, 290
  See also Art of War, The; Camouflage;
  Espionage
Miller, Angela, 1
Miller, Mark, 201
Mimicry, 14, 24, 41, 86, **192–194,** 218,
  229, 248, 278, 290, 301
  See also Camouflage; Deception in
  animals
Minimization, 24, 26, 52, 58, 83, 95,
  144, 148, 184, **194–195,** 200,
  262, 305
Minnesota Multiphasic Personality
  Inventory-2 (MMPI-2), 120

Misinformation, 7, 8, 14, 15, 48, 60, 71,
    88, 101, 125, 126, 127, 128, 129, 130,
    134, 141, 183, 247, 248, 257, 279, 285,
    290, 294
Misperception, 44, 58, 111, 141,
    142, 243
Models of lying, **195–197**
    Activation-Decision-Construction-
        Action Theory, 195, 196, 197
    Cognitive Load Approach, 195, 196
    Cognitive Strain Model, 159, 195, 196
    Information Manipulation Theory 2,
        195, 196, 197, 238
    Strategic Model, 159, 195, 196
    Working Memory Model, 195, 196, 197
Morality, 66, 67, 178, 209, 234, 236
    types in childhood development, 66
    See also Conscience
Motivational impairment effect, **198–199,**
    230, 297
Motives for lying, **199–202**
Mudrack, Peter, 166
Munchausen by proxy. *See* Munchausen
    syndrome
Munchausen syndrome, 179, **202–204**
Mutually beneficial lies. *See* Prosocial lies
Mythomania. *See* Compulsive lying

Nahari, Galit, 255
Narcissism, 30, 31, 53, 81, 82, 115,
    141, 177, 181, **205–206,** 226, 227,
    283, 294
    entitlement, 200, 205
    exhibitionism, 205
    Narcissism Personality Inventory, 205
    self-sufficiency, 205
    vanity, 205
    See also Dark Triad
Narcissistic personality disorder, 63, 120
Nash, William, 2
National Institute of Health, 147
Negative emotion words, 160, 163
Negative feedback cycle, 70, 110, 169
Negative reinforcement, 181
Negotiations, 12, 13, 16, 25, 27, 33, 68,
    102, 155, 174, 178, 214, 258, 282,
    289, 291
Neuroimaging, 206, 207, 254
Neuropsychological, 120, 179, 180,
    221, 222
    research, 221, 222
Neuroscience, **206–208**

transcranial direct current stimulation,
    207
transcranial magnetic stimulation, 207
white matter, 207
Neurotic, 166, 226, 271
Neuroticism, 166, 226
Neutral expressions, 109
Ni, Preston, 181
Nihei, Yoshiaki, 276
Noble lies, **208–209**
    Plato, 208, 209
    Republic, The, 208
    Socrates, 208
Nodding, 11, 23, 96, 210
Nonverbal behavior, 5, 16, 22, 23, 60, 64,
    79, 85, 96, 99, 107, 121, 168, 198,
    209–211, 218, 253, 260, 286, 292,
    301, 302, 303, 308
Nonverbal cues, 6, 37, 41, 59, 97, 98,
    118, 187, 199, 210, 211, 218, 219,
    225, 303, 307
Norris, Gareth, 271
Nyhan, Brendan, 127

Obstruction of justice, 239
    See also Fifth Amendment
Occasional liars, 242, 243
Occasional lies, 154
    See also White Lies
Omission, lies of, 21, 44, 59, 60, 98, 124,
    182, **213–214,** 238, 243
Online dating, 46, 47, 163, **214–216,** 283
Openness, 29, 75, 110, 175, 188, 226, 227
Optimism bias, **216–217**
Organisms, 41, 192, 193
    See also Animals
Orlins, Emily, 237
O'Sullivan, Maureen, 98, 108, 190, 224,
    225, 306, 307, 308
Otgaar, Henry, 94, 133
Othello Error, 37, **218–219**
    Othello, 218
    Shakespeare, William, 218
Other-oriented lies, 183

Palacio, Dylan, 295
Palsane, Madan, 57
Paltering, 213–214, 225, 238
    See also Omission, lies of
Paraverbal
    behavior, 26, 97, 99, 121, 301, 302
    cues, 27, 98, 124, 125, 196

Paraverbal communication. *See* Vocal changes when lying
Parental rights, 136
Parenting, 53, 174, 258, 262
Parents, 67, 100, 135, 136, 144, 154, 155, 166, 170–175, 180, 203, 223, 235, 241, 250, 275
  abusive, 136
  American or U.S., 171
  authoritarian, 174
  authoritative, 173, 174
  Chinese, 171
  permissive, 174
  See also Age differences; Lying to children; Lying to parents
Parietal cortex, 54, 254
Park, Chris, 235
Parkinson's disease, 207, **221–223**
Parnell, John, 49
Passive-aggressive, 181
Paternalistic lies, 209, **223–224**
Paterson, Helen, 301
Pathological liars, 43, 207, 242
  See also Antisocial personality disorder
Pathological lying, 34, 62
  See also Compulsive lying
Patterson, Francine, 244
Pennebaker, James W., 159, 162–163
  See also Linguistic Inquiry and Word Count analysis program
Performance, 1, 24, 45, 49, 50, 89, 95, 169, 170, 179, 185, 198, 205, 211, 217, 221, 237, 295, 307
  See also Motivational impairment effect
Perjury, 136, 137, **224–226**
Personality, 30, 31, 53, 69, 81, 82, 83, 115, 120, 141, 162, 165, 166, 170, 172, 177, 179, 181, 187, 205, 206, **226–228,** 235, 264, 271, 294, 303, 307
  agreeableness, 82, 206, 226–227, 262
  conscientiousness, 68, 81, 226–227, 271
  differences, 226, 303
  extraversion, 187, 226–227
  introversion, 187, 226
  neuroticism, 166, 226, 271
  openness, 29, 75, 110, 174, 188, 226–227
  psychopathy, 30, 31, 81–82, 115, 177, 226–227, 230, 241, 294
  tests, 120, 170, 179, 307
  See also Antisocial personality disorder; Borderline personality disorder; Dark Triad; Locus of control;

Machiavellianism; Narcissism; Trolling
Person-centered perspective, 201
Perspective-taking, 16, 291
Philosophy, 12, 116
  See also Ethics
Phishing, 46, 51, 82, 90, 139, 140, 183, 184, 188, **228–229,** 270
  clone phishing, 228
  spear phishing, 82, 140, 228
  whaling, 228
  See also Catfishing; Clickbait; Fraud; Scams
Physical health, 57, 68, 69, 70, 76, 77, 110, 111, 121, 156, 216, 217, 236
Physiological response, 64, 65, 72, 73, 115, 120, 131, 186, 196, 198, 218, 219, 230–231, 239, 240, 241, 268, 270, 302, 303, 304
  See also Control Questions Test; Othello Error; Physiology; Polygraph tests
Physiology, 57, 65, **230–231,** 240
Piltdown Man, 145, **231–233**
  See also Hoax
Placebo effect, **233–234,** 298
Plagiarism, 1, 2, 45, 147, **234–236**
  See also Academic cheating
Polite lies, 5, 16, 37, 38, 45, 69, 100, 101, 173, **236–238**
  See also Butler lies; Prosocial lying; White lies
Politics, 7, 8, 9, 13, 14, 21, 25, 28, 32, 61, 62, 71, 74, 90, 102, 103, 104, 112, 113, 114, 116, 127, 128, 130, 141, 142, 144, 145, 146, 159, 163, 218, 228, **238–239,** 246, 247, 248, 251, 252, 259, 262, 272, 273, 280, 282, 285, 286, 288, 289, 294
Polygraph tests, 64, 72, 73, 91, 99, 170, 230, **239–241,** 268, 269, 270
  See also Behavior Analysis Interview; Concealed Information Test; Control Questions Test; Saxe, Leonard
Porter, Stephen, 198
Positron emission tomography (PET), 206, 207, 208
Powell, Walter, 280
Prefrontal cortex, 5, 100, 124, 206, 207, 208, 221, 222
Premack, David, 87, 244, 290
Premeditation, 5, 25, 30, 35, 42, 54, 71, 109, 134, 201, 269

Preoccupation Model of Secrecy, 197
Prevalence of lying, 32, 44, 183, **241–244**
Primary lies, 100
Primates, 87, **244–245,** 290, 291
 See also Deception in animals
Prisoner's Dilemma, **245–247**
 tit-for-tat strategy, 246
Prolific liars, 76, 242–243, 29
Propaganda, 128, 130, 208, **247–249,** 285, 286, 287
Prosocial lies, 27, 30, 31, 45, 68, 96, 99, 100, 243
Prosocial lying, 27, 68, 69, 70, **249–250**
Pseudologia fantastica, 62, 63
 See also Borderline personality disorder; Compulsive lying
Psychoanalytical, 201, 274
Psychological health, 38, 57, 70, 110, 194, 201, 226, 227, 272, 273
Psychological perspectives, 201, 233
Psychopathy, 30, 31, 81–82, 115, 177, 226–227, 230, 241, 294
Psychosis, 202
Psychoticism, 227
Puffery, **250–252**
 See also Exaggeration
Punishment, 2, 5, 26, 27, 30, 33, 41, 45, 50, 53, 60, 62, 67, 84, 86, 87, 89, 90, 94, 95, 100, 116, 119, 131, 134, 136, 154, 155, 167, 169, 171, 172, 174, 188, 191, 199, 200, 201, 224, 225, 235, 236, 237, 245, 246, 268, 269, 270, 275, 295
Pyramid schemes. *See* Scams

Rate of speech, 23, 97, 137, 210, 301, 302, 308
Rationalization, 1, 21, 56, 58, 59, 67, 70, 76, 77, 93, 127, 148, 180, 192, 194, 195, 213, 259, 260, 269, 272, 273, 274, 295, 296
Reaction time, 5, 186, 187, 196, 207, 222, **253–254**
Reality monitoring, 160, **254–256,** 303
Reasoning, 7, 8, 58, 66, 92, 143, 159, 181, 255, 258, 276, 286, 287, 288, 296
Receptor sites, 92, 234
Recursive awareness, 119, 168, 244, **256–258**
Red herring, **258–259**
Regression, 181
Reid Technique, 199, **260–261**
Relational lies, 154, 155, 199

Relationship health, 28, 63, 81, 110, 114, 174, 175, 252
Religion, 66, 91, 119, 145, 208, 247, 248, 273, 294
 religious laws, 208
 religious leaders, 208, 273
Repression, 91, 133, 274
Response latency, 23, 97, 186, 187, 301, 302
Reverse psychology, **261–263**
Rewards, 1, 5, 16, 20, 30, 50, 51, 56, 67, 69, 70, 86, 87, 139, 149, 154, 164, 167, 173, 179, 180, 188, 200, 201, 206, 207, 221, 222, 226, 237, 246, 254, 262, 268, 275
Robles, Jessica, 262
Rogers, Todd, 213
Romanov, Anastasia. *See* Anderson, Anna; Impersonator
Romantic relationships, 28, 29, 44, 46, 53, 61, 83, 113, 141, 153, 177, 178, 214, 215, **263–265,** 269, 296
Rosenberg, Erika, 188
Rowatt, Wade, 83
Ruffman, Ted, 292

Saarni, Carolyn, 100, **267–268**
 disappointing gift task, 100, 267
Sadism, 294
Santos, Rachel, 171
Sato, Taku, 276
Sauerland, Melanie, 123
Saunders, Rhodri, 147
Savulescu, Julian, 147
Saxe, Leonard, **268–270**
Schizophrenia, 71, 91, 202
Scams, 2, 19, 47, 151, 183, 188, **270–272,** 284
Schipani, Cindy, 75
Schneider, Sandra, 58
Schuman, Stanley, 298
Schweitzer, Maurice, 249
Secret societies. *See* Espionage
Seery, Mark, 53
Self-assessment, 25, 85, 205, 262
Self-awareness, 86, 281, 290
Self-concept, 58, 88, 148, 149, 195
Self-deception, 20, 24, 27, 56, 58, 76, 91, 94, 95, 110, 114, 123, 148, 205, 206, 216, 217, **272–274,** 306
 See also Hypocrisy; Narcissism; Optimism bias

Self-esteem, 24, 25, 27, 29, 30, 34, 43, 45,
    46, 53, 57, 58, 61, 63, 68, 69, 70, 71,
    77, 78, 83, 96, 110, 113, 141, 148, 149,
    152, 153, 171, 180, 181, 195,
    200, 201, 202, 206, 213, 214, 216,
    226, 227, 242, 249, 264, 272, 273,
    275, 283, 305
Self-focus, 30, 177
Self-references, 160, 163
Self-serving lies, 183, 275
    See also Black lies; Instrumental lies
Semantics, 2, 3, 4, 213
Sense of self, 34, 81, 82, 201, 205, 206,
    242, 273
Serota, Kim, 241–243
Sex differences in lying behavior, 268,
    275–276
Shaffer, David R., 137
Shalvi, Shaul, 75
Shaw, Julia, 131, 133
Sherlock Holmes effect, **276–278**
Shiv, Baba, 306
Shu, Lisa, 67
Signaling theory, **278–279**
Singer, Mark, 49
Skepticism, 4, 46, 164, 188, 225, 251
Slander. See also Defamation; Fake news
Slessor, Gillian, 121
Slovenko, Ralph, 104
Smith, Edward, 270
Smith, Madeline, 243
Smith, Rachelle, 60, 101, 125, 257, 289
Smoke and mirrors, **279–281**
Snook, Brent, 52
Snow, Nancy, 248
Snyder, Scott, 34
Social health, 46
Social intelligence, 49, 177, 256, 258,
    281–283
Social media, 14, 25, 46, 59, 127, 128,
    129, 130, 145, 182, 183, 200, 215,
    283–284, 286, 287, 295
Sociopathic liars, 11, 242
    See also Antisocial personality disorder;
    Compulsive lying; Gaslighting
Sociopathy. See Antisocial personality
    disorder
Sockpuppets, 14, 90, 248, **285–286**
    Barron, John, 285
    50 Cent Party, 285
    Furtado, Tad, 285
    Mackey, John, 285

meatpuppet, 285
strawman sockpuppet, 285
Sokol, Daniel K., 93
Sterk, Claire, 280
Strategic Model, 159, 195, 196
Striatum, 206, 207, 254
Students, 1–2, 20, 26, 38, 44, 56, 79, 147,
    159, 184, 223, 235–236, 241, 259,
    269, 307
Su, Sarena, 251
Subtle movements, 85, 210
Suchotzki, Kristina, 186, 253
Sun Tzu, 12–13, 290
    See also Art of War, The
Superiority, 102, 181, 205
Suspension of disbelief, **286–288**
Sweating, 97, 125, 191, 210, 211, 239, 241

Tactical deception, 12, 60, 86, 87, 102,
    118, 168, 169, 174, 244, 280, 281,
    289–290, 291
    Trojan Horse, 290
    See also Art of War, The
Tang, Honghong, 148
Teodorescu, Kinneret, 275
Theory of mind, 5, 15, 27, 35, 86, 87, 92,
    100, 101, 118, 154, 168, 236, 237, 256,
    257, 267, 268, 281, **290–292**
Thinking cues, 107
Threats, 2, 11, 29, 33, 35, 52, 53, 81, 103,
    111, 115, 136, 153, 155, 170, 171, 180,
    196, 228, 229, 231, 240, 248, 260, 261,
    262, 269, 272, 296
    See also Coercion
Toma, Catalina, 215
Transparent lies, 16, 292
Transparent lies and the illusion of
    transparency, **292–293**
Treason. See Espionage
Trick, 5, 33, 102, 107, 125, 144, 195, 270
Trolling, 283, **294–295**
Trump, Donald, 7, 21, 32, 127, 130,
    248, 285
Trust bias, 231
Truth bias, 6, 15, 97, 108, 118, 131, 188,
    225, 263, 295, 297, 303
    See also Truth-Default Theory
Truth-Default Theory (TDT), 238,
    295–298
    veracity effect, 297
Truth Wizard, 99, 108, 306, 307–308
    Ellory, Renee, 308

Eyes for Lies, 308
    See also Ekman, Paul; Wizard's Project
Turner, Ronny, 143
Tunnel vision, 198, 199
Tuskegee Syphilis Study, 88, **298–299**
Tzu, Sun, 12–13, 290
    See also Art of War, The

Van Bockstaele, Bram, 55
Van Oorsouw, Kim, 94
Veracity effect. *See* Truth-Default Theory
Verschuere, Bruno, 186, 253
Villar, Gina, 301–302
Vishwanath, Arun, 183
Vocal changes when lying, **301–302,** 303
Vocal pitch, 16, 36, 97, 98, 121, 124, 210,
    211, 301–302
Vrij, Aldert, 23, 85, 297, **303–304**

Walczyk, Jeffrey, 196
Wang, Shun, 148
Warneken, Felix, 237
Warren, Danielle, 139

Weisel, Ori, 75
Wetherell, Marmaduke, 145, 164, 165
    See also Hoax; Loch Ness Monster
White lies, 27, 30, 31, 45, 69, 76, 93, 110,
    172, 173, 198, 200, 222, 223, 230,
    242, 243, 249, 291, 296, **305–306**
    See also Butler lies; Polite lies;
    Prosocial lying
Willie, Tiara, 53
Wizard's Project, 108, **306–308**
Woodruff, Guy, 87, 244, 290
Working memory, 5, 27, 187, 195, 196, 197,
    207, 275
Wright, Elizabeth, 283, 284
Wright, Robert, 58

Xie, Ninghui, 251

Yang, Defeng, 251
Yellow journalism. *See* Fake news
Yu, Hui, 294

Zvi, Lisa, 205

About the Author

Rachelle M. Smith, PhD, is professor of psychology at Husson University in Bangor, Maine. Her previous book with ABC-CLIO is titled *The Biology of Beauty: The Science behind Human Attractiveness.* She has published research articles on deception such as "Development of Tactical Deception from 4 to 8 Years of Age" and "Development of Children's Ability to Infer Intentions from Nonverbal Cues." She is also coauthor of a book chapter in *The Cambridge Handbook of Evolutionary Perspectives on Human Behavior* titled "Ontogeny of Tactical Deception."

www.ingramcontent.com/pod-product-compliance
Lightning Source LLC
Chambersburg PA
CBHW080412270326
41929CB00018B/2991